VIOLENCE AND THE SACRED

❧ RENE GIRARD

Violence and the Sacred

❧ *Translated by Patrick Gregory*

The Johns Hopkins University Press
Baltimore

This book has been brought to publication with the generous
assistance of the Andrew W. Mellon Foundation.

Originally published in Paris in 1972 as *La Violence et le sacré*
© 1972 By Editions Bernard Grasset
English translation copyright © 1977 by The Johns Hopkins University Press
All rights reserved
Printed in the United States of America on acid-free paper

The Johns Hopkins University Press
2715 North Charles Street
Baltimore, Maryland 21218-4319
The Johns Hopkins Press Ltd., London

Originally published, 1977
Johns Hopkins Paperbacks edition, 1979
05 04 03 02 01 00 99 98 97 96   13 12 11 10 9

Library of Congress Cataloging-in-Publication Data

Girard, René, 1923–
    Violence and the sacred.

    Translation of La violence et le sacré.
    Bibliography: p.319.
    Includes index.
    1. Rites and ceremonies. 2. Sacrifice. I. Title.
BL600.G5413   291.3′4   77-4539
ISBN 0-8018-1963-6 (hardcover)
ISBN 0-8018-2218-1 (paperback)

A catalog record for this book is available from the British Library.

Contents

Acknowledgments

My thanks are due to the Guggenheim Foundation for the fellowship, and to the State University of New York at Buffalo (Faculty of Arts and Letters) for the sabbatical leave that enabled me to complete the present book. I wish to express my appreciation to Martine Bell, not only for typing and proofreading but also for her thoughtful examination of the manuscript and bibliographical materials and a careful preparation of the index. My gratitude also goes to all my friends, and especially to Eugenio Donato and Josue Harari, whose constant collaboration and numerous suggestions have been extremely helpful.

VIOLENCE AND THE SACRED

Chapter One

Sacrifice

IN MANY RITUALS the sacrificial act assumes two opposing aspects, appearing at times as a sacred obligation to be neglected at grave peril, at other times as a sort of criminal activity entailing perils of equal gravity.

To account for this dual aspect of ritual sacrifice—the legitimate and the illegitimate, the public and the all but covert—Henri Hubert and Marcel Mauss, in their "Essay on the Nature and Function of Sacrifice,"[1] adduce the sacred character of the victim. Because the victim is sacred, it is criminal to kill him—but the victim is sacred only because he is to be killed. Here is a circular line of reasoning that at a somewhat later date would be dignified by the sonorous term *ambivalence*. Persuasive and authoritative as that term still appears, it has been so extraordinarily abused in our century that perhaps we may now recognize how little light it sheds on the subject of sacrifice. Certainly it provides no real explanation. When we speak of ambivalence, we are only pointing out a problem that remains to be solved.

If sacrifice resembles criminal violence, we may say that there is, inversely, hardly any form of violence that cannot be described in terms of sacrifice—as Greek tragedy clearly reveals. It has often been observed that the tragic poets cast a glimmering veil of rhetoric over the sordid realities of life. True enough—but sacrifice and murder would not lend themselves to this game of reciprocal substitution if they were not in some way related. Although it is so obvious that it may hardly seem worth mentioning, where sacrifice is concerned first appearances count for little, are quickly brushed aside—and should therefore receive special attention. Once one has made up one's mind that sacrifice is an institution essentially if not entirely symbolic, one can say anything whatsoever about it. It is a subject that lends itself to insubstantial theorizing.

Sacrifice contains an element of mystery. And if the pieties of classical humanists lull our curiosity to sleep, the company of the ancient

---

[1] Henri Hubert and Marcel Mauss, *Sacrifice: Its Nature and Function* (Chicago, 1968).

authors keeps it alert. The ancient mystery remains as impenetrable as ever. From the manner in which the moderns treat the subject of sacrifice, it would be hard to know whether distraction, detachment, or some sort of secret discretion shapes their thinking. There seems to be yet another mystery here. Why, for example, do we never explore the relationship between sacrifice and violence?

Recent studies suggest that the physiology of violence varies little from one individual to another, even from one culture to another. According to Anthony Storr, nothing resembles an angry cat or man so much as another angry cat or man.[2] If violence did indeed play a role in sacrifice, at least at one particular stage of the ritual, we would have a significant clue to the whole subject. Here would be a factor to some extent independent of those cultural variables that are often unknown to us, or only dimly known, or perhaps less familiar than we like to think.

Once aroused, the urge to violence triggers certain physical changes that prepare men's bodies for battle. This set toward violence lingers on; it should not be regarded as a simple reflex that ceases with the removal of the initial stimulus. Storr remarks that it is more difficult to quell an impulse toward violence than to rouse it, especially within the normal framework of social behavior.

Violence is frequently called irrational. It has its reasons, however, and can marshal some rather convincing ones when the need arises. Yet these reasons cannot be taken seriously, no matter how valid they may appear. Violence itself will discard them if the initial object remains persistently out of reach and continues to provoke hostility. When unappeased, violence seeks and always finds a surrogate victim. The creature that excited its fury is abruptly replaced by another, chosen only because it is vulnerable and close at hand.

There are many indications that this tendency to seek out surrogate objects is not limited to human violence. Konrad Lorenz makes reference to a species of fish that, if deprived of its natural enemies (the male rivals with whom it habitually disputes territorial rights), turns its aggression against the members of its own family and destroys them.[3] Joseph de Maistre discusses the choice of animal victims that display human characteristics—an attempt, as it were, to deceive the violent impulse: "The sacrificial animals were always those most prized for their usefulness: the gentlest, most innocent creatures, whose habits and instincts brought them most closely into harmony with man. . . .

---

[2] Anthony Storr, *Human Aggression* (New York, 1968).

[3] Konrad Lorenz, *On Aggression*, trans. Marjorie Kerr Wilson (New York, 1966).

From the animal realm were chosen as victims those who were, if we might use the phrase, the most *human* in nature."[4]

Modern ethnology offers many examples of this sort of intuitive behavior. In some pastoral communities where sacrifice is practiced, the cattle are intimately associated with the daily life of the inhabitants. Two peoples of the Upper Nile, for example—the Nuers, observed by E. E. Evans-Pritchard, and the Dinka, studied at a somewhat later date by Godfrey Lienhardt—maintain a bovine society in their midst that parallels their own and is structured in the same fashion.[5]

The Nuer vocabulary is rich in words describing the ways of cattle and covering the economic and practical, as well as the poetic and ritualistic, aspects of these beasts. This wealth of expression makes possible a precise and finely nuanced relationship between the cattle, on the one hand, and the human community on the other. The animals' color, the shape of their horns, their age, sex, and lineage are all duly noted and remembered, sometimes as far back as five generations. The cattle are thereby differentiated in such a way as to create a scale of values that approximates human distinctions and represents a virtual duplicate of human society. Among the names bestowed on each man is one that also belongs to the animal whose place in the herd is most similar to the place the man occupies in the tribe.

The quarrels between various subgroups of the tribes frequently involve cattle. All fines and interest payments are computed in terms of head of cattle, and dowries are apportioned in herds. In fact, Evans-Pritchard maintains that in order to understand the Nuer, one must *"chercher la vache"*—"look to the cows." A sort of "symbiosis" (the term is also Evans-Pritchard's) exists between this tribe and their cattle, offering an extreme and almost grotesque example of the closeness that characteristically prevails between pastoral peoples and their flocks.

Fieldwork and subsequent theoretical speculation lead us back to the hypothesis of substitution as the basis for the practice of sacrifice. This notion pervades ancient literature on the subject—which may be one reason, in fact, why many modern theorists reject the concept out of hand or give it only scant attention. Hubert and Mauss, for instance, view the idea with suspicion, undoubtedly because they feel that it

[4] Joseph de Maistre, "Eclaircissement sur les sacrifices," *Les Soirées de Saint-Pétersbourg* (Lyons, 1890), 2:341–42. Here, and throughout the book, translations are by Patrick Gregory unless an English-language reference is cited.

[5] E. E. Evans-Pritchard, The Nuer (Oxford, 1940); Godfrey Lienhardt, *Divinity and Experience: The Religion of the Dinka* (Oxford, 1961).

introduces into the discussion religious and moral values that are incompatible with true scientific inquiry. And to be sure, Joseph de Maistre takes the view that the ritual victim is an "innocent" creature who pays a debt for the "guilty" party. I propose an hypothesis that does away with this moral distinction. As I see it, the relationship between the potential victim and the actual victim cannot be defined in terms of innocence or guilt. There is no question of "expiation." Rather, society is seeking to deflect upon a relatively indifferent victim, a "sacrificeable" victim, the violence that would otherwise be vented on its own members, the people it most desires to protect.

The qualities that lend violence its particular terror—its blind brutality, the fundamental absurdity of its manifestations—have a reverse side. With these qualities goes the strange propensity to seize upon surrogate victims, to actually conspire with the enemy and at the right moment toss him a morsel that will serve to satisfy his raging hunger. The fairy tales of childhood in which the wolf, ogre, or dragon gobbles up a large stone in place of a small child could well be said to have a sacrificial cast.

VIOLENCE IS NOT TO BE DENIED, but it can be diverted to another object, something it can sink its teeth into. Such, perhaps, is one of the meanings of the story of Cain and Abel. The Bible offers us no background on the two brothers except the bare fact that Cain is a tiller of the soil who gives the fruits of his labor to God, whereas Abel is a shepherd who regularly sacrifices the first-born of his herds. One of the brothers kills the other, and the murderer is the one who does not have the violence-outlet of animal sacrifice at his disposal. This difference between sacrificial and nonsacrificial cults determines, in effect, God's judgement in favor of Abel. To say that God accedes to Abel's sacrificial offerings but rejects the offerings of Cain is simply another way of saying—from the viewpoint of the divinity—that Cain is a murderer, whereas his brother is not.

A frequent motif in the Old Testament, as well as in Greek myth, is that of brothers at odds with one another. Their fatal penchant for violence can only be diverted by the intervention of a third party, the sacrificial victim or victims. Cain's "jealousy" of his brother is only another term for his one characteristic trait: his lack of a sacrificial outlet.

According to Moslem tradition, God delivered to Abraham the ram previously sacrificed by Abel. This ram was to take the place of Abraham's son Isaac; having already saved one human life, the same animal would now save another. What we have here is no mystical hocus-pocus, but an intuitive insight into the essential function of sacrifice, gleaned exclusively from the scant references in the Bible.

Another familiar biblical scene takes on new meaning in the light of our theory of sacrificial substitution, and it can serve in turn to illuminate some aspects of the theory. The scene is that in which Jacob receives the blessing of his father Isaac.

Isaac is an old man. He senses the approach of death and summons his eldest son, Esau, on whom he intends to bestow his final blessing. First, however, he instructs Esau to bring back some venison from the hunt, so as to make a "savory meat." This request is overheard by the younger brother, Jacob, who hastens to report it to his mother, Rebekah. Rebekah takes two kids from the family flock, slaughters them, and prepares the savory meat dish, which Jacob, in the guise of his elder brother, then presents to his father.

Isaac is blind. Nevertheless Jacob fears he will be recognized, for he is a "smooth man," while his brother Esau is a "hairy man." "My father peradventure will feel me, and I shall seem to him as a deceiver; and I shall bring a curse upon me, not a blessing." Rebekah has the idea of covering Jacob's hands and the back of his neck with the skins of the slaughtered goats, and when the old man runs his hands over his younger son, he is completely taken in by the imposture. Jacob receives the blessing that Isaac had intended for Esau.

The kids serve in two different ways to dupe the father—or, in other terms, to divert from the son the violence directed toward him. In order to receive his father's blessing rather than his curse, Jacob must present to Isaac the freshly slaughtered kids made into a "savory meat." Then the son must seek refuge, literally, in the skins of the sacrificed animals. The animals thus interpose themselves between father and son. They serve as a sort of insulation, preventing the direct contact that could lead only to violence.

Two sorts of substitution are telescoped here: that of one brother for another, and that of an animal for a man. Only the first receives explicit recognition in the text; however, this first one serves as the screen upon which the shadow of the second is projected.

Once we have focused attention on the sacrificial victim, the object originally singled out for violence fades from view. Sacrificial substitution implies a degree of misunderstanding. Its vitality as an institution depends on its ability to conceal the displacement upon which the rite is based. It must never lose sight entirely, however, of the original object, or cease to be aware of the act of transference from that object to the surrogate victim; without that awareness no substitution can take place and the sacrifice loses all efficacy. The biblical passage discussed above meets both requirements. The narrative does not refer directly to the strange deception underlying the sacrificial substitution, nor does it allow this deception to pass entirely unnoticed. Rather, it mixes the act of substitution with another act of substitution, permitting us a fleeting, sidelong glimpse of the process. The narrative itself, then, might be said to partake of a sacrificial quality; it claims to reveal one act of substitution while employing this first substitution to half-conceal another. There is reason to believe that the narrative touches upon the mythic origins of the sacrificial system.

The figure of Jacob has long been linked with the devious character of sacrificial violence. In Greek culture Odysseus plays a similar role. The story of Jacob's benediction can be compared to the episode of the Cyclops in the *Odyssey*, where a splendidly executed ruse enables the hero to escape the clutches of a monster.

Odysseus and his shipmates are shut up in the Cyclops' cave. Every day the giant devours one of the crew; the survivors finally manage to blind their tormentor with a flaming stake. Mad with pain and anger, the Cyclops bars the entrance of the cave to prevent the men from escaping. However, he lets pass his flock of sheep, which go out daily to pasture. In a gesture reminiscent of the blind Isaac, the Cyclops runs his hands over the back of each sheep as it leaves the cave to make sure that it carries no passenger. Odysseus, however, has outwitted his captor, and he rides to freedom by clinging to the thick wool on the underside of one of the rams.

A comparison of the two scenes, one from Genesis and the other from the *Odyssey*, lends credence to the theory of their sacrificial origins. In each case an animal intervenes at the crucial moment to prevent violence from attaining its designated victim. The two texts are mutually revealing: the Cyclops of the *Odyssey* underlines the fearful menace that hangs over the hero (and that remains obscure in the Genesis story); and the slaughter of the kids in Genesis, along with the offering of the "savory meat," clearly implies the sacrificial character of the flock, an aspect that might go unnoticed in the *Odyssey*.

SACRIFICE HAS OFTEN BEEN DESCRIBED as an act of mediation between a sacrificer and a "deity." Because the very concept of a deity, much less a deity who receives blood sacrifices, has little reality in this day and age, the entire institution of sacrifice is relegated by most modern theorists to the realm of the imagination. The approach of Hubert and Mauss leads to the judgement of Claude Lévi-Strauss in *La Pensée sauvage*: because sacrificial rites have no basis in reality, we have every reason to label them meaningless.

The attempt to link sacrifice to a nonexistent deity brings to mind

Paul Valéry's description of poetry as a purely solipsistic activity practiced by the more able solely out of love for art, while the less able persist in the belief that they are actually communicating with someone!

The two ancient narratives examined above make unmistakable reference to the act of sacrifice, but neither makes so much as a passing mention of a deity. If a god had intervened in either incident, its significance would have been diminished rather than increased, and the reader would have been led to conclude, in accordance with the beliefs common to late antiquity and to the modern world, that sacrifice has no real function in society. Divine intervention would have meant the elimination of the pervasive aura of dread, along with its firmly structured economy of violence. We would have then been thrown back upon a formalistic critical approach that would in no way further our understanding.

As we have seen, the sacrificial process requires a certain degree of *misunderstanding*. The celebrants do not and must not comprehend the true role of the sacrificial act. The theological basis of the sacrifice has a crucial role in fostering this misunderstanding. It is the god who supposedly demands the victims; he alone, in principle, who savors the smoke from the altars and requisitions the slaughtered flesh. It is to appease his anger that the killing goes on, that the victims multiply. Interpreters who think they question the primacy of the divine sufficiently by declaring the whole affair "imaginary" may well remain the prisoners of the theology they have not really analyzed. The problem then becomes, how can a real institution be constructed on a purely illusory basis? It is not to be wondered at if the outer shell finally gives way, bringing down with it even the most solid aspects of the institution.

Instead of rejecting the theological basis outright, qua abstraction (which is the same, in effect, as passively accepting it), let us expose its assumptions to a critical examination. Let us try to uncover the societal conflicts that the sacrificial act and its theological interpretations at once dissimulate and appease. We must break with the formalistic tradition of Hubert and Mauss.

The interpretation of sacrifice as an act of violence inflicted on a surrogate victim has recently been advanced once again. Godfrey Lienhardt (in *Divinity and Experience*) and Victor Turner (in a number of works, especially *The Drums of Affliction*), drawing from fieldwork, portray sacrifice as practiced among the Dinka and the Ndembu as a deliberate act of collective substitution performed at the expense of the victim and absorbing all the internal tensions, feuds, and rivalries pent up within the community.

Sacrifice plays a very real role in these societies, and the problem of substitution concerns the entire community. The victim is not a substitute for some particularly endangered individual, nor is it offered up to some individual of particularly bloodthirsty temperament. Rather, it is a substitute for all the members of the community, offered up by the members themselves. The sacrifice serves to protect the entire community from *its own* violence; it prompts the entire community to choose victims outside itself. The elements of dissension scattered throughout the community are drawn to the person of the sacrificial victim and eliminated, at least temporarily, by its sacrifice.

If we turn our attention from the theological superstructure of the act—that is, from an interpretive version of the event that is often accepted as the final statement on sacrifice—we quickly perceive yet another level of religious discourse, in theory subordinated to the theological dimension, but in reality quite independent of it. This has to do with the social function of the act, an aspect far more accessible to the modern mind.

It is easy to ridicule a religion by concentrating on its more eccentric rites, rites such as the sacrifices performed to induce rain or bring fine weather. There is in fact no object or endeavor in whose name a sacrifice cannot be made, especially when the social basis of the act has begun to blur. Nevertheless, there is a common denominator that determines the efficacy of all sacrifices and that becomes increasingly apparent as the institution grows in vigor. This common denominator is internal violence—all the dissensions, rivalries, jealousies, and quarrels within the community that the sacrifices are designed to suppress. The purpose of the sacrifice is to restore harmony to the community, to reinforce the social fabric. Everything else derives from that. If once we take this fundamental approach to sacrifice, choosing the road that violence opens before us, we can see that there is no aspect of human existence foreign to the subject, not even material prosperity. When men no longer live in harmony with one another, the sun still shines and the rain falls, to be sure, but the fields are less well tended, the harvests less abundant.

The classic literature of China explicitly acknowledges the propitiatory function of sacrificial rites. Such practices "pacify the country and make the people settled. . . . It is through the sacrifices that the unity of the people is strengthened" (CH'U YU II, 2). The *Book of Rites* affirms that sacrificial ceremonies, music, punishments, and laws have one and the same end: to unite society and establish order.[6]

In attempting to formulate the fundamental principles of sacrifice

[6] A. R. Radcliffe-Brown, *Structure and Function in Primitive Society* (Glencoe, Ill., 1952), p. 158.

without reference to the ritualistic framework in which the sacrifice takes place, we run the risk of appearing simplistic. Such an effort smacks strongly of "psychologizing." Clearly, it would be inexact to compare the sacrificial act to the spontaneous gesture of the man who kicks his dog because he dares not kick his wife or boss. However, there are Greek myths that are hardly more than colossal variants of such gestures. Such a one is the story of Ajax. Furious at the leaders of the Greek army, who refused to award him Achilles' weapons, Ajax slaughters the herd of sheep intended as provisions for the army. In his mad rage he mistakes these gentle creatures for the warriors on whom he means to vent his rage. The slaughtered animals belong to a species traditionally utilized by the Greeks for sacrificial purposes; but because the massacre takes place outside the ritual framework, Ajax is taken for a madman. The myth is not, strictly speaking, about the sacrificial process; but it is certainly not irrelevant to it. The institution of sacrifice is based on effects analogous to those produced by Ajax's anger—but structured, channeled and held in check by fixed laws.

In the ritualistic societies most familiar to us—those of the Jews and of the Greeks of the classical age—the sacrificial victims are almost always animals. However, there are other societies in which human victims are substituted for the individuals who are threatened by violence.

Even in fifth century Greece—the Athens of the great tragedians—human sacrifice had not, it seems, completely disappeared. The practice was perpetuated in the form of the pharmakos, maintained by the city at its own expense and slaughtered at the appointed festivals as well as at a moment of civic disaster. If examined closely for traces of human sacrifice, Greek tragedy offers some remarkable revelations. It is clear, for example, that the story of Medea parallels that of Ajax on the sacrificial level, although here we are dealing with human rather than with animal sacrifice. In Euripides' *Medea* the principle of human substitution of one victim for another appears in its most savage form. Frightened by the intensity of Medea's rage against her faithless husband, Jason, the nurse begs the children's tutor to keep his charges out of their mother's way:

> I am sure her anger will not subside until it has found a victim. Let us pray that the victim is at least one of our enemies![7]

Because the object of her hatred is out of reach, Medea substitutes her own children. It is difficult for us to see anything resembling a religious act in Medea's insane behavior. Nonetheless, infanticide has its

---

[7] Here, and throughout the book, quotations from the Greek plays have been translated by Patrick Gregory, from the original Greek.

place among ritualistic practices; the practice is too well documented in too many cultures (including the Jewish and the ancient Greek) for us to exclude it from consideration here. Medea's crime is to ritual infanticide what the massacre of sheep in the *Ajax* is to animal sacrifice. Medea prepares for the death of her children like a priest preparing for a sacrifice. Before the fateful act, she issues the traditional ritual announcement: all those whose presence might in any way hinder the effectiveness of the ceremony are requested to remove themselves from the premises.

Medea, like Ajax, reminds us of a fundamental truth about violence; if left unappeased, violence will accumulate until it overflows its confines and floods the surrounding area. The role of sacrifice is to stem this rising tide of indiscriminate substitutions and redirect violence into "proper" channels.

Ajax has details that underline the close relationship between the sacrificial substitution of animals and of humans. Before he sets upon the flock of sheep, Ajax momentarily contemplates the sacrifice of his own son. The boy's mother does not take this threat lightly; she whisks the child away.

In a general study of sacrifice there is little reason to differentiate between human and animal victims. When the principle of the substitution is *physical resemblance* between the vicarious victim and its prototypes, the mere fact that both victims are human beings seems to suffice. Thus, it is hardly surprising that in some societies whole categories of human beings are systematically reserved for sacrificial purposes in order to protect other categories.

I do not mean to minimize the gap that exists between the societies that practice human sacrifice and those that do not. However, this gap should not prevent us from perceiving what they have in common. Strictly speaking, there is no essential difference between animal sacrifice and human sacrifice, and in many cases one is substituted for the other. Our tendency to insist on differences that have little reality when discussing the institution of sacrifice—our reluctance, for example, to equate animal with human sacrifice—is undoubtedly a factor in the extraordinary misunderstandings that still persist in that area of human culture.

This reluctance to consider all forms of sacrifice as a single phenomenon is nothing new. Joseph de Maistre, having defined the principle of sacrificial substitution, makes the bold and wholly unsubstantiated assertion that this principle does not apply to human sacrifice. One cannot, he insists, kill a man to save a man. Yet this assertion is repeatedly contradicted by Greek tragedy, implicitly in a play like *Medea*, and explicitly elsewhere in Euripides.

In Euripides' *Electra*, Clytemnestra explains that the sacrifice of her daughter Iphigenia would have been justified if it had been performed to save human lives. The tragedian thus enlightens us, by way of Clytemnestra, on the "normal" function of human sacrifice—the function de Maistre had refused to acknowledge. If, says Clytemnestra, Agamemnon had permitted his daughter to die:

> . . . in order to prevent the sack of the city, to help his home, to rescue his children, sacrificing one to save the others, I could then have pardoned him. But for the sake of brazen Helen . . . !

Without ever expressly excluding the subject of human sacrifice from their research—and indeed, on what grounds could they do so?— modern scholars, notably Hubert and Mauss, mention it but rarely in their theoretical discussions. On the other hand, the scholars who do concern themselves with human sacrifice tend to concentrate on it to the exclusion of everything else, dwelling at length on the "sadistic" or "barbarous" aspects of the custom. Here, again, one particular form of sacrifice is isolated from the subject as a whole.

This dividing of sacrifice into two categories, human and animal, has itself a sacrificial character, in a strictly ritualistic sense. The division is based in effect on a value judgement, on the preconception that one category of victim—the human being—is quite unsuitable for sacrificial purposes, while another category—the animal—is eminently sacrificeable. We encounter here a survival of the sacrificial mode of thinking that perpetuates a misunderstanding about the institution as a whole. It is not a question of rejecting the value judgment on which this misunderstanding is based, but of putting it, so to speak, in parentheses, of recognizing that as far as the institution is concerned, such judgments are purely arbitrary. All reduction into categories, whether implicit or explicit, must be avoided; all victims, animal or human, must be treated in the same fashion if we wish to apprehend the criteria by which victims are selected (if indeed such criteria exist) and discover (if such a thing is possible) a universal principle for their selection.

We have remarked that all victims, even the animal ones, bear a certain *resemblance* to the object they replace; otherwise the violent impulse would remain unsatisfied. But this resemblance must not be carried to the extreme of complete assimilation, or it would lead to disastrous confusion. In the case of animal victims the difference is always clear, and no such confusion is possible. Although they do their best to empathize with their cattle, the Nuers never quite manage to mistake a man for a cow—the proof being that they always sacrifice the latter, never the former. I am not lapsing into the trap of Lévy

Bruhl's "primitive mentality." I am not saying that primitive man is less capable of making distinctions than we moderns.

In order for a species or category of living creature, human or animal, to appear suitable for sacrifice, it must bear a sharp resemblance to the *human* categories excluded from the ranks of the "sacrificeable," while still maintaining a degree of difference that forbids all possible confusion. As I have said, no mistake is possible in the case of animal sacrifice. But it is quite another case with human victims. If we look at the extremely wide spectrum of human victims sacrificed by various societies, the list seems heterogeneous, to say the least. It includes prisoners of war, slaves, small children, unmarried adolescents, and the handicapped; it ranges from the very dregs of society, such as the Greek pharmakos, to the king himself.

Is it possible to detect a unifying factor in this disparate group? We notice at first glance beings who are either outside or on the fringes of society: prisoners of war, slaves, pharmakos. In many primitive societies children who have not yet undergone the rites of initiation have no proper place in the community; their rights and duties are almost nonexistent. What we are dealing with, therefore, are exterior or marginal individuals, incapable of establishing or sharing the social bonds that link the rest of the inhabitants. Their status as foreigners or enemies, their servile condition, or simply their age prevents these future victims from fully integrating themselves into the community.

But what about the king? Is he not at the very heart of the community? Undoubtedly—but it is precisely his position at the center that serves to isolate him from his fellow men, to render him casteless. He escapes from society, so to speak, via the roof, just as the pharmakos escapes through the cellar. The king has a sort of foil, however, in the person of his fool. The fool shares his master's status as an outsider—an isolation whose literal truth is often of greater significance than the easily reversible symbolic values often attributed to it. From every point of view the fool is eminently "sacrificeable," and the king can use him to vent his own anger. But it sometimes happens that the king himself is sacrificed, and that (among certain African societies) in a thoroughly regulated and highly ritualistic manner.[8]

It is clearly legitimate to define the difference between sacrificeable and nonsacrificeable individuals in terms of their degree of integration, but such a definition is not yet sufficient. In many cultures women are not considered full-fledged members of their society; yet women are never, or rarely, selected as sacrificial victims. There may be a simple explanation for this fact. The married woman retains her ties with her

---

[8] Cf. Chapter 4, pp. 104–10.

parents' clan even after she has become in some respects the property of her husband and his family. To kill her would be to run the risk of one of the two groups' interpreting her sacrifice as an act of murder committing it to a reciprocal act of revenge. The notion of vengeance casts a new light on the matter. All our sacrificial victims, whether chosen from one of the human categories enumerated above or, *a fortiori*, from the animal realm, are invariably distinguishable from the nonsacrificeable beings by one essential characteristic: between these victims and the community a crucial social link is missing, so they can be exposed to violence without fear of reprisal. Their death does not automatically entail an act of vengeance.

The considerable importance this freedom from reprisal has for the sacrificial process makes us understand that sacrifice is primarily an act of violence without risk of vengeance. We also understand the paradox —not without its comic aspects on occasion—of the frequent references to vengeance in the course of sacrificial rites, the veritable obsession with vengeance when no chance of vengeance exists:

> For the act they were about to commit elaborate excuses were offered; they shuddered at the prospect of the sheep's death, they wept over it as though they were its parents. Before the blow was struck, they implored the beast's forgiveness. They then addressed themselves to the species to which the beast belonged, as if addressing a large family clan, beseeching it not to seek vengeance for the act that was about to be inflicted on one of its members. In the same vein the actual murderer was punished in some manner, either beaten or sent into exile.[9]

It is the entire species *considered as a large family clan* that the sacrificers beseech not to seek vengeance. By incorporating the element of reprisal into the ceremony, the participants are hinting broadly at the true function of the rite, the kind of action it was designed to circumvent and the criteria that determined the choice of victim. The desire to commit an act of violence on those near us cannot be suppressed without a conflict; we must divert that impulse, therefore, toward the sacrificial victim, the creature we can strike down without fear of reprisal, since he lacks a champion.

Like everything that touches on the essential nature of the sacrificial act, the true distinction between the sacrificeable and the nonsacrificeable is never clearly articulated. Oddities and inexplicable anomalies confuse the picture. For instance, some animal species will be formally excluded from sacrifice, but the exclusion of members of the community is never mentioned. In constantly drawing attention to the truly maniacal aspects of sacrifice, modern theorists only serve to per-

---

[9] Hubert and Mauss, *Sacrifice*, p. 33.

petuate an old misunderstanding in new terms. Men can dispose of their violence more efficiently if they regard the process not as something emanating from within themselves, but as a necessity imposed from without, a divine decree whose least infraction calls down terrible punishment. When they banish sacrificial practices from the "real," everyday world, modern theorists continue to misrepresent the violence of sacrifice.

The function of sacrifice is to quell violence within the community and to prevent conflicts from erupting. Yet societies like our own, which do not, strictly speaking, practice sacrificial rites, seem to get along without them. Violence undoubtedly exists within our society, but not to such an extent that the society itself is threatened with extinction. The simple fact that sacrificial practices, and other rites as well, can disappear without catastrophic results should in part explain the failure of ethnology and theology to come to grips with these cultural phenomena, and explain as well our modern reluctance to attribute a real function to them. After all, it is hard to maintain that institutions for which, as it seems, we have no need are actually indispensable.

It may be that a basic difference exists between a society like ours and societies imbued with religion—a difference that is partially hidden from us by rites, particularly by rites of sacrifice, that play a compensatory role. This difference would help explain why the actual function of sacrifice still eludes us.

When internal strife, previously sublimated by means of sacrificial practices, rises to the surface, it manifests itself in interfamily vendettas or blood feuds. This kind of violence is virtually nonexistent in our own culture. And perhaps it is here that we should look for the fundamental difference between primitive societies and our own; we should examine the specific ailments to which we are immune and which sacrifice manages to control, if not to eliminate.

Why does the spirit of revenge, wherever it breaks out, constitute such an intolerable menace? Perhaps because the only satisfactory revenge for spilt blood is spilling the blood of the killer; and in the blood feud there is no clear distinction between the act for which the killer is being punished and the punishment itself. Vengeance professes to be an act of reprisal, and every reprisal calls for another reprisal. The crime to which the act of vengeance addresses itself is almost never an unprecedented offense; in almost every case it has been committed in revenge for some prior crime.

Vengeance, then, is an interminable, infinitely repetitive process. Every time it turns up in some part of the community, it threatens to

involve the whole social body. There is the risk that the act of vengeance will initiate a chain reaction whose consequences will quickly
prove fatal to any society of modest size. The multiplication of reprisals instantaneously puts the very existence of a society in jeopardy,
and that is why it is universally proscribed.

Curiously enough, it is in the very communities where the proscription is most strictly enforced that vengeance seems to hold sway. Even
when it remains in the background, its role in the community unacknowledged, the specter of vengeance plays an important role in
shaping the relationships among individuals. That is not to say that the
prohibition against acts of vengeance is taken lightly. Precisely because
murder inspires horror and because men must be forcibly restrained
from murder, vengeance is inflicted on all those who commit it. The
obligation never to shed blood cannot be distinguished from the obligation to exact vengeance on those who shed it. If men wish to prevent
an interminable outbreak of vengeance (just as today we wish to prevent nuclear war), it is not enough to convince their fellows that
violence is detestable—for it is precisely because they detest violence
that men make a duty of vengeance.

In a world still haunted by the specter of vengeance it is difficult to
theorize about vengeance without resorting to equivocations or paradoxes. In Greek tragedy, for instance, there is not—and cannot be—
any consistent stand on the subject. To attempt to extract a coherent
theory of vengeance from the drama is to miss the essence of tragedy.
For in tragedy each character passionately embraces or rejects vengeance depending on the position he occupies at any given moment in
the scheme of the drama.

Vengeance is a vicious circle whose effect on primitive societies can
only be surmised. For us the circle has been broken. We owe our good
fortune to one of our social institutions above all: our judicial system,
which serves to deflect the menace of vengeance. The system does not
suppress vengeance; rather, it effectively limits it to a single act of
reprisal, enacted by a sovereign authority specializing in this particular
function. The decisions of the judiciary are invariably presented as the
final word on vengeance.

Vocabulary is perhaps more revealing here than judicial theories.
Once the concept of interminable revenge has been formally rejected,
it is referred to as *private* vengeance. The term implies the existence of
a *public* vengeance, a counterpart never made explicit. By definition,
primitive societies have only private vengeance. Thus, public vengeance is the exclusive property of well-policed societies, and our society calls it the judicial system.

Our penal system operates according to principles of justice that are in no real conflict with the concept of revenge. The same principle is at work in all systems of violent retribution. Either the principle is just, and justice is therefore inherent in the idea of vengeance, or there is no justice to be found anywhere. He who exacts his own vengeance is said to "take the law into his own hands." There is no difference of principle between private and public vengeance; but on the social level, the difference is enormous. Under the pyblic system, an act of vengeance is no longer avenged; the process is terminated, the danger of escalation averted.

The absence of a judicial system in primitive societies has been confirmed by ethnologists. Malinowski concludes that "the 'criminal' aspect of law in savage communities is perhaps even vaguer than the civil one; the idea of 'justice' in our sense [is] hardly applicable and the means of restoring a disturbed tribal equilibrium [are] slow and cumbersome."[10]

Radcliffe-Brown's conclusions are identical, and summon up, as such conclusions must, the specter of perpetual vengeance: "Thus, though the Andaman Islanders had a well-developed social conscience, that is, a system of moral notions as to what is right and wrong, there was no such thing as punishment of a crime by the society. If one person injured another it was left to the injured one to seek vengeance if he wished and if he dared. There were probably always some who would side with the criminal, their attachment to him overcoming their disapproval of his actions."[11]

The anthropologist Robert Lowie speaks of the "administering of justice" in reference to primitive societies. He distinguishes two types of societies, those that possess a "central authority," and those that do not. Among the latter it is the parental group, he declares, that exercises the judicial power, and *this group confronts the other group in the same way that a sovereign state confronts the outside world.* There can be no true "administering of justice," no judicial system without a superior tribunal capable of arbitrating between even the most powerful groups. Only that superior tribunal can remove the possibility of blood feud or perpetual vendetta. Lowie himself recognizes that this condition is not always met: "From the supreme law of group solidarity it follows that when an individual has injured a member of another group, his own group shield him while the opposing group support the injured man's claims for compensation or revenge. Thence there may develop blood-feuds and civil wars. . . . The Chukchi generally make

[10] Bronislaw Malinowski, *Crime and Custom in Savage Society* (Totowa, N.J., 1967), p. 94.
[11] A. R. Radcliffe-Brown, *The Andaman Islanders* (New York, 1964), p. 52.

peace after the first act of retribution, but among the Ifugao the struggle may go on almost interminably. . . ."[12]

To speak here of the "administering of justice" is to abuse the meaning of the words. The desire to find in primitive societies virtues equal or superior to our own as regards the control of violence must not lead us to minimize the differences. Lowie's terminology simply perpetuates a widely accepted way of thinking by which the right to vengeance *takes the place* of a judicial system wherever such a system is lacking. This theory, which seems securely anchored to common sense, is in fact erroneous and gives rise to an infinite number of errors. Such thinking reflects the ignorance of a society—our own—that has been the beneficiary of a judicial system for so many years that it is no longer conscious of the system's real achievements.

If vengeance is an unending process it can hardly be invoked to restrain the violent impulses of society. In fact, it is vengeance itself that must be restrained. Lowie bears witness to the truth of this proposition every time he gives an example of the "administering of justice," even in those societies that, according to him, possess a "central authority." It is not the lack of any abstract principle of justice that is important, but the fact that the so-called legal reprisals are always in the hands of the victims themselves and those near to them. As long as there exists no sovereign and independent body capable of taking the place of the injured party and taking upon itself the responsibility for revenge, the danger of interminable escalation remains. Efforts to modify the punishment or to hold vengeance in check can only result in a situation that is precarious at best. Such efforts ultimately require a spirit of conciliation that may indeed be present, but may equally well be lacking. As I have said, it is inexact to speak of the administering of justice, even in connection with such institutional concepts as "an eye for an eye" or the various forms of trial by combat. In such cases it seems wise to adhere to Malinowski's conclusion: "The means of restoring a disturbed tribal equilibrium [are] slow and cumbersome. . . . We have not found any arrangement or usage which could be classed as a form of 'administration of justice,' according to a code and by fixed methods."[13]

If primitive societies have no tried and true remedies for dealing with an outbreak of violence, no certain cure once the social equilibrium has been upset, we can assume that *preventive* measures will play an essential role. Here again I return to the concept of sacrifice as I earlier defined it: an instrument of prevention in the struggle against violence.

[12] Robert Lowie, *Primitive Society* (New York, 1970), p. 400.
[13] Malinowski, *Crime and Custom in Savage Society*, pp. 94, 98.

In a universe where the slightest dispute can lead to disaster—just as a slight cut can prove fatal to a hemophiliac—the rites of sacrifice serve to polarize the community's aggressive impulses and redirect them toward victims that may be actual or figurative, animate or inanimate, but that are always incapable of propagating further vengeance. The sacrificial process furnishes an outlet for those violent impulses that cannot be mastered by self-restraint; a partial outlet, to be sure, but always renewable, and one whose efficacy has been attested by an impressive number of reliable witnesses. The sacrificial process prevents the spread of violence by keeping vengeance in check.

In societies that practice sacrifice there is no critical situation to which the rites are not applicable, but there are certain crises that seem to be particularly amenable to sacrificial mediation. In these crises the social fabric of the community is threatened; dissension and discord are rife. The more critical the situation, the more "precious" the sacrificial victim must be.

It is significant that sacrifice has languished in societies with a firmly established judicial system—ancient Greece and Rome, for example. In such societies the essential purpose of sacrifice has disappeared. It may still be practiced for a while, but in diminished and debilitated form. And it is precisely under such circumstances that sacrifice usually comes to our notice, and our doubts as to the "real" function of religious institutions are only reinforced.

Our original proposition stands: ritual in general, and sacrificial rites in particular, assume essential roles in societies that lack a firm judicial system. It must not be assumed, however, that sacrifice simply "replaces" a judicial system. One can scarcely speak of replacing something that never existed to begin with. Then, too, a judicial system is ultimately irreplaceable, short of a unanimous and entirely voluntary renunciation of all violent actions.

When we minimize the dangers implicit in vengeance we risk losing sight of the true function of sacrifice. Because revenge is rarely encountered in our society, we seldom have occasion to consider how societies lacking a judicial system of punishment manage to hold it in check. Our ignorance engages us in a false line of thought that is seldom, if ever, challenged. Certainly we have no need of religion to help us solve a problem, runaway vengeance, whose very existence eludes us. And because we have no need for it, religion itself appears senseless. The efficiency of our judicial solution conceals the problem, and the elimination of the problem conceals from us the role played by religion.

The air of mystery that primitive societies acquire for us is undoubtedly due in large part to this misunderstanding. It is undoubtedly responsible for our extreme views of these societies, our insistence on portraying them alternately as vastly superior or flagrantly inferior to our own. One factor alone might well be responsible for our oscillation between extremes, our radical evaluations: the absence in such societies of a judicial system. No one can assess with certainty the amount of violence present in another individual, much less in another society. We can be sure, however, that in a society lacking a judicial system the violence will not appear in the same places or take the same forms as in our own. We generally limit our area of inquiry to the most conspicuous and accessible aspects of these societies. Thus, it is not unnatural that they should seem to us either horribly barbarous or blissfully utopian.

In primitive societies the risk of unleashed violence is so great and the cure so problematic that the emphasis naturally falls on prevention. The preventive measures naturally fall within the domain of religion, where they can on occasion assume a violent character. Violence and the sacred are inseparable. But the covert appropriation by sacrifice of certain properties of violence—particularly the ability of violence to move from one object to another—is hidden from sight by the awesome machinery of ritual.

Primitive societies are not given over to violence. Nor are they necessarily less violent or less "hypocritical" than our own society. Of course, to be truly comprehensive we ought to take into consideration *all* forms of violence, more or less ritualized, that divert a menace from nearby objects to more distant objects. We ought, for instance, to consider war. War is clearly not restricted to one particular type of society. Yet the multiplication of new weapons and techniques does not constitute a fundamental difference between primitive and modern warfare. On the other hand, if we compare societies that adhere to a judicial system with societies that practise sacrificial rites, the difference between the two is such that we can indeed consider the absence or presence of these institutions as a basis for distinguishing primitive societies from "civilized" ones. These are the institutions we must scrutinize in order to arrive, not at some sort of value judgement, but at an objective knowledge of the respective societies to which they belong.

In primitive societies the exercise of preventive measures is not confined exclusively to the domain of religion. The way in which these measures are made manifest in normal social intercourse made a lasting impression on the minds and imaginations of the first European observers and established a prototype of "primitive" psychology and behavior which, if not universally applicable, is still not wholly illusory.

When the least false step can have dire consequences, human relationships may well be marked by a prudence that seems to us excessive and accompanied by precautions that appear incomprehensible. It is in this sense that we must understand the lengthy palavers that precede any undertaking not sanctified by custom, in this sense that we must understand primitive man's reluctance to engage in nonritualized games or contests. In a society where every action or gesture may have irreparable consequences it is not surprising that the members should display a "noble gravity" of bearing beside which our own demeanor appears ridiculous. The commercial, administrative, or ideological concerns that make such overwhelming demands on our time and attention seem utterly frivolous in comparison to primitive man's primary concerns.

Primitive societies do not have built into their structure an automatic brake against violence; but we do, in the form of powerful institutions whose grip grows progressively tighter as their role grows progressively less apparent. The constant presence of a restraining force allows modern man safely to transgress the limits imposed on primitive peoples without even being aware of the fact. In "policed" societies the relationships between individuals, including total strangers, is characterized by an extraordinary air of informality, flexibility, and even audacity.

Religion invariably strives to subdue violence, to keep it from running wild. Paradoxically, the religious and moral authorities in a community attempt to instill nonviolence, as an active force into daily life and as a mediating force into ritual life, through the application of violence. Sacrificial rites serve to connect the moral and religious aspects of daily life, but only by means of a lengthy and hazardous detour. Moreover, it must be kept in mind that the efficacy of the rites depends on their being performed in the spirit of *pietas*, which marks all aspects of religious life. We are beginning to understand why the sacrificial act appears as both sinful and saintly, an illegal as well as a legitimate exercise of violence. However, we are still far from a full understanding of the act itself.

Primitive religion tames, trains, arms, and directs violent impulses as a defensive force against those forms of violence that society regards as inadmissible. It postulates a strange mixture of violence and nonviolence. The same can perhaps be said of our own judicial system of control.

There may be a certain connection between all the various methods employed by man since the beginning of time to avoid being caught up in an interminable round of revenge. They can be grouped into three general categories: (1) preventive measures in which sacrificial rites divert the spirit of revenge into other channels; (2) the harnessing or hobbling of vengeance by means of compensatory measures, trials by combat, etc., whose curative effects remain precarious; (3) the establishment of a judicial system—the most efficient of all curative procedures.

We have listed the methods in ascending order of effectiveness. The evolution from preventive to curative procedures is reflected in the course of history or, at any rate, in the course of the history of the Western world. The initial curative procedures mark an intermediary stage between a purely religious orientation and the recognition of a judicial system's superior efficiency. These methods are inherently ritualistic in character, and are often associated with sacrificial practices.

The curative procedures employed by primitive societies appear rudimentary to us. We tend to regard them as fumbling efforts to improvise a judicial system. Certainly their pragmatic aspects are clearly visible, oriented as they are not toward the guilty parties, but toward the victims—since it is the latter who pose the most immediate threat. The injured parties must be accorded a careful measure of satisfaction, just enough to appease their own desire for revenge but not so much as to awaken the desire elsewhere. It is not a question of codifying good and evil or of inspiring respect for some abstract concept of justice; rather, it is a question of securing the safety of the group by checking the impulse for revenge. The preferred method involves a reconciliation between parties based on some sort of mutual compensation. If reconciliation is impossible, however, an armed encounter can be arranged in such a manner that the violence is wholly self-contained. This encounter can take place within an enclosed space and can involve prescribed regulations and specifically designated combatants. Its purpose is to cut violence short.

To be sure, all these curative measures are steps in the direction of a legal system. But the evolution, if indeed evolution is the proper term, is not continuous. The break comes at the moment when the intervention of an independent legal authority becomes *constraining*. Only then are men freed from the terrible obligations of vengeance. Retribution in its judicial guise loses its terrible urgency. Its meaning remains the same, but this meaning becomes increasingly indistinct or even fades from view. In fact, the system functions best when everyone concerned is least aware that it involves retribution. The system can—and as soon as it can it will—reorganize itself around the accused and the concept of guilt. In fact, retribution still holds sway, but forged into a principle of abstract justice that all men are obliged to uphold and respect.

We have seen that the "curative" measures, ostensibly designed to temper the impulse toward vengeance, become increasingly mysterious in their workings as they progress in efficiency. As the focal point of the system shifts away from religion and the preventive approach is translated into judicial retribution, the aura of misunderstanding that has always formed a protective veil around the institution of sacrifice shifts as well, and becomes associated in turn with the machinery of the law.

As soon as the judicial system gains supremacy, its machinery disappears from sight. Like sacrifice, it conceals—even as it also reveals—its resemblance to vengeance, differing only in that it is not self-perpetuating and its decisions discourage reprisals. In the case of sacrifice, the designated victim does not become the object of vengeance because he is a replacement, is not the "right" victim. In the judicial system the violence does indeed fall on the "right" victim; but it falls with such force, such resounding authority, that no retort is possible.

It can be argued that the function of the judicial system is not really concealed; and we can hardly be unaware that the judicial process is more concerned with the general security of the community than with any abstract notion of justice. Nonetheless, we believe that the system is founded on a unique principle of justice unknown to primitive societies. The scholarly literature on the subject seems to bear out this belief. It has long been assumed that a decisive difference between primitive and civilized man is the former's general inability to identify the guilty party and to adhere to the principle of guilt. Such an assumption only confuses the issue. If primitive man insists on averting his attention from the wrongdoer, with an obstinacy that strikes us as either idiotic or perverse, it is because he wishes above all to avoid fueling the fires of vengeance.

If our own system seems more rational, it is because it conforms more strictly to the principle of vengeance. Its insistence on the punishment of the guilty party underlines this fact. Instead of following the example of religion and attempting to forestall acts of revenge, to mitigate or sabotage its effects or to redirect them to secondary objects, our judicial system *rationalizes* revenge and succeeds in limiting and isolating its effects in accordance with social demands. The system treats the disease without fear of contagion and provides a highly effective technique for the cure and, as a secondary effect, the prevention of violence.

This rationalistic approach to vengeance might seem to stem from a peculiarly intimate relationship between the community and the judicial system. In fact, it is the result not of any familiar interchange between the two, but of the recognition of the sovereignty and independence of the judiciary, whose decisions no group, not even the collectivity as a body, can challenge. (At least, that is the principle.) The judicial authority is beholden to no one. It is thus at the disposal of everyone, and it is universally respected. The judicial system never hesitates to confront violence head on, because it possesses a monopoly on the means of revenge. Thanks to this monopoly, the system generally succeeds in stifling the impulse to vengeance rather than spreading or aggravating it, as a similar intervention on the part of the aggrieved party would invariably do.

In the final analysis, then, the judicial system and the institution of sacrifice share the same function, but the judicial system is infinitely more effective. However, it can only exist in conjunction with a firmly established political power. And like all modern technological advances, it is a two-edged sword, which can be used to oppress as well as to liberate. Certainly that is the way it is seen by primitive cultures, whose view on the matter is indubitably more objective than our own.

If the function of the system has now become apparent, that is because it no longer enjoys the obscurity it needs to operate effectively. A clear view of the inner workings indicates a crisis in the system; it is a sign of disintegration. No matter how sturdy it may seem, the apparatus that serves to hide the true nature of legal and illegal violence from view eventually wears thin. The underlying truth breaks through, and we find ourselves face to face with the specter of reciprocal reprisal. This is not a purely theoretical concept belonging to the intellectual and scholarly realm, but a sinister reality; a vicious circle we thought we had escaped, but one we find has tightened itself, all unsuspected, around us.

The procedures that keep men's violence in bounds have one thing in common: they are no strangers to the ways of violence. There is reason to believe that they are all rooted in religion. As we have seen, the various forms of prevention go hand in hand with religious practices. The curative procedures are also imbued with religious concepts —both the rudimentary sacrificial rites and the more advanced judicial forms. *Religion* in its broadest sense, then, must be another term for that obscurity that surrounds man's efforts to defend himself by curative or preventative means against his own violence. It is that enigmatic quality that pervades the judicial system when that system replaces sacrifice. This obscurity coincides with the transcendental effectiveness of a violence that is holy, legal, and legitimate successfully opposed to a violence that is unjust, illegal, and illegitimate.

In the same way that sacrificial victims must in principle meet the approval of the divinity before being offered as a sacrifice, the judicial system appeals to a theology as a guarantee of justice. Even when this theology disappears, as has happened in our culture, the transcendental quality of the system remains intact. Centuries can pass before men realize that there is no real difference between their principle of justice and the concept of revenge.

Only the transcendental quality of the system, acknowledged by all, can assure the prevention or cure of violence. This is the case no matter what the consecrating institution may be. Only by opting for a sanctified, legitimate form of violence and preventing it from becoming an object of disputes and recriminations can the system save itself from the vicious circle of revenge.

A unique generative force exists that we can only qualify as religious in a sense deeper than the theological one. It remains concealed and draws its strength from this concealment, even as its self-created shelter begins to crumble. The acknowledgment of such a force allows us to assess our modern ignorance—ignorance in regard to violence as well as religion. Religion shelters us from violence just as violence seeks shelter in religion. If we fail to understand certain religious practices it is not because we are outside their sphere of influence but because we are still to a very real extent enclosed within them. The solemn debates on the death of God and of man are perhaps beside the point. They remain theological at bottom, and by extension sacrificial; that is, they draw a veil over the subject of vengeance, which threatens to become quite real once again, in the form not of a philosophical debate but of unlimited violence, in a world with no absolute values. As soon as the essential quality of transcendence—religious, humanistic, or whatever—is lost, there are no longer any terms by which to define the legitimate form of violence and to recognize it among the multitude of illicit forms. The definition of legitimate and illegitimate forms then becomes a matter of mere opinion, with each man free to reach his own decision. In other words, the question is thrown to the winds. Henceforth there are as many legitimate forms of violence as there are men to implement them; legitimacy as a principle no longer exists. Only the introduction of some transcendental quality that will persuade men of the fundamental difference between sacrifice and revenge, between a judicial system and vengeance, can succeed in bypassing violence.

All this explains why our penetration and demystification of the system necessarily coincides with the disintegration of that system. The act of demystification retains a sacrificial quality and remains essentially religious in character for at least as long as it fails to come to a conclusion—as long, that is, as the process purports to be nonviolent, or less violent than the system itself. In fact, demystification leads to constantly increasing violence, a violence perhaps less "hypocritical" than the violence it seeks to expose, but more energetic, more virulent, and the harbinger of something far worse—a violence that knows no bounds.

While acknowledging the differences, both functional and mythical, between vengeance, sacrifice, and legal punishment, it is important to recognize their fundamental identity. Precisely because these three institutions are essentially the same they tend to adopt the same types of violent response in times of crisis. Seen in the abstract, such an assertion may seem hyperbolic or simply unbelievable. It can only be appreciated by means of concrete examples. Only then will the utility of the comparison become apparent; customs and institutions that have remained incomprehensible, unclassifiable, and "aberrant" heretofore make sense when seen in the light of this identity.

Robert Lowie, discussing collective reactions to an act of violence, brings out a fact well worth noting here: "The Chukchi generally make peace after the first act of retribution. . . . While the Ifugao tend to protect a kinsman under almost all circumstances, the Chukchi often avert a feud by killing a member of the family."[14]

Whether it be through sacrificial killing or legal punishment, the problem is to forestall a series of reprisals. As the above quotation shows, Lowie is well aware of this aspect. In killing one of their own, the Chukchi abort the issue; by offering a victim to their potential enemies they enjoin them not to seek vengeance, not to commit an act that would constitute a fresh affront and oblige the other side to seek further retribution. This expiatory procedure brings to mind the sacrificial process; the fact that the victim is someone other than the guilty party drives the resemblance home.

The Chukchi practice cannot, however, be classified as sacrificial. A properly conducted ritual killing is never openly linked to another bloodletting of irregular character. It never allows itself to pass as a deliberate act of retribution. Because this link is consistently missing, the meaning of the sacrificial process has always eluded us, and the relationship between sacrifice and violence has remained obscure. Now the meaning is made clear, and in a manner too spectacular for the act to be mistaken for mere ritual.

Should one then classify this custom among legal punishments? Can one properly refer to it as an "execution of justice?" Probably not; after all, the victim of the second murder was in no way responsible for the first. To be sure, Lowie invokes the concept of "collective responsibility," but this is not a satisfactory explanation. Collective responsibility never specifically excludes the true culprit, and that is

[14] Lowie, *Primitive Society*, p. 400.

precisely what is being done here. Even if this exclusion is not clearly spelled out, there is sufficient evidence for us to assume that in many instances the true culprit is systematically spared. As a cultural attitude, this certainly demands attention.

To refer in this context to the so-called primitive mentality, to some "possible confusion between the individual and the group," is to hedge the issue. If the Chukchi choose to spare the culprit it is not because they cannot distinguish where the guilt lies. On the contrary, they perceive it with the utmost clarity. It is precisely because they see that the guilty party is guilty that they choose to spare him. The Chukchi believe that they have good reasons to act as they do, and it is these reasons we must now examine.

To make a victim out of the guilty party is to play vengeance's role, to submit to the demands of violence. By killing, not the murderer himself, but someone close to him, an act of perfect reciprocity is avoided and the necessity for revenge by-passed. If the counterviolence were inflicted on the aggressor himself, it would by this very act participate in, and become indistinguishable from, the original act of violence. In short, it would become an act of pure vengeance, requiring yet another act of vengeance and transforming itself into the very thing it was designed to prevent.

Only violence can put an end to violence, and that is why violence is self-propagating. Everyone wants to strike the last blow, and reprisal can thus follow reprisal without any true conclusion ever being reached.

In excluding the actual guilty party from reprisals the Chukchi hope to avoid the vicious cycle of revenge. They try to cover their tracks— but not entirely, for they do not want to deprive their act of its primordial meaning as a response to an initial killing, as the payment of a debt contracted by one of their number. To quell the passions aroused by this crime an act is required that bears some resemblance to the vengeance sought by the plaintiffs but that does not quite qualify as an act of revenge. The act resembles both a legal punishment and a sacrifice, and yet it cannot be assimilated to either. The act described here resembles a legal punishment in that it constitutes an act of reparation, a violent retribution; and the Chukchi show no hesitation in imposing on themselves the same loss they have inflicted on others. Their action resembles a sacrifice in that the victim of the second murder is not responsible for the first.

So flagrant a disregard of the principle of guilt strikes us as absurd. We hold that principle in such high esteem that any deviation from it appears to us an aberration of the intellect or malfunction of the senses. Yet our line of reasoning is rejected by the "primitives" because it involves too strict an application of the doctrine of vengeance and is thus fraught with peril.

When we require a direct link between guilt and punishment we believe that we adhere to a fundamental truth that has somehow eluded the primitive mind. In fact, we are ignoring a problem that poses a very real threat to all primitive societies: escalating revenge, unleashed violence—a problem the seeming extravagances of their customs and the violence of their religious practices are specifically designed to meet.

In Greek culture in particular, physical contact with the anathema is avoided. Behind this peculiar prohibition lurks a fear perhaps analogous to the one that inspires the Chukchi custom. To do violence to a violent person is to be contaminated by his violence. It is best, therefore, to arrange matters so that nobody, except perhaps the culprit himself, is directly responsible for his death, so that nobody is obliged to raise a finger against him. He may be abandoned without provisions in mid-ocean, or stranded on top of a mountain, or forced to hurl himself from a cliff. The custom of exposure, as a means of getting rid of malformed children, seems to find its origin in this same fear.

All such customs may appear to us unreasonable and absurd. In fact they adhere to a coherent logic. All of them concern themselves with formulating and practicing a form of violence incapable of serving as a connecting link between the violent act that preceded and the one that must follow. The aim is to achieve a radically new type of violence, truly decisive and self-contained, a form of violence that will put an end once and for all to violence itself.

Primitive peoples try to break the symmetry of reprisal by addressing themselves directly to the question of form. Unlike us, they perceive recurrent patterns, and they attempt to halt this recurrence by introducing something different into the picture. Modern man has long since lost his fear of reciprocal violence, which, after all, provides our judicial system with its structure. Because the overwhelming authority of the judiciary prevents its sentence from becoming the first step in an endless series of reprisals, we can no longer appreciate primitive man's deep-seated fear of pure, unadulterated vengeance. The Chukchi's behavior or the Greeks' cautious treatment of the anathema strike us as puzzling.

Of course, the Chukchi solution is not to be confused with retaliatory vengeance, ritual sacrifice, or legal punishment. And yet it is reminiscent of all these institutions. Their solution seems to occur at the point where all three intersect. Unless the modern mind can cope with the fact that the three are indeed capable of intersecting, it is not likely to shed much light on the questions that concern us here.

〰〰 THE CHUKCHI SOLUTION is fraught with psycho-
logical implications, all of rather limited interest. For example, it can be
said that in choosing to kill someone close to the culprit rather than the
culprit himself the Chukchi are trying to be conciliatory without risk-
ing a loss of face. That is indeed possible, but there are many other
possibilities as well. It is easy to lose one's way in a maze of psychological speculation. The religious structure clearly transcends all "psychological" interpretations; it neither requires nor contradicts them.

The essential religious concern here is ritual impurity. And the cause
of ritual impurity is violence. In many cases, this fact seems self-
evident.

Two men come to blows; blood is spilt; both men are thus rendered
impure. Their impurity is contagious, and anyone who remains in their
presence risks becoming a party to their quarrel. The only sure way to
avoid contagion is to flee the scene of violence. There is no question
here of duty or morality. Contamination is a terrible thing, and only
those who are already contaminated would wilfully expose themselves
to it.

If even an accidental contact with a "contaminated" being can
spread the impurity, it goes without saying that a violent and hostile
encounter will guarantee infection. Therefore, the Chukchi reason,
whenever violence is inevitable, it is best that the victim be *pure*,
untainted by any involvement in the dispute. As we can see, these
notions of impurity and contagion play an active role in social relations
and are firmly rooted in reality. It is precisely this basis in reality that
scholars have long denied. Modern observers—particularly Frazer's
contemporaries and disciples—were totally blind to the reality that lay
behind these ideas, because it was not *their* reality and because primitive religion succeeded in camouflaging its social function. Concepts
such as impurity and contagion, because they translate human relations
into material terms, provide a sort of camouflage. The peril that overshadows all human relations and that stems from these relations is
presented either in a purely material or in a wholly otherworldly guise.
The notion of ritual impurity can degenerate until it is nothing more
than a terror-stricken belief in the malevolent results of physical contact. Violence has been transformed into a sort of seminal fluid that
impregnates objects on contact and whose diffusion, like electricity or
Balzacian "magnetism," is determined by physical laws. Far from dis-
sipating the ignorance that surrounds these concepts, modern thinking
only reinforces the confusion. By denying religion any basis in reality,
by viewing it as a sort of bedtime story for children, we collaborate
with violence in its game of deception.

In many religious communities—among the ancient Greeks, for instance—when a man has hanged himself, his body becomes impure. So too does the rope from which he dangles, the tree to which the rope is attached, and the field where the tree stands. The taint of impurity diminishes, however, as one draws away from the body. It is as if the scene of a violent act, and the objects with which the violence has been committed, send out emanations that penetrate everything in the immediate area, growing gradually weaker through time and space.

When a town has undergone a terrible bloodletting, and emissaries from that town are sent to another community, they are considered impure. Every effort is made to avoid touching them, talking to them, remaining in their presence any longer than necessary. After their departure rites of purification are undertaken: sacrifices offered, lustral water sprinkled about.

While Frazer and his disciples tend to view this fear of infection by the "impure" as a prime example of the "irrational" and "superstitious" element of religious thought, other observers regard it as an anticipation of sound scientific principles. They point out the striking resemblance between the precautions that modern medicine takes against bacterial infection and the ritualistic avoidance of pollution.

In some societies contagious diseases—smallpox, for instance—have their own particular gods. During his illness the patient is dedicated to the god; that is, he is isolated from the community and put under the supervision of an "initiate," or priest of the god, someone who has contracted the illness and survived it. This man now partakes of the god's power; he is immune to the effects of the divine violence.

It is easy to see why some observers have concluded that these impurity rituals reveal some sort of vague intuitive knowledge of microbiology; that the rituals, in short, are grounded in fact. Against this view it is argued that the procedures that are supposed to protect the believers from ritual impurity often disregard, or even flout, the principles of modern hygiene. This argument is not wholly satisfactory, however, for it fails to take into account the possible parallels between ritualistic precautions and the first tentative measures taken in the early days of public hygiene—in the nineteenth century, for example.

The theory that regards religious terrors or taboos as a sort of proto-science has hit on something of real interest, but too indefinite and limited to be of much use in our investigation. Such a theory can only arise in a culture that regards *sickness* as the sole fatal influence, the sole enemy man has to conquer. Clearly, medical considerations are not excluded from the primitive concept of contagion, and the prevention of epidemics plays a definite role in impurity rites. But these factors play only a minor role in primitive culture. They arouse our interest precisely because they offer the sole instance in which the modern scientific notion of contagion, which is exclusively pathological, coincides with the primitive concept, which is far broader in scope.

The aspects of religion in which contagion seems to have some reality for us are hard to distinguish from those in which it ceases to have any reality. That is not to say that primitive religion is afflicted with the sort of "confusion" that Frazer or Lévy-Bruhl attributed to it. The assimilation of contagious diseases and all forms of violence—the latter also regarded as contagious in nature—is based on a number of complementary inferences that combine to form a strikingly coherent picture.

A primitive society, a society that lacks a legal system, is exposed to the sudden escalation of violence. Such a society is compelled to adopt attitudes we may well find incomprehensible. Our incomprehension seems to stem from two main factors. In the first place, we know absolutely nothing about the contagion of violence, not even whether it actually exists. In the second place, the primitive people themselves recognize this violence only in an almost entirely dehumanized form; that is, under the deceptive guise of the *sacred*.

Considered all together, the ritual precautions against violence are firmly rooted in reality, absurd though some of them may appear to our own eyes. If the sacrificial catharsis actually succeeds in preventing the unlimited propagation of violence, a sort of *infection* is in fact being checked.

From the outset of this study, after all, I have regarded violence as something eminently communicable. The tendency of violence to hurl itself on a surrogate if deprived of its original object can surely be described as a contaminating process. Violence too long held in check will overflow its bounds—and woe to those who happen to be nearby. Ritual precautions are intended both to prevent this flooding and to offer protection, insofar as it is possible, to those who find themselves in the path of ritual impurity—that is, caught in the floodtide of violence.

The slightest outbreak of violence can bring about a catastrophic escalation. Though we may tend to lose sight of this fact in our own daily lives, we are intellectually aware of its validity, and are often reminded that there is something infectious about the spectacle of violence. Indeed, at times it is impossible to stay immune from the infection. Where violence is concerned, intolerance can prove as fatal an attitude as tolerance, for when it breaks out it can happen that those who oppose its progress do more to assure its triumph than those who endorse it. There is no universal rule for quelling violence, no principle of guaranteed effectiveness. At times all the remedies, harsh as well as gentle, seem efficacious; at other times, every measure seems to heighten the fever it is striving to abate.

Inevitably the moment comes when violence can only be countered by more violence. Whether we fail or succeed in our effort to subdue it, the real victor is always violence itself. The *mimetic* attributes of violence are extraordinary—sometimes direct and positive, at other times indirect and negative. The more men strive to curb their violent impulses, the more these impulses seem to prosper. The very weapons used to combat violence are turned against their users. Violence is like a raging fire that feeds on the very objects intended to smother its flames.

The metaphor of fire could well give way to metaphors of tempest, flood, earthquake. Like the plague, the resemblance violence bears to these natural cataclysms is not limited to the realm of poetic imagery. In acknowledging that fact, however, we do not mean to endorse the theory that sees in the sacred a simple transfiguration of natural phenomena.

The sacred consists of all those forces whose dominance over man increases or seems to increase in proportion to man's effort to master them. Tempests, forest fires, and plagues, among other phenomena, may be classified as sacred. Far outranking these, however, though in a far less obvious manner, stands human violence—violence seen as something exterior to man and henceforth as a part of all the other outside forces that threaten mankind. Violence is the heart and secret soul of the sacred.

We have yet to learn how man succeeds in positing his own violence as an independent being. Once he has accomplished this feat, however, the sacred presence invades his universe, mysteriously infects, without participating in it, and buffets him about rather in the manner of a plague or other natural disaster. Once all this has occurred, man is confronted with a group of phenomena that, despite their heterogeneous appearance, exhibit remarkable similarities.

As a general practice, it is wise to avoid contact with the sick if one wishes to stay healthy. Similarly, it is wise to steer clear of homicides if one is eager not to be killed.

As we see it, these are two distinct types of "contagion." Modern science concerns itself exclusively with one type, and has established its reality beyond all dispute. However, the other type could well be of greater importance to the members of a society that we have defined as primitive—that is, a society lacking legal sanctions.

Religious thought encompasses a large body of phenomena under the heading of ritual impurity—phenomena that seem disparate and absurd from the viewpoint of modern science but whose relationship and reality become perfectly clear when tested for the presence of basic violence, the prime ingredient and ultimate resource of the whole system.

There are undeniable similarities, for instance, between a bout of serious illness and an act of violence wilfully perpetrated by an enemy. The sufferings of the invalid are analogous to those of the wounded victim; and if the invalid runs the risk of dying, so too do all those who are involved in one fashion or another, either actively or passively, in a violent action. Death is nothing more than the worst form of violence that can befall a man. It is no less reasonable, therefore, to lump together all the possible causes of death, pathological and otherwise, than it is to create a separate category for only one of them: sickness.

To understand religious thought requires an empirical approach. The goal of religious thinking is exactly the same as that of technological research—namely, practical action. Whenever man is truly concerned with obtaining concrete results, whenever he is hard pressed by reality, he abandons abstract speculation and reverts to a mode of response that becomes increasingly cautious and conservative as the forces he hopes to subdue, or at least to outrun, draw ever nearer.

In its simplest, perhaps most elementary form, religion manifests little curiosity about the origins of those terrible forces that visit their fury on mankind but seems to concentrate its attention on determining a regular sequential pattern that will enable man to anticipate these onslaughts and take measures against them.

Religious empiricism invariably leads to one conclusion: it is essential to keep as far away as possible from sacred things, always to avoid direct contact with them. Naturally, such thinking occasionally coincides with medical empiricism or with scientific empiricism in general. This is why some observers insist on regarding religious empiricism as a preliminary stage of science.

This same empiricism, however, can sometimes reach conclusions so utterly foreign to our own way of thinking and can show itself so narrow, inflexible and myopic in its attitudes that we are tempted to attribute its functioning to some sort of psychological malaise. Such a reaction leads us to regard primitive society as an "ailing" society, beside which our "civilized" society presents a picture of radiant health.

The adherents of this theory show no hesitation in standing these categories on their heads, however, whenever the need arises. Thus, on occasion, it is "civilization" that is sick; and because civilized society is the antithesis of primitive society, it now appears that the primitive sphere must be the healthy one. Manipulate them as one will, it looks as if the concepts of sickness and health are not very useful in clarifying the relationship between primitive societies and our own.

Ritual precautions that appear lunatic or at least highly exaggerated in a modern context are in fact quite reasonable when viewed in their proper context—that is, in the context of religion's complete unaware-ness of the violence it makes sacred. When men believe that they can actually feel the breath of a Homeric Cyclops at their backs, they are apt to resort to all means at their disposal, to embrace all possible precautions. It seems safer to overreact than to underreact.

This religious attitude is not dissimilar to that of medicine when suddenly confronted with an unknown disease. An epidemic breaks out; the doctors and scientists are unable to isolate the pathogenic agent. Under the circumstances, what should they do? Clearly they must adopt, not *some* of the precautionary measures employed against familiar diseases, but *all* of them, without exception. Ideally, they would invent entirely new measures, since the enemy they are fighting is itself employing new weapons.

Once the microbe has been identified, it is seen that some of the measures employed were completely useless and should be abandoned in any future dealings with the disease. Yet it must be admitted that as long as the cause of the illness was unknown, their use was fully justified.

We must be careful not to push our metaphor too far. Neither primitive nor modern man has yet succeeded in identifying the mi-crobe responsible for the dread disease of violence. Western civiliza-tion is hindered in its efforts to isolate and analyze the causes and to examine them in any but the most superficial manner because it has enjoyed until this day a mysterious immunity from the most virulent forms of violence—an immunity not, it seems, of our society's making, but one that has perhaps resulted in the making of our society.

AMONG PRIMITIVE TABOOS the one that has per-haps been most analyzed is the taboo surrounding menstrual blood. Menstrual blood is regarded as impure; menstruating women are segre-gated from the community. They are forbidden to touch any objects of communal usage, sometimes even their own food, for risk of contami-nation.

If we wish to understand why menstruation is considered "impure," we must consider it within the general category of bloodletting. Most primitive peoples take the utmost care to avoid contact with blood. Spilt blood of any origin, unless it has been associated with a sacrificial act, is considered impure. This universal attribution of impurity to spilt blood springs directly from the definition we have just proposed: wherever violence threatens, ritual impurity is present. When men are enjoying peace and security, blood is a rare sight. When violence is unloosed, however, blood appears everywhere—on the ground, underfoot, forming great pools. Its very fluidity gives form to the contagious nature of violence. Its presence proclaims murder and announces new upheavals to come. Blood stains everything it touches the color of violence and death. Its very appearance seems, as the saying goes, to "cry out for vengeance."

Any bloodletting is frightening. It is only natural, therefore, that menstrual bleeding should awaken fear. However, there is another, complicating element at work here. Although menstrual bleeding can be readily distinguished from blood spilt in a murder or an accident and can thus be dissociated from those virulent forms of violence, it is in many societies regarded as the most impure of impurities. We can only assume that this extreme reaction has to do with the sexual aspect of menstruation.

Sexuality is one of those primary forces whose sovereignty over man is assured by man's firm belief in his sovereignty over it. The most extreme forms of violence can never be directly sexual because they are collective in nature. The group is quite capable of perpetrating a single, coherent act of violence, whose force is increased with the addition of each individual quotient of violence; but sexuality is never truly collective. That fact alone explains why sexual interpretations of the sacred invariably ignore or play down the role of violence, whereas an interpretation based on violence readily grants sexuality the prominent place it occupies in all primitive religions. We are tempted to conclude that violence is impure because of its relation to sexuality. Yet only the reverse proposition can withstand close scrutiny. Sexuality is impure because it has to do with violence.

Such an idea seems to run counter to the spirit of contemporary humanism, which has settled into a friendly accord with the pan-sexualism of the psychoanalysts and remains unruffled even by the death-wish theory. Nonetheless, the signs are too numerous and too clear to be ignored. We have conceded that menstrual blood has a direct relationship to sexuality; we also contend that its relationship to unleashed violence is even closer. The blood of a murdered man is impure. This impurity cannot be derived from the impurity attributed to menstrual blood. On the other hand, to understand the impurity of menstrual blood we must trace its relationship to blood spilt by violence, as well as to sexuality. The fact that the sexual organs of women periodically emit a flow of blood has always made a great impression on men; it seems to confirm an affinity between sexuality and those diverse forms of violence that invariably lead to bloodshed.

To understand the nature and extent of this affinity we must return to that solid core of "common sense" that plays a far greater role in religious thinking than fashionable theorists are willing to acknowledge. In fact, the notion that the beliefs of all mankind are a grand mystification that we alone have succeeded in penetrating is a hardy perennial—as well as being, to say the least, somewhat arrogant. The problem at hand is not the arrogance of Western science nor its blatant "imperialism," but rather its sheer inadequacy. It is precisely when the need to understand becomes most urgent that the explanations proposed in the domain of religion become most unsatisfactory.

The connection between sexuality and religion is a heritage common to all religions and is supported by an impressive array of convergent facts. Sex and violence frequently come to grips in such direct forms as abduction, rape, defloration, and various sadistic practices, as well as in indirect actions of indefinite consequences. Sex is at the origin of various illnesses, real or imaginary; it culminates in the bloody labors of childbirth, which may entail the death of mother, child, or both together. Even within the ritualistic framework of marriage, when all the matrimonial vows and other interdictions have been conscientiously observed, sexuality is accompanied by violence; and as soon as one trespasses beyond the limits of matrimony to engage in illicit relationships—incest, adultery, and the like—the violence, and the impurity resulting from this violence, grows more potent and extreme. Sexuality leads to quarrels, jealous rages, mortal combats. It is a permanent source of disorder even within the most harmonious of communities.

In refusing to admit an association between sexuality and violence— an association readily acknowledged by men over the course of several millennia—modern thinkers are attempting to prove their broadmindedness and liberality. Their stance has led to numerous misconceptions. Like violence, sexual desire tends to fasten upon surrogate objects if the object to which it was originally attracted remains inaccessible; it willingly accepts substitutes. And again like violence, repressed sexual desire accumulates energy that sooner or later bursts forth, causing tremendous havoc. It is also worth noting that the shift from violence to sexuality and from sexuality to violence is easily effected, even by the most "normal" of individuals, totally lacking in perversion. Thwarted sexuality leads naturally to violence, just as lovers' quarrels often end in an amorous embrace. Recent scientific findings seem to justify the primitive perspective on many points. Sexual excitement and violent impulses manifest themselves in the same manner. In both instances, the majority of discernible bodily reactions are identical.[15]

Before we attempt to explain away the taboo on menstrual blood by means of some all-inclusive, generalized interpretation—before, for example, we invoke those "phantasms" that play the same role in our consciousness as do the enchanters' tricks" in Don Quixote's—we should make quite sure that we have first exhausted all direct avenues to comprehension. In fact, there is nothing incomprehensible about the viewpoint that sees menstrual blood as a physical representation of sexual violence. We ought, however, to go further: to inquire whether this process of symbolization does not respond to some half-suppressed desire to place the blame for all forms of violence on women. By means of this taboo a transfer of violence has been effected and a monopoly established that is clearly detrimental to the female sex.

THE TAINT OF impurity cannot always be avoided; even the most careful precautions are no security against it. And the least contact with the infection can contaminate the entire community.

How can one cleanse the infected members of all trace of pollution? Does there exist some miraculous substance potent enough not only to resist infection but also to purify, if need be, the contaminated blood? Only blood itself, blood whose purity has been guaranteed by the performance of appropriate rites—the blood, in short, of sacrificial victims—can accomplish this feat.

Behind this astonishing paradox, the menace of violent action can be discerned. All concepts of impurity stem ultimately from the community's fear of a perpetual cycle of violence arising in its midst. The menace is always the same and provokes the same set of responses, the same sacrificial gestures designed to redirect the violence onto inconsequential victims. The idea of ritual purification is far more than mere shadow play or illusion.

The function of ritual is to "purify" violence; that is, to "trick" violence into spending itself on victims whose death will provoke no reprisals. Because the secret of this mechanism is unknown to the participants in the rites, religion tries to account for its own operation metaphorically, using for that purpose the objects and materials involved in that operation. The properties of blood, for example, vividly illustrate the entire operation of violence. We have already spoken of blood spilt by mischance or malice. Blood that dries on the victim soon loses its viscous quality and becomes first a dark sore, then a roughened scab. Blood that is allowed to congeal on its victim is the impure

[15] Storr, *Human Aggression*, pp. 18–19.

product of violence, illness, or death. In contrast to this contaminated substance is the fresh blood of newly slaughtered victims, crimson and free flowing. This blood is never allowed to congeal, but is removed without trace as soon as the rites have been concluded.

The physical metamorphosis of spilt blood can stand for the double nature of violence. Some religious practices make elaborate use of this duality. Blood serves to illustrate the point that the same substance can stain or cleanse, contaminate or purify, drive men to fury and murder or appease their anger and restore them to life.

We are not dealing here with one of Gaston Bachelard's "material metaphors," a poetic recreation of little real consequence. Nor does Laura Makarius's suggestion that the ambiguous character of blood is in fact the ultimate reality behind the constant reversals of primitive religion seem wholly apposite here.[16] Both authors lose sight of a crucial point: the paradoxical nature of violence. Although religion grasps this paradox—and that only tentatively—mostly by means of such symbolic representations as that of blood, it differs radically from modern theory, which speaks of "phantasms" and "poetry" and does not even realize how real the sacrificial process can be and how appropriate the major metaphors and symbols through which it is expressed.

Even the wildest aberrations of religious thought still manage to bear witness to the fact that evil and the violent measures taken to combat evil are essentially the same. At times violence appears to man in its most terrifying aspect, wantonly sowing chaos and destruction; at other times it appears in the guise of peacemaker, graciously distributing the fruits of sacrifice.

The secret of the dual nature of violence still eludes men. Beneficial violence must be carefully distinguished from harmful violence, and the former continually promoted at the expense of the latter. Ritual is nothing more than the regular exercise of "good" violence. As we have remarked, if sacrificial violence is to be effective it must resemble the nonsacrificial variety as closely as possible. That is why some rites may seem to us nothing more than senseless inversions of prohibited acts. For instance, in some societies menstrual blood is regarded as a beneficial substance when employed in certain rites but retains its baleful character in other contexts.

The two-in-one nature of blood—that is, of violence—is strikingly illustrated in Euripides' *Ion*. The Athenian queen, Creusa, plots to do away with the hero by means of an exotic talisman: two drops of blood from the deadly Gorgon. One drop is a deadly poison, the other

16 Cf. Laura Makarius, "Les Tabous du forgeron," *Diogène* 62 (April–June 1968).

a miraculous healing agent. The queen's old slave asks her the origin of
this substance:

> *Creusa:* When the fatal blow was struck a drop spurted
> from the hollow vein. . . .
> *Slave:* How is it used? What are its properties?
> *Creusa:* It wards off all sickness and nourishes life.
> *Slave:* And the other drop?
> *Creusa:* It kills. It is made from the Gorgon's venomous
> serpents.
> *Slave:* Do you carry them mixed together or separate?
> *Creusa:* Are good and evil to be mixed together?
> Separate, of course.

Nothing could seem more alike than two drops of blood, yet in this
case nothing could be more different. It is only too easy to blend them
together and produce a substance that would efface all distinction between the pure and the impure. Then the difference between "good"
and "bad" violence would be eliminated as well. As long as purity and
impurity remain distinct, even the worst pollution can be washed
away; but once they are allowed to mingle, purification is no longer
possible.

Chapter Two

The Sacrificial Crisis

AS WE HAVE SEEN, the proper functioning of the sacrificial process requires not only the complete separation of the sacrificed victim from those beings for whom the victim is a substitute but also a similarity between both parties. This dual requirement can be fulfilled only through a delicately balanced mechanism of associations.

Any change, however slight, in the hierarchical classification of living creatures risks undermining the whole sacrificial structure. The sheer repetition of the sacrificial act—the repeated slaughter of the same type of victim—inevitably brings about such change. But the inability to adapt to new conditions is a trait characteristic of religion in general. If, as is often the case, we encounter the institution of sacrifice either in an advanced state of decay or reduced to relative insignificance, it is because it has already undergone a good deal of wear and tear.

Whether the slippage in the mechanism is due to "too little" or "too much" contact between the victim and those whom the victim represents, the results are the same. The elimination of violence is no longer effected; on the contrary, conflicts within the community multiply, and the menace of chain reactions looms ever larger.

If the gap between the victim and the community is allowed to grow too wide, all similarity will be destroyed. The victim will no longer be capable of attracting the violent impulses to itself; the sacrifice will cease to serve as a "good conductor," in the sense that metal is a good conductor of electricity. On the other hand, if there is *too much* continuity the violence will overflow its channels. "Impure" violence will mingle with the "sacred" violence of the rites, turning the latter into a scandalous accomplice in the process of pollution, even a kind of catalyst in the propagation of further impurity.

These are postulates that seem to take form a priori from our earlier conclusions. They can also be discerned in literature—in the adaptations of certain myths in classical Greek tragedy, in particular in Euripides' version of the legend of Heracles.

Euripides' *Heracles* contains no tragic conflict, no debate between

39

declared adversaries. The real subject of the play is the failure of a sacrifice, the act of sacrificial violence that suddenly *goes wrong*. Heracles, returning home after the completion of his labors, finds his wife and children in the power of a usurper named Lycus, who is preparing to offer them as sacrificial victims. Heracles kills Lycus. After this most recent act of violence, committed in the heart of the city, the hero's need to purify himself is greater than ever, and he sets about preparing a sacrifice of his own. His wife and children are with him when Heracles, suddenly seized by madness, mistakes them for his enemies and *sacrifices* them.

Heracles' misidentification of his family is attributed to Lyssa, goddess of madness, who is operating as an emissary of two other goddesses, Iris and Hera, who bear Heracles ill will. The preparations for the sacrifice provide an imposing setting for the homicidal outburst; it is unlikely that their dramatic significance passed unnoticed by the author. In fact, it is Euripides himself who directs our attention to the ritualistic origins of the onslaught. After the massacre, Heracles' father, Amphitryon, asks his son: "My child, what happened to you? How could this horror have taken place? Was it perhaps the spilt blood that turned your head?" Heracles, who is just returning to consciousness and remembers nothing, inquires in turn: "Where did the madness overtake me? Where did it strike me down?" Amphitryon replies: "Near the altar, where you were purifying your hands over the sacred flames."

The sacrifice contemplated by the hero succeeded only too well in polarizing the forces of violence. Indeed, it produced a superabundance of violence of a particularly virulent kind. As Amphitryon suggested, the blood shed in the course of the terrible labors and in the city itself finally turned the hero's head. Instead of drawing off the violence and allowing it to ebb away, the rites brought a veritable flood of violence down on the victim. The sacrificial rites were no longer able to accomplish their task; they swelled the surging tide of impure violence instead of channeling it. The mechanism of substitutions had gone astray, and those whom the sacrifice was designed to protect became its victims.

The difference between sacrificial and nonsacrificial violence is anything but exact; it is even arbitrary. At times the difference threatens to disappear entirely. There is no such thing as truly "pure" violence. Nevertheless, sacrificial violence can, in the proper circumstances, serve as an agent of purification. That is why those who perform the rites are obliged to purify themselves at the conclusion of the sacrifice. The procedure followed is reminiscent of atomic power plants; when the expert has finished decontaminating the installation, he must himself be decontaminated. And accidents can always happen.

The catastrophic inversion of the sacrificial act would appear to be an essential element in the Heracles myth. The motif reappears, thinly concealed behind secondary themes, in another episode of his story, in Sophocles' *The Women of Trachis.*

Heracles had mortally wounded the centaur Nessus, who had assaulted Heracles' wife, Deianira. Before dying, the centaur gave the young woman a shirt smeared with his sperm—or, in Sophocles' version, smeared with his blood mixed with the blood of a Hydra. (Once again, as in the *Ion*, we encounter the theme of the two kinds of blood mingling to form one.)

The subject of the tragedy, as in Euripides' *Heracles*, is the return of the hero. In this instance Heracles is bringing with him a pretty young captive, of whom Deianira is jealous. Deianira sends a servant to her husband with a welcoming gift, the shirt of Nessus. With his dying breath the centaur had told her that the shirt would assure the wearer's eternal fidelity to her; but he cautioned her to keep it well out of the way of any flame or source of heat.

Heracles puts on the shirt, and soon afterward lights a fire for the rites of sacrificial purification. The flames activate the poison in the shirt; it is the rite itself that unlooses the evil. Heracles, contorted with pain, presently ends his life on the pyre he has begged his son to prepare. Before dying, Heracles kills the servant who delivered the shirt to him; this death, along with his own and the subsequent suicide of his wife, contributes to the cycle of violence heralded by Heracles' return and the failure of the sacrifice. Once again, violence has struck the beings who sought the protection of sacrificial rites.

A number of sacrifice motifs intermingle in these two plays. A special sort of impurity clings to the warrior returning to his homeland, still tainted with the slaughter of war. In the case of Heracles, his sanguinary labors render him particularly impure.

The returning warrior risks carrying the seed of violence into the very heart of his city. The myth of Horatius, as explicated by Georges Dumézil, illustrates this theme: Horatius kills his sister before any ritual purification has been performed. In the case of Heracles the impurity triumphs over the rite itself.

If we examine the mechanism of violence in these two tragedies, we notice that when the sacrifice goes wrong it sets off a chain reaction of the sort defined in the first chapter. The murder of Lycus is presented in the Euripides play as a last "labor" of the hero, a still-rational prelude to the insane outburst that follows. Seen from the perspective of the ritualist, it might well constitute a first link of impure violence.

With this incident, as we have noted, violence invades the heart of the city. This initial murder corresponds to the death of the old servant in *The Women of Trachis*.

Supernatural intervention plays no part in these episodes, except perhaps to cast a thin veil over the true subject: the sacrificial celebration that has gone wrong. The goddess Lyssa, Nessus' shirt—these add nothing to the meaning of the two stories; rather, they act as a veil, and as soon as the veil is drawn aside we encounter the same theme of "good" violence turning into "bad." The mythological accompaniments of the stories can be seen as redundant. Lyssa, the goddess of madness, sounds more like a refugee from an allegorical tale than a real goddess, and Nessus' shirt joins company with all the acts of violence that Heracles carries on his back.

The theme of the Warrior's Return is not, strictly speaking, mythological, and readily lends itself to sociological or psychological interpretations. The conquering hero who threatens to destroy the liberty of his homeland belongs to history, not myth. Certainly that is the way Corneille seems to approach the subject in *Horace*, although in his version of the tale the ideology is somewhat reversed—the returning warrior is rightly shocked by his sister's lack of patriotism. We could easily translate the "case histories" of Heracles and Horatius into psychological or psychoanalytical terms and come up with numerous working theories, each at variance with the other. But we should avoid this temptation, for in debating the relative merits of each theory we would lose sight of the role played by ritual—a subject that has nothing to do with such debates, even though it may, as we shall see, open the way to them. Being more *primitive*, ritualistic action is hospitable to all ideological interpretations and dependent on none. It has only one axiom: the contagious nature of the violence encountered by the warrior in battle—and only one prescription: the proper performance of ritual purification. Its sole purpose is to prevent the resurgence of violence and its spread throughout the community.

The two tragedies we have been discussing present in anecdotal form, as if dealing exclusively with exceptional individuals, events that are significant because they affect the community as a whole. Sacrifice is a social act, and when it goes amiss the consequences are not limited to some "exceptional" individual singled out by Destiny.

Historians seem to agree that Greek tragedy belonged to a period of transition between the dominance of an archaic theocracy and the emergence of a new, "modern" order based on statism and laws. Before its decline the archaic order must have enjoyed a certain stability; and this stability must have reposed on its religious element—that is, on the sacrificial rites.

Although they predate the tragedians, the pre-Socratics are often regarded as the philosophers of classical tragedy. In their writings we can find echoes of the religious crisis we are attempting to define. The fifth fragment of Heraclitus quite clearly deals with the decay of sacrificial rites, with their inability to purify what is impure. Religious beliefs are compromised by the decadent state of the ritual: "In vain do they strive for purification by besmirching themselves with blood, as the man who has bathed in the mire seeks to cleanse himself with mud. Such antics can only strike the beholder as utter folly! In addressing their prayers to images of the gods, they might just as well be speaking to the walls, without seeking to know the true nature of gods or heroes."

The difference between blood spilt for ritual and for criminal purposes no longer holds. The Heraclitus fragment appears in even sharper relief when compared to analogous passages in the Old Testament. The preexilian prophets Amos, Isaiah, and Micah denounce in vehement terms the impotence of the sacrificial process and ritual in general. In the most explicit manner they link the decay of religious practices to the deterioration of contemporary behavior. Inevitably, the eroding of the sacrificial system seems to result in the emergence of reciprocal violence. Neighbors who had previously discharged their mutual aggressions on a third party, joining together in the sacrifice of an "outside" victim, now turn to sacrificing one another. Empedocles' *Purifications* brings us even closer to the problem:

136. When will the sinister noise of this carnage cease? Can you not see that you are devouring one another with your callous hearts?
137. The father seizes hold of the son, who has changed form; in his mad delusion he kills him, murmuring prayers. The son cries out, imploring his insane executioner to spare him. But the father hears him not, and cuts his throat, and spreads a great feast in his palace. In the same way the son takes hold of the father, the children their mother, one slaughtering the other and devouring their own flesh and blood.

The concept of a "sacrificial crisis" may be useful in clarifying certain aspects of Greek tragedy. To a real extent it is sacrificial religion that provides the language for these dramas; the criminal in the plays sees himself not so much as a righter-of-wrongs as a performer-of-sacrifices. We always view the "tragic flaw" from the perspective of the new, emergent order; never from that of the old order in the final stages of decay. The reason for this approach is clear: modern thought has never been able to attribute any real function to the practice of sacrifice, and because the nature of the practice eludes us, we naturally find it difficult to determine when and if this practice is in the process of disintegration. In the case of Greek tragedy it is not enough merely to believe in the existence of the old order; we must look deeper if we hope to discover the religious problems of the era. Unlike the Jewish prophets, whose viewpoint was historical, the Greek tragedians evoked their own sacrificial crisis in terms of legendary figures whose forms were fixed by tradition.

All the bloody events that serve as background to the plays—the plagues and pestilences, civil and foreign wars—undoubtedly reflect the contemporary scene, but the images are unclear, as if viewed through a glass darkly. Each time, for example, a play of Euripides deals with the collapse of a royal house (as in *Heracles, Iphigenia in Aulis*, or *The Bacchae*), we are convinced that the poet is suggesting that the scene before our eyes is only the tip of the iceberg, that the real issue is the fate of the entire community. At the moment when Heracles is slaughtering his family offstage, the chorus cries out: "Look, look! The tempest is shaking the house; the roof is falling in."

If the tragic crisis is indeed to be described in terms of the sacrificial crisis, its relationship to sacrifice should be apparent in all aspects of tragedy—either conveyed directly through explicit reference or perceived indirectly, in broad outline, underlying the texture of the drama.

If the art of tragedy is to be defined in a single phrase, we might do worse than call attention to one of its most characteristic traits: the opposition of symmetrical elements. There is no aspect of the plot, form, or language of a tragedy in which this symmetrical pattern does not recur. The third actor, for instance, hardly constitutes the innovation that critics have claimed. Third actor or no third actor, the core of the drama remains the tragic dialogue; that is, the fateful confrontation during which the two protagonists exchange insults and accusations with increasing earnestness and rapidity. The Greek public brought to these verbal contests the same educated sense of appreciation that French audiences many centuries later evinced for their own classic drama—for Théramène's famous speech from the last act of *Phèdre*, for example, or for almost any passage from *Le Cid*.

The symmetry of the tragic dialogue is perfectly mirrored by the stichomythia, in which the two protagonists address one another in alternating lines. In tragic dialogue hot words are substituted for cold steel. But whether the violence is physical or verbal, the suspense remains the same. The adversaries match blow for blow, and they seem so evenly matched that it is impossible to predict the outcome of the battle. The structural similarity between the two forms of violence is illustrated by the description of the duel between the brothers Eteocles and Polyneices in Euripides' *Phoenician Women*. There is nothing in this account that does not apply equally to both brothers: their parries, thrusts, and feints, their gestures and postures, are identical: "If either saw the other's eye peer over the rim of his shield, He raised his spear."

Polyneices loses his spear in the fight, and so does Eteocles. Both are wounded. Each blow upsets the equilibrium, threatening to decide the outcome then and there. It is immediately followed by a new blow that not only redresses the balance but creates a symmetrical disequilibrium that is itself, naturally enough, of short duration. The tragic suspense follows the rhythm of these rapid exchanges, each one of which promises to bring matters to a head—but never quite does so. "They struggle now on even terms, each having spent his spear. Swords are unsheathed, and the two brothers are locked in close combat. Shield clashes with shield, and a great clamor engulfs them both." Even death fails to tip the balance. "They hit the dust and lay together side by side; and their heritage was still unclaimed."

The death of the brothers resolves nothing; it simply perpetuates the symmetry of the battle. Each had been his army's champion, and the two armies now resume the struggle, reestablish the symmetry. Oddly enough, however, the conflict is now transferred to a purely verbal plane, transforming itself into a true tragic dialogue. Tragedy now assumes its proper function as a verbal extension of physical combat, an interminable debate set off by the chronically indecisive character of an act of violence committed previously:

> The soldiers then leapt to their feet, and the argument began. We claimed that our king had won; they claimed the victory for Polyneices. The captains quarreled, too. Some said that Polyneices had struck the first blow; others replied that death had snatched the palm of victory from both claimants.

The indecisiveness of the first combat spreads quite naturally to the second, which then sows it abroad. The tragic dialogue is a debate without resolution. Each side resolutely continues to deploy the same arguments, emphases, goals; *Gleichgewicht* is Hölderlin's word for it. Tragedy is the balancing of the scale, not of justice but of violence. No sooner is something added to one side of the scale than its equivalent is contributed to the other. The same insults and accusations fly from one combatant to the other, as a ball flies from one player to another in tennis. The conflict stretches on interminably because between the two adversaries there is no difference whatsoever.

The equilibrium in the struggle has often been attributed to a so-called tragic impartiality; Hölderlin's word is *Impartialität*. I do not find this interpretation quite satisfactory. Impartiality implies a deliberate refusal to take sides, a firm commitment to treat both contestants equally. The impartial party is not eager to resolve the issue, does not want to know if there is a resolution; nor does he maintain that resolution is impossible. His impartiality-at-any-price is not unfrequently simply an unsubstantiated assertion of superiority. One of the adversaries is right, the other wrong, and the onlooker is obliged to take sides; either that, or the rights and wrongs are so evenly distributed between the two factions that taking sides is impossible. The self-proclaimed advocate of impartiality does not want to commit himself to either course of action. If pushed toward one camp, he seeks refuge in the other. Men always find it distasteful to admit that the "reasons" on both sides of a dispute are equally valid—which is to say that *violence operates without reason.*

Tragedy begins at that point where the illusion of impartiality, as well as the illusions of the adversaries, collapses. For example, in *Oedipus the King*, Oedipus, Creon, and Tiresias are each in turn drawn into a conflict that each had thought to resolve in the role of impartial mediator.

It is not clear to what extent the tragedians themselves managed to remain impartial. For example, Euripides in *The Phoenician Women* barely conceals his preference for Eteocles—or perhaps we should say his preference for the Athenian public's approval. In any case, his partiality is superficial. The preferences registered for one side or another never prevent the authors from constantly underlining the symmetrical relationship between the adversaries.

At the very moment when they appear to be abandoning impartiality, the tragedians do their utmost to deprive the audience of any means of taking sides. Aeschylus, Sophocles, and Euripides all utilize the same procedures and almost identical phraseology to convey symmetry, identity, reciprocity. We encounter here an aspect of tragic art that has been largely overlooked by contemporary criticism. Nowadays critics tend to assess a work of art on the basis of its *originality*. To the extent that an author cannot claim exclusive rights to his themes, his style, and his esthetic effects, his work is deemed deficient. In the domain of esthetics, singularity reigns supreme.

Such criteria cannot apply, of course, to Greek tragedy, whose authors were not committed to the doctrine of originality at any price. Nevertheless, our frustrated individualism still exerts a deleterious effect on modern interpretations of Greek tragedy.

It is readily apparent that Aeschylus, Sophocles, and Euripides shared certain literary traits and that the characters in their plays have certain characteristics in common. Yet there is no reason to label these resemblances mere stereotypes. It is my belief that these "stereotypes" contain the very essence of Greek tragedy. And if the tragic element in these plays still eludes us, it is because we have obstinately averted our attention from these similarities.

The tragedians portray men and women caught up in a form of violence too impersonal in its workings, too brutal in its results, to allow any sort of value judgement, any sort of distinction, subtle or simplistic, to be drawn between "good" and "wicked" characters. That is why most modern interpretations go astray; we have still not extricated ourselves entirely from the "Manichean" frame of reference that gained sway in the Romantic era and still exerts its influence today.

In Greek tragedy violence invariably effaces the differences between antagonists. The sheer impossibility of asserting their differences fuels the rage of Eteocles and Polyneices. In Euripides' *Heracles* the hero kills Lycus to keep him from sacrificing his family, and next he does what he wanted to prevent his enemy from doing, thereby falling victim to the ironic humor of a Destiny that seems to work hand in glove with violence. In the end it is Heracles who carries out the crime meditated by his counterpart. The more a tragic conflict is prolonged, the more likely it is to culminate in a violent mimesis; the resemblance between the combatants grows ever stronger until each presents a mirror image of the other. There is a scientific corollary: modern research suggests that individuals of quite different make-up and background respond to violence in essentially the same way.

It is the act of reprisal, the repetition of imitative acts of violence, that characterizes tragic plotting. The destruction of differences is particularly spectacular when the hierarchichal distance between the characters, the amount of respect due from one to the other, is great— between father and son, for instance. This scandalous effacement of distinctions is apparent in Euripides' *Alcestis*. Father and son are engaged in a tragic dialogue; each accuses the other of fleeing from death and leaving the heroine to die. The symmetry is perfect, emphasized by the symmetrical interventions of the members of the Chorus, who first castigate the son ("Young man, remember to whom you are speaking; do not insult your father"), and then rebuke the father ("Enough has been said on this subject; cease, we pray you, to abuse your own son.").

In *Oedipus the King* Sophocles frequently puts in Oedipus's mouth words that emphasize his resemblance to his father: resemblance in desires, suspicions, and course of action. If the hero throws himself impetuously into the investigation that causes his downfall, it is because he is reacting just as Laius did in seeking out the potential assassin who, according to the oracles, would replace him on the throne of Thebes and in the bed of the queen.

Oedipus finally kills Laius, but it is Laius who, at the crossroads, first raised his hand against his son. The patricide thus takes part in a reciprocal exchange of murderous gestures. It is an act of reprisal in a universe based on reprisals.

At the core of the Oedipus myth, as Sophocles presents it, is the proposition that all masculine relationships are based on reciprocal acts of violence. Laius, taking his cue from the oracle, violently rejects Oedipus out of fear that his son will seize his throne and invade his conjugal bed. Oedipus, taking his cue from the oracle, does away with Laius, violently rebuffs the sphinx, then takes their places—as king and "scourge of the city," respectively. Again, Oedipus, taking his cue from the oracle, plots the death of that unknown figure who may be seeking to usurp his own position. Oedipus, Creon, and Tiresias, each taking his cue from the oracle, seek one another's downfall.

All these acts of violence gradually wear away the differences that exist not only in the same family but throughout the community. The tragic combat between Oedipus and Tiresias pits the community's chief spiritual leaders against one another. The enraged Oedipus seeks to strip the aura of "mystery" from his rival, to prove that he is a false prophet, nothing more:

> Come tell us: have you truly shown yourself a prophet? When the terrible sphinx held sway over our countrymen, did you ever whisper the words that would have delivered them? That riddle was not to be answered by anyone; the gift of prophecy was called for. Yet that gift was clearly not yours to give; nor was it ever granted to you, either by the birds or by the gods.

Confronted by the king's frustration and rage at being unable to uncover the truth, Tiresias launches his own challenge. The terms are much the same: "If you are so clever at solving enigmas, why are you powerless to solve this one?" Both parties in this tragic dialogue have recourse to the same tactics, use the same weapons, and strive for the same goal: destruction of the adversary. Tiresias poses as the champion of tradition, taking up the cudgels on behalf of the oracles flouted by Oedipus. However, in so doing he shows himself insolent to royal authority. Although the targets are individuals, it is the institutions that receive the blows. Legitimate authority trembles on its pedestal, and the combatants finally assist in the downfall of the very order they strove to maintain. The impiety referred to by the chorus—the neglect of the oracles, the general decadence that pervades the religion of the community—are surely part of the same phenomenon that works away at the undermining of family relationships, as well as of religious and social hierarchies.

The *sacrificial crisis*, that is, the disappearance of the sacrificial rites, coincides with the disappearance of the difference between impure violence and purifying violence. When this difference has been effaced, purification is no longer possible and impure, contagious, reciprocal violence spreads throughout the community.

The sacrificial distinction, the distinction between the pure and the impure, cannot be obliterated without obliterating all other differences as well. One and the same process of violent reciprocity engulfs the whole. The sacrificial crisis can be defined, therefore, as a crisis of distinctions—that is, a crisis affecting the cultural order. This cultural order is nothing more than a regulated system of distinctions in which the differences among individuals are used to establish their "identity" and their mutual relationships.

In the first chapter the danger threatening the community with the decay of sacrificial practices was portrayed in terms of physical violence, of cyclical vengeance set off by a chain reaction. We now discover more insidious forms of the same evil. When the religious framework of a society starts to totter, it is not exclusively or immediately the physical security of the society that is threatened; rather, the whole cultural foundation of the society is put in jeopardy. The institutions lose their vitality; the protective façade of the society gives way; social values are rapidly eroded, and the whole cultural structure seems on the verge of collapse.

The hidden violence of the sacrificial crisis eventually succeeds in destroying distinctions, and this destruction in turn fuels the renewed violence. In short, it seems that anything that adversely affects the institution of sacrifice will ultimately pose a threat to the very basis of the community, to the principles on which its social harmony and equilibrium depend.

A SINGLE PRINCIPLE is at work in primitive religion and classical tragedy alike, a principle implicit but fundamental. Order, peace, and fecundity depend on cultural distinctions; it is not these distinctions but the loss of them that gives birth to fierce rivalries and sets members of the same family or social group at one another's throats.

Modern society aspires to equality among men and tends instinctively to regard all differences, even those unrelated to the economic or social status of men, as obstacles in the path of human happiness. This modern ideal exerts an obvious influence on ethnological approaches, although more often on the level of technical procedure than that of explicit principle. The permutations of this ideal are complex, rich in potential contradictions, and difficult to characterize briefly.

Suffice it to say that an "antidifferential" prejudice often falsifies the ethnological outlook not only on the origins of discord and conflict but also on all religious modes. Although usually implicit, its principles are explicitly set forth in Victor Turner's *The Ritual Process:* "Structural differentiation, both vertical and horizontal, is the foundation of strife and factionalism, and of struggles in dyadic relations between incumbents of positions or rivals for positions."¹ When differences come unhinged they are generally identified as the cause of those rivalries for which they also furnish the stakes. This has not always been their role. As in the case of sacrificial rites, when they no longer serve as a dam against violence, they serve to swell the flood.

In order to rid ourselves of some fashionable intellectual attitudes— useful enough in their place, but not always relevant in dealing with the past—we might turn to Shakespeare, who in the course of the famous speech of Ulysses in *Troilus and Cressida* makes some interesting observations on the interaction of violence and "differences." The point of view of primitive religion and Greek tragedy could not be better summarized than by this speech.

The Greek army has been besieging Troy for a long time and is growing demoralized through want of action. In commenting on their position, Ulysses strays from the particular to a general reflection on the role of "Degree," or distinctions, in human endeavors. "Degree," or *gradus*, is the underlying principle of all order, natural and cultural. It permits individuals to find a place for themselves in society; it lends a meaning to things, arranging them in proper sequence within a hierarchy; it defines the objects and moral standards that men alter, manipulate, and transform. The musical metaphor describes that order as a "structure," in the modern sense of the word, a system of chords thrown into disharmony by the sudden intervention of reciprocal violence:

> . . . O when Degree is shaked
> Which is the ladder to all high designs,
> The enterprise is sick! How could communities,
> Degrees in schools, and brotherhoods in cities,
> Peaceful commerce from dividable shores,
> The primogenitive and due of birth,
> Prerogative of age, crowns, sceptres, laurels,
> But by degree, stand in authentic place?
> Take but degree away, untune that string,
> And, hark, what discord follows! Each thing meets
> In mere oppugnancy: the bounded waters

¹ Victor Turner, *The Ritual Process* (Chicago, 1969), p. 179.

Should lift their bosoms higher than the shores,
And make a sop of all this solid globe:
Strength should be lord of imbecility,
And the rude son should strike his father dead:
Force should be right; or rather, right and wrong
Between whose endless jar justice resides,
Should lose their names, and so should justice too.

As in Greek tragedy and primitive religion, it is not the differences but the loss of them that gives rise to violence and chaos, that inspires Ulysses' plaint. This loss forces men into a perpetual confrontation, one that strips them of all their distinctive characteristics—in short, of their "identities." Language itself is put in jeopardy. "Each thing meets/In mere oppugnancy:" the adversaries are reduced to indefinite objects, "things" that wantonly collide with each other like loose cargo on the decks of a storm-tossed ship. The metaphor of the floodtide that transforms the earth's surface to a muddy mass is frequently employed by Shakespeare to designate the undifferentiated state of the world that is also portrayed in Genesis and that we have attributed to the sacrificial crisis.

In this situation no one and nothing is spared; coherent thinking collapses and rational activities are abandoned. All associative forms are dissolved or become antagonistic; all values, spiritual or material, perish. Of course, formal education, as represented by academic "degrees," is rendered useless, because its value derives from the now inoperative principle of universal differentiation. To say that this speech merely reflects a Renaissance commonplace, the great chain of being, is unsatisfactory. Who has ever seen a great chain of being collapse?

Ulysses is a career soldier, authoritarian in temper and conservative in inclination. Nevertheless, the order he is committed to defend is secretly acknowledged as arbitrary. The end of distinctions means the triumph of the strong over the weak, the pitting of father against son—the end of all human justice, which is here unexpectedly defined in terms of "differences" among individuals. If perfect equilibrium invariably leads to violence, as in Greek tragedy, it follows that the relative nonviolence guaranteed by human justice must be defined as a sort of imbalance, a difference between "good" and "evil" parallel to the sacrificial difference between "pure" and "impure." The idea of justice as a balanced scale, an exercise in exquisite impartiality, is utterly foreign to this theory, which sees the roots of justice in differences among men and the demise of justice in the elimination of these differences. Whenever the terrible equilibrium of tragedy prevails, all talk of right and wrong is futile. At that point in the conflict one can only say to the combatants: Make friends or pursue your own ruin.

❧❦   IF THE TWO-IN-ONE crisis that we have described is indeed a fundamental reality—if the collapse of the cultural structure of a society leads to reciprocal violence and if this collapse encourages the spread of violence everywhere—then we ought to see signs of this reality outside the restricted realms of Greek tragedy or Shakespearean drama. The closer our contact with primitive societies, the more rapidly these societies tend to lose their distinctive qualities; but this loss is in some cases effected through a *sacrificial crisis*. And in some cases these crises have been directly observed by ethnologists. Scholarly literature on the subject is rather extensive; rarely, however, does a coherent picture emerge. More often than not the accounts are fragmentary, mingled with commentary relating to purely structural matters. A remarkable exception, well worth our attention here, is Jules Henry's *Jungle People*, which deals with the Kaingang Indians of Santa Katarina in Brazil.[2] The author came to live with the Indians shortly after they had been transferred to a reservation, when the consequences of that last and radical change had not yet completely taken hold. He was thus able to observe at first hand, or through the testimony of witnesses, the process I call the sacrificial crisis.

The extreme poverty of the Kaingang culture on a religious as well as a technological level made a strong impression on Henry, who attributed it to the blood feuds (that is, the cyclical vengeance) carried on among close relatives. To describe the effects of this reciprocal violence he instinctively turned to the hyperbolic imagery of the great myths, in particular to the image of plague: "Feuds spread, cleaving the society asunder like a deadly axe, blighting its life like the plague."[3]

These are the very symptoms that we have made bold to identify with the sacrificial crisis, or crisis of distinctions. The Kaingang seem to have abandoned all their old mythology in favor of stories of actual acts of revenge. When discussing internecine murders, "they seem to be fitting together the parts of a machine, the intricate workings of which they know precisely. Their absorbed interest in the history of their own destruction has impressed on their minds with flawless clarity the multitudinous cross-workings of feuds."[4]

Although the Kaingang blood feuds represent the decadence of a system that once enjoyed relative stability, the feuds still retain some remnant of their original "sacrificial" nature. They constitute, in fact, a more forceful, more violent—and therefore less effective—effort to keep a grip on the "good" violence, with all its protective and con-

[2] Jules Henry, *Jungle People* (New York, 1964).
[3] Ibid., p. 50.
[4] Ibid., p. 51.

straining powers. Indeed, the "bad" violence does not yet penetrate the defenses of those Indians who are said to "travel together"; that is, go out together on hunting expeditions. However, this group is always small in number, and the relative peace that reigns within it is in sharp contrast to the violence that rages triumphantly outside—*between* the different groups.

Within the group there is a spirit of conciliation. The most inflammatory challenges pass unacknowledged; adultery, which provokes an instant and bloody reprisal among members of rival groups, is openly tolerated. As long as violence does not cross a certain threshold of intensity, it remains sacrificial and defines an inner circle of nonviolence essential to the accomplishment of basic social functions—that is, to the survival of the society. Nonetheless, the moment arrives when the inner group is contaminated. As soon as they are installed on a reservation, members of a group tend to turn against one another. They can no longer polarize their aggressions against outside enemies, the "others," the "different men."[5]

The chain of killings finally reaches the heart of the individual group. At this point, the very basis of the social life of the group is challenged. In the case of the Kaingang, outside factors—primarily the Brazilian authorities—intervened assuring the physical survival of the last remnants of the Kaingang while guaranteeing the extinction of their culture.

In acknowledging the existence of an internal process of self-destruction among the Kaingang, we are not attempting to diminish or dismiss the part played by the white man in this tragedy. The problem of Brazilian responsibility would not be resolved even if the new settlers had refrained from using hired assassins to speed up the process of destruction. Indeed, it is worth asking whether the impetus behind the Kaingang's dismemberment of their culture and the inexorable character of their self-destruction were not ultimately due to the pressure of a foreign culture. Even if this were the case, cyclical violence still presents a threat to any society, whether or not it is under pressure from a foreign culture or from any other external interference. The process is basically internal.

Such is Henry's conclusion after contemplating the terrible plight of the Kaingang. He uses the phrase "social suicide," and we must admit that the potentiality for such self-destruction always exists. In the course of history a number of communities doubtless succumbed to

---

[5] The Kaingang use one and the same term to refer to (1) differences of all kinds; (2) men of rival groups, who are always close relatives; (3) Brazilians, the traditional enemy; and (4) the dead and all mythological figures, demonic and divine, generally spoken of as "different things."

their own violent impulses and disappeared without a trace. Even if we have certain reservations about his interpretation of the case under discussion, Henry's conclusions have direct pertinence to numberless groups of human beings whose histories remain unknown. "This group, excellently suited in their physical and psychological endowments to cope with the rigors of their natural environment, were yet unable to withstand the internal forces that were disrupting their society, and having no culturally standardized devices to deal with them, were committing social suicide."[6]

The fear generated by the kill-or-be-killed syndrome, the tendency to "anticipate" violence by lashing out first (akin to our contemporary concept of "preventive war") cannot be explained in purely psychological terms. The notion of a *sacrificial crisis* is designed to dissipate the psychological illusion; even in those instances when Henry borrows the language of psychology, it is clear that he does not share the illusion. In a universe both deprived of any transcendental code of justice and exposed to violence, everybody has reason to fear the worst. The difference between a projection of one's own paranoia and an objective evaluation of circumstances has been worn away.[7]

Once that crucial distinction has vanished, both psychology and sociology falter. The professional observer who distributes good or bad marks to individuals and cultures on the basis of their "normality" and "abnormality" is obliged to make his observations from the particular perspective of someone *who does not run the risk of being killed.* Psychologists and other social scientists ordinarily suppose a peaceable substructure for their subjects; indeed, they tend to take this pacific quality for granted. Yet nothing in their mode of reasoning, which they like to regard as radically "enlightened," solidly based, and free of idealistic nonsense, justifies such an assumption—as Henry's study makes clear: "With a single murder the murderer enters a locked system. He must kill and kill again, he must plan whole massacres lest a single survivor remain to avenge his kin."[8]

Henry encountered some particularly bloodthirsty specimens among the Kaingang, but he also fell in with individual members of the tribe

---

[6] Henry, *Jungle People*, p. 7.

[7] "When Yakwa says to me, 'My cousin wants to kill me,' I know he wants to kill his cousin, who slaughtered his pigs for rooting up his corn; and when he says, 'Eduardo (the Agent) is angry with me,' I realize that he is angry with the Agent for not having given him a shirt. Yakwa's state of mind is a pale reflection of the Kaingang habit of projecting their own hate and fear into the minds of those whom they hate and fear. Yet one cannot always be sure that it is just a projection, for in these feuds currents of danger may radiate from any number of points of conflict, and there is often good and sufficient cause for any fear" (ibid., p. 54).

[8] Ibid., p. 53.

who were peaceable and perspicacious and who sought in vain to free themselves from the machinery of destruction. *"Kaingang murderers are like characters of a Greek tragedy in the grip of a natural law whose processes once started can never be stayed."*[9]

ALTHOUGH THEY APPROACHED THE SUB-ject more obliquely, the Greek tragedians were concerned, like Jules Henry, with the destruction of a cultural order. The violent reciprocity that engulfs their characters is a manifestation of this destructive process. Our own concern with sacrificial matters shows the vital role the ritualistic crisis—the abolition of all distinctions—plays in the formation of tragedy. In turn, a study of tragedy can clarify the nature of this crisis and those aspects of primitive religion that are inseparably linked to it. For in the final analysis, the sole purpose of religion is to prevent the recurrence of reciprocal violence.

I am inclined, then, to assert that tragedy opens a royal way to the great dilemmas of religious ethnology. Such a stand will no doubt elicit the scorn of "scientific" researchers as well as fervent Hellenophiles, from the defenders of traditional humanism to the disciples of Nietzsche and Heidegger. The scientifically inclined have a tendency to regard literary folk as dubious company, whose society grows increasingly dangerous as their own efforts remain obstinately theoretical. As for the Hellenophiles, they are quick to see blasphemy in any parallel drawn between classical Greece and primitive societies.

It is essential to make it clear, once and for all, that to draw on tragic literature does not mean to relinquish scholarly standards of research; nor does it constitute a purely "esthetic" approach to the subject. At the same time we must manage to appease the men of letters who tremble at the thought of applying scientific methods of any kind to literature, convinced as they are that such methods can only lead to facile "reductionism" of the works of art, to sterile analyses that disregard the spirit of the literature. The conflict between the "two cultures," science and literature, rests on a common failure, a negative complicity shared by literary critics and religious specialists. Neither group perceives the underlying principle on which their objects are based. The tragedians seem to have labored in vain to make this principle manifest. They never achieve more than partial success, and their efforts are perpetually undone by the differentiations imposed on their work by literary critics and social scientists.

Ethnologists are not unaware that ritual impurity is linked to the dissolution of distinctions between individuals and institutions.[10] How-

9 Ibid.
10 Cf. Mary Douglas, *Purity and Danger* (London, 1966).

ever, they fail to recognize the dangers inherent in this dissolution. As we have noted, the modern mind has difficulty conceiving of violence in terms of a loss of distinctions, or of a loss of distinctions in terms of violence. Tragedy can help to resolve this difficulty if we agree to view the plays from a radical perspective. Tragic drama addresses itself to a burning issue—in fact, to *the* burning issue. The issue is never directly alluded to in the plays, and for good reason, since it has to do with the dissolution by reciprocal violence of those very values and distinctions around which the conflict of the plays supposedly revolves. Because this subject is taboo—and even more than taboo, almost unspeakable in the language devoted to distinctions—literary critics proceed to obscure with their own meticulously differentiated categories the relative lack of difference between antagonists that characterizes a tragic confrontation in classical drama.

The primitive mind, in contrast, has no difficulty imagining an affiliation between violence and nondifferentiation and, indeed, is often obsessed by the possible consequences of such a union. Natural differences are conceived in terms of cultural differences, and vice versa. Where we would view the loss of a distinctive quality as a wholly natural phenomenon having no bearing on human relationships, the primitive man might well view this occurrence with deep dread. Because there is no real difference between the various modes of differentiation, there is in consequence no difference between the manner in which things fail to differ; the disappearance of natural differences can thus bring to mind the dissolution of regulations pertaining to the individual's proper place in society—that is, can instigate a sacrificial crisis.

Once we have grasped this fact, certain religious phenomena never explained by traditional approaches suddenly become intelligible. A brief glance at one of the more spectacular of these phenomena will, I think, serve to demonstrate the usefulness of applying the tragic tradition to religious ethnology.

In some primitive societies twins inspire a particular terror. It is not unusual for one of the twins, and often both, to be put to death. The origin of this terror has long puzzled ethnologists.

Today the enigma is presented as a problem of classification. Two individuals suddenly appear, where only one had been expected; in those societies that permit them to survive, twins often display a single social personality. The problem of classification as defined by structuralism does not justify the death of the twins. The reasons that prompt men to do away with certain of their children are undoubtedly bad reasons, but they are not frivolous ones. Culture is not merely a jigsaw puzzle where the extra pieces are discarded once the picture has been completed. If the problem of classification becomes crucial, that is because its implications are crucial.

Twins invariably share a cultural identity, and they often have a striking physical resemblance to each other. Wherever differences are lacking, violence threatens. Between the biological twins and the sociological twins there arises a confusion that grows more troubled as the question of differences reaches a crisis. It is only natural that twins should awaken fear, for they are harbingers of indiscriminate violence, the greatest menace to primitive societies. As soon as the twins of violence appear they multiply prodigiously, by scissiparity, as it were, and produce a sacrificial crisis. It is essential to prevent the spread of this highly contagious disease. When faced with biological twins the normal reaction of the culture is simply to avoid contagion. The way primitive societies attempt to accomplish this offers a graphic demonstration of the kind of danger they associate with twins. In societies where their very existence is considered dangerous, the infants are "exposed"; that is, abandoned outside the community under conditions that make their death inevitable. Any act of *direct* physical violence against the anathema is scrupulously avoided. Any such act would only serve to entrap the perpetrators in a vicious circle of violence—the trap "bad" violence sets for the community and baits with the birth of twins.

An inventory of the customs, prescriptions, and interdictions relating to twins in those societies where they are regarded with dread reveals one common concern: the fear of pollution. The divergences from one culture to the next are easily explained in terms of the religious attitudes defined above, which pertain to the strictly empirical—that is, terrorstricken—character of the precautions taken against "bad" violence. In the case of twins, the precautions are misdirected; nevertheless, they become quite intelligible once we recognize the terror that inspires them. Although the menace is somewhat differently perceived from society to society, it is fundamentally the same everywhere, and a challenge with which all religious institutions are obliged to cope.

The Nyakyusa maintain that the parents of twins are contaminated by "bad" violence, and there is a certain logic about that notion, since the parents are, after all, responsible for engendering the twins. In reference to the twins the parents are designated by a term that is applied to all threatening individuals, all monstrous or terrifying creatures. In order to prevent the spread of pollution the parents are required to isolate themselves and submit to rites of purification; only then are they allowed to rejoin the community.[11]

It is not unreasonable to believe that the relatives and close friends of the twins' parents, as well as their immediate neighbors, are those most directly exposed to the infection. "Bad" violence is by definition a force that works on various levels—physical, familial, social—and spreads from one to the other.

Twins are impure in the same way that a warrior steeped in carnage is impure, or an incestuous couple, or a menstruating woman. All forms of violence lead back to violence. We overlook this fact because the primitive concept of a link between the loss of distinctions and violence is strange to us; but we need only consider the calamities primitive people associate with twins to perceive the logic of this concept. Deadly epidemics can result from contact with twins, as can mysterious illnesses that cause sterility in women and animals. Even more significant to us is the role of twins in provoking discord among neighbors, a fatal collapse of ritual, the transgression of interdictions—in short, their part in instigating a sacrificial crisis.

As we have seen, the sacred embraces all those forces that threaten to harm man or trouble his peace. Natural forces and sickness are not distinguished from the threat of a violent disintegration of the community. Although man-made violence plays a dominant role in the dialectics of the sacred and is never completely omitted from the warnings issued by religion, it tends to be relegated to the background and treated as if it emanated from outside man. One might say that it has been deliberately hidden away almost out of sight behind forces that are genuinely exterior to man.

Behind the image of twins lurks the baleful aspect of the sacred, perceived as a disparate but formidably unified force. The sacrificial crisis can be viewed as a general offensive of violence directed against the community, and there is reason to fear that the birth of twins might herald this crisis.

In the primitive societies where twins are not killed they often enjoy a privileged position. This reversal corresponds to the attitudes we have noted in regard to menstrual blood. Any phenomenon linked to impure violence is capable of being inverted and rendered beneficent; but this can take place only within the immutable and rigorous framework of ritual practice. The purifying and pacifying aspects of violence take precedence over its destructive aspects. The apparition of twins, then, if properly handled, may in certain societies be seen to presage good events, not bad ones.

[11] Monica Wilson, *Rituals of Kinship among the Nyakyusa* (Oxford, 1957).

જ∙⊁⊀ IF THE STATEMENTS ABOVE ARE VALID, two brothers need not be twins for their resemblances to arouse anxiety. We can assume almost a priori that in some societies the mere fact of familial similarity is cause for alarm. The verification of such a hypothesis would, I believe, confirm the inadequacy of previous theories regarding twins. If the twin phobia can be extended to other members of the family it can no longer be explained solely in terms of "a problem of classification." Twins could no longer be said to cause alarm because two individuals had turned up where only one was expected; their *physical resemblance* would now be perceived as the disruptive factor.

At this point we may well wonder how something so commonplace as the resemblance between siblings can be officially proscribed without causing enormous inconvenience, not to say total chaos. After all, a community cannot categorize a majority of its inhabitants as probationary criminals without creating an intolerable situation. Nevertheless, the phobia of resemblance is a fact. Malinowski's *The Father in Primitive Psychology* offers formal proof. The study demonstrates how the phobia can perpetuate itself without disastrous consequences. The ingenuity of man, or rather of his cultural systems, copes with the problem by categorically denying the existence of the dreaded phenomenon, or even its possibility:

> In a matrilineal society, as in the Trobriands, where all maternal relatives are considered to be of the "same body," and the father to be a "stranger," we would naturally expect and have no doubt that the facial and bodily similarity would be traced to the mother's family alone. The contrary is the case, and this is affirmed with an extremely strong social emphasis. Not only is it a household dogma, so to speak, that a child never resembles its mother, any of its brothers or sisters, or any of its maternal kinsmen, but it is extremely bad form and a great offence to hint at any such similarity. . . .
>
> I was introduced to this rule of *savoir vivre* in the usual way by making a *faux pas*. One of my bodyguards in Omarakana, named Moradeda, was endowed with a peculiar cast of features which had struck me at first sight. . . . One day I was struck by the appearance of an exact counterpart to Moradeda and asked his name and whereabouts. When I was told that he was my friend's elder brother, living in a distant village, I exclaimed: "Ah, truly! I asked about you because your face is alike—alike to that of Moradeda." There came such a hush over all the assembly that I noticed it at once. The man turned round and left us, while part of the company present, after looking away in a manner half-embarrassed, half-offended, soon dispersed. I was then told by my confidential informants that I had committed a breach of custom, that I had perpetrated

what is called "*taputaki migila*," a technical expression referring only to this act, which might be translated: "to-defile-by-comparing-to-a-kins-man-his-face." What astonished me in this discussion was, that in spite of the striking resemblance between the two brothers, my informants refused to admit it. In fact, they treated the question as if no one could possibly ever resemble his brother, or, for the matter of that, any mater-nal kinsman. I made my informants quite angry and displeased with me by arguing the point.

This incident taught me never to hint at such a resemblance in the presence of the people concerned. But I thrashed the matter out well with many natives in subsequent general conversations. I found that every one in the Trobriands will, in the teeth of all the evidence, deny stoutly that similarity can exist between matrilineal kinsmen. You simply irritate and insult a Trobriander if you point to striking instances, exactly as you irritate your next-door neighbor in our own society if you bring before him a glaring truth which contradicts some of his cherished opinions, political, religious, or moral, or which is still worse, runs counter to his personal interests.[12]

Negation here serves as affirmation. There would be nothing unto-ward in mentioning resemblances if they were not a matter of great importance. To accuse two close relatives of resembling one another is to assert that they are a menace to the community, the carriers of an infectious disease. Malinowski tells us further that the accusation is a traditional form of insult among the Trobriands, the most wounding at their disposal. His account inspires confidence precisely because he presents the phenomenon as a complete enigma, proposing no interpre-tation of his own.

On the other hand, the Trobriands not only tolerate references to the resemblance between fathers and children but virtually demand its acknowledgment. This society formally denies the father's role in the reproductive process; between father and children, then, no parental link is said to exist.

Malinowski's description demonstrates that a paternal resemblance is perceived by the Trobriands, paradoxically enough, *in terms of differ-ences*. It is the father who serves to differentiate the children from one another. He is literally the bearer of a difference, among whose charac-teristics we recognize the phallic element so dear to psychoanalysts. Because the father sleeps with the mother, because he is so often near her, he is said to "mold the face of the child." Malinowski informs us that the word *kuli*—"coagulate," "mold," "leave an impression"— recurred constantly in the discussions of resemblances. The father evidently represents form, the mother matter. In this capacity the

[12] Bronislaw Malinowski, *The Father in Primitive Psychology* (New York, 1966), pp. 88–91.

father makes the children different from their mother and from one another. That explains why the children resemble him, and why *a resemblance to the father, common to all children, does not imply a resemblance of one child to another:* "It was often pointed out to me how strongly one or the other of the sons of To'uluwa, chief of Omarakana, resembled his father. . . . Whenever I pointed out that this similarity to the father implied similarity among each other, such a heresy was indignantly repudiated."[13]

At this point it seems appropriate to juxtapose the basic mythical theme of *enemy brothers* with the phobia concerning twins and other fraternal resemblances. Clyde Kluckhohn asserts that the most common of all mythical conflicts is the struggle between brothers, which generally ends in fratricide. In some regions of black Africa the mythical protagonists are brothers "born in immediate sequence."[14] If I understand this phrase correctly, it includes twins but is not strictly limited to them. The continuity between the theme of twins and the fraternal motif in general is not peculiar to the Trobriand Islands.

Even when the brothers are not twins, the difference between them is less than that between all other degrees of relations. They share the same mother, father, gender; in most instances they occupy the same position in respect to other relatives, both close and distant. Brothers seem to have more rights, duties, and functions in common than other family members. Twins are in a sense reinforced brothers whose final objective difference, that of age, has been removed; it is virtually impossible to distinguish between them.

We instinctively tend to regard the fraternal relationship as an affectionate one; yet the mythological, historical, and literary examples that spring to mind tell a different story: Cain and Abel, Jacob and Esau, Eteocles and Polyneices, Romulus and Remus, Richard the Lion-Hearted and John Lackland. The proliferation of enemy brothers in Greek myth and in dramatic adaptations of myth implies the continual presence of a sacrificial crisis, repeatedly alluded to in the same symbolic terms. The fraternal theme is no less "contagious" qua theme for being buried deep in the text than is the malevolent violence that accompanies it. In fact, the theme itself is a form of violence.

When Polyneices departs from Thebes, leaving his brother to take his turn on the throne, he carries the fraternal conflict with him as an integral part of his being. Everywhere he goes he literally draws from the earth the brother who seems expressly designed to thwart him, just

[13] Ibid., p. 92.
[14] Clyde Kluckhohn, "Recurrent Themes in Myths and Mythmaking," in *Myth and Mythmaking*, ed. Henry A. Murray (Boston, 1968), p. 52.

as Cadmus sowed the dragon's teeth and brought forth a harvest of fully armed warriors ready to do battle with one another.

An oracle had announced to Adrastus that his two daughters would marry a lion and a wild boar respectively—animals very different in appearance, but of equally violent temper. In Euripides' *Supplices* Adrastus recounts how he came upon his future sons-in-law Polyneices and Tydeus, both poverty-stricken exiles who were fighting for shelter outside his door:

Adrastus: The two exiles came to my door one night.
Theseus: Which two? What were their names?
Adrastus: Tydeus and Polyneices. And each fell on the other's throat.
Theseus: And you recognized them as the beasts for whom your daughters were destined?
Adrastus: They looked exactly like two wild beasts.
Theseus: How had they wandered so far from their homeland?
Adrastus: Tydeus was banished for having killed a kinsman.
Theseus: And Oedipus's son, why had he left Thebes?
Adrastus: A father's curse: that he should kill his brother.

The ferocity of the two young men, the symmetry of their family situations, and their forthcoming marriages to two sisters—reconstituting, as it were, a properly "fraternal" relationship—all conspire to recreate the Polyneices/Eteocles relationship and, indeed, all other instances of fraternal rivalry.

Once our attention has been drawn to the "distinctive" traits of fraternal strife we seem to rediscover them, recurring singly or in clusters, throughout classical myth and tragedy. In addition to true brothers, such as Eteocles and Polyneices, we find brothers-in-law (that is, quasi-brothers), like Polyneices and Tydeus, Oedipus and Creon; or other close relatives of the same generation, like the first cousins Pentheus and Dionysus. Ultimately, the insufficient difference in the family relationships serves to symbolize the dissolution of family distinctions; in other words, it *desymbolizes*. Such relationships thus finally contribute to the symmetry of conflicts that is concealed in myth, but vigorously proclaimed in tragedy, which betrays this hidden process simply by *representing* the mythological material on stage.

Nothing can be further from the truth than the statement that tragedy lacks universality because it is totally preoccupied with family distinctions. It is the elimination of these distinctions that leads directly to fraternal strife and to the religious phobia regarding twins. The two themes are essentially the same; however, there is a shade of difference between them that deserves our attention.

Twins offer a symbolic representation, sometimes remarkably eloquent, of the symmetrical conflict and identity crisis that characterize the sacrificial crisis. But the resemblance is entirely accidental. There is no real connection between biological and sociological twins; twins are no more predisposed to violence than any other men—or, at least, any other brothers. There is something decidedly arbitrary about the relationship between sacrificial crises and the essential quality of twinship, which is not of the same order of arbitrariness as that of the linguistic sign, since the representative element is always present. Ultimately, the classic definition of the symbol seems to apply to the correspondence between twins and the sacrificial crisis.

In the case of fraternal strife the representative element becomes blurred. Fraternal relationships normally take form within the framework of the family, where differences, no matter how small, are readily recognized and acknowledged. In passing from twins to the general category of brothers, we lose something on the level of symbolic representation, but gain something on that of social reality; in fact, the shift puts our feet securely on the ground. Because in most societies the fraternal relationship implies only a minimum of differences, it obviously constitutes a vulnerable point in a system structured on differences, a point dangerously exposed to the onset of a sacrificial crisis. The fear of twins, qua twins, is clearly mythic and has little basis in reality, but one can hardly say the same for the thematic concern with fraternal rivalry. It is not only in myths that brothers are simultaneously drawn together and driven apart by something they both ardently desire and which they will not or cannot share—a throne, a woman or, in more general terms, a paternal heritage.

Rival brothers, unlike twins, straddle both forms of "desymbolization," the purely symbolic and the concrete variety—the variety that constitutes the true sacrificial crisis. In some African monarchies the death of the king precipitates a struggle for the succession and transforms the king's sons into *fraternal enemies*. It is difficult if not impossible to determine to what extent this struggle is symbolic, a matter of ritual, and to what extent it is a real historical event, pregnant with unforeseen consequences. In other words, it is hard to know whether one is dealing with a real-life struggle or with ritual mimicry whose cathartic effects are believed to ward off the impending crisis it imitates so faithfully.

If we have difficulty grasping what twins, or even rival brothers, represent, it is because we do not consider their presence a genuine threat. We cannot imagine how the mere appearance of a pair of twins or rival brothers can convey the entire course of sacrificial crisis; how the pair can *epitomize the entire crisis*, in terms not of formal rhetoric but of real violence. Any violent effacement of differences, even if initially restricted to a single pair of twins, reaches out to destroy a whole society.

We cannot be held entirely responsible for our lack of comprehension. None of the mythological themes can, by itself, point to the truth concerning the sacrificial crisis. In the case of twins, symmetry and identity are represented in extraordinarily explicit terms; nondifference is present in concrete, literal form, but this form is itself so exceptional as to constitute a new difference. Thus the *representation* of nondifference ultimately becomes the very exemplar of difference, a classic monstrosity that plays a vital role in sacred ritual.

In the case of enemy brothers the domestic context in which they operate brings us back into contact with reality: we are no longer dealing with outlandish phenomena that provoke either amusement or dread. But the very concreteness of the conflict tends to efface its symbolic significance; to lend it the character of a real historical event. With enemy brothers, as with twins, the sign cannot fail to betray the thing signified because that "thing" is the destruction of all signification. It is violent reciprocity, on the rampage everywhere, that truly destroys differences; yet this process can never be fully signified. Either a degree of difference survives and we remain within the framework of a cultural order, surrounded by meanings that ought to have been wiped out. Or perhaps all differences have indeed been effaced, but the nondifference immediately appears as a new and outlandish difference, a monstrosity such as twins, for example.

Being made up of differences, language finds it almost impossible to express undifferentiation directly. Whatever it may say on the subject, language invariably says at once too much and too little, even in such concise statements as "Each thing meets/In mere oppugnancy" or "sound and fury,/Signifying nothing."

No matter how diligently language attempts to catch hold of it, the reality of the sacrificial crisis invariably slips through its grasp. It invites anecdotal history on the one hand, and on the other, a visitation of monsters and grotesques. Mythology succumbs to the latter; tragedy is constantly threatened by the former.

Monstrosities recur throughout mythology. From this we can only conclude that myths make constant reference to the sacrificial crisis, but do so only in order to disguise the issue. Myths are the retrospective transfiguration of sacrificial crises, the reinterpretation of these crises in the light of the cultural order that has arisen from them.

The traces of sacrificial crisis are less distinct in myth than in tragedy. Or rather, tragedy is by its very nature a partial deciphering of mythological motifs. The poet brings the sacrificial crisis back to life; he pieces together the scattered fragments of reciprocity and balances

elements thrown out of kilter in the process of being "mythologized."
He whistles up a storm of violent reciprocity, and differences are
swept away in this storm just as they were previously dissolved in the
real crisis that must have generated the mythological transfiguration.

Tragedy envelops all human relationships in a single tragic antagonism. It does not differentiate between the fraternal conflict of
Eteocles and Polyneices, the father-son conflict of *Alcestis* or *Oedipus
the King*, the conflict between men who share no ancestral ties, such as
Oedipus and Tiresias. The rivalry of the two prophets is indistinguishable from the rivalry between brothers. Tragedy tends to restore violence to mythological themes. It in part fulfills the dire forebodings
primitive men experience at the sight of twins. It spreads the pollution
abroad and multiplies the mirror images of violence.

Tragedy has a particular affinity for myth, but that does not mean it
takes the same course. The term *desymbolism* is more appropriate to
tragedy than is *symbolism*. It is because most of the symbols of the
sacrificial crisis—in particular the symbol of the enemy brother—lend
themselves so readily to *both* the tragic and the ritual situations that
tragedy has been able to operate, at least to some extent, within and
also contrary to mythological patterns. I have already noted this dual
aspect of symbolic reference in connection with the monarchic succession in certain African states; it is virtually impossible to determine
whether the fraternal rivalry that occurs in that connection is ritualistic or part of the "tragedy of history."

Symbolized reality becomes, paradoxically, the loss of all symbolism;
the loss of differences is necessarily betrayed by the differentiated
expression of language. The process is a peculiar one, utterly foreign to
our usual notions of symbolism. Only a close reading of tragedy, a
radically "symmetrical" reading, will help us to understand the phenomenon, to penetrate to the source of tragic inspiration. If the tragic
poet touches upon the violent reciprocity underlying all myths, it is
because he perceives these myths in a context of weakening distinctions and growing violence. His work is inseparable, then, from a new
sacrificial crisis, the one referred to at the opening of this chapter.

To know violence is to experience it. Tragedy is therefore directly
linked to violence; it is a child of the sacrificial crisis. The relationship
between tragedy and myth as it is now taking shape can perhaps be
understood more easily if we consider an analogous relationship, that
of the Old Testament prophets to the Pentateuchal texts they cite as
exemplars. For example, we find in Jeremiah (9:3–5):

Beware a brother,
for every brother plays the role of Jacob,

and every friend spreads scandal.
One deceives the other. . . .
Fraud upon fraud, deceit upon deceit.

The concept of enemy brothers previously mentioned in connection with Jacob is precisely the same as the concept governing Euripides' version of the Eteocles/Polyneices story. It is the symmetry of the conflict that defines the fraternal relationship, and this symmetry, originally limited to a few tragic heroes, now reaches out to include the entire community. It loses its particularized quality and acquires a predominantly social meaning. The allusion to Jacob is subordinated to the main design, which is the description of the sacrificial crisis; violence engulfs the whole society, all its members confronting one another as enemy brothers. Specific stylistic effects underline the symmetry and mirror the violent reciprocity: 'One deceives the other. . . . Fraud upon fraud, deceit upon deceit."

The books of the Old Testament are rooted in sacrificial crises, each distinct from the other and separated by long intervals of time, but analogous in at least some respects. The earlier crises are reinterpreted in the light of the later ones. And the experience of previous crises is of great value in coping with subsequent ones. Jeremiah's treatment of the historical figure of Jacob seems to bear this out. Contact has been established between the time of Genesis and the crisis of the sixth century; as a result, light is shed on both eras. Like tragedy, the prophetic act constitutes a return to violent reciprocity; so it, too, levels all mythological distinctions and does so even more effectively than tragedy. However, this leads us to a subject that deserves separate consideration, a subject I will turn to in another work.

Although the source of inspiration emerges more dimly and indirectly in tragedy than in biblical examples, the pattern is the same. The passage quoted above might well be taken for a fragment of a tragic drama drawn from the Book of Genesis—a tragedy of enemy brothers, perhaps Jacob and Esau.

Tragic and prophetic inspiration do not draw strength from historical or philological sources but from a direct intuitive grasp of the role played by violence in the cultural order and in disorder as well, in mythology and in the sacrificial crisis. England, in the throes of religious upheaval, provided Shakespeare with such an inspiration for his *Troilus and Cressida*. There is no reason to believe that advances in scholarship will, by the process of continuous enrichment so dear to the positivist cause, increase our understanding of the great tragedies; for however real and valuable this process may be, it fails to touch on the true tragic spirit. This spirit, never widespread even in periods of crisis, vanishes without a trace during periods of cultural stability.

At a given moment the violent effacement of distinctions ceases and the process begins to reverse itself, giving way to mythical elaboration. Mythical elaboration gives way in turn to the inverse operation of tragic inspiration. What sets off these metamorphoses? What mechanism governs the shift from cultural order to disorder? This is the question that concerns us; and this question elicits yet another, which touches on the final stages of the sacrificial crisis. Once violence has penetrated a community it engages in an orgy of self-propagation. There appears to be no way of bringing the reprisals to a halt before the community has been annihilated.

If there are really such events as sacrificial crises, some sort of braking mechanism, an automatic control that goes into effect before everything is destroyed, must be built into them. In the final stages of a sacrificial crisis the very viability of human society is put in question. Our task is to discover what these final stages involve and what makes them possible. It is likely that they must serve as a point of departure for both ritual and myth. Everything we can learn about this phase of the crisis, then, will enhance our knowledge of the nature of ritual and myth.

To find an answer to these questions let us address ourselves to one myth in particular, the story of Oedipus. Our previous investigations gave us reason to believe that the most useful approach lay by way of tragedy. We will turn our attention, therefore, to Sophocles' *Oedipus the King*.

⚜ *Chapter Three*

Oedipus and the Surrogate Victim

⚜ SOPHOCLES IS OFTEN PRAISED for having created in Oedipus a highly individualized character. Here, it is said, is a hero who is very much his own man. And what sort of a man is he? It is traditional to note both his "generosity," and his "impulsiveness." At the opening of the play we admire his "noble serenity," as he dedicates himself to solving the mystery of the plague that afflicts his subjects. But the least obstacle, delay, or provocation suffices to upset his poise. The diagnosis seems clear: Oedipus is prone to fits of anger. The king himself acknowledges this fault, presenting it, so it seems, as that unique but fatal flaw without which a hero cannot attain tragic stature.

The "noble serenity" is in evidence first; the fits of anger follow. Tiresias provokes the initial outburst, Creon the second. In Oedipus's own account of his past life he informs us that he has frequently succumbed to this "flaw." He admits to overreacting to hasty phrases heedlessly uttered; a drinking companion in Corinth had blurted out some remark casting doubt on Oedipus's parentage; Oedipus reacted with an outburst of anger that precipitated his departure from the city. And it was in a fit of anger that he struck down at the crossroads an old man who blocked his way.

The description of his character seems unambiguous, and *anger* is surely as good a word as any to use in describing the *personal* reactions of the hero. However, we cannot help asking ourselves whether these tantrums really serve to distinguish Oedipus from the other characters. In other words, can they be said to perform the differential function upon which the whole concept of "character" is based?

If we look closely at the myth we notice that "anger" crops up everywhere. It was a kind of suppressed anger that incited Oedipus's companion at Corinth to cast doubt on the hero's parentage. At the fateful crossroads it was anger that goaded Laius initially to raise a hand against his son. It was yet an earlier act of anger, preceding any actions by Oedipus, that prompted the father's decision to do away with his infant son.

It is clear that Oedipus has no monopoly on anger in the play. Whatever the author's intentions, there would be no tragic debate if the other protagonists did not become angry in turn. It is true that these outbursts only occur after a certain delay; and it is tempting to regard them as "justified reprisals," warranted by Oedipus's inexcusable and provoking displays of temper. But we have seen that Oedipus's anger is never without antecedents; it is always preceded and determined by an initial outburst. Even that initial anger is never truly the original anger. In the domain of impure violence, any search for origins leads back to myth. One cannot engage in a search of this sort, much less place any credence in the ultimate success of such a search, without destroying violent reciprocity; without, in short, having recourse to those very mythological distinctions from which tragedy is striving to extricate itself.

Tiresias and Creon keep their tempers at the 'outset: their initial serenity is matched by Oedipus's own serenity in the first episode. In fact, we have to do with an alternation of calm and anger. The only distinction between Oedipus and his adversaries is that Oedipus initiates the contest, triggering the tragic plot. He thus has a certain head start on the others. But though the action does not occur simultaneously, its symmetry is absolute. Each protagonist in turn occupies the same position in regard to the same object. This object is none other than the particular tragic conflict whose association with the plague we have already noted and will explore in more detail further on. At first, each of the protagonists believes that he can quell the violence; at the end each succumbs to it. All are drawn unwittingly into the structure of violent reciprocity—which they always think they are outside of, because they all initially come from the outside and mistake this positional and temporary advantage for a permanent and fundamental superiority.

The three protagonists believe themselves to be above the battle. After all, Oedipus is not from Thebes, Creon is not king, and Tiresias is soaring aloft, high amid the clouds. Creon returns from Thebes armed with the latest oracle. Oedipus and especially Tiresias bring to bear their formidable divinatory skills. In this capacity they possess all the prestige of the modern "expert," whose services are reserved for exceptionally difficult cases. Each believes himself to be an impartial observer, detached from the action; each wants to assume the role of arbitrator and judge. The solemnity of the three sages rapidly gives way to fury, however, when each sees his prestige challenged—if only by the silence of the other two.

The force exerted by the three men in the struggle corresponds to each man's illusion of superiority, his hubris. In other words, nobody possesses sophrosyne, and on that level, too, the differences among them are illusory or quickly effaced. The passage from calm to anger is in each case rendered inevitable. It seems arbitrary, therefore, to relegate to Oedipus, as a distinctive "character trait," an attribute shared equally by all—especially if this common attribute is drawn from the tragic context of the play and provides a more coherent interpretation than the psychological approach allows.

Far from bringing differences into sharp relief, the plunge into opposition reduces the protagonists to a uniform condition of violence; they are engulfed in the same storm of passion. A single glance at an Oedipus drunk with violence and eager to engage him in "dialogue" convinces Tiresias that he has been led astray. But the knowledge comes too late: "Alas, alas, how terrible to know the truth, when this knowledge serves for naught. I was not totally ignorant of this truth, but had thrust it from my mind. Otherwise I would not have come."

Tragedy is not a matter of differing opinions. The symmetrical quality of the conflict determines the limits of the tragic inspiration. And in asserting that there is no difference between the antagonists in a tragedy, we are saying that ultimately there is no difference between the "true" and the "false" prophet. The statement seems ridiculous, even unthinkable, at first glance. For does not Tiresias proclaim the truth about Oedipus at the outset, while Oedipus is vilifying Tiresias with odious calumnies?

With Tiresias's entrance our quest for symmetry receives a sharp rebuff. As soon as it catches sight of this stately personage, the chorus exclaims:

> Here approaches the most inspired of prophets,
> he alone who is the keeper of hidden truth.

Clearly we are dealing here with the infallible and omniscient prophet, the sole possessor of an indubitable verity, long ripened in the keeping. For once, it seems, difference has triumphed. However, some lines further on this difference is eclipsed; we encounter a resurgence of reciprocity, more explicit than ever. Tiresias himself rejects the traditional interpretation of his role, the very one proposed by the chorus. In reply to Oedipus, who has questioned him derisively on the origins of his prophetic gifts, Tiresias denies that he possesses any truth except the truth conferred on him by Oedipus himself:

Oedipus: Who taught you truth? Was it part of your training as a prophet?
Tiresias: You taught me, in forcing me to speak against my will.

If we take Tiresias's reply literally, the terrible charges of patricide and incest that he has just leveled at Oedipus did not stem from any supernatural source of information. The accusation is simply an act of reprisal arising from the hostile exchange of a tragic debate. Oedipus unintentionally initiates the process by forcing Tiresias to speak. He accuses Tiresias of having had a part in the murder of Laius; he prods Tiresias into reprisal, into hurling the accusation back at him.

The only difference between the initial accusation and the counter-charge is the paradoxical quality of the latter. This quality, which could well be a weakness, in fact becomes an added strength. Tiresias, not content to answer Oedipus's "You are guilty," by echoing, "You are guilty," underlines what from his point of view is the most scandalous aspect of the accusation—a guilty man is leveling the charge: "You pronounce me guilty and think yourself innocent whereas, O wondrous world, the guilty one is you. The criminal you pursue is none other than Oedipus."

To accuse the other of Laius's murder is to attribute to him sole responsibility for the sacrificial crisis; but as we have seen, everybody shares equal responsibility, because everybody participates in the destruction of a cultural order. The blows exchanged by enemy brothers may not always land on their mark, but every one of them deals a staggering blow to the institutions of monarchy and religion. Each party progresses rapidly in uncovering the truth about the other, without ever recognizing the truth about himself.

Each sees in the other the usurper of a legitimacy that he thinks he is defending but that he is in fact undermining. Anything one may affirm or deny about either of the adversaries seems instantly applicable to the other. Reciprocity is busy aiding each party in his own destruction. The tragic debate is clearly the verbal equivalent of the fight between such enemy brothers as Eteocles and Polyneices.

In a series of replies Tiresias warns Oedipus of the purely reciprocal nature of the approaching tragedy; that is, of the blows that each will inflict on the other. As far as I know, nobody has proposed a satisfactory interpretation of these lines. The very rhythm of the phrases, their symmetrical effects, anticipate and provoke the tragic debate. We see here violent reciprocity in action, canceling all distinctions between the two men:

> Enough. Let me go home now. If you follow my advice, we will both find it easier to bear our separate destinies. . . .
>
> Ah! I see that your own words fall wide of the mark; and I fear to have no better success with mine. . . .
>
> I do not want to inflict pain on either of us. . . .

You reproach me for my stubbornness, but refuse to see the stubbornness
that dwells within you; and therefore out of stubbornness cast blame on
me. . . .

The violent elimination of differences between the antagonists, their
total identity, suddenly illuminates these responses, which give perfect
expression to the true nature of tragic relationships. The fact that these
responses, even today, still seem obscure, confirms our lack of understanding. It should be said, however, that there is good reason for this
lack: one cannot persevere in bringing to light the symmetrical quality
of tragedy—as we are now doing—without contradicting the fundamental implications of the myth.

If the myth does not explicitly set forth the problem of differences,
it nonetheless manages to resolve the problem in a matter both brutal
and categorical. The solution involves patricide and incest. In the
mythical version of the story the issue of reciprocity—the identity of
Oedipus with the others—never arises. One can assert with lotal conviction that Oedipus is unique in at least one respect: he alone is guilty
of patricide and incest. He is presented as a monstrous exception to the
general run of mankind; he resembles nobody, and nobody resembles
him.

The tragedian's version of the Oedipus story differs radically from
the myth; indeed, it is impossible to do justice to this presentation
without abandoning the myth altogether. Interpreters of Sophocles'
play invariably devise compromises that conceal the underlying contradiction between the tragedy and the myth. I shall not have recourse
to these venerable compromises, nor try to invent new ones. My quest
leads elsewhere; I intend to trace the tragic vein to its source, if only to
see where it leads. I hope this exploration will yield something of value
about the genesis of the myth.

First let us return to the issues of patricide and incest and attempt to
determine whether these crimes can be attributed to one particular
protagonist, and to *one alone*. As we have seen, the tragedy transforms
the murder of Laius, and the patricide and incest themselves, into an
exchange of mutual incriminations. Oedipus and Tiresias each attempt
to place the blame for the city's plight on the other; the accusations of
patricide and incest are only especially striking contributions to a conventional exchange of incivilities. At this stage of the debate there is no
reason to assume that either party is more guilty of any crime than the
other. Both sides seem equally matched; neither seems able to gain the
upper hand. The myth breaks the deadlock, however, and does so
unequivocally. We must now, in the light of our understanding of

tragic reciprocity, examine on what basis and under what conditions the myth succeeds in intervening decisively in the struggle.

At this point a strange and well-nigh fantastic thought suggests itself. If we eliminate the testimony brought against Oedipus in the second half of the tragedy, then the conclusion of the myth, far from seeming a sudden lightning flash of the truth, striking down the guilty party and illuminating all the mortal participants, seems nothing more than the camouflaged victory of one version of the story over the other, the polemical version over its rival—the community's formal acceptance of Tiresias's and Creon's version of the story, thereafter held to be the true and universal version, the verity behind the myth itself.

At this point the reader may well suspect that I harbor some strange illusions about the "historical" potential of these texts and about the information that one may reasonably expect to draw out of them. I hope that what follows will help to dissipate these fears. However, before proceeding I feel obliged to address myself to another type of objection that the present inquiry seems certain to attract.

Literary criticism concerns itself with tragedy; mythology is outside its proper bailiwick. Students of mythology, on the other hand, exclude tragedy from their area of concern and even display on occasion a hostile attitude toward it.

This division of labor harks back to Aristotle, who declares in the *Poetics* that the competent tragic poet will avoid manipulating the myths and limit his borrowings from them to certain "subjects." This interdict of Aristotle still stands in the way of our confronting the symmetrical quality of tragedy and the mythical concern with differences, which protects "literature" from "mythology" and also protects their respective specialists from the subversive consequences that might result from a confrontation.

It is precisely this confrontation I want to emphasize. Indeed, one cannot but wonder how attentive readers of *Oedipus the King* have managed to overlook it. At the climactic moment of the tragic struggle Sophocles has inserted into his text two replies that seem to pertain directly to our reading. Oedipus's imminent fall has nothing to do with any heinous sin; rather, it should be regarded as the outcome of a tragic encounter in which Oedipus has met defeat. Oedipus replies to the chorus, which has pleaded with him to spare Creon: "What you are asking, if the truth be told, is neither more nor less than my death or exile."

The chorus insists that Creon does not deserve punishment; he should be allowed to withdraw in peace. Oedipus yields to their request, but reluctantly, and he reminds the chorus once again of the true nature of this struggle whose outcome is still unclear. To spare an enemy brother from death or exile is to condemn oneself to death or exile: "Well, then, let him depart—though his departure means my certain death, or else my ignominious expulsion from Thebes."

Should we follow tradition and attribute such responses to the "tragic illusion"? In that case the whole play and its wondrous equilibrium must also be a figment of this same illusion. We will be on safer ground, I believe, if we turn our attention from "tragic illusion" to tragic vision. I cannot help feeling that Sophocles himself is prompting us to do so.

Yet Sophocles himself remains elusive. Tragic subversion has its limits; if the playwright challenges the basis of the myth, he only dares to do so in muted and devious fashion. He does not want to compromise his own enterprise or demolish the mythological framework in which he operates.

We are left with no model or guide; we are engaged in a cultural activity that remains undefined, and we can have recourse to no known critical discipline. What we are about to do is as novel to tragedy or literary criticism as it is to psychoanalysis or ethnology.

We must return once again to the so-called crimes of the son of Laius. The act of regicide is the exact equivalent, vis-à-vis the polis, of the act of patricide vis-à-vis the family. In both cases the criminal strikes at the most fundamental, essential, and inviolable distinction within the group. He becomes, literally, the slayer of distinctions.

Patricide represents the establishment of violent reciprocity between father and son, the reduction of the paternal relationship to "fraternal" revenge. This reciprocity is explicitly indicated in the tragedy; as we have noted, Laius displays violence towards Oedipus even before his son actually attacks him.

When it has succeeded in abolishing even the traditional father-son relationship, violent reciprocity is left in sole command of the battlefield. Its victory could hardly be more complete, for in pitting father against son it has chosen as the basis of their rivalry an object solemnly consecrated as belonging to the father and formally forbidden the son: that is, the father's wife and son's mother. Incest is also a form of violence, an extreme form, and it plays in consequence an extreme role in the destruction of differences. It destroys that other crucial family distinction, that between the mother and her children. Between patricide and incest, the violent abolition of all family differences is achieved. The process that links violence to the loss of distinctions will naturally perceive incest and patricide as its ultimate goals. No possibility of difference then remains; no aspect of life is immune from the onslaught of violence.[1]

Patricide and incest will thus be defined in terms of their consequences. Oedipus's monstrosity is contagious; it infects first of all those beings engendered by him. The essential task is to separate once more the two strains of blood whose poisonous blend is now perpetuated by the natural process of generation. Incestuous propagation leads to formless duplications, sinister repetitions, a dark mixture of unnamable things. In short, the incestuous creature exposes the community to the same danger as do twins. These are indeed the manifestations, real and transfigured, of the sacrificial crisis always referred to by primitive societies in connection with incest. Indeed, the mothers of twins are often suspected of having conceived their children in incestuous fashion.

Sophocles attributes Oedipus's incest to the influence of the god Hymen, who after all is directly implicated in the affair as the god of matrimonial laws and the regulator of family distinctions.

> Hymen, O Hymen, to whom I owe my birth, and who, having engendered me, employed the same seed in the same place to cast upon the outraged world a monstrous commingling of fathers, brothers, sons; of brides, wives, and mothers!

In contradistinction to the Ulysses of Shakespeare and his crisis of *Degree*, the Oedipus myth (note that we are not referring here to the tragedy) makes no effort to link patricide and incest to anything else, not even to Laius's abortive attempt at infanticide. They are presented as separate events, so anomalous that it is impossible to think of them as part of the tumult that rages around them, involving elements of conflicting symmetry. The dual disasters, incest and patricide, seem to be

---

[1] In an essay entitled "Ambiguïté et renversement: sur la structure énigmatique *d'Oedipe Roi*," Jean-Pierre Vernant has aptly defined this loss of cultural difference. Patricide and incest, he writes, "constitute . . . a direct violation of the game of draughts in which each piece stands, in relation to the others, at a specified place on the draught board of the city." In effect, the results of the two crimes are always expressed in terms of lost distinctions: "The equalization of Oedipus and his sons is expressed in a series of brutal images: the father has sown his children in the same place where he himself was sown; Jocasta is a wife: not wife but mother, whose furrows have yielded a double harvest of father and children; she has been sown, and from these same furrows, these 'equal' furrows, he has obtained his children. But it is left to Tiresias to endow this talk of equality with its true tragic weight when he addressed Oedipus in the following terms: Evils will befall you which 'will establish an equality between yourself and your children'" (in *Echanges et communications*, ed. Jean Pouillon and Pierre Maranda [The Hague, 1970], p. 425).

divorced from all context and visited on Oedipus alone either by pure chance or at the bidding of Destiny or some other sacred force.

Patricide and incest serve the same purpose here as do twins in many primitive religions. The crimes of Oedipus signify the abolishment of differences, but because the nondifference is attributed to a particular individual, it is transformed into a new distinction, signifying the monstrosity of Oedipus's situation. The nondifference became the responsibility, not of society at large, but of a single individual.

Patricide and incest thus play the same role in the Oedipus myth as do the other mythical and ritual motifs considered previously. They serve to conceal the sacrificial crisis far more effectively than they reveal it. To be sure, they manage to express both aspects of the crisis, both reciprocity and forced similarities; but they do so in a way that strikes terror into the beholder and suggests that they are the exclusive responsibility of a particular individual. We lose sight of the fact that this same reciprocity operates among every member of the community and signifies the existence of a sacrificial crisis.

Another thematic device, in addition to patricide and incest, cloaks the sacrificial crisis in parallel and inverse fashion: the motif of the plague or epidemic.

We have already referred to various epidemics as "symbols" of the sacrificial crisis. Even if Sophocles had in mind the famous Athenian plague of 430 B.C., he clearly did not mean to limit his reference to one specific microbiotic visitation. The epidemic that interrupts all the vital functions of the city is surely not unrelated to violence and the loss of distinctions. The oracle itself explains matters: it is the infectious presence of a *murderer* that has brought on the disaster.

The play makes it clear that the infection and the onslaught of reciprocal violence are one and the same. The process by which the three protagonists are each in turn tainted with violence corresponds to the progress of the disease, always quick to lay low those who would contain it. Without explicitly declaring the identical nature of the two strains, the text nonetheless calls attention to their parallel qualities. Begging Oedipus and Creon to end their quarrel, the chorus exclaims: "The sight of this dying country fills me with anguish. Must we now add to our misery the miseries which flow from you?"

In tragedy, and outside it as well, plague is a symbol for the sacrificial crisis; that is, it serves the same function as patricide and incest. It seems reasonable to ask why two different symbols are used when one would do, and whether these two symbols really play identical roles.

We need only compare the two themes—plague and patricide/incest —to remark how they differ and what this difference implies. Vital aspects of the sacrificial crisis are apparent in both symbolic presentations, but they are differently distributed. The plague motif illuminates but a single aspect: the collective character of the disaster, its universally contagious nature. This motif ignores violence ?nd the nondifferential character of the crisis. With the patricide/incest motif, on the other hand, violence and nondifference are presented in magnified and highly concentrated form, but limited to a single individual. Here it is the collective element that has been ignored.

Both the patricide/incest and the plague motifs serve to disguise the presence of the sacrificial crisis, but the disguises are not the same. When viewed separately, each appears unrecognizable, without form. One complements the other, however, and when they are brought together and uniformly applied to all members of the community, the shape and substance of the crisis becomes clear. Once again it is impossible to make any affirmative or negative judgements about the participants. The responsibility for the events is evenly distributed among all.

If the crisis has dropped from sight, if universal reciprocity is eliminated, it is because of the unequal distribution of the very real parts of the crisis. In fact, nothing has been truly abolished, nothing added, but everything has been *misplaced*. The whole process of mythical formulation leads to a transferral of violent undifferentiation from all the Thebans to the person of Oedipus. Oedipus becomes the repository of all the community's ills.

In the myth, the fearful transgression of a single individual is substituted for the universal onslaught of reciprocal violence. Oedipus is responsible for the ills that have befallen his people. He has become a prime example of the human scapegoat.

At the conclusion of his drama Sophocles has Oedipus address the Thebans in the terms best calculated to quell their doubts and fears. He assures them that all the evils abroad in the community are the sole responsibility of the surrogate victim, and that he alone, as that victim, must assume the consequences for these ills: "Believe me, you have nothing more to fear. My ills are mine alone, no other mortal is fit to bear them." Oedipus is indeed the responsible party, so responsible that he frees the community from all accountability. The concept of the plague is a result of this situation. The plague is what remains of the sacrificial crisis when it has been emptied of all violence. It calls to mind the passivity of the "patient" in the modern world of medicine. Everyone is sick. Nobody owes anybody anything by way of recompense or atonement—except, of course, Oedipus.

If the community is to be freed of all responsibility for its unhappy condition and the sacrificial crisis converted into a physical disorder, a plague, the crisis must first be stripped of its violence. Or rather, this violence must be deflected to some individual—in this case, Oedipus. In the course of the tragic debate all the characters do their utmost to assist in this process. As we have seen, the inquest on Laius's death is in fact an investigation into the general subject of the sacrificial crisis; and it is clearly a matter of pinning the responsibility for the troubled state of the community on some individual, of framing a reply to the mythical question *par excellence*: "Who initiated the crisis?" Oedipus fails to fix the blame on Creon or Tiresias. Creon and Tiresias are successful in their efforts to fix the blame on him. The entire investigation is a feverish hunt for a scapegoat, which finally turns against the very man who first loosed the hounds.

Having oscillated freely among the three protagonists, the full burden of guilt finally settles on one. It might very well have settled on another, or on none. What is the mysterious mechanism that determines how the guilt shall fall?

The attribution of guilt that henceforth passes for "true" differs in no way from those attributions that will henceforth be regarded as "false," except that in the case of the "true" guilt no voice is raised to protest any aspect of the charge. A particular version of events succeeds in imposing itself; it loses its polemical nature in becoming the acknowledged basis of the myth, in becoming the myth itself. The mythical attribution can only be defined as a phenomenon of unanimity. At the point where two, three, or hundreds of symmetrical and inverted accusations meet, one alone makes itself heard and the others fall silent. The old pattern of each against another gives way to the unified antagonism of all against one.

How does it happen that the community's sense of unity, destroyed by the sacrificial crisis, is suddenly, almost miraculously, restored? Here we are in the very midst of the crisis, when all the circumstances seem to militate against any unified course of action. It is impossible to find two men who agree on anything, and each member of the community seems intent on transferring the collective burden of responsibility to the shoulders of his enemy brother. Chaos reigns. No connecting thread, however tenuous, links the conflicts, antagonisms, and obsessions that beset each individual.

Yet at this very moment, when all seems lost, when the irrational runs amok amid an infinite diversity of opinions, the resolution of the dilemma is at hand. The whole community now hurls itself into the violent unanimity that is destined to liberate it.

What is the source of this mysterious unanimity? The antagonists caught up in the sacrificial crisis invariably believe themselves separated by insurmountable differences. In reality, however, these differences gradually wear away. Everywhere we now encounter the same desire, the same antagonism, the same strategies—the same illusion of rigid differentiation within a pattern of ever-expanding uniformity. As the crisis grows more acute, the community members are transformed into "twins," matching images of violence. I would be tempted to say that they are each *doubles* of the other.

In Romantic literature, in the animistic theory of primitive religious practices and in modern psychiatry, the term *double* is perceived as essentially unreal, a projection of the imagination. I mean something different here. Although *doubles*, in my use of the term, convey certain hallucinatory associations (which I shall discuss further on), they are in themselves not at all imaginary—no more than the tragic symmetry of which they form the ideal expression is imaginary.

If violence is a great leveler of men and everybody becomes the double, or "twin," of his antagonist, it seems to follow that all the doubles are identical and that any one can at any given moment become the double of all the others; that is, the sole object of universal obsession and hatred. A single victim can be substituted for all the potential victims, for all the enemy brothers that each member is striving to banish from the community; he can be substituted, in fact, for each and every member of the community. Each member's hostility, caused by clashing against others, becomes converted from an individual feeling to a communal force unanimously directed against a single individual. The slightest hint, the most groundless accusation, can circulate with vertiginous speed and is transformed into irrefutable proof. The corporate sense of conviction snowballs, each member taking confidence from his neighbor by a rapid process of mimesis. The firm conviction of the group is based on no other evidence than the unshakable unanimity of its own illogic.

The universal spread of "doubles," the complete effacement of differences, heightening antagonisms but also making them interchangeable, is the prerequisite for the establishment of violent unanimity. For order to be reborn, disorder must first triumph; for myths to achieve their complete integration, they must first suffer total disintegration.

Where only shortly before a thousand individual conflicts had raged unchecked between a thousand enemy brothers, there now reappears a true community, united in its hatred for one alone of its number. All the rancors scattered at random among the divergent individuals, all the differing antagonisms, now converge on an isolated and unique figure, the *surrogate victim.*

The general direction of the present hypothesis should now be abundantly clear; any community that has fallen prey to violence or has been stricken by some overwhelming catastrophe hurls itself blindly into the search for a scapegoat. Its members instinctively seek an immediate and violent cure for the onslaught of unbearable violence and strive desperately to convince themselves that all their ills are the fault of a lone individual who can be easily disposed of.

Such circumstances bring to mind the forms of violence that break out spontaneously in countries convulsed by crisis: lynchings, pogroms, etc. It is perhaps worth noting that these forms of collective violence generally justify themselves by making accusations of an Oedipal variety: parricide, incest, infanticide.

Such comparisons are of only limited value, but they shed some light. They reveal a hidden connection among certain tragedies that at first glance seem utterly foreign to one another. It is impossible to say whether Sophocles was aware of the full implications of his theme, though to judge from the passages we have cited from *Oedipus the King*, it is difficult to believe that he shared our ignorance. It could well be that the tragic inspiration was neither more nor less than the sudden inkling of the origins of certain mythological themes. This view seems to find support in other tragedies besides *Oedipus* and other tragedians besides Sophocles—in particular in the work of Euripides.

The heroine of *Andromache* is Neoptolemus's mistress; Hermione is his wife. The two women, prime examples of enemy sisters, engage in a tragic debate. The humiliated wife accuses her rival of the "typical" crimes of parricide and incest, those with which Tiresias charged Oedipus at the same crucial moment of another tragedy:

> Have you, woman, no shame at all? You do not scruple to sleep with the son of your husband's murderer [Neoptolemus's father Achilles had killed Hector] or to bear his children. Such is the way of barbarians: the father sleeps with the daughter, the son with the mother, the brother with the sister. And they think nothing of killing one another, nor does their law condemn the practice. We want no such customs here.

The "substitution" is clear. The foreigner, Andromache, is made to appear the incarnation of the sacrificial crisis that threatens the community. She is declared capable of committing precisely those crimes that figure so predominantly in mythology and that consequently form the subject of classical tragedy. Hermione's ominous final phrase, "We want no such customs here," already hints at the collective fury and fear that might be launched against Andromache at Hermione's instigation. Already the mechanism has been put in motion for the selection of a surrogate victim.

It is difficult to believe that Euripides did not know what he was doing when he framed these passages, that he was unaware of the close relationship between the genesis of mythology and the collective mechanism he alludes to here; nor can I believe that he was not attempting to issue a warning to his public, to instill a sense of uneasiness without defining the problem precisely or confronting it directly.

We like to believe that we are well acquainted with the mechanisms of collective violence. In fact we know them only in their most degenerate forms, as poor imitations of the collective machinery that processed such mythological material as the story of Oedipus. In the following pages *violent unanimity* will, I believe, reveal itself as the fundamental phenomenon of primitive religion; although wherever it plays a crucial role it is completely, or almost completely, absorbed by the mythological forms it engenders. We perceive only its marginal and bastardized manifestations, which are unproductive as far as myths and ritual are concerned.

It is generally assumed that collective violence—in particular, the pitting of all against one—is an aberration in the history of a society; a perversion more or less pathological in nature, whose study can hardly be expected to yield anything of sociological significance. Our rationalist bent (about which I will have more to say further on) leads to an innocence of outlook that refuses to concede to collective violence anything more than a limited and fleeting influence, a "cathartic" action similar, in its most extreme forms, to the catharsis of the sacrificial ritual. However, the fact that the Oedipus myth has survived over several millenia and that modern culture continues to hold it dear would suggest that the effects of collective violence are greatly underestimated.

The mechanism of reciprocal violence can be described as a vicious circle. Once a community enters the circle, it is unable to extricate itself. We can define this circle in terms of vengeance and reprisals, and we can offer diverse psychological descriptions of these reactions. As long as a working capital of accumulated hatred and suspicion exists at the center of the community, it will continue to increase no matter what men do. Each person prepares himself for the probable aggression of his neighbors and interprets his neighbor's preparations as confirmation of the latter's aggressiveness. In more general terms, the mimetic character of violence is so intense that once violence is installed in a community, it cannot burn itself out.

To escape from the circle it is first necessary to remove from the scene all those forms of violence that tend to become self-propagating and to spawn new, imitative forms.

When a community succeeds in convincing itself that one alone of its number is responsible for the violent mimesis besetting it; when it is able to view this member as the single "polluted" enemy who is contaminating the rest; and when the citizens are truly unanimous in this conviction—then the belief becomes a reality, for there will no longer exist elsewhere in the community a form of violence to be followed or opposed, which is to say, imitated and propagated. In destroying the surrogate victim, men believe that they are ridding themselves of some present ill. And indeed they *are*, for they are effectively doing away with those forms of violence that beguile the imagination and provoke emulation.

It may seem absurd to assign any practical purpose to the concept of the surrogate victim. Yet we have only to substitute the word *violence*, as it is used in these pages, for the particular *ills* or *sins* that the victim is supposed to take upon himself to realize that we are indeed dealing, not simply with an illusion and a mystification, but with the most formidable and influential illusion and mystification in the whole range of human experience, one whose consequences are real and manifold.

Because modern man clings to the belief that knowledge is in itself a "good thing," he grants little or no importance to a procedure, such as the one involving the surrogate victim, that only serves to conceal the existence of man's violent impulses. The optimistic falsification could well constitute the worst sort of ignorance. Indeed, the formidable effectiveness of the process derives from its depriving men of knowledge: knowledge of the violence inherent in themselves with which they have never come to terms.

As Oedipus and Tiresias show us, the knowledge of these violent impulses continues to expand in the course of the sacrificial crisis. However, far from restoring peace, the knowledge only increases the antagonists' awareness of the *other's* violence, thereby serving to intensify the controversy. This baleful knowledge, this lucidity that is only another manifestation of violence, is succeeded by an all-inclusive ignorance. At a single blow, collective violence wipes out all memory of the past. Now we see why the sacrificial crisis is never described in myths and ritual as it really is. There human violence is envisioned as issuing from some force exterior to man. It is one with religion, as well as with those forces that really do emanate from without human will: death, illness, natural phenomena.

Men cannot confront the naked truth of their own violence without the risk of abandoning themselves to it entirely. They have never had a very clear idea of this violence, and it is possible that the survival of all human societies of the past was dependent on this fundamental lack of understanding.

The Oedipus myth, as we have attempted to explain it in the preceding pages, follows a structural pattern that conforms to that of the surrogate victim. Let us now try to determine whether the pattern recurs in other myths. From what we have seen, it seems likely that the process of finding a surrogate victim constitutes a major means, perhaps the sole means, by which men expell from their consciousness the truth about their violent nature—that knowledge of past violence which, if not shifted to a single "guilty" figure, would poison both the present and the future.

The Thebans—religious believers—sought a cure for their ills in a formal acceptance of the myth, in making it the indisputable version of the events that had recently convulsed the city and in making it the charter for a new cultural order—by convincing themselves, in short, that all their miseries were due exclusively to the plague. Such an attitude requires absolute faith in the guilt of the surrogate victim. And the very first results, the sudden restoration of peace, seemed to confirm the identification of the guilty party and also the general correctness of the diagnosis. The crisis is seen as a mysterious illness introduced into the community by an outsider. The cure lies in ridding the community of the sole malignant element.

The curative process is not an illusion, and if we give our attention to the matter we see that no attempt has been made to conceal that process. In fact, it is constantly mentioned, but in a language and with a thematic content of its own derivation. Naturally, this process manages to encompass the oracular pronouncement reported by Creon: the cure must depend on the identification and expulsion of the individual whose presence pollutes the community. In other terms, everybody must agree on the selection of the guilty individual. The surrogate victim plays the same role on the collective level as the objects the shamans claim to extract from their patients play on the individual level—objects that are then identified as the cause of the illness.

Later on (in Chapter 9) we shall see that the same forces are at work in both cases; but though similar, the two facets of the metaphor are not equivalent. The mechanism of violent unanimity is not modeled on the technique of the shamans, nor is it basically metaphorical in nature; on the other hand, there is reason to believe that the technique of the shamans is modeled on the mechanism of unanimity, interpreted in mythical fashion. Parricide and incest provide the community with exactly what it needs to represent and exorcise the effects of the sacrificial crisis. The myth is there to prove that we are dealing with a spontaneous process of collective self-mystification, the nature of which escapes not only its direct but also its indirect beneficiaries—the Freudian psychoanalyst, for instance. As far as can be ascertained the operation does not make use of vulgar dissimulation or willful manipulation of the facts concerning the sacrificial crisis. Because the violence is unanimously ordained, it effectively restores peace and order. And the false premises that it maintains acquire, in consequence, an impregnable authority. These premises serve to hide from sight the unanimous resolution as well as the sacrificial crisis. The resolution serves as the framework of the myth, invisible as long as the structure remains intact. There would be no *themes* without the structural support of the *anathema*. The anathema's true object is not Oedipus, who is only one thematic element among others, but the unanimous quality of his selection which, if it is to remain effective, must be shielded from scrutiny, protected from any outside contact or intervention. This anathema still operates today in the form of neglect, through our total indifference to the concept of collective violence and our refusal to attach any significance to the phenomenon, even when it thrusts itself upon our attention.

The structure of the myth remains unshaken even today. Transferring it intact into the realm of the imaginary only serves to strengthen it, to render it even less susceptible to analysis. No interpretation has penetrated to the core of the myth. Even Freud's famous explanation of the Oedipus story, the most brilliant and misleading of many, failed to establish the true identity of the object being "suppressed": not the desire for patricide or incest but the violence that lurked behind these all-too-visible motifs, the menace of total destruction that was diverted and concealed by means of the surrogate victim.

My hypothesis does not require that the mythological text offer a *thematic* treatment of condemnation or expulsion directly related to the underlying source of violence. Quite the contrary. The absence of this theme in certain versions of the myth by no means invalidates my theory. All traces of collective violence can, and may, be eliminated. This does not mean that the effects of the violence have been spent; in fact, they are stronger than ever. In order for the anathema to deploy its full force, it must slip from sight and from conscious memory.

It is not the absence of the anathema from tragedy, but rather its presence, that would pose a problem were it not for our belief that the tragic muse effects a partial demolition of the myth. The traces of religious anathema unearthed in tragedy should be regarded not as anachronistic survivals from a primitive past but as being in the nature of an archaeological find. The *anathema* of *Oedipus the King* should be viewed as part of Sophocles' reading of the myth, a reading perhaps more radical in its implications than we originally imagined. The poet puts some very revealing words in Oedipus's mouth: "Quickly, in the name of the gods! hide me somewhere far away from here. Kill me, or hurl me into the sea, where I will never be seen again."

The extent of the poet's understanding of the myth and its origins is hard to ascertain, but it does not have to be complete for tragedy to represent a progress in the direction of mythical dismantling. The mechanism that produces the surrogate victim is dependent on no one particular theme because it has engendered them all; it cannot be comprehended by means of a purely thematic or structural interpretation of the play.

❧ UNTIL NOW WE HAVE SEEN OEDIPUS only in terms of his polluted presence, as a receptacle for universal shame. And prior to the onslaught of collective violence, the hero of *Oedipus the King* is just that. Another Oedipus emerges, however, from the final operation; a "definitive" Oedipus, first glimpsed in the final tragedy of the Oedipus cycle, *Oedipus at Colonus*.

In the opening episodes we are still dealing with the original, polluted figure, whose appearance within their boundaries fills the inhabitants of Colonus with dread. As the play progresses, however, a remarkable change takes place. Oedipus is still a dangerous, even a terrifying figure, but he has also become very precious to the community. Colonus and Thebes begin to squabble over the future possession of the patricide's corpse, which is already looked upon as a valuable relic.

What has brought about this change? Initially, Oedipus was associated with the evil aspects of the crisis. He possessed no positive qualities. If his exile was a "good" thing, it was so in a purely negative sense, as the amputation of a gangrenous limb is "good" for an afflicted body. In *Oedipus at Colonus*, however, the scope of the drama has been enlarged. Having plunged the community into strife, the surrogate victim restores peace and order by his departure. Whereas all the previous acts of violence compounded the violence, the violence directed against the surrogate victim banished all trace of violence. The explanation for this extraordinary difference falls naturally within the domain of religion, whose concern with the problem is far from idle, since its solution touches on the well-being, if not the survival, of the community. Because human thought has never succeeded in grasping the mechanism of violent unanimity, it naturally turns toward the victim and seeks to determine whether he is not somehow responsible for the miraculous consequences of his own death or exile. Attention is drawn not only to the distinctive traits of the decisive act—the form of the murder, for example—but also to the victim's personality. Because the violence directed against the victim was intended to restore order and tranquillity, it seems only logical to attribute the happy result to the victim himself.

At the supreme moment of the crisis, the very instant when reciprocal violence is abruptly transformed into unanimous violence, the two faces of violence seem to be juxtaposed; the extremes meet. The surrogate victim serves as catalyst in this metamorphosis. And in performing this function he seems to combine in his person the most pernicious and most beneficial aspect of violence. He becomes the incarnation, as it were, of a game men feign to ignore, one whose basic rules are indeed unknown to them: the game of their own violence.[2]

It is not enough to say that the surrogate victim "symbolizes" the change from reciprocal violence and destruction to unanimous accord and construction; after all, the victim is directly responsible for this change and is an integral part of the process. From the purely religious point of view, the surrogate victim—or, more simply, the final victim —inevitably appears as a being who submits to violence without provoking a reprisal; a supernatural being who sows violence to reap peace; a mysterious savior who visits affliction on mankind in order subsequently to restore it to good health.

To our modern way of thinking a hero cannot be "good" without ceasing to be "evil," and vice versa. Religious empiricism sees matters in a different light; in a sense, it confines itself to recording events as it sees them. Oedipus is initially an evil force and subsequently a beneficial one. It is not a question of "exonerating" him, because the question of blaming him, in the modern moralistic sense of the term, never arises. Nor for that matter does religious empiricism show any interest in initiating one of those programs of "rehabilitation" so fashionable today among thinkers who claim to have freed themselves from the shackles of morality. The claims of religious thought are too modest, too tempered by fear, for its proponents to assume such lofty attitudes. The mysterious union of the most evil and most beneficial forces is of vital concern to the community, and can neither be challenged nor ignored. Nevertheless, it is a paradox that totally escapes human comprehension; and religion humbly acknowledges its impotence. The beneficial Oedipus at Colonus supercedes the earlier, evil Oedipus, but he does not negate him. How could he negate him, since it was the expulsion of a *guilty* Oedipus that prompted the departure of violence? The peaceful outcome of his expulsion confirms the justice of the sentence passed on him, his unanimous conviction for patricide and incest. If Oedipus is indeed the savior of the community, it is because he is a patricidal and incestuous son.

Sophocles' two Oedipus tragedies show a pattern of transgression and salvation long familiar to scholars. Such a pattern is to be found in

[2] We will see further on that this phenomenon of the transformation of secular into sacred elements is facilitated by hallucinatory effects that are basic to the primordial religious experience. However, it is not essential to have experienced these effects to grasp the main principles of primitive religious systems. The logic of such systems is now open to view.

innumerable tales from folklore and mythology; in fairy stories, legends, and even in works of literature. A source of violence and disorder during his sojourn among men, the hero appears as a redeemer as soon as he has been eliminated, invariably by violent means.

It also happens that the hero, while remaining a transgressor, is cast primarily as a destroyer of monsters. Oedipus appears in this role in the episode of the Sphinx. The Sphinx plays a role similar to that of the plague, terrorizing all Thebes and demanding a periodic tribute of victims.

We must now inquire whether the explanation I have proposed for the principal episode of the Oedipus myth is equally applicable to similar mythological tales; in other words, whether we are in each instance dealing with a different manifestation of the surrogate victim. Indeed, in all such myths the hero draws to himself a violent reaction, whose effects are felt throughout the community. He unwittingly conjures up a baleful, infectious force that his own death—or triumph—transforms into a guarantee of order and tranquillity.

The plague motif is only one of many that could serve equally well to conceal the presence of the sacrificial crisis and its violent outcome. For example, there are stories of collective salvation, in which the death of a single victim serves to appease the anger of some god or spirit. A lone individual, who may or may not have been guilty of some past crime, is offered up to a ferocious monster or demon in order to appease him, and he ends up killing that monster as he is killed by him.

The functioning of the surrogate victim explains the principal motifs of the Oedipus myth and illuminates the genesis and structure of these motifs. Moreover, I believe that this same process serves to explain a great many other myths; so many, in fact, that we cannot help wondering whether it might not be the structural mold of all mythology. Nor do my speculations stop here. If the generating spark of religion itself and the transcendental force that characterizes it are in fact the product of violent unanimity—of social unity forged or reforged by the "expulsion" of the surrogate victim—then even more momentous matters are at issue. If this is indeed the case we will find ourselves dealing not only with myths but also with rituals and the whole question of religion.

At present I have done little more than outline a hypothesis, some of whose elements are still lacking. In the chapters to come I hope to fill out this theory, to make clear what must now of necessity seem somewhat obscure. The first task, however, is to examine the basis of my hypothesis and attempt to situate it in the context of contemporary thought.

Even at this stage it is apparent, I believe, that the hypothesis casts light on certain passages in mythological literature. Heraclitus, who has been called the "philosopher of tragedy" and who has equal claim to the title "philosopher of myth," seems to have been on the track of the same structuring force I am now pursuing. Perhaps I anticipate, but I cannot refrain from mentioning that certain fragments of Heraclitus, until now mute and indecipherable, suddenly assume an obvious meaning in the light of my hypothesis. Does not Fragment 60 display a clear summation of the origins of myth, of the role of violence in the engendering of the gods and of distinctions? Does it not offer a resumé of all the questions that have been addressed in this chapter?

> Strife is the father and king of all. Some it makes gods, others men; some slaves, and others free.

Chapter Four

The Origins of Myth
and Ritual

꧁ IN THE STUDY OF PRIMITIVE RELIGION two theories have long held sway. The older attributes the origins of ritual to myth, seeking in the mythological construct either some real event grounded in historical fact or a specific belief that gave birth to ritualistic practices. The more recent theory reverses the procedure, attributing to ritual not only the origin of myth but also the origin of the gods, and—in Greece—of tragedy and other cultural forms as well. Hubert and Mauss belong to the latter school of thought. In sacrifice they see the genesis of the gods: "The repetition of these ceremonies in which, either by custom or for any other reason, an identical victim reappears at regular intervals, ends by creating a sort of personality. The accumulation of past sacrifices thus culminates in the creation of a god, while the individual rite preserves its secondary effects.[1]

Sacrifice is here visualized as engendering religion. This means, of course, that we cannot expect to learn anything about the origin of sacrifice itself from Hubert and Mauss; for when a phenomenon is used to explain other phenomena, it can generally be assumed that no explanation of the explanatory phenomenon will be forthcoming. The latter becomes a kind of unformulated dogma to be accepted on pure faith. Whatever makes other things clear does not need, apparently, to be made clear itself.

Hubert and Mauss have nothing to say about the origins of sacrificial practice and very little about its nature and function, even though their discussion is entitled *Sacrifice: Its Nature and Function*. As we have already seen, the notion that sacrifice serves primarily to bring us into contact with the "gods" makes little sense. For even if the gods are imaged forth at the conclusion of a long series of sacrifices, what are we to make of the preliminary rounds? What were the sacrificers thinking about at a time when they did not yet possess gods with

[1] Hubert and Mauss, *Sacrifice*, p. 81.

whom to "communicate"? Why—for whom—were those rites performed under the vast celestial void? The passion that prompts modern
antitheists to shift all blame onto the "gods" must not lead us astray.
Sacrifice deals with humankind, and it is in human terms that we must
attempt to comprehend it.

Hubert and Mauss's failure to come to grips with the origin and
function of sacrifice makes their accurate description of its operation
even more remarkable. One cannot attribute this accuracy to some a
priori concept, for sacrifice still awaits its proper interpretation.

The resemblances among the rites practiced in disparate cultures are
striking, and the variations from one culture to another are never
sufficient to disguise the basic similarities. Hubert and Mauss can thus
feel justified in describing the sacrificial process outside the context of
any specific culture, as if it were some kind of technique. And a
technique it truly is; but does this technique, as these two authors
contend, have no real object and serve no function in the social process? How can an institution that is ultimately judged fantastical and
imaginary manifest such remarkable similarities from culture to culture? It is no longer a question of appealing to "diffusionist" theories—
they had already been discredited, and with good reason, at the time
Hubert and Mauss were writing.

The more one reflects on these structural similarities, the more one is
tempted to qualify them as not merely surprising, but downright
miraculous. And while admiring the descriptive powers of Hubert and
Mauss, one cannot help wishing they shared that irrepressible inquisi-
tiveness that characterized some of their predecessors. Yet it was
undoubtedly necessary to set aside a great many problems in order to
schematize certain forms of analysis—and that is precisely what these
two authors did. Undoubtedly a provisional limiting of the field of
study serves to bring into relief certain areas that had previously been
neglected and misunderstood.

In scientific research, as in warfare, it is always prudent—for the
sake of morale—to represent strategic retreats in a positive light. All
the same, workers in the field must take care not to mistake these
retreats for glorious victories. In all the social sciences today the tendencies apparent in the work of Hubert and Mauss seem to have swept
the field. It is no longer a question of relating ritual to myth or even
myth to ritual. Such procedures invariably produced a circular train of
argument, from which the only means of escape seemed to lie in designating some arbitrary point of departure. It is good that this futile
mode of thought has been abandoned. Another positive development is
the recognition that if a solution to the problem exists, it exists at the
center of the circle, not on the periphery. What is decidedly not good

is the conclusion that either this center is totally inaccessible or there is no center at all.

Such pessimistic suppositions, based on past failures, purport to be ultrascientific but are in fact questions of philosophy and temperament. Past failures prove nothing outside their own context. It is foolhardy to condemn the search for a real origin simply because the search has not been successful so far. Antimetaphysical speculation is, after all, another form of metaphysics. At any moment a new theory may arise that will provide a satisfactory—that is, a scientific—answer to the question of the origins, nature, and function not only of sacrifice but also of religion in general.

It is not enough to declare certain problems null and void, after a cursory and purely "symbolic" investigation, in order to lay claim to a scientific approach. Science is not a refuge for philosophic skepticism, a pose of sage resignation. All great discoveries begin with a sense of curiosity that is today often dismissed as childish and a faith in the resources of language, even the most commonplace language, that is often condemned as naive. When the *nil admirari* of those bourgeois dandys caricatured by Stendhal passes for the last word in understanding, we have just cause for alarm. The relative failure of Frazer, Freud, or Robertson Smith is no reason to regard their insistence on getting to the bottom of things as foolish or outdated. To assert that there is nothing to be gained by seeking out the function and origin of ritual is to say that the language of religion is destined to remain forever a dead letter, a kind of gibberish—cleverly codified perhaps, but devoid of any real meaning.

From time to time a voice is heard calling our attention to the very strangeness of institutions such as sacrifice and attempting to satisfy our deep need to find a firm basis in reality for these institutions. Adolphe Jensen, for one, managed to reopen the great inquiries of the past—and it is perhaps for that very reason that his work has received so little notice from contemporary scholars. Jensen writes:

> Man must have been subjected to some particularly overwhelming experiences to have been led to introduce such cruel practices into his life. What could have been the reasons?
>
> What could have persuaded men to kill their fellow-beings—not in the wanton, amoral manner of barbarians succumbing to their instincts, but as a reflex of the awakened consciousness of the creator of cultural forms, seeking to comprehend the innermost nature of the world and to transmit this knowledge to future generations by means of dramatic representations? . . . Mythological thought always returns to what happened *initially*, to the act of creation, justly assuming that this occurrence sheds the brightest, most revealing light on a given subject. . . .

> If murder plays such a decisive role in the sacrificial rite, this means that it must have played a particularly important part in the initial impulse.[2]

I do not deny the utility of recent descriptive contributions. But I believe the time has come for us to ask ourselves, once again, whether something of vital importance did indeed take place *initially*. We must return to the traditional questions, reframing them in terms of the rigorous methodology of our own times.

Once we have determined the underlying principle of our search, we should consider the a priori conditions that any theory must fulfill to command our scrutiny. If sacrifice has a real origin, the memory of which myths keep alive in one way and rituals commemorate in another, then it seems clear that we are dealing with an event that initially made a very strong impression. Very strong, but not unforgettable—for in the end it is forgotten. But this impression, although subject to later modification, lives on in the religious observances and perhaps in all the cultural manifestations of the society. There is no need to postulate some form of individual or collective subconscious to account for its survival.

The extraordinary number of commemorative rites that have to do with killing leads us to imagine that the original event must have been a murder. Freud, in *Totem and Taboo*, lucidly perceived this necessity. And the remarkable similarities among the sacrificial rites of various localities suggest that the murder was always of the same general type. This does not mean that the murder was a single historical event or that it belongs exclusively to prehistory. Although the event looks exceptional from the perspective of any given society, it seems quite commonplace in a broad, comparative context.

The sacrificial crisis and the surrogate-victim mechanism fulfill all the conditions required of a satisfactory hypothesis.

But, it may be protested, if such an event had actually taken place, science would already have discovered it. This assertion fails to take into account an extraordinary deficiency of modern science. The presence of a religious element at the source of all human societies is indubitable; yet, of all social institutions, religion is the only one to which science has been unable to attribute a genuine objective, a real function. I contend that the objective of ritual is the proper reenactment of the surrogate-victim mechanism; its function is to perpetuate or renew the effects of this mechanism; that is, to keep violence *outside* the community.

---

[2] Adolphe E. Jensen, *Mythes et cultes chez les peuples primitifs* (Paris, 1954), pp. 206–7.

⧜ I BEGAN BY REMARKING on the cathartic func-
tion of sacrifice, and went on to define the sacrificial crisis as the loss of
this function, as well as of all cultural distinctions. If the unanimous
violence directed against the surrogate victim succeeds in bringing this
crisis to an end, clearly this violence must be at the origin of a new
sacrificial system. If the surrogate victim can interrupt the destructur-
ing process, it must be at the origin of structure. We shall see further
on whether it is possible to verify this assertion with regard to those
rites and regulations that are essential to a cultural order—festivals,
rites of passage, proscriptions against incest, etc. At present we have
good reason to believe that the violence directed against the surrogate
victim might well be radically generative in that, by putting an end to
the vicious and destructive cycle of violence, it simultaneously initiates
another and constructive cycle, that of the sacrificial rite—which protects the community from that same violence and allows culture to
flourish.

If this is true, the generative violence constitutes at least the indirect
origin of all those things that men hold most dear and that they strive
most ardently to preserve. This notion is affirmed, though in a veiled
and transfigured manner, by the many etiological myths that deal with
the murder of one mythological character by other mythological characters. That event is conceived as the origin of the cultural order; the
dead divinity becomes the source not only of sacred rites but also of
matrimonial regulations and proscriptions of every kind; in short, of all
those cultural forms that give man his unique humanity.

In some cases the mythological characters are said to grant men
whatever they need to live in society; in other cases they deny them
these same benefits. In either case men manage to obtain what they
require, sometimes by theft or trickery, but not before one of the
mythological characters has been isolated from the others and subjected to some unusual accident or misfortune. This accident may be
fatal; sometimes it is merely ludicrous. We must recognize in it a mask
of the collective violence that terminates the crisis. Sometimes the
central figure breaks away from the group and flees, taking with him
the object in dispute. Generally he is overtaken and put to death;
occasionally he is merely wounded or beaten. Sometimes it is he who
demands to be beaten, and at each blow extraordinary benefits accrue,
giving rise to a fertility and an abundance that assures the harmonious
functioning of the cultural order.

The mythical narrative sometimes takes the form of a contest or
game, a quasi-sportive or pugilistic event that evokes the rivalries inherent in the sacrificial crisis. Behind all these themes one can detect

the outline of reciprocal violence, gradually transformed into a unanimous act. It is certainly astonishing that all human activities, and even the course of nature itself, are subordinated to this metamorphosis of violence taking place at the heart of the community. When relationships between men are troubled, when men cease to cooperate among themselves and to come to terms with one another, there is no human enterprise that does not suffer. Even the success of the hunt, of fishing expeditions, of food gathering is put in question. Therefore, the benefits attributed to the generative violence extend beyond mankind to nature itself. The act of collective murder is seen as the source of all abundance; the principle of procreation is attributed to it, and all those plants that are useful to man; everything beneficial and nutritive is said to take root in the body of the primordial victim.

Even Hubert and Mauss cite facts that should serve to bring socially aware investigators into direct contact with social realities. Side by side with myths in which the element of generative mob action is barely discernible, there exist others in which its presence is explicitly acknowledged. Such transparent myths are by no means confined to those cultures we Western humanists might be tempted to qualify as primitive or crude. Hubert and Mauss offer an exemplary specimen from Greece: "At Troezen, in the peribolos of the temple of Hippolytos, the death of the foreign goddesses Damia and Auxesia was commemorated by an annual festival, the *lithobolia*. According to tradition, the two virgin goddesses from Crete were stoned to death in the course of an uprising. These foreigners represent *the* foreigner, the passerby who often plays a role in the harvest festivals; and the lapidation is a sacrificial rite."[3]

Associated with the Oedipus myth are rites, like those involving the pharmakos, whose true significance becomes clear in the light of the above comments. The city of Athens prudently kept on hand a number of unfortunate souls, whom it maintained at public expense, for appointed times as well as in certain emergencies. Whenever some calamity threatened—plague, famine, foreign invasion, or internal dissension—there was always a pharmakos at the disposal of the community.

The complete explanation of the Oedipus myth—that is, the determining of the precise function of the surrogate victim—permits us to understand the aim of the sacrificers. They are striving to produce a replica, as faithful as possible in every detail, of a previous crisis that was resolved by means of a spontaneously unanimous victimization. All the dangers, real and imaginary, that threaten the community are sub-

[3] Hubert and Mauss, *Sacrifice*, p. 83.

sumed in the most terrible danger that can confront a society: the sacrificial crisis. The rite is therefore a repetition of the original, spontaneous "lynching" that restored order in the community by reestablishing, around the figure of the surrogate victim, that sentiment of social accord that had been destroyed in the onslaught of reciprocal violence. Like Oedipus, the victim is considered a polluted object, whose living presence contaminates everything that comes in contact with it and whose death purges the community of its ills—as the subsequent restoration of public tranquillity clearly testifies. That is why the pharmakos was paraded about the city. He was used as a kind of sponge to sop up impurities, and afterward he was expelled from the community or killed in a ceremony that involved the entire populace.

If my thesis is correct, the pharmakos, like Oedipus himself, has a dual connotation. On the one hand he is a woebegone figure, an object of scorn who is also weighed down with guilt; a butt for all sorts of gibes, insults, and of course, outbursts of violence. On the other hand, we find him surrounded by a quasi-religious aura of veneration; he has become a sort of cult object. This duality reflects the metamorphosis the ritual victim is designed to effect; the victim draws to itself all the violence infecting the original victim and through its own death transforms this baneful violence into beneficial violence, into harmony and abundance.

It is not surprising that the word *pharmakon* in classical Greek means both poison and the antidote for poison, both sickness and cure —in short, any substance capable of perpetrating a very good or very bad action, according to the circumstances and the dosage. The *pharmakon* is thus a magic drug or volatile elixir, whose administration had best be left by ordinary men in the hands of those who enjoy special knowledge and exceptional powers—priests, magicians, shamans, doctors, and so on.[4]

The comparison of Oedipus and the pharmakos is not meant to imply that we accept the views of certain scholars (most notably the early-twentieth-century Cambridge Ritualists) who have proposed a purely ritualistic interpretation of tragedy. It is evident that the Oedipus myth is intimately associated with rites analogous to those involving the pharmakos, but we must take care not to confuse the myth and ritual, on the one hand, with the essentially antimythical and antiritualistic inspiration of the drama on the other. The Cambridge Ritualists and their disciples have based their interpretation of the role of the pharmakos on the idea that seasonal change—the "death" and "resurrection" of nature—constitutes the original model for the rite, its deep-

4 Cf. Chapter 11, pp. 296–97.

seated meaning. In fact, there is nothing in nature that could encourage or even suggest such an atrocious sort of ritual killing as the death of the pharmakos. In my opinion, the sole possible model remains the sacrificial crisis and its resolution. Nature enters the picture later, when the ritualistic mind succeeds in detecting certain similarities between nature's rhythms and the community's alternating pattern of order and disorder. The *modus operandi* of violence—sometimes reciprocal and pernicious, sometimes unanimous and beneficial—is then taken as the model for the entire universe.

To portray tragedy as a repetition and an adaptation of the seasonal rites, a sort of *sacre du printemps*, is surely to strip it of those very elements that mark it as tragedy. This remains true even if it is correct ultimately to confer on tragedy a quasi-ritualistic value in Western culture. Frazer and the Cambridge Ritualists center their interpretation on seasonal and agricultural connotations that do play an important role in many festivals but that are ultimately derived, like all other connotations, from the victimization mechanism. The connection between the drama and the major mythological themes is undeniable, but in order to grasp its full significance we must transcend the approach that limits itself to thematic analysis and renounce those prejudices that might lead us to portray the "scapegoat" purely as a product of blind superstition, a nonfunctional device bereft of any operative value. In the scapegoat theme we should recognize the very real metamorphosis of reciprocal violence into restraining violence through the agency of unanimity. This unique mechanism structures all cultural values even as it conceals itself behind them; it is associated even more fundamentally with the double-edged images of myths and rituals. Sophocles "appends" nothing to the scapegoat theme; its "broader meaning" is not simply tacked on, nor has the tragic poet on his own initiative turned Oedipus into a "reflection of the human condition." Scapegoat effects are more deeply rooted in the human condition than we are willing to admit.[5]

My hypothesis is becoming at once broader and more precise. It should permit us to see through certain previously impenetrable reli-

[5] A number of French scholars have detected in the Oedipus of both myth and tragedy a pharmakos and a "scapegoat." According to Marie Delcourt, the institution of the scapegoat explains the fate of the infant Oedipus, abandoned by his parents: "Oedipus is offered as a scapegoat by a father called *Laius*, that is to say *Publius*, the representative of the people." The murder by exposure of weak or ill-formed infants was extremely widespread and is certainly associated with the concept of the surrogate victim—that is, with the unanimous basis of all sacrificial rites. It is the indication of that unanimity among the general populace that Marie Delcourt has touched upon here (*Légendes et cultes de héros en Grèce* [Paris, 1942], p. 102. Cf. also her *Oedipe et la légende du conquérant* [Paris, 1944]).

gious acts, such as the execution of the pharmakos, and to discern their perfectly intelligible aims. As we will soon discover, this same hypothesis pertains not only to rites as a general category, but also to their most minute details. Hitherto I have examined only those sacrifices that involve human victims. The link between the rite and the functioning of violent unanimity is especially apparent when the original victim also happens to have been a human being. In such instances, the effort at imitation is easy to discern.

We should now ask ourselves whether animal sacrifices, too, cannot be defined as the mimesis of an initial collective murder. In my first chapter I suggested that there was no essential difference between human and animal sacrifice. If this is true, the origin of all sacrifices must be the same. The celebrated Judaic scapegoat and all animal rites of the same type lend strong support to my hypothesis. But there is surely no harm in pausing a moment longer to examine a "classical" case of animal sacrifice in order to demonstrate, if possible, its direct connection with the execution of a surrogate victim. If it can be shown that the sacrificial rites are indeed striving to reproduce the mechanism of violent unanimity and that the surrogate victim is indeed the key to all these rites, considerable new light will be shed on the matter of animal sacrifice.

Let us turn our attention to one of those rare societies in which sacrifice survives to this day as a living institution and whose customs have been diligently recorded by a trained ethnologist. In *Divinity and Experience*, Godfrey Lienhardt describes in detail several sacrificial ceremonies that he witnessed among the Dinka. I will summarize the general substance of his descriptions, taking care to emphasize those points that seem especially significant.

The insistent rhythm of choral incantations gradually captures the attention of a crowd of bystanders who at first appeared scattered and self-absorbed. Participants begin to brandish weapons in mock warfare. A few isolated individuals strike out at others, but without any real hostility. In these preparatory stages violence is, therefore, already present in a ritual form, but it is still manifestly reciprocal; the ritualistic imitation deals first with the sacrificial crisis itself, with the chaotic antecedents to the unanimous resolution. From time to time somebody detaches himself from the group to beat the cow or calf that has been

More recently, Jean-Pierre Vernant has taken up these ideas and exploits some of their possibilities in his thematic analysis of *Oedipus the King:* "Divine ruler and pharmakos: these are the two faces of Oedipus. It is this duality that accounts for his enigmatic aspect, that unites in him, like an ambiguous phrase, two inverse images superimposed one upon the other. To this inversion in Oedipus's nature Sophocles appends a broader meaning: the hero as a reflection of the human condition" (Vernant, "Ambiguité et renversement," p. 1271).

tied to a nearby stake, or to hurl insults at it. There is nothing static or stilted about the performance; it succeeds in giving shape to a collective impulse that gradually triumphs over the forces of dispersion and discord by bringing corporate violence to bear on a ritual victim. In this rite the metamorphosis of reciprocal violence into unilateral violence is explicitly and dramatically reenacted. And it seems to me that the same can be seen to hold true for an infinite number of rites if one keeps a sharp eye out for signs (often, admittedly, fragmentary and elusive) that reveal the functioning of this particular metamorphosis. In the often-cited example of the Greek Bouphonia, the participants make a point of quarreling among themselves before turning their attention to the designated victim. All the mock battles that generally take place prior to sacrificial ceremonies and all the ritual dances whose formal symmetry is reflected in a perpetual confrontation between the performers lend themselves to an interpretation in which the performances are seen as imitative responses to a sacrificial crisis.

In the Dinka sacrifice it seems that the paroxysm takes place not at the death of the victim, but in the course of the ritual curses pronounced before its death. One gets the impression that these curses are in themselves able to destroy the victim; that it is, as in tragedy, for all practical purposes killed by words. And these words, even if they are not firmly fixed by custom, are fundamentally identical to the accusations hurled by Tiresias against Oedipus. The actual execution sometimes consists of a veritable stampede of the entire group directed against the victim. In this case, it is the victim's genitals that are singled out. The same is true of the pharmakos who is whipped on his sexual organs with herbaceous plants. There is thus some reason to believe that the animal victim is a stand-in for an original victim accused, like Oedipus, of patricide, incest, or of some other sexual transgression that signifies the violent abolition of distinctions—the major cause of cultural disintegration. The means of dispatching the victim may vary depending on the nature of the crime; but the death sentence itself remains invariable. The ritualistic mentality imagines that this death will result in benefits too great to be ascribed to a simple punitive measure. These benefits must be real. But the ritualistic mentality does not understand why they have accrued; the only explanations it can offer are mythic. However, this same mentality has a good notion of how these benefits are obtained, and it tries unceasingly to repeat the fruitful process.

The scorn, hostility, and cruelty displayed toward the animal prior to the ritualistic slaughter are replaced upon its death by a show of ritualistic veneration. In bearing away into death the scourge of reciprocal violence, the victim has performed its assigned function.

Henceforth the victim will incarnate violence in both its guises, beneficial and baneful; that is, it will personify the All-Powerful who rules from on high. Having been so flagrantly abused, it is only reasonable that the victim should be greatly honored—just as it was reasonable to banish Oedipus when he seemed the bearer of ill fortune and reasonable to honor him when his departure assured the community's well-being. That adopting the former attitude assures the latter result seems to confirm the rationality of the plan, despite its contradictory appearance.

Lienhardt himself defines the victim as a scapegoat who becomes the receptacle of human passions. We are dealing here with an animal *pharmakos*, a calf or cow that assumes, not some vague and ill-defined sins, but the very real (though often hidden) hostilities that *all the members of the community feel for one another*. Our portrayal of sacrifice as an imitation and reenactment of spontaneous collective violence in no way conflicts with the definition I proposed in Chapter 1. In fact, spontaneous violence contains an element of appeasement that can also be found in ritual sacrifice, though in diluted form. In the original event, it is unleashed violence that is checked and at the same time partially appeased; in the ritual reenactment, it is the more or less latent aggressions that are dealt with.

The community is both attracted and repelled by its own origins. It feels the constant need to reexperience them, albeit in veiled and transfigured form. By means of rites the community manages to cajole and somewhat subdue the forces of destruction. But the true nature and real function of these forces will always elude its grasp, precisely because the source of the evil is the community itself. The only way in which the ritualistic imagination can succeed in its self-appointed task —a task both painstaking and elusive—is by allowing violence a certain amount of free play, *as in the original instance*, but not too much; that is, by exercising its memory of the collective expulsion on carefully designated objects and within a rigorous framework.

In societies where sacrifice is still a living institution it displays the cathartic function I attributed to it in my first chapter. The catharsis is performed in a structural setting so strikingly similar to that of unanimous violence that one can only conclude that it is a deliberate, if not an entirely exact, imitation of unanimous violence.

ANY THESIS THAT MAINTAINS that ritual is the imitation and reenactment of spontaneous, unanimous violence may well seem fanciful, even fantastic, as long as one considers a few isolated rites. But when one widens the scope of the inquiry, supporting evidence appears at every turn. Seen from a broad perspective, certain mythological and ritualistic analogies, previous overlooked, leap into view. Even a cursory examination reveals that the theme of unanimity recurs with extraordinary frequency in all aspects of religious life, in rituals, and in myths. It recurs in cultures so far apart, in forms so disparate, and in texts so diverse in nature that it is impossible to explain it away through some diffusionist theory.

As noted above, the Dinka sacrificial execution often takes the form of a stampede of young men, who trample the beast down and crush him by their sheer mass. When the animal is too large to be killed in this way, he is slaughtered in a more conventional manner; but a simulated stampede is still performed as a prelude to the slaughter. The sacrificial ceremony requires a show of collective participation, if only in purely symbolic form. This association of the collectivity with the killing of the sacrificial victim is found in numerous instances—notably in the Dionysiac *sparagmos*, which I will discuss later on.[6] All the participants, without exception, are required to take part in the death scene. The same is true for the Arabian camel sacrifice described in Robertson Smith's *Religion of the Semites*, and for a good many other sacrificial rituals.

It is a unanimous group that Odysseus and his companions plunge the red-hot stake into the Cyclops' eye. It is as a unanimous group that the gods of some of the generative myths conspire and bring about the death of one of their divine colleagues. In Hindu mythology the same motif recurs. The *Yadjour-Veda* speaks of a sacrificial ceremony in which a god, Soma, is to be put to death by the other gods. Mithra at first refuses to join his divine companions in the act, but he is finally persuaded to do so by the argument that the sacrifice will be totally ineffective if not performed by all. This myth offers a prescription for the correct performance of a sacrifice. Unanimity is a formal requirement; the abstention of a single participant renders the sacrifice even worse than useless—it make it dangerous.

In the story of the murder of Hainuwele, mythological heroine of the Ceram Islanders, the sacrificers stamp on her grave in a manner that emphatically underlines the unanimous and collective character of the enterprise. The signs of unanimity displayed in some local myth can reappear in identical form in a ritual peformed by some other community. For example, the Ngadju-Dayaks of Borneo first sacrifice slaves, then perform a burial rite that involves all the participants' stamping on the graves. In fact, the Ngadju-Dayaks demand total participation in all their sacrificial rites. The long drawn out agony of the

[6] Cf. Chapter 5, 131.

slaves' execution yields nothing to psychological explanations. What counts is the communal gesture of unanimity; therefore, all the participants in the sacrifice are required to strike the victim before its death. The ritualistic structure of the ceremony is strictly regulated and reflects the hierarchical distinctions that govern the cultural order. Animal sacrifices are performed in the same manner.[7]

Even in a society such as the Kaingang, wracked by reciprocal violence, the demand for unanimity reappears in bastard form: "The murderers never wanted to act alone. They insisted on the collaboration of the members of the group. To demand that the final blow be delivered by someone else is the usual practice at Kaingang murders."[8] There is no question of denying the psychological significance of such accounts; quite the contrary. In the absence of any collective structuralization, our only recourse is the psychological interpretation. No ritual context is available; evil violence runs wild.

THE FUNCTION OF SACRIFICE, as defined in Chapter 1, not only allows for but requires a surrogate victim—in other words, violent unanimity. In ritual sacrifice the victim, when actually put to death, diverts violence from its forbidden objectives within the community. But for whom, precisely, is this victim substituted? Heretofore we could only conceive of this substitution in terms of individual psychological mechanisms, which clearly do not provide an adequate picture of the process. If there were no surrogate victim to transform the sacrifice from an essentially private concern into one involving the whole community, we would be obliged to regard the victim as a substitute for particular individuals who have somehow provoked the sacrificer's anger. If the transfer is purely personal, as it is in psychoanalysis, then sacrifice cannot be a true social institution involving the entire community. But sacrifice, as we know, is essentially a communal institution. "Individualization" marks a later, decadent stage in its evolution, a development contrary to its original spirit.

To understand how and why sacrifice functions as it does, we should consider the proposition that the ritual victim is never substituted for some particular member of the community or even for the community as a whole: *it is always substituted for the surrogate victim.* As this victim itself serves as a substitute for all the members of the community, the sacrificial substitution does indeed play the role that we

---

[7] H. Shärer, "Die Bedeutung des Menschenopfers im Dagakischen Toten Kult," *Mitteilungen der deutschen Gesellschaft für Volkerkunde* 10 (1940). Cited by Jensen, *Mythes et cultes chez les peuples primitifs,* p. 198.

[8] Jules Henry, *Jungle People* (New York, 1964), p. 123.

have attributed to it, protecting all the members of the community from their respective violence—but always through the intermediary of the surrogate victim.

This observation should clear me of any suspicion of "psychologizing" while eliminating a serious objection to basing the present theory on sacrificial substitution. If the entire community were not already subsumed under a single head, that of the surrogate victim, it would be impossible to attribute to the sacrificial substitution the significance we have claimed for it, impossible to establish a social basis for the institution.

The original act of violence is unique and spontaneous. Ritual sacrifices, however, are multiple, endlessly repeated. All those aspects of the original act that had escaped man's control—the choice of time and place, the selection of the victim—are now premeditated and fixed by custom. The ritual process aims at removing all element of chance and seeks to extract from the original violence some technique of cathartic appeasement. The diluted force of the sacrificial ritual cannot be attributed to imperfections in its imitative technique. After all, the rite is designed to function during periods of relative calm; as we have seen, its role is not curative, but preventive. If it were more "effective" than it in fact is—if it did not limit itself to appropriate sacrificial victims but instead, like the original act of violence, vented its force on a participating member of the community—then it would lose all effectiveness, for it would bring to pass the very thing it was supposed to prevent: a relapse into the sacrificial crisis. The sacrificial process is as fully adapted to its normal function as collective murder is to its abnormal and normative function. There is every reason to believe that the minor catharsis of the sacrificial act is derived from that major catharsis circumscribed by collective murder.

Ritual sacrifice is founded on a double substitution. The first, which passes unperceived, is the substitution of one member of the community for all, brought about through the operation of the surrogate victim. The second, the only truly "ritualistic" substitution, is superimposed on the first. It is the substitution of a victim belonging to a predetermined sacrificial category for the original victim. The surrogate victim comes from inside the community, and the ritual victim must come from outside; otherwise the community might find it difficult to unite against it.

How, it may be asked, does the second substitution graft itself onto the first? How does the original violence succeed in imposing a centrifugal force on the rite? In short, how does the sacrificial technique operate? I will attempt to return to these questions, but at this point I wish to draw attention to the essentially mimetic character of sacrifice with regard to the original, generative act of violence. Thanks to this mimetic aspect we can understand how the sacrificial process can exist and function, without being obliged to attribute to the ritualistic mind a manipulative ability or a clairvoyance that it most certainly does not possess.

It is entirely possible to regard the sacrificial rite as a commemoration of a real event without reducing it to the triviality of one of our own national holidays; or, for that matter, without ascribing it to some neurotic compulsion, as psychoanalysts are wont to do. A trace of very real violence persists in the rite, and there is no doubt that the rite succeeds at least partially because of its grim associations, its lingering fascination; but its essential orientation is peaceful. Even the most violent rites are specifically designed to abolish violence. To see these rites as expressions of man's pathological morbidity is to miss the point.

It goes without saying that the rite has its violent aspects, but these always involve a *lesser* violence, proffered as a bulwark against a far more virulent violence. Moreover, the rite aims at the most profound state of peace known to any community: the peace that follows the sacrificial crisis and results from the unanimous accord generated by the surrogate victim. To banish the evil emanations that accumulate within the community and to recapture the freshness of this original experience are one and the same task. Whether order reigns supreme or whether its reign is already challenged, the same model, the same plan of action is invariably proposed. It is the plan, associated with the victorious resolution of all communal crises, that involves violence against the surrogate victim.

WE ARE EVOLVING A THEORY of myth and ritual —in short, of religion as a whole. Up to this point the analyses of the crucial role attributed to the surrogate victim and to unanimous violence may have appeared too summary, too incomplete for this theory to seem much more than a working hypothesis. At this stage of our exposition we can hardly hope to have banished all the reader's doubts. A thesis that attributes a *real* origin to religion demands the abandonment of too many currently accepted ideas and the rethinking of too many fundamental concepts to be readily accepted, expecially when it is not susceptible to direct verification. If ritual imitation no longer recalls precisely what it is imitating, if the secret of the primordial event has been allowed to slip from its memory, then the rite involves a form of delusion that has never subsequently been understood.

No single rite will reproduce, point for point, the operations my hypothesis proposes as the origin of all rites. A delusion concerning its own factual basis—*not* the absence of that basis—is characteristic of religion. And the source of this delusion is none other than the surrogate victim; or rather, the fact, which remains unperceived, that the surrogate victim is arbitrarily chosen. The ritualistic mind strives to reproduce the operation of violent unanimity without understanding its mimetic nature. If my hypothesis is correct, no single religious form will suffice to illuminate the whole picture, but a multiplicity of examples will cast light on its various aspects until everything gradually becomes clear and certainty prevails.

In order to verify my hypothesis, then, it must be applied to many different forms of ritual and myth, as far apart in content, history, and geography as possible. If it is correct, the complex rites will provide the most striking confirmation. The more complex a system, the more numerous will be the elements it strives to reproduce in the operation analyzed above. As most of these elements are, in principle, already in our possession, the most difficult problems should resolve themselves of their own accord. The scattered fragments of the system should cohere, and the unintelligible become intelligible.

The sacred monarchies of continental Africa have long resisted all attempts at analysis. In discussing the complexity of their structures, scholars have had recourse to such adjectives as "strange" and "aberrant." In an era when it was still believed possible to classify all rituals under more or less logical headings, the African rites were generally grouped under the rubric "Exceptions."

In one important group, situated between Egypt and Swaziland, the king is required to commit an act of incest, either real or symbolic, on certain solemn occasions—notably, at his enthronement or in the course of the periodic rites of renewal. Among the king's possible partners are virtually all the women formally forbidden him by matrimonial regulations: mother, sisters, daughters, nieces, cousins, etc. Sometimes the parentage is real, sometimes classificatory. In societies where the incestuous act is no longer actually consummated—if, indeed, it ever was—a symbolism of incest persists. As Luc de Heusch has pointed out, the important role played by the queen mother in these societies can only be understood in the context of ritual incest.[9]

In order to understand royal incest we must take care not to wrench it from its context, as is too often done by writers captivated by its sensational aspects. This rite forms part of an overall ritualistic procedure that prescribes the other transgressions the king must commit before he takes office. For example, he must eat certain forbidden foods, and commit certain acts of violence. In some instances, he is literally bathed in blood and fed concoctions whose ingredients

[9] Luc de Heusch, *Essai sur le symbolisme de l'inceste royal en Afrique* (Brussels, 1958).

(bloody offal and refuse of all kinds) indicate their evil character. In some societies the whole enthronement ceremony takes place in an atmosphere of blood-stained confusion. It is not a question, then, of one particular forbidden act or of one act being particularly forbidden. On occasion the king is required to commit all the forbidden acts that are imaginable and possible for him to commit. The encyclopedic character of the transgressions, as well as the eclectic nature of the incestuous act, betray who it is that the king is supposed to incarnate: the paragon of transgressors, the man who holds nothing sacred and who fearlessly assumes every form of hubris.

We are not dealing here with royal peccadilloes in the class, let us say, of Louis XIV's mistresses—objects of amused forebearance, perhaps, but accorded no official position by the community. The African peoples close their eyes to nothing; in fact, they keep them wide open, and incest, in their judgment, often constitutes the *sine qua non* of accession to the throne. That is not to say that such infractions are no longer considered reprehensible when committed by a king. On the contrary, it is because of their ability to remain reprehensible that these infractions are selected. These acts bestow on the king a particularly potent form of pollution, which is repeatedly alluded to in the symbolic imagery of the ceremonies: "Among the Bushongs, for example, where rats are regarded as *nyec* (disgusting) and held as taboo, the king is formally presented at his coronation with a basket full of these rodents."[10] The theme of the leper-king is sometimes associated with this same ceremony; the new king is proclaimed the descendant and heir of a royal leper who was the first to occupy the throne.[11]

The cultures that practice royal incest sometimes offer an interpretation of it that cannot be taken seriously. It is asserted that the king chooses a wife from among his close relatives in order to preserve the purity of the royal blood. This explanation will not do. Clearly the incest, as well as the other "forbidden" acts, are designed to make the king the very incarnation of impurity. It is because of this impurity that the king, in the course of the enthronement and renewal ceremonies, is subjected to the ritualistic insults and abuse of his people. A hostile crowd denounces the misconduct of this miscreant, who is as yet nothing more than a criminal and a social outcast. In some instances the royal army stages a mock attack on the king's personal bodyguard and even on the king himself.

If one chooses to make a criminal of one's king and requires him to violate the most sacred laws, in particular the laws of exogamy, it

[10] J. Vansina, "Initiation Rite of the Bushong," Africa 25 (1955): 149–50. Quoted by Laura Makarius, "Du roi magique au roi divin," *Annales* 25, no. 3 (1970):677.
[11] Makarius, "Du roi magique au roi divin," p. 670.

cannot be for the pleasure of "pardoning" him or of displaying one's generosity of spirit. On the contrary: all this takes place because punishment of the severest sort seems to be in order, and the needful insults and hostilities find their outlet in sacrificial ceremonies in which the king plays the chief role—the role of the original victim. I have insisted on the need to view royal incest in its proper ritual context. This context is not limited to the act itself; it appears also to include the real or symbolic sacrifice of the monarch. And the sacrifice of the king is clearly a punishment for his transgressions. The idea that the king is sacrificed because he has lost his strength or virility is as fanciful as the theory that royal incest preserves the purity of the family strain. Both theories are tardy afterthoughts, designed to supply an ideological basis for the rites. Few ethnologists take them seriously, and ethnological evidence offers good reason to doubt them. In Ruanda, for example, the king and the queen mother—clearly an incestuous couple—must periodically submit to a sacrificial rite that can only be regarded as a symbolic punishment for incest: "The royal pair appeared in public, bound like captives condemned to death. A bull and a cow, their substitutes, were clubbed to the ground and slaughtered. The king then mounted the flanks of the bull and some of the bull's blood was poured over him *so as to carry the symbolic resemblance between the two as far as possible.*"[12]

It should now be clear what scenario the king is acting out and what place incest occupies in the plot. This scenario is very like the Oedipus myth—not by reason of historical affiliation, but because the mythic and ritualistic imaginations are using the same model in both cases. Behind the pageantry of the African monarchies lurks the specter of the sacrificial crisis, suddenly resolved by the unanimity arising from the generative act of violence. Each African king is a new Oedipus, obliged to play out his own myth from beginning to end, because ritualistic theory sees in this enactment the means of renewing and perpetuating a cultural order that is constantly on the brink of destruction. As in the case of Oedipus, there was a charge of incest associated with the original act of mob violence and serving as its justification, an accusation seemingly confirmed by the effective results of the collective action. The king is thus required to do *what he was originally accused of* and to do it not to public acclaim, but to the angry protests that accompanied the *original* accusation. In principle the charge of incest will at each successive enthronement give rise to the same indignation, the same collective violence that on the original occasion ac-

[12] Luc de Heusch, "Aspects de la sacralité du pouvoir en Afrique," in *Le Pouvoir et le sacré* (Brussels, 1962). Cited in L. de Lagger, *Le Ruanda ancient* (Namur, 1939), pp. 209–16.

companied the slaughter that allayed the universal rage and led to the triumphant advent of the cultural order.

The relationship between royal incest and a prior accusation of incest is often confirmed by an etiological myth. H. J. Krige and J. D. Krige report such a myth among the Lovedu.[13] Incest presides over the birth of society; it is the bearer of peace and abundance to mankind. But incest is neither a first cause nor an essential condition. Although it may initially appear to offer justification for the act of sacrifice, on a deeper level it is the act of sacrifice that justifies the incest. The king reigns only by virtue of his future death; he is no more and no less than a victim awaiting sacrifice, a condemned man about to be executed. The sacrifice itself is not the first, but a ritualized form of the *original* outburst of violent unanimity.

Although the king is required to eat disgusting concoctions and commit all sorts of violent crimes, there is no reason to associate his performance with the avant-garde theater or to see him as a sort of antihero of the contemporary counterculture. The spirit behind these rites has nothing in common with such modern phenomena. Rather than welcome the powers of evil with open arms, the rites seek to exorcise them. The king must show himself "worthy" of his punishment—fully as worthy as the original outcast from whom the ceremony derives. It is important to cultivate the future victim's supposed potential for evil, to transform him into a monster of iniquity—not for esthetic reasons, but to enable him to polarize, to literally draw to himself, all the infectious strains in the community and transform them into sources of peace and fecundity. The principle of this metamorphosis has its source in the sacrifice of the monarch and subsequently pervades his entire existence on earth. The investiture hymn of the Mossis (Ouagadougous) expresses with classic concision a dynamic formula for salvation that only my hypothesis of the surrogate victim can render intelligible:

> You are a turd,
> You are a heap of refuse,
> You have come to kill us,
> You have come to save us.[14]

The king has a genuine function identical to that of any sacrificial victim. He is the catalyst who converts sterile, infectious violence into positive cultural values. The monarchy might be compared to the factories that convert household refuse into fertilizer. In both cases the

---

[13] H. J. Krige and J. D. Krige, "The Lovedu of Transvaal," in *African Worlds* (London, 1954).
[14] T. Theuws, "Naître et mourir dans le rituel Luba," *Zaïre* 14, 2/3 (Brussels) (1960):172. Quoted by Makarius, "Du roi magique au roi divin," p. 685.

resulting products are too potent to be applied at full strength; they must be used with moderation and caution and on occasion be mixed with neutral agents. The king "fertilizes" a farmer's field from a safe distance; if he passes too close the surface will be singed; if he walks on it, a blight will ensue.

The parallelism between the Oedipus myth and these African observances is striking. There is no theme in the myth or the tragedy that does not find an echo here. In certain cases the regulations relating to incest seem to reflect the double motif of infanticide and parricide, as in the formal edict that forever separates the king from his son. In other societies one can detect reflections of the other double motifs of the myth. Like the son of Laius, the king of the Nyoros has "two little mothers", and the chief of the Jukuns has two mistresses, whom Luc de Heusch compares to the Nyoro pair.[15]

---

[15] *Moro-Naba*, film by J. Rouch and D. Zahan. Produced by Comité du film ethnolographique de l'I.F.A.N. Cited by Makarius, "Du roi magique au roi divin," p. 685. This parallelism is undoubtedly rooted in the presence of a sacred monarchy of the African type in archaic Greece. Yet no matter how legitimate and even necessary this historical hypothesis may be, it does not really serve to explain the Oedipus myth. In order to explain the relationship between the myth, ritual, and tragedy, as well as its parallelism with the African observances, we must have perceived the real mechanism that hides behind all these cultural accretions—in particular the sacred monarchy, which can by no means be considered the irreducible element in the analysis. We must grasp the role of the surrogate victim, that is, the conclusion of a crisis of reciprocal violence, brought about through unanimous accord directed or redirected against a victim. In "Ambiguïté et renversement," (pp. 1271–72), Jean-Pierre Vernant has brought together many mythological and ritualistic details that forcefully suggest the inadequacy of certain fashionable psychological assumptions and the obstacles they present to a true appreciation of the "scapegoat's" role and associated phenomena:

> The polarity between the king and the scapegoat (a polarity the tragedy situates at the very heart of the figure of Oedipus) was hardly invented by Sophocles. It is ingrained in the religious practices and social theories of the Greeks. The poet has lent it new meaning, however, in making it the symbol of man's fundamental ambiguity. If Sophocles chose the *tyrannos-pharmakos* to illustrate what we have called the "reversal" theme, it was because these two opposing figures appear symmetrical and to some degree interchangeable. Each regards itself as an *individual* responsible for the *collective* salvation of the group. In the works of Homer and Hesiod it is the king, an offspring of Zeus, who is responsible for the fertility of the soil, the herds, and the women. As long as he shows himself irreproachable (*amumòn*) in the dispensing of justice, his people prosper; but if he falters, the whole community pays the penalty for the failing of this one individual. The gods then visit misfortune on all—*limos* and *loimos*, "famine" and "plague." The men kill each other, the women cease to bear children, the earth remains sterile and the flocks and herds no longer reproduce. When such a divine calamity descends on a people their natural recourse is to sacrifice their king. For if the king is responsible for the community's fertility and this fertility ceases, that indicates that the power invested in him as sovereign has somehow become inverted; his justice turns to crime, his integrity to corruption, and the best (*aristos*) seems to be replaced by the worst (*kakistos*). The legends of Lycurgus, Athamas, and Oinoclus therefore involve, as a means of putting the *loimos* to rout, the lapidation of the king,

Behind the Athenian pharmakos, behind the Oedipus myth, there is real violence at work, reciprocal violence brought to an end by the unanimous slaughter of the surrogate victim. In almost every case the enthronement or renewal rituals—and in some cases the actual, definitive death of the monarch—are accompanied by mock combats between two factions. These ritual confrontations, sometimes enlisting the participation of the whole community, recall the chaos and factionalism whose only cure lies in the surrogate victim. And if this violent treatment of a surrogate victim serves as a model everywhere, it is because it has actually proved effective in restoring peace and unity. Only the social utility of this collective violence can account for a politicoritualistic scheme that consists not only of constantly repeating the process but also of making the surrogate victim the sole arbitrator of all conflicts, proclaiming it a veritable incarnation of absolute sovereignty.

In many cases succession to the throne entails a ritual battle between father and son or between sons. Luc de Heusch offers a description of such a struggle: "The death of the king triggers a war of succession, a war whose ritualistic character can hardly be underestimated. The princes reputedly employ their most potent magic medicines to eliminate their fraternal rivals. At the core of this royal magic contest in Nkole appears the old theme of *enemy brothers*. Factions congregate around the various claimants, and the surviving brother is accorded the throne." As we remarked earlier, in a conflict whose course is no longer strictly regulated by a predetermined model, the ritualistic ele-

his ritual murder, or the sacrifice of his son. But there are also instances where a member of the community is delegated to assume the role of the unworthy king, the antisovereign. The king then unloads on this inverted image of himself all his negative attributes. We now have the true pharmakos: the king's double, but in reverse. He is similar to those mock kings who are crowned at carnival time, when everything is set topsy-turvy and social hierarchies turned upside down; when sexual prohibitions are lifted, and theft permitted; when servants take the place of their masters and women exchange clothing with men; when, in short, the throne is yielded only to the basest, ugliest, most ridiculous and criminal of beings. But once the carnival is over the antiking is expelled from the community or put to death, and his disappearance puts an end to all the disorder that his person served to symbolize for the community and also to purge for it.

Vernant's observations on Oedipus and the African monarchies are equally applicable to many other cases, for they ultimately concern the ritualistic response to the presence of violence. Once we recognize the role of unanimity in the operation of the surrogate victim, it becomes clear that in these instances we are not dealing with gratuitous elaborations of superstition. That is why Sophocles' version should not be looked upon as something entirely new that adds a further dimension to the myth but as a reduction, the partial demolishing of its mythological meaning, both in regard to modern psychology and sociology and in regard to other ancient myths. The poet lends no "new meaning" to the royal scapegoat, he simply draws nearer the universal source of meanings.

ments disintegrate into actual events and it becomes impossible to distinguish history from ritual. This confusion is in itself revealing. A rite retains its vitality only as long as it serves to channel political and social conflicts of unquestionable reality in a specific direction. On the other hand, it remains a rite only as long as it manages to restrict the conflictual modes of expression to rigorously determined forms.

ᴼᴄᴽᴁ WHEREVER WE POSSESS DETAILED DESCRIP-tions of specific renewal rites, we observe that they, too, follow the general pattern of the sacrificial crisis, incorporating its original violence. These rites are to royalty as a whole what the microcosm is to the macrocosm. The royal rites of Incwala, in Swaziland, have received particularly careful attention.[16]

As the rites begin the king retires to his sacred enclosure, where he imbibes various noxious potions and commits incest with a tribal sister. These actions are intended to augment the king's *silwane*, a term whose literal translation is "to be like a savage beast." Although this attribute is not the exclusive property of the king, it serves to set him apart from his subjects. The king's *silwane* is always superior to anyone else's, even that of his bravest warrior.

During this preparatory period the people intone a hymn, the *simémo*, which expresses their hatred of the king and their desire to see him expelled from the community. From time to time the monarch, more "savage-beastly" than ever, puts in an appearance. His nudity and the black paint with which he has decorated his body serve as a symbol of defiance. There then takes place a mock battle between the people and the royal clan in which the very person of the king is at stake. Fortified in their turn with magic potions, and swollen with *silwane*—though to a lesser extent than their chief—the armed warriors encircle the sacred enclosure and endeavor, as it seems, to take possession of the king, who is protected by his entourage.

In the course of the rites (presented here in abridged form), a symbolic execution of the king also occurs. With a touch of his wand the royal incarnation of violence transfers his own *silwane* to a cow, thus transforming the animal into a "raging bull," which is then put to death. As in the Dinka sacrifices, the warriors hurl themselves *all together* and *without weapons* onto the beast, belaboring it with their fists.

[16] T. O. Beidelman, "Swazi Royal Ritual," *Africa* 36 (1966):373–405; P. A. W. Cook, "The Inqwala Ceremony of the Swazi," *Bantu Studies* 4 (1930):205–10; M. Gluckman, *Rituals of Rebellion in South-East Africa* (Manchester, 1954); H. Kuper, "A Ritual Kingship among the Swazi," *Africa* 14 (1944:230–56; H. Kuper, *The Swazi: A South African Kingdom* (New York, 1964); E. Norbeck, "African Rituals of Conflict," *American Anthropologist* 65 (1963):1254–79.

During the ceremony the distance between the king, his entourage, the warriors, and the rest of his subjects is temporarily effaced. This loss of differences has nothing to do with "fraternization." Rather, it is the result of the violence that engulfs all the participants. T. O. Beidelman defines this portion of the rites as a *dissolving of distinctions*.[17] Victor Turner describes the Incwala as a play of kingship, in the Shakespearean sense of the expression.

The ceremony unleashes an increasing exaltation, a dynamism that draws its energy from the very forces it puts in play; forces that initially seem to claim the king as their victim but from which he eventually emerges as the absolute ruler. At first almost sacrificed himself, the king then presides at rites which show him to be the sacrificer *par excellence*. There is nothing surprising about this duality; it simply confirms the role we attributed to the surrogate victim, its ability to master all violence. Even when he is a victim, the king remains the final arbiter of the contest and can intervene at any point. He plays all the roles, and no form of violence, no matter how extreme or eccentric, is foreign to him.

At the height of the battle between the warriors and the king, the king withdraws once more to his enclosure. He reemerges armed with a gourd, which he hurls at the shields of his assailants. After this attack, the groups disband. H. Kuper's native informants told him that in time of war, any warrior struck by the royal gourd would forfeit his life. In the light of this information, the anthropologist suggests that we look upon the warrior whom the king singles out to be struck by the gourd as a sort of national scapegoat. This amounts to seeing him as a *double* for the king, a man who symbolically dies in his place, as the cow had done earlier in the ceremony.

The Incwala rites begin at the end of an old year and close at the beginning of a new year. A relationship exists between the crisis commemorated by the rites and the end of a temporal cycle. The rites follow certain natural rhythms, but these rhythms can scarcely be regarded as a prime factor in the ceremonies even if they occasionally seem to overshadow the violence. For it is the violence whose very presence establishes the essential function of all myths and rituals: to disguise, to divert, and to banish disorder from the community. At the close of the ceremonies a great bonfire is lit, and on it are consumed all the pollutions accumulated in the course of the rites and in the course of the past year. A symbolism of cleansing and purification pervades all the important stages of the ceremony.

[17] Beidelman, "Swazi Royal Ritual," p. 391, n. 1.

TO BE PROPERLY UNDERSTOOD royal incest must be perceived as part of a ritual pattern that is identical with the monarchy itself. The king must be looked upon as a future sacrificial object; that is, as the replacement for the surrogate victim. Incest, then, plays a relatively minor role in the proceedings. Its purpose is to augment the effectiveness of the sacrifice. And although the sacrifice, directly linked as it is to spontaneous collective violence, is perfectly intelligible without reference to incest, the incest is unintelligible without reference to sacrifice.

To be sure, the sacrificial element can disappear completely, while the incest or incest symbolism persists. This does not mean, however, that the sacrifice is subsidiary to the incest or that the incest can be considered without reference to the sacrifice. Rather, the participants have moved so far from the origin of events that they now regard their own rites from the same general perspective as Western observers (one is almost tempted to say "Western voyeurs"). The incest persists *owing to its very strangeness*. In the collapse of ritual—which in one sense is not really a collapse, since it prolongs and reinforces the original delusion—incest alone survives; it alone is remembered when all else has been forgotten. The African monarchy has now been reduced to a tourist attraction. In addition, modern ethnology has almost invariably isolated institutional incest from its context; it consistently fails to appreciate its meaning because it insists on viewing incest as an autonomous event, something so remarkable that it should have a significance all its own, without reference to the surrounding phenomena. Psychoanalysts perpetuate this error; one might say they are its chief perpetrators.

It is by means of incest that the king assumes the mantle of royalty, but the act itself is "royal" only in its demanding the death of those who commit it, in its harkening back to the original victim. This becomes apparent when we turn to a rather remarkable exception in the midst of those societies that prescribe royal incest; namely, a society in which the practice is formally and absolutely forbidden. One might suppose that such a refusal simply entails a reversion to the general rule that prohibits incest. But matters are not that simple. The practice is not merely rejected and forbidden as it would be in most societies, but these measures are accompanied by extraordinary precautions. The monarch's entourage undertakes to remove all his close relatives from his presence, and he is forced to imbibe, not fortifying potions, but debilitating ones. All of which means, of course, that an aura of incest surrounds the throne, an aura no less strong than those in the neighboring monarchies where royal incest is obligatory.[18] These special precautionary measures are justified solely by the king's dangerous vulnerability to this particular transgression. Thus, it might be said that the basic criterion of royalty remains the same. Even in a society that formally excludes incest, the king replaces an original victim who is believed to have violated the rules of exogamy. It is as the heir and successor of this victim that the king is considered particularly susceptible to incest. The copy is assumed to have all the qualities of the original.

The general rule proscribing the practice of incest is here reaffirmed, but in such a peculiar manner that we can only regard it as an exception to the exception and classify it with the cultures that practice royal incest. The essential question is this: Why is the repetition of an incestuous act—invariably traced back to some original banished transgressor, some founding father or mythic hero of the community— regarded as salubrious by one society and noxious by its neighbor? A contradiction of this kind among communities whose religious outlooks, with the exception of their treatment of incest, are so very similar, seems to defy all efforts at rational inquiry.

The distribution of a religious theme such as royal incest throughout a cultural milieu of a certain range and variety suggests that "influences," in the traditional sense of the word, are at work. The incest theme cannot be "original" to each of these cultures; that much seems clear. Does this mean that my general hypothesis no longer applies?

I maintain that the original act of violence is the matrix of *all* ritual and mythological significations. Strictly speaking, this is only true of an act whose violence is absolute, so to speak: perfect, completely spontaneous, extreme. Between this instance of complete originality and the mechanical repetition of rites at the other end of the scale, we can assume the existence of an infinite number of intermediary forms.

---

18 "The Nioka impose continence on their chief for the rest of his life. He is obliged to send away all the women of his household, wear a penis sheath at all times, and take sedative drugs. Among the Njumbas of Kasaï, the 'chief wife' (the first wife of the chief) is required to take medications that produce not only sterility but a complete suppression of the menstrual cycle. The excessive character of these customs can be readily explained in terms of the conflict between a tradition of royal incest and the desire to allow no breach of the exogamic prohibition. The Pendes, in fact, regard any hint of royal incest with great severity, and they dismissed a chieftain from his position because he had once, as a warrior, treated his sister for an abdominal abscess: 'You have seen the nakedness of your sister; you are no longer fit to be our chief" (Makarius, "Du roi magique au roi divin," p. 671). On the Pendes, see L. Sousberge, "Etuis péniens ou gaines de chasteté chez les ba-Pende," *Africa* 24 (1954), and "Structures de parenté et alliance d'après les formules Pende," *Mémoires de l'Académie royale des sciences coloniales belges* 4, no. 1 (1951).

The fact that certain religious and cultural themes pervade a vast area does not exclude the possibility that truly spontaneous collective violence, working through one of the intermediary forms and endowed with real (if limited) creative powers on the mythic and religious level, might occur in many places. This would explain the many variants of the same myth, the same cults, from locality to locality, and also the claim made by various places to be the birthplace of the same god.

It should be noted, however, that even though the myths and rituals are susceptible to infinite variation in detail, they all revolve around a few major themes, one of which is incest. As soon as a community begins to regard an isolated individual as responsible for a sacrificial crisis—that is, responsible for the disintegration of distinctions within the community—it follows that this same individual is accused of violating society's most fundamental rules, the rules of kinship. In short, the individual is considered essentially "incestuous" in nature. The theme of the incestuous outcast is not universal, but it is found in many widely scattered cultural areas. The fact that the theme turns up spontaneously in so many different places is not incompatible with the notion of cultural diffusion within a broad geographical expanse.

The surrogate-victim hypothesis offers a means of traversing the vast theoretical terrain between the passivity and excessively rigid continuity of the diffusionist theories, on the one hand, and the equally rigid discontinuity of modern formalism, on the other. While not excluding borrowings from other cultures, my hypothesis confers on these borrowed elements a large degree of autonomy within their new setting. This accounts for the strange contradiction of the strict requirement and the formal prohibition of royal incest existing side by side in neighboring societies. In each instance we can see the same incest theme, but reinterpreted in terms of local experience.

The ritualistic imagination strives to repeat the original generative process. The unanimity that regulates, pacifies, and reconciles supplants the opposite situation, displacing the paroxysm of violence that divides, destroys, and levels. The transition from disruptive violence to order and peace is almost instantaneous. The two different faces of the primordial experience are juxtaposed; unanimity is attained in the course of a brief and terrifying meeting of opposites. All sacrificial rites, then, reproduce certain forms of violence and appropriate certain associations that seem more suitable to the sacrificial crisis itself than to its cure. Incest is an example. In societies where it is an accepted practice, royal incest is regarded as a means of salvation and, in consequence, an institution to be carefully preserved. Such a reaction is perfectly intelligible.

The primary—in fact, the sole—purpose of the rite is to prevent the return of the sacrificial crisis. Incest is a product of this crisis, and even when it is attributed to the surrogate victim it still signifies the crisis; it retains a sinister connotation. We can understand, therefore, that the ritualistic mind might refuse to consider incest as a contribution to the community's salvation even in its association with the surrogate victim. It might persist in regarding incest, even when committed by the representative and heir of the original victim, as the ultimate act of evil, capable of plunging the community into a highly contagious form of violence.

Incest, then, is simply another aspect of the affliction that the rites are designed to prevent. But they attempt to prevent it by means of a cure that is intimately associated with the most virulent form of the affliction. The ritualistic mind thus finds itself obliged to separate what cannot be separated, and the solution must ultimately be an arbitrary one. The ritualistic mind is perhaps more willing than we are to admit that good and evil are simply two aspects of the same reality, but eventually it must distinguish between them; even in the ritualistic framework, where there are fewer differences than in any other area of human culture, a distinction between the two must be apparent. The purpose of the rite is to consolidate this difference, newly restored after the terrible undifferentiation of the crisis. There is nothing arbitrary or imaginary about the difference between violence and nonviolence, but men always treat it as a difference within a process that is violent from beginning to end. That is how the rite is made possible. The rite selects a certain form of violence as "good," as necessary to the unity of the community, and sets up in opposition to it another sort of violence that is deemed "bad," because it is affiliated to violent reciprocity. In the same way the rite can designate certain forms of incest as "good"—for example, royal incest—and others as "bad." It can equally well decide that all forms of incest are "bad," and refuse to admit even royal incest among those actions which, if not actually sacrificial in character, are still capable of contributing to the sacrificial powers of the monarch.

Given the fundamental importance to mankind of the transformation of bad violence into good and the equally fundamental inability of men to solve the mystery of this transformation, it is not surprising that men are doomed to ritual; nor is it surprising that the resulting rites assume forms that are both highly analogous and highly diverse.

That the ritualistic imagination can confront royal incest and derive two diametrically opposed solutions from it demonstrates both the arbitrary and the fundamental character of the difference between good (that is, sacrificial) and bad violence. In each culture, the inverse solution can be felt behind each chosen solution. In societies where it is an accepted and even an obligatory practice, incest, even royal incest, still retains a sinister connotation; it invites punishment and justifies the death of the king. But in societies where it is forbidden, incest has a certain beneficial quality, in that the king is perceived as having a special predilection for incest, and nothing closely associated to the king can be completely bad since the king brings unity and salvation to the community.

Although incest may have contradictory associations, it is not simply a pawn on a structural chessboard, to be moved about at will. Nor can it be added or subtracted from the cultural picture simply to satisfy the whims of intellectual fashion. We must take care that a formal structuralistic approach does not strip it completely of its dramatic impact; nor must we permit psychoanalysis to pass it off as the meaning of meanings.

IT IS IN THE DOMAIN of general anthropology that orthodox Freudianism is most vulnerable. There is no formal psychoanalytical explanation of royal incest, not even of the Oedipus myth; no explanation of the interesting similarities between the Oedipus myth and the African monarchies. With brilliant intuition, Freud pointed the way toward patricide and incest, but his disciples failed to follow his lead. Instead of conceding the impotence of psychoanalysis in dealing with the subject, most scholars, even those hostile to psychoanalysis, tacitly acknowledge its privilege to deal with anything remotely concerned with incest. Nobody can approach the question of royal incest without saluting the stately ghost of Freud. Yet psychoanalysis has never said, and never can say, anything decisive on the subject of royal incest, anything that could add substantially to our understanding or, for that matter, approach the Master at his best.

The almost total absence of the incest motif in late-nineteenth-century Western culture led Freud to conclude that all human society is warped by a universal desire, universally suppressed, to commit maternal incest. The presence of incest in the mythology and rituals of primitive peoples seemed to Freud an irrefutable proof of his hypothesis. But psychoanalysis has never managed to explain why the absence of incest in one culture has exactly the same significance as the presence of incest in another. There is no doubt that Freud's hypothesis was mistaken; but he often had good reasons for being wrong, whereas those who denounce his errors often have the wrong reasons for being right.

Freud perceived that the incest and patricide motifs of the Oedipus myth concealed something essential to the understanding of all aspects of culture. The cultural context in which he functioned led him to believe that the crimes attributed to the surrogate victim were indeed the hidden desires of all men, the secret source of human conduct. Some of the cultural phenomena of the period could be at least partially explained in terms of the absence of patricidal or incestuous manifestations. Psychoanalysis could not claim equal success, as limited as this success might be, in its approach to myths and religion. When patricide and incest are openly displayed, it is hard to see what it is they are hiding—some still better hidden instance of incest or patricide, perhaps? Even if one concedes such a theory, it in no way serves to explain the other themes of the myth, or even incest itself when it appears in a real form within a ritualistic framework.[19]

Until some other approach succeeds where psychoanalysis has failed, the claims of psychoanalysis will continue to influence us. However, once the Freudian interpretation of mythological and ritual incest has been replaced by another explanation, at once very close to and very far removed from the Freudian viewpoint, many thematic aspects of the issue will suddenly become clear, and we will have good cause to believe that Freud's theory has finally had its day.

In the African monarchies as in the Oedipus myth, incest—maternal or otherwise—is not primary matter, absolute and irreducible. It is an allusion that can readily be translated into other terms. The same is true of patricide, or any of the crimes, perversions, and monstrosities with which mythology abounds. All these motifs, and others as well, serve to conceal and disguise rather than reveal the violent elimination of differences. It is this particular violence that is the suppressed matter of the myths; not suppressed desire, but terror, terror of absolute violence. And who would deny that far stronger than desire, in fact

---

[19] The most favorable situation for psychoanalytic theories of this sort would be the total absence of incest and patricide from the entire corpus of mythology and ritual. However, psychoanalysis could also adjust to its constant presence, to a continual intrusion of incest and patricide motifs. The truth lies between these extremes. Patricide figures in mythology and ritual, but hardly more than any other type of criminal activity; the same applies to incest. Among the different kinds of incest, maternal incest will at most play the role of *primus inter pares*, unless it is replaced by the incestuous relationship with a sister or some other relative; but never so fully or so systematically that one can attribute it merely to a reflex of the "unconscious."
A statistical survey has been made dealing with violence between relations in myths of the "Oedipus type." These myths were drawn from some fifty selected cultures, more or less evenly distributed within the six broad cultural regions defined by Murdock. Clyde Kluckhohn sums up the results: "One can make a good case for 'antagonism against close relatives—*usually* of the same sex' as a prominent motif, and a fair case for physical violence against such relatives. But neither parricide nor Raglan's regicide motifs will stand up literally without a great deal of farfetched interpretation" ("Recurrent Themes in Myths and Mythmaking," pp. 53–54).

the only force that can snuff out desire, is that nameless but irresistible terror?

Widespread patricide and incest signify the final stages of the sacrificial crisis. Limited to a single individual, patricide and incest shift the whole burden of the crisis onto a surrogate victim. The hidden basis of myths is not sexual; it cannot be, for that motif is openly revealed. Nonetheless, sexuality is important insofar as it stimulates violence and provides occasions for it to vent its force. Like other natural phenomena, sexuality is a real presence in myths. In fact, it plays a more important role in them than does nature itself, but a role that is not truly decisive. Sexuality becomes almost completely explicit in the incest motif. There it is associated with a purely individual violence, one, however, that still masks the collective violence. This violence would surely wipe out the community were it not for the religious delusion that the surrogate victim provides.

The theory that mythological themes serve to express man's fear of natural phenomena has in the twentieth century given way to the idea that these same themes conceal man's fear of the purely sexual and "incestuous" nature of his desires. The two theories are themselves mythic; like the other theories we have discussed, they function within the context of myth and help to perpetuate the delusions of myth. However, the two theories should not be put on the same footing. Freud is less "mythic" than his predecessors; sex is more involved in human violence than are thunder and earthquakes, closer to the hidden sources of mythic elaboration. "Naked" or "pure" sexuality is directly connected to violence. It is the final veil shielding violence from sight; at the same time it is the beginning of violence's revelation. Historically, these two aspects of sexuality often dominate in turn; periods of "sexual liberation" often precede some violent outburst. This is true even in the chronological sequence of Freud's own work. The dynamism of this work tends to transcend the initial pansexualism to engage itself in the ambiguous enterprise of *Totem and Taboo* or the radical concept of the "death wish." We can thus look on Freud's work as a step toward the revelation of something far more profound than the theory of suppressed desires, a theory whose inadequacy he may have dimly perceived; toward, in fact, the absolute violence still concealed by a certain delusion, the nature of which remains in the broad sense "sacrificial."

Dionysus

ᘿᑕᗐᐄ ALMOST EVERY SOCIETY HAS FESTIVALS that have retained a ritualistic character over the centuries. Of particular interest to the modern inquirer are observances involving the deliberate violation of established laws; for example, celebrations in which sexual promiscuity is not only tolerated but prescribed or in which incest becomes the required practice.

Such violations must be viewed in their broadest context: that of the overall elimination of differences. Family and social hierarchies are temporarily suppressed or inverted; children no longer respect their parents, servants their masters, vassals their lords. This motif is reflected in the esthetics of the holiday—the display of clashing colors, the parading of transvestite figures, the slapstick antics of piebald "fools." For the duration of the festival unnatural acts and outrageous behavior are permitted, even encouraged.

As one might expect, this destruction of differences is often accompanied by violence and strife. Subordinates hurl insults at their superiors; various social factions exchange gibes and abuse. Disputes rage in the midst of disorder. In many instances the motif of rivalry makes its appearance in the guise of a contest, game, or sporting event that has assumed a quasi-ritualistic cast. Work is suspended, and the celebrants give themselves over to drunken revelry and the consumption of all the food amassed over the course of many months.

I have no doubt that these festivities commemorate a sacrificial crisis. It may seem strange to memorialize a traumatic event in such an uproarious manner, but the explanation lies ready to hand. The specifically "festive" aspects of the celebration, those that most effectively capture the attention, that dominate the spectacle, and that are the only ones to survive the evolutionary transformations of the festival—these aspects have nothing to do with the festival's underlying cause. The fundamental purpose of the festival is to set the stage for a sacrificial act that marks at once the climax and the termination of the festivities. Roger Caillois has pointed out the sacrificial origin of festivals.[1] If the crisis brought on by the loss of distinctions and the subsequent advent of reciprocal violence can be celebrated in such a jubilant fashion, it is because these holocausts are seen in retrospect as the initial stages of a cathartic process. The beneficial character of the generative unanimity tends to be projected onto the past, affecting the initial impression of the crisis and making it seem other than it was. The violent dismissal of distinctions now acquires a favorable connotation, which will eventually manifest itself as a festive display.

I have already advanced a number of interpretations that may prove relevant to the subject of festivals. For example, ritual incest ultimately acquires a beneficial aspect that seems to be almost wholly independent of its sacrificial quality. In certain societies the aristocrats, and even the artisans, have recourse to ritual incest, more or less furtively, to bring them good luck before a difficult or hazardous undertaking. The rites performed during the enthronement of certain African monarchs or in the course of renewal ceremonies often resemble festival practices. Conversely, in festivals in which the monarch plays no direct role we encounter a substitute king—sometimes a "king of fools"—who is himself nothing more than a sacrificial victim endowed with sacral privileges; at the conclusion of the festivities, he or his representative will be sacrificed. The king's sovereignty—real or imagined, permanent or temporary—seems to derive from an original, generative act of violence inflicted on a surrogate victim.

The function of the festival is no different from the function of other sacrificial rites. As Emile Durkheim perceived, the festival revitalizes the cultural order by reenacting its conception, reproducing an experience that is viewed as the source of health and abundance; reenacting, in fact, the moment when the fear of falling into interminable violence is most intense and the community is therefore most closely drawn together.

Primitive peoples regard their cultural tradition as a fragile and precious inheritance to be carefully nurtured and protected from any change, for change could only serve to damage it, perhaps mortally. The skepticism and resentment we moderns feel toward taboos of any kind, which feelings we tend to assume are shared by primitive peoples, play no part in their festivities. The often-cited syndrome of "release of tensions" or that much-ridden hobby-horse of psycho-sociologists, the "necessary outlet," has relevance only to a single aspect of the ritual process, and an exclusive emphasis on these syndromes distorts the original spirit of the ritual.

Festivals are based on the assumption that there is a direct link

[1] Roger Caillois, *Man and the Sacred*, trans. Meyer Barash (Glencoe, Ill., 1959), chap. 4, pp. 97–127.

between the sacrificial crisis and its resolution. The crisis is inseparable from its happy ending and becomes itself a cause for jubilation. But this interpretation is not the only one possible. As we have already noticed in the case of royal incest, religious thinking on the relationship between the crisis and its conclusion can result in two divergent viewpoints. Either it is the continuity between crisis and conclusion that strikes the imagination, or it is the rupture; in each instance, the resulting interpretation must be both partially true and partially false. Yet religious thinking tends to adopt one or another of the two solutions and cling to it for dear life—even if, at the outset, the choice could easily have gone the other way.

It can be assumed almost a priori that certain societies will opt for the second solution, the one that emphasizes the rupture between the crisis and the founding violence. In such cases another kind of festival will arise, one that, in comparison with the festival we have been describing, might perhaps be called an antifestival. The rites of sacrificial expulsion are not preceded by a period of frenzied anarchy, but by an extreme austerity and an increased rigor in the observance of all interdicts. Extraordinary precautions are taken to prevent the community from falling prey once again to reciprocal violence.

In fact, both solutions can be observed. In some societies we encounter ritual occasions that resemble festivals—there is the same periodicity, the same interruption of normal activities, the same rites of sacrificial expulsion—and yet are so very different from festivals that they constitute a vexing problem for ethnologists, one similar to the enigma of royal incest, which is accepted in some societies and forbidden in others. Far from being temporarily suspended, in the antifestival all cultural prohibitions are strongly reinforced.

The rites of the Swazi Incwala correspond closely to the definition of the antifestival. Throughout the period of observance all sexual activity, including the most legitimate, is forbidden. Sleeping late in the morning is regarded as a crime, and physical contact between individuals is to be avoided, even physical contact with one's own body (the celebrants are not supposed to wash or to scratch themselves). A threat of imminent pollution—that is, of violence—hangs over the entire community. All singing and loud noise are prohibited. Children are scolded if they grow noisy at play.

In *The Golden Bough* Frazer offers a fine example of an antifestival. For several weeks in the year the Cape tribe on the Gold Coast permit no sound of tom-toms or musket fire. Public conversations are forbidden. If a dispute arises and voices are raised, the contesting parties are summoned before the chieftain, who deals out stiff fines to everyone involved. To avoid arguments over strayed livestock, all lost animals become the property of their finders, and the original owners are obliged to relinquish all claim.

It seems clear that such measures are intended to prevent the outbreak of widespread violence. Frazer offers no explanation for them, but his anthropological intuition (far superior to his theorizing) prompted him to classify these practices under the rubric of festivals. The logic of the antifestival is as strict as that of the festival. The goal is to reproduce the beneficial effects of violent unanimity while abbreviating as much as possible the terrible preliminaries—which, in the case of the antifestival, are perceived in a negative light. The longer the interval between any two purifying rituals, the greater the danger of a violent explosion. Impurities accumulate; and in the period immediately preceding the celebration of the rite, a period saturated with the memory of the sacrificial crisis, everyone moves with extreme caution. It is as if the community had suddenly become an arsenal piled high with gunpowder. The Saturnalia has been transformed into its opposite, the feast changed to a fast; but the purpose of the ritual remains the same.

In addition to the festival and the antifestival, one finds, as might have been expected, "mixed" ceremonies resulting from a more complex, more nuanced concept of the relationship between the crisis and the restoration of order, a concept that takes into account both the continuity and the discontinuity between them. In some instances at least these variations can be seen as a late development, resulting from the sheer remoteness of the original violence; that is, from the cumulative effect of mythological elaboration.

All too often we go astray when examining the nature of the festival and allow our attention to be diverted to secondary aspects. Under these circumstances the events hidden behind the rite become increasingly inaccessible, and the rite's unity of purpose splinters into many incompatible segments. At the very point when the religious aspects of the rite have begun to reflect an ignorance equal to our own, the rite suddenly appears to have a timely and original function, whereas this function is in fact belated and derivative. The asceticism and mortifications of the antifestivals seems very far removed from the kind of activity we associate with a festival. We fail to grasp that they share a common origin and that in those communities where the ritual has retained its greatest vitality they often achieve a "dialectical" equilibrium. The more the rites diverge from their true function, the more differentiated they appear and the more interesting they become to scholars, who can sort them out in different categories.

Modern scholarship, notably since Frazer, is no longer unaware that certain festivals entailed human sacrifice. Nonetheless, we are still far from suspecting that the distinctive traits of this practice and their innumerable variations can be traced back directly or indirectly to a generative act of collective violence, a liberating gesture of mob anger. The origin of the festival can still be discerned, even in those instances where sacrificial immolation has been eliminated from the proceedings. The disappearance of the sacrificial event may lead to new rites whose sacrificial character is easily identifiable—rites of exorcism, for example. These rites occupy the same place as the vanished sacrifice, and even when they are not directly linked to sacrifice they serve the same function in the ceremonies. In short, they can be said to be a replacement for the sacrifice.

What is the correct procedure for ridding a person or place of devils and evil spirits? Often it is a matter of shouting, clanging weapons or cooking vessels, and beating the air with a stick. Nothing seems more natural than to take a broom to the devil—if, that is, one is stupid enough to believe in his existence. The modern intellectual, the "liberated" Frazerian, therefore concludes that primitives liken the spirit of evil to some great beast that takes to its heels when frightened. The rationalistic mind does not bother with customs that seem not only puerile in conception but lacking all reason.

In this case as in many others a complacent intellect and the seeming "naturalness" of the circumstances can serve to conceal their most interesting aspects. In principle, the act of exorcism is an act of violence perpetrated against the devil or his associates. In some festivals this terminal violence is preceded by mock combat *between the exorcists themselves*. We recognize here a pattern repeated in many sacrificial rites: the actual immolation is preceded by ritual disputes between the sacrificers, in which the violence is to some extent simulated. This phenomenon of mock combat must stem in all instances from the same general source.

In an example adduced by Frazer, the young men of the village go from house to house, pausing at each to perform the rites of exorcism. The tour begins with a quarrel about which house to visit first. (As a good positivist, Frazer takes care to include even those details that do not fit neatly into his own scheme; for this reason alone he deserves our gratitude and respect.) The preliminary quarrel is a reminder of the sacrificial crisis; the sacrifice or exorcism that follows emulates the unanimous violence which is, in effect, promptly grafted onto the reciprocal violence and distinguished from it only by its miraculous results.

At the conclusion of the quarrel unanimity is achieved, and the moment has come for the surrogate victim, for the performance of the sacrifice. The object of the quarrel is ostensibly the sacrifice itself; that is, the selection of the victim. In the course of the quarrel each disputant strives to put in a final word, reducing his antagonist to silence; each wants to get in the decisive blow, the one that permits no response and that will therefore serve as a model for the rite itself.

Greek legends often contain vague reference to a sacrifice—a human sacrifice—offered by a community, city, or army to some god. The persons involved agree on the need for such a sacrifice but disagree on the choice of victim. To understand the situation the investigator must reverse the order of events. First comes the violence, spontaneous and senseless; then comes the sacrificial explanation, genuinely sacrificial in that it conceals the senseless and basically intolerable aspect of the violence. The sacrificial explanation is rooted in an act of terminal violence, violence that can only be labeled sacrificial retrospectively, because it brought all hostilities to an end. These stories may represent the minimal form of mythological fabrication. A collective murder that brings about the restoration of order imposes a kind of ritualistic framework on the savage fury of the group, all of whose members are out for one another's blood. Murder becomes sacrifice; the angry free-for-all that preceded it is transformed into a ritual dispute over the choice of the most suitable victim, one that satisfies the piety of the faithful or has been selected by the god. In effect, the real question behind these preliminaries is, Who will kill whom?

The dispute concerning *the first dwelling to be exorcised* screens the same conflictual process, leading to the violent resolution of the crisis. Exorcism represents the last chain in a series of reprisals.

Having succumbed to reciprocal violence, the celebrants as a group vent their fury *on the empty air.* We see here manifested a truth common to all rites, but never more clearly displayed than in this type of exorcism. Ritual violence awakens no hostility, confronts no antagonist; as long as their blows are directed *as a group* against an insubstantial presence, which for excellent reasons shows no tendency to retaliate in kind, the exorcists are not likely to resume their quarrel. And here the rite reveals its origin and function. The unanimity attained through the intervention of the surrogate victim must not be lost. The community stands united before the onslaught of "evil spirits" and remains faithful to its vow to reject mutual hostility. The rite reaffirms and reinforces this resolution. And religious thought returns again and again to that supreme wonder, that last word of violence, which is all the more precious for being pronounced so late in the day. Sacrifice is the boon worthy above all others of being preserved, celebrated and memorialized, reiterated and reenacted in a thousand different forms, for it alone can prevent transcendental violence from turning back into reciprocal violence, the violence that really hurts, setting man against man and threatening the total destruction of the community.

❧ THIS GENERAL THEORY of the sacrificial crisis and violent unanimity seems to clarify aspects of the festival that have hitherto remained obscure. As the ritualistic aspects of the festival dwindle, it degenerates into a communal "letting off of steam"—the very idea of the festival held dear by modern scholars. The gradual loss of ritualistic structure and the constantly increasing misunderstandings surrounding the festival seem to go hand in hand. The disintegration of myths and rituals, and indeed of religious thought in general, leads not to genuine demythologizing, but to the outbreak of a new sacrificial crisis.

The joyous, peaceful facade of the deritualized festival, stripped of any reference to a surrogate victim and its unifying powers, rests on the framework of a sacrificial crisis attended by reciprocal violence. That is why genuine artists can still sense that tragedy lurks somewhere behind the bland festivals, the tawdry utopianism of the "leisure society." The more trivial, vulgar, and banal holidays become, the more acutely one senses the approach of something uncanny and terrifying. The theme of holiday-gone-wrong dominates Fellini's films and has recently surfaced in various different forms in the work of many other artists.

The holiday-gone-wrong serves nicely to symbolize decadence. As an artistic motif it is rich in fruitful paradoxes. What is more, it is a very real part of the scene in any decadent society. To ascertain this we have only to look at the festal practices of obviously failing societies, such as the Yanomamö, who are torn apart by perpetual civil war, or even more strikingly, of societies in the final stages of disintegration, such as the Kaingang. The festival as celebrated in these societies has lost all its ritual characteristics; it has "gone wrong" in the sense that it has reverted to its violent origins. Instead of holding violence in check, the ceremonies inaugurate a new cycle of revenge. By a process of inversion that can befall all rites and that we have already had occasion to observe in the case of sacrificial rites, the festival ceases to function as a preventive measure and lends its support to the forces of destruction:

> The killing was to be done in traditional Kaingáng style; they [the future victims] were to be invited to a festa, made to drink, and then slaughtered. Although the Kaingáng associate festas with quarreling and murder they never refused an invitation to one even though they knew their lives were in danger. One might imagine that at a festa where large

sections of the tribe came together to enjoy themselves the bonds of kinship would be renewed and strengthened and old attachments of man for man would draw new warmth from the general good feeling.

Although this was true of some Kaingáng festas they were as often the scene of violent quarreling and disruption as they were of friendliness and solidarity. The men and women got drunk, and the men boasted to their children of their invulnerability and their deeds of blood. The men 'told their *waikayu*' [hubris] 'walking about, shaking either clubs or lances, slashing at the air, crying out the deeds they had done and the murders they would yet commit. As the beer and the excitement mounted to their heads they turned on their neighbors and quarreled with them because they suspected them of adultery with their wives or because they themselves had had affairs with their neighbors' wives and themselves felt suspected and hated.[2]

Kaingang folklore abounds in accounts of festivals that turn into massacres, and the Kaingang expression "We shall make beer for him" has decidedly sinister connotations.

ᨓᨑ LET US NOW APPLY our newfound concept of the festival to the myth of Dionysus, as portrayed in Euripides' tragedy *The Bacchae*. This analysis will concern itself with issues referred to in the discussion of the Oedipus myth; I hope it will help to clarify my thesis of the role of violence while also directing attention to new problems of significance.

A bacchanal is a festival in the sense just defined; it displays all the characteristics previously discussed. *The Bacchae* begins as a ritual bacchanal. The poet underlines the destruction of distinctions as the god sweeps away all the barriers that usually divide mortals: wealth, age, sex, and so on. Everyone is called on to worship Dionysus; the chorus proclaims that graybeards will now mingle with youths, women will be on a par with men.

The bacchanal portrayed by Euripides involves the women of Thebes. Having established his worship in Asia, Dionysus arrives in his native city in the guise of a young disciple of his own cult who exerts a potent influence over almost everyone who encounters him. Seized by the spirit of the god, Dionysus's own aunt Agauë, his cousin Ino, and all the women of Thebes desert hearth and home to wander the slopes of Mount Cithaeron, celebrating the first bacchanal.

Idyllic at first, the bacchantes' revel soon becomes a bloodthirsty nightmare. The delirious women hurl themselves indiscriminately on men and beasts. Only Pentheus, king of Thebes and son of Agauë,

[2] Henry, *Jungle People*, pp. 56–57.

persists in denying the divinity of his cousin. Like Tiresias and Creon in *Oedipus the King*, Pentheus is an outsider who, before succumbing to the universal frenzy, lucidly defines the situation: "I have just returned from my travels to hear news of the strange illness that afflicts our city."

The "strange illness" is clearly the sacrificial crisis. It has struck with lightning speed, inciting its victims to irrational acts. The sacrificial crisis makes no distinction between those who submit to its demands out of prudence or opportunism—like the two old men—and the only man who has the boldness to reject it—the unfortunate Pentheus. Whether one chooses to fight or to submit, violence triumphs.

Throughout the tragedy the Bacchic spirit is presented as indistinguishable from the infectious evil. Pentheus rebukes his grandfather, who has attempted to persuade him to join in worshiping the god: "Do not breathe your infection on me; go and play the bacchant." The Dionysiac outbreak spells the disintegration of social institutions and the collapse of the cultural order; both of which disasters are dramatically symbolized by the destruction of the royal palace at the climax of the action. It is futile to attempt to restrain the god of violence. Pentheus tries to imprison the defiant youth whose form Dionysus has assumed; but even as everything around him is engulfed in flame, the god steps forth unharmed from the ruins.

The Bacchae takes as its subject a festival that goes wrong. And we will hardly be surprised at this unpleasant turn of events when we consider that this bacchanal is none other than the original bacchanal; that is, the sacrificial crisis. The tragedy seems to offer strong evidence in support of my theory of the meaning of festivals. It traces the festival back to its violent beginnings, back to its origins in reciprocal violence. Euripides subjects the myth and worship of Dionysus to the same sort of treatment that Sophocles applied to the Oedipus myth. He brings into play the conflictual symmetry behind the mythological message (and, as with Oedipus, behind the rite)—a message that conceals this symmetry at least as much as it displays it.

The playwright's task was made easier because the bacchanal perpetuates an essential aspect of the sacrificial crisis: the destruction of differences. Beginning as a gesture of harmony, the Dionysiac elimination of distinctions rapidly degenerates into a particularly virulent form of violent nondifferentiation. The abolishment of sexual differences, which appears in the ritual bacchanal as a celebration of love and brotherhood, becomes in the tragedy an act of hostility. The women take up the most violent masculine activities, hunting and warfare. They deride men for their weakness and femininity. Dionysus, in the guise of a long-haired adolescent, personally takes a hand in fomenting the disorder. Pentheus, having reproached the god for his effeminate appearance, is seized by the desire to disguise himself in woman's dress so that he can spy on the bacchantes on the slopes of Mount Cithaeron.

We also find in *The Bacchae* reference to that loss of distinction between man and beast that is always linked to violence. The bacchantes hurl themselves on a herd of cattle, which they mistake for prying men, and tear them apart with their bare hands. And Pentheus, mad with rage, imprisons a bull in his stable in the belief that he has captured Dionysus himself. Agaüe commits the inverse error: when the bacchantes discover her son Pentheus spying on them, she mistakes him for a "young lion" and strikes the first blow to kill him.

Another difference that tends to disappear in the course of the tragedy is the seemingly indelible distinction between man and god—in this instance, between Pentheus and Dionysus. There is no aspect of Dionysus that fails to find a reflection in Pentheus. Dionysus is a dual figure. On the one hand, there is the Dionysus of the Maenads, the defender of divine and human laws, the jealous guardian of legality; on the other, there is the subversive *agent-provocateur* of the tragedy, the figure we have considered above. This same duality can be seen in Pentheus. The king of Thebes introduces himself to us as a pious conservative, a guardian of traditional values. Yet the chorus denounces him as a bold lawbreaker whose blasphemy exposes the city to divine retribution. There is no doubt that Pentheus contributes to the chaos he claims to oppose. He dons the garb of a bacchant and becomes possessed by Dionysus; that is, by violence—a violence that eliminates all distinctions between creatures, whether "men" or "gods," through the paradoxical means of fierce antagonism.

The characteristics of each protagonist are all reproduced, to a degree, in the other. For example, the divinity of Dionysus is counterbalanced by a secret humanity implied by his appearance as a long-haired youth. Similarly, the humanity of Pentheus is counterbalanced, if not by divinity, at least by a delusion of divinity, revealed in the superhuman claims that accompany his final submission to the Dionysiac spirit: "Could I not lift up on my shoulders Cithaeron and all its groves, with all the reveling bacchantes?"

In the Dionysiac frenzy all differences between man and god tend to disappear. If there is a voice of Dionysiac orthodoxy in the play it can only be that of the Lydian Maenads, who address us in unequivocal terms. God-inspired madness has made each celebrant another Dionysus. The Lydian chorus declares, "Who leads the dance becomes a Bromios!"

It has been said that the delirium of Pentheus and the Theban bacchantes is due to a culpable hubris, whereas everything relating to Dionysus and his Maenads is truly divine. Even the worst forms of violence are legitimate because god is god and man is man. There is some apparent truth in that. As far as the overall plot of the play is concerned, the difference between man and god is never lost sight of; in fact, it is strongly proclaimed at the beginning and end of the tragedy. Yet in the middle all differences mingle and dissolve, including the distinction between human and divine.

As we have seen, tragic inspiration leads to the same results in *The Bacchae* as in *Oedipus the King*. Mythological and ritual values are abolished by reciprocal violence. The subjective nature of all differences is exposed. We are compelled to confront a vital question pertaining to myth and the cultural order. Sophocles stopped just short of framing this question and concludes by reaffirming the compromised mythological values. Euripides follows the same procedure in *The Bacchae*. The symmetry is so implacably applied that in the end it dissolves the difference between man and god. Divinity becomes nothing more than a prize in the struggle between two rivals: "You know . . . how happy you are when a great crowd greets you at your doors, and all the city glorifies the name of Pentheus. Bacchus also loves such honors, I am sure. . . ."

In any case, at the end of the play the uniqueness of the deity is reaffirmed, and in terrifying fashion. It is made abundantly clear that no real contest ever existed between the omnipotent Dionysus and the culpably weak Pentheus. The triumph of difference once again shields from sight the recently exposed tragic symmetry. Once again tragedy seems to oscillate between audacity and indecision. In the case of Sophocles the conflict between the symmetry of the tragic action and the dissymmetry of the mythological content is our only reason for believing that the poet, knowingly or unknowingly, recoiled before an act of even greater audacity. In the case of *The Bacchae* the same textual conflict is present, and we are led by the same process to a similar conclusion: Euripides, too, backed off from commiting an act of even greater audacity. But this time the backing off is not performed in silence. His tragedies contain numerous passages whose emphatic tone and repetition of theme clearly mark them as expressions of the poet's decision to retreat and his attempts to justify himself:

Human wisdom is not wisdom, and to aspire to more than man's due is to shorten life, is to sacrifice the fruit at hand for what is out of reach. I think it is sheer madness or plain stupidity to act in such a manner. . . . Keep heart and mind aloof from overreaching intellects. The beliefs and practices common to the common man are good enough for me.

Scholars are far from agreement on the interpretation of such passages, and much of the modern debate on Euripides centers on this problem. It may be that the whole question has been falsified by a postulate implicitly accepted by all the commentators. This postulate relates to the type of knowledge the poet has declined to confront. We have taken it for granted that such knowledge cannot be unknown to us; the idea that anyone so remote from "modern thought" as Euripides could have perceived a danger wholly unsuspected by us, could have anticipated a truth whose existence has escaped us completely, hardly seems worth consideration.

Modern critics are convinced that Euripides drew back before that same skepticism of which they are themselves the proud proponents—an intellectual viewpoint that denies the existence of a real basis for religion and declares the whole institution purely "imaginary." Euripides, they suggest, hesitated from conventional propriety or simple prejudice to acknowledge that religion was nothing more than mystification, an illusion specifically designed to offer consolation or impose restraints. Timidity kept him from acknowledging that religion was a figment of the imagination.

The modern intellectual is a romantic soul who likes to think of himself as the boldest iconoclast in history. At times he cannot but challenge the high place accorded Euripides by tradition and wonder whether the poet is not essentially too "bourgeois" in spirit to warrant such esteem.

But Euripides speaks less in terms of religious "faith," in the modern sense, than in terms of the transgressing of limits, of the fearsome knowledge that exists beyond these limits. We do not seem to be dealing in his case with a simple choice between belief and disbelief—two equally abstract concepts. Something else is at play, something more to the point than sterile religious scepticism. This something else, still to be discerned, is nonetheless near at hand, in the text of *The Bacchae*.

THE MURDER OF PENTHEUS serves as both culmination and resolution of a crisis provoked by the god himself in "revenge" for the Thebans' failure to pay homage to him, and especially for the resistance of his own family. Having brought about Pentheus' death, the god banishes the rest of the family from the city. Peace and harmony now return to Thebes, which will henceforth honor the god in the manner ordained by him.

The murder thus appears as the outcome of a divine plan and, at the same time, the result of a spontaneous outburst. The divine plan falls within the formalized framework of ritual sacrifice. In this instance the god himself is the sacrificer and prepares the future victim; the sacrificial act ordained by him coincides with the act of revenge that will appease his anger. Under the pretext of arranging his costume and coiffure, Dionysus manages to touch Pentheus ritualistically on his head, waist, and feet. The murder itself is performed in accordance with Dionysiac practice; it includes the distinctive *sparagmos*, or dismemberment, which we have already encountered in other sacrificial contexts. In addition (1) all the bacchantes participate in the killing. This satisfies the requirements of unanimity, which figures in so many rituals. And (2) no weapon is used; the victim is torn apart by the women's bare hands. Such a performance is not peculiar to the Dionysiac cult. We have already cited two examples of collective murders without weapons, one in a Dinka sacrifice and the other part of the Swazi Incwala, where a cow is substituted for the king; there are many similar examples. The assertion—made by Rudolf Otto, among others— that the Dionysiac rites were unique can easily be disproved. There is no aspect of the Dionysiac myth or ritual that does not find a distinct echo in many primitive societies.

The Euripidean version of the myth emphasizes the spontaneous aspect of the ritualistic proceedings and thus affords us a fleeting glimpse—or at least a strong intimation—of a real relationship between the rite and a past event, grounded in fact and partially reconstituted by the dramatist. The dismemberment of a living victim by unarmed assailants, each participating wholly in the act, takes on a clear meaning. Even without Euripides' detailed description we can imagine the original scene. It would not have been a case of premeditated assassination. Everything suggests a crowd whose intentions were initially pacific; a disorganized mob that for unknown reasons (of no real importance to our argument) came to a high pitch of mass hysteria. The crowd finally hurled itself on one individual; even though he had no particular qualifications for this role, he served to polarize all the fears, anxieties, and hostilities of the crowd. His violent death provided the necessary outlet for the mass anguish, and restored peace.[3]

The ritual *sparagmos* reenacts with scrupulous exactitude the mob violence that brought riot and disorder to an end. In the ritual performance, the community tries to mimic the gestures that effected its salvation. It is also trying, paradoxically enough, to recapture through ritual the element of complete spontaneity. Here, as elsewhere, tragedy occupies an ambiguous, intermediary position between the ritual performance and the spontaneous model that the ritual attempts to reproduce. From the point of view of established religious doctrine,

[3] The best treatment of the crowd's role in abolishing differences is Elias Canetti's *Crowds and Power*, trans. Carol Stewart (New York, 1966).

Dionysus is wholly responsible for Pentheus' murder. After all, the god is master of events; it is he who prepares from afar the details of the first sacrifice, his own sacrificial enterprise that is the most awesome and effective of all sacrifices, the one that truly mends the shattered community. But from the point of view of a religion-in-the-making, the murder of Pentheus appears as a spontaneous resolution that could be neither planned nor anticipated.

The collective violence is openly displayed, but the essential process —the arbitrary choice of the victim and the sacrificial substitution that restores unity—remains concealed. The actual expulsion of the victim recedes from sight and maintains its efficiency by appearing only in the guise of institutionalized sacrifice. From the viewpoint of the sacrificial crisis, the relationship between the *doubles*, Dionysus and Pentheus, is reciprocal in a double sense. There is no reason why it should be Dionysus rather than Pentheus who sacrifices his companion. Yet from the viewpoint of established religion, even if this reciprocity is at one level acknowledged and the sacrificer and his victim are recognized as *doubles*, on another and more basic level this same reciprocity is abolished. The direction must not be allowed to reverse itself; it has been fixed once and for all, and the expulsion is always understood to have *already* taken place.

We cannot hope to understand the rite merely by attributing it to psychic motivations, either conscious or unconscious. And in spite of all appearances, gratuitous sadism plays no part in the procedure. The rite is directed toward order and tranquillity, not violence. It strives to achieve violence solely in order to eliminate it. Nothing is more naive or, in the final analysis, more futile than the speculations psychological theorists derive from the brutality of a rite such as the *sparagmos*.

The Bacchae offers ample evidence in support of my definition of sacrifice. Euripides' tragedy and the whole cult of Dionysus seem to provide strong support for the hypothesis that traces myth and ritual to a generative act of unanimity.

THE IMPARTIAL READER, approaching the play free of the influence of Nietzsche or Rudolf Otto, is always struck by the sheer perfidy of Dionysus's role. Throughout the play the god wanders from place to place, engendering violence and crime with the artfulness of a satanic seducer. Only the quixotic masochism of our own age, the result of a long immunity to the violence that threatens primitive societies, allows us to see anything attractive in the Dionysus of *The Bacchae*. It seems clear that Euripides shares none of our illusions, which would be comic if they were less disquieting.

The god has no proper being outside the realm of violence. All his attributes are linked to violence; if he is associated with the gift of prophetic inspiration (like the Delphic Apollo who figures in the Oedipus myth), it is because prophetic inspiration is part of the sacrificial crisis. And if he later appears as the god of wine, that is probably a more sedate version of his original designation as the god of homicidal fury. Certainly there is nothing in the ancient Dionysiac tradition that alludes directly to viniculture or the production of wine.[4] In *The Bacchae* the epiphany of the god arises from the catastrophic consequences of the sacrificial crisis, which is symbolized by the destruction of Pentheus's palace:

> *Chorus:* Divine tremor, shake the floor of the earth!
> *Dionysus:* See! The palace of Pentheus trembles. It falls! Dionysus is standing there! Bow down before him!
> *Chorus:* We bow down before him. Ah, see the marble friezes fall! Bromios will shout with triumph within!
> *Dionysus:* Let divine lightning be the torch! Now set afire the ruins of Pentheus's palace.
> *Chorus:* Ah, ah! Look, look! Around the sacred tomb of Semele the ever-smouldering fire leaps in flame! Prostrate yourselves before your god, O Maenads. The palace falls! He is coming, the son of Zeus!

It may seem surprising, even scandalous, that the incarnation of the most terrible forms of violence should be an object of veneration as well as of fear. In this case, however, it is not the worshipers who are naive, but the bewildered observers.

If we examine more closely the specific types of violence associated with the god, we find that an overall pattern appears. This pattern seems to confirm our interpretation of Pentheus's murder as a Dionysiac sacrifice. Under the name of *Bromios*—the Noisemaker, the Earthshaker—Dionysus presides over disasters that have nothing to do with the thunderstorms and earthquakes beloved of nineteenth-century scholars but that in fact always involve a mob impelled by sheer panic to the performance of extraordinary acts. Tiresias defines Dionysus as the god of mob hysteria, of sudden onslaughts of collective fear: "Soldiers in full battle array and poised for combat are transfixed by panic before a lance has touched them. This hysteria is Dionysus's work."

Such statements, added to the ones we have already collected and to

---

[4] Cf. Henri Jeanmaire, *Dionysos: Histoire du culte de Bacchus* (Paris, 1970), p. 23.

the body of evidence drawn from other rites, leads to the inescapable conclusion that *Dionysus is the god of decisive mob action.* Once stated, it should be easy to see why such a god is called for and why he is revered. He claims legitimacy not from his ability to disturb the peace but from his ability to restore the peace he has himself disturbed —thereby justifying, a posteriori, having disturbed it in the first place. Divine intervention is transformed into legitimate anger against a blasphemous hubris, which, until the crucial display of unanimity, seemed to implicate the god himself.

Textual criticism confirms the theories that portray the Dionysiac cult as a consequence of major political and social upheavals. In spite of its limitations, a work like Erwin Rohde's *Psyche* manifests a profound intuitive grasp of reality. In the absence of new documentary evidence the traditional historical method can make little progress. Only a comparative analysis of texts and of significant religious phenomena (a method utilized by Rohde, but on too small a scale) can substantially increase our knowledge.[5]

Along with any known historical context, we can infer behind a myth like that of *The Bacchae* a sudden outbreak of violence so extreme as to threaten the very existence of the community. This threat will eventually be withdrawn, as rapidly as it appeared, thanks to a type of mob violence that reconciles all members of the community because it involves the participation of all. The metamorphosis from peaceable citizens into raging beasts is too terrifying and too transitory for the community to accept it as issuing from within itself. As soon as calm has been miraculously restored, the past tumult will be looked upon as a supreme example of divine intervention. Angered at discovering himself ignored or misrepresented, a god has made known his wishes in a thoroughly godlike manner. Having accepted a final victim, a victim of his own choice in which he may also be incarnated, he silently withdraws from the scene. He will be as benevolent from afar as he was terrible in propinquity.

Religion, then, is far from "useless." It humanizes violence; it protects man from his own violence by taking it out of his hands, transforming it into a transcendent and ever-present danger to be kept in check by the appropriate rites appropriately observed and by a modest and prudent demeanor. Religious misinterpretation is a truly construc-

---

[5] Erwin Rohde, *Psyche: The Cult of Souls and Belief in Immortality among the Greeks*, trans. W. B. Hillis from the 8th ed. (London and New York, 1925). In his remarkable *Dionysos*, Jeanmaire offers a critical appraisal of the sociological approach. His thesis, which emphasizes ecstatic aspects of the cult and the signs of possession, can be reconciled with an awareness of social and historical aspects through my hypothesis of the sacrificial crisis and unanimous generative violence.

tive force, for it purges man of the suspicions that would poison his existence if he were to remain conscious of the crisis as it actually took place.

To think religiously is to envision the city's destiny in terms of that violence whose mastery over man increases as man believes he has gained mastery over it. To think religiously (in the primitive sense) is to see violence as something superhuman, to be kept always at a distance and ultimately renounced. When the fearful adoration of this power begins to diminish and all distinctions begin to disappear, the ritual sacrifices lose their force; their potency is no longer recognized by the entire community. Each member tries to correct the situation individually, and none succeeds. The withering away of the transcendental influence means that there is no longer the slightest difference between a desire to save the city and unbridled ambition, between genuine piety and the desire to claim divine status for oneself. Everyone looks on a rival enterprise as evidence of blasphemous designs. (It was at such a moment that all the distinctions between Dionysus and Pentheus were effaced.) Men set to quarreling about the gods, and their skepticism leads to a new sacrificial crisis that will appear— retrospectively, in the light of a new manifestation of unanimous violence—as a new act of divine intervention and divine revenge.

Men would not be able to shake loose the violence between them, to make of it a separate entity both sovereign and redemptory, without the surrogate victim. Also, violence itself offers a sort of respite, the fresh beginning of a cycle of ritual after a cycle of violence. Violence will come to an end only after it has had the last word and that word has been accepted as divine. The meaning of this word must remain hidden, the mechanism of unanimity remain concealed. For religion protects man as long as its ultimate foundations are not revealed. To drive the monster from its secret lair is to risk loosing it on mankind. To remove men's ignorance is only to risk exposing them to an even greater peril. The only barrier against human violence is raised on misconception. In fact, the sacrificial crisis is simply another form of that knowledge which grows greater as the reciprocal violence grows more intense but which never leads to the whole truth. It is the knowledge of violence, along with the violence itself, that the act of expulsion succeeds in shunting outside the realm of consciousness. From the very fact that it belies the overt mythological messages, tragic drama opens a vast abyss before the poet; but he always draws back at the last moment. He is exposed to a form of hubris more dangerous than any contracted by his characters; it has to do with a truth that is felt to be infinitely destructive, even if it is not fully understood—and its destructiveness is as obvious to ancient religious thought as it is to modern philosophers. Thus, we are dealing with an interdiction that still applies to ourselves and that modern thought has not yet invalidated. The fact that this secret has been subjected to exceptional pressure in the play must prompt the following lines:

> May our thoughts never aspire to anything higher than the laws! What does it cost man to acknowledge the full sovereignty of the gods? That which has always been held as true owes its strength to Nature.

FOR DIONYSUS AS FOR OEDIPUS, the mythic elaboration, the transfiguring medium of the story, leads to the reorganization of certain elements that properly pertain to collective phenomena anterior to the myth, elements that would be wholly unsuitable, even unintelligible, if they were evenly distributed among the characters; if, that is, the reciprocal nature of the violence were duly acknowledged. In both cases reciprocity yields to difference, and this difference severs the god or mythic hero from the community, while drawing to him all the community's violent impulses. Henceforth the role of violence in the crisis—in addition to its function in purely ritualistic or sacrificial terms—will be recalled solely as that of a passive agent of contagion: the plague in the Oedipus myth, or the fraternal nondifferentiation, or the Dionysiac bacchanal.

All the elements that enter into the composition of the myth are borrowed from the reality of the crisis; nothing has been added, nothing taken away; no conscious alterations have been made. Mythological elaboration is an unconscious process based on the surrogate victim and nourished by the presence of violence. This presence is not "repressed," not cast off on the unconscious; rather, it is detached from man and made divine.

Tragic inspiration dissolves fictive differences in reciprocal violence; it demystifies the double illusion of a violent divinity and an innocent community. The mixed choruses at the festivals of Dionysus and the temporary permission granted women to drink wine are faint echoes of a more awesome type of intoxication. Tragic inspiration demystifies the bacchanal; consequently, it destroys the delusion based on the collective transference upon which a major portion of the rite depends. The rite is not oriented toward violence, but toward peace. The tragic demystification discloses a bacchanal that is pure frenzy, naked violence. And the process of tragic demystification is itself violent, for it cannot but weaken the rites and contribute to their "going wrong." Far from toiling in the cause of peace and universal understanding, as a world blind to the social role of human violence likes to believe, antireligious demystification is every bit as ambiguous as religion itself. If it takes up arms against a certain type of violence, it may well bring about another, undoubtedly more destructive type. Unlike the moderns, Euripides confronts this ambiguity head on, and that is why he never advances in one direction without subsequently retracing his steps in another. In his oscillations between "audacity" and "timidity," he appears to be alternately defending and denouncing the bacchanal. At the beginning of the play the bacchanal is presented in a favorable light by Cadmus and Tiresias, who both make speeches in praise of Dionysus. Euripides seems anxious to defend the cult against those who would associate Dionysiac nondifferentiation with promiscuity and violence. The bacchantes are presented as models of tranquillity and decorum, and the hostile aspersions cast on the cult are indignantly rejected by the poet.

The defense of the bacchantes, however, is immediately belied by events. As Marie Delcourt-Curvers remarks in her introduction to the play, we wonder "what meaning the poet intended to give to the antics of Agaüe and her companions—innocent at first (to the point of seeming slightly ridiculous), then disquieting, and finally murderous; so that having doubted the very existence of a "problem of *The Bacchae*," we are forced to acknowledge both the problem and our inability to resolve it."[6]

The rite may stem from violence and be steeped in violence, but it still aspires to peace. In fact, it is a means of promoting harmony between the members of the community. Euripides tried to save the rite from the destruction visited on all religious concepts by sacrificial crises and the tragic mode. But this effort was doomed to failure: the poet's tragic inspiration all too easily overcame his good intentions; and once the sacrificial and nonsacrificial have been mixed—like the two drops of Gorgon's blood—there is no separating them.

The "problem of *The Bacchae*" would never have arisen if Euripides had fully acceded to the violent origin of the rite, the playing out of violence, and had acknowledged the generative act of unanimity preserved by the rite, lost in the onslaught of reciprocal violence and recovered through the mechanism of the surrogate victim. He could then have demonstrated that the good and bad aspects of the bacchanal correspond to the two faces of the generative act. The same creatures who are at each others' throats during the course of a sacrificial crisis are fully capable of coexisting, before and after the crisis, in the relative harmony of a ritualistic order.

Indeed, there would have been no problem if Euripides had been

---

6 *Euripide*, ed. and trans. Marie Delcourt-Curvers (Paris, 1962).

able to adopt the perspective of primitive religion, openly espousing the sacred while stripping man of his violence and reattributing it to divine influences. Again, there would have been no "problem of *The Bacchae*" if the play had been able to bring his perplexities to rest with one of the intermediate positions between the two extremes of the religious solution, which transfers the whole burden of violence to the divinity, and the unadorned truth, which passes the violence back to man.

In this intermediate system, which is the system of modern man, the opposition between violent disjunction and peaceful harmony—a difference that should unfold in the course of time, as a diachronic process—is transmuted into a synchronic difference. We enter a universe populated by "good" and "evil" influences—the only universe in which we feel truly at home.

Such a universe is adumbrated in *The Bacchae*. All the elements of its establishment are there: the concept of an "impious revolt" against the gods; the partitioning of the god's retinue into "authentic" (Lydian) and "inauthentic (Theban) maenads. However, at the core of the tragic action all distinctions between a "good" and a "bad" Dionysiac possession—between enthusiasm rewarded as a prize to the faithful and enthusiasm meted out as a punishment to the wicked—are effaced. The Manichaean division between good and evil is no sooner proposed than it vanishes from sight.

This division, it should be noted, is reflected in the continuing hunt for a scapegoat on the cultural and ideological level, a hunt that has gone on long after Pentheus met his fate on the slopes of Mount Cithaeron.

To resolve the problem of *The Bacchae*, we would need to establish a system of differentiation that did not dissolve under scrutiny and that permitted us to affirm the play's literary, psychological, and moral coherence. Such a system would be based, once again, on recourse to *arbitrary* violence.

The foundations of *The Bacchae* have not been uncovered, but they have been soundly shaken. It is not Euripides' "psychological" approach that is ultimately responsible for the incoherence of the tragedy, its oscillation between "audacity" and "timidity." Rather, it is the "shaking of degrees," which Euripides cannot and will not explicitly acknowledge but which blunts all distinctions and multiplies all meanings, allowing none of them to remain unshaken.

The tragedy never succeeds in finding its equilibrium; but then, there is no place for equilibrium in the drama. It is from this that the play's fertile incoherence stems—an incoherence very different from the sterile coherence of lesser works of art, "intellectually" and "esthetically" beyond reproach. There is no point in trying to resolve the "problem of *The Bacchae*," any more than there is in trying to resolve the opposition between the symmetry of the tragic action and the dissymetry of the mythological message in *Oedipus the King*. Ultimately these two problems are one. Instead of trying to force tragedy to conform to our trivial and insignificant criterion of coherence, we should concentrate on the logical flaws of tragedy and try to penetrate the inviolate interiors of the myths, to see how they are put together. We must generalize the problem of *The Bacchae* so that it applies to all cultures—religious and nonreligious, primitive and nonprimitive. Our problem then will relate to culture's violent origins, previously hidden but now discernible in the rapid disintegration of the last sacrificial practices of the modern world.

THE PREPONDERANCE OF WOMEN in the Dionysiac cult remains a subject of conjecture. We may well wonder, without retracting any of our previous suppositions, whether the charges brought against the women—their responsibility for Pentheus's murder, the homicidal frenzy that characterizes their behavior throughout the original bacchanal (that is, throughout the sacrificial crisis)—are not every bit as false as the idyllic portrait of the bacchanal, at the beginning of the play, as a rustic interlude amid the flowers and forests of Cithaeron.

The two protagonists are male, but behind them there are only women and old men. Homicidal fury is very real during the crisis, but it pertains to the entire community; the violence directed against the surrogate victim cannot be limited strictly to the women. We may therefore wonder whether the preponderance of women does not constitute a secondary mythological displacement, an effort to exonerate from the accusation of violence, not mankind as a whole, but adult males, who have the greatest need to forget their role in the crisis because, in fact, they must have been largely responsible for it. They alone risk plunging the community into the chaos of reciprocal violence.

We can therefore postulate a mythological substitution of women for men in regard to violence. That is not to say that the women's link to Mount Cithaeron was pure invention. Myths invent nothing; but the true meaning of this mass migration of women, accompanied by their children and perhaps by old men, may well have been as badly distorted by the tragic handling as by pastoral idealizing. We are told that the exodus from the city was prompted by divine inspiration and Dionysiac enthusiasm. Thus, exodus becomes a characteristic trait of the crisis, but it is neither a triumphal procession nor an irresistible charge. Rather, it is likely to have been a frantic flight of those members of the community whose age or sex prevented them from bearing arms. The weaker leave the field to the stronger, who spread terror throughout the city.

Anthropological evidence seems to support this hypothesis. Napoleon Chagnon describes a festival organized by a number of closely related Yanomamö communities. The program of entertainment included a series of "chest pounding duels," ostensibly of friendly intent and traditional to the occasion. At the moment when the imminent defeat of one team threatened to turn the contest into a bloody battle, "the women and children began to cry, knowing that the situation was getting serious, and they grouped into the farthest corners of their houses near the exits." Shortly after, while the warriors of both factions were preparing for combat and gathering their poisoned arrows, "the women and children . . . began fleeing from the village, screaming and wailing."[7]

The role played by women in the religious and cultural structure of a society—or rather, the minor importance of that role—is graphically illustrated by the social framework prevailing in certain South American villages—in those of Bororo, for example.[8] The village is laid out in the form of an almost perfect circle, divided up according to social categories. In the center is the men's house; entrance is forbidden to women. Cultural and religious activities consist for the main part of a complex system of comings and goings confined entirely to the men, with the central house serving as a sort of general meeting place. The women inhabit the houses on the periphery of the circle and unlike the men, they never move to another house. This immobility of the women was one of the factors that led early researchers to affirm the existence of a "matriarchy." In fact, far from attesting to women's importance, this very stability suggests that women are only passive spectators at a masculine tragicomedy. The elegant dance ritual practiced by the men in time of order and tranquillity amounts to a precautionary measure designed to prevent the violent encounters that occur in times of turbulence. The physical structure of the Bororo village seems to reflect the centrifugal inclinations of its weakest inhabitants, the women, by making the center an exclusively masculine preserve. This inclination is universal; it was observed by Chagnon in its most literal form during the Yanomamö festival, and it can be surmised behind the less convincing aspects of the Dionysus myth.

The motionless groups of women, gathered together in the periph-

---

[7] Napoleon Chagnon, *Yanomamö, the Fierce People* (New York, 1968), p. 116.
[8] Cf. Claude Lévi-Strauss, *Tristes Tropiques*, trans. John Weightman and Doreen Weightman (New York, 1975), chap. 22.

eral houses, bring powerfully to mind the people who cluster on side-walks or at street corners whenever "something is going on—"usually some dispute or brawl. The desire not to miss any part of the show balanced by the desire to remain at a safe distance from the action causes the spectators to form themselves into a circle around the object of interest. Psychoanalysts will note, of course, that the men's house has been inserted like a phallus in the feminine circle; but this observation scarcely helps to explain the situation. Beyond the sexual symbolism is the violence that gives shape to the events and that literally inscribes itself—first as a cultural order, then as sexuality hidden behind that order, and finally and openly as violence, which underlies all possible meanings and remains indecipherable as long as any other meaning overlays it.

Returning to the subject of Dionysus, we repeat that the presence of the women outside the city might well represent a *real* circumstance of the original crisis, transfigured by a mythological operation analogous to, but distinct from, the one we have already analyzed. A transfer of violence can be assumed, parallel to the one that engenders the god but of less consequence. We are dealing here with a mythological elaboration that probably took place early, at an epoch when the divinity had not yet absorbed the most violent and repulsive aspects of the sacrificial crisis. The characteristic features of the crisis are not yet sufficiently blurred and indistinct for men to be willing to acknowledge them as their own.

The tendency to attribute to women what is probably a masculine trait of violence can be related to a major thematic motif of *The Bacchae*: the loss of sexual differentiation. As we have remarked, one of the effects of the sacrificial crisis is a certain feminization of the men, accompanied by a masculinization of the women. For the idea that men behave like women and women like men is substituted the idea that the sinister Dionysiac practices are almost exclusively women's work. The abolishment of sexual differences—for that matter, of all differences—is a reciprocal phenomenon, and the mythological redistribution has been carried out, as always, at the expense of reciprocity. The symmetrical elements regroup under a nonsymmetrical form; a form reassuring to male dignity and authority, for it grants what amounts to a virtual monopoly on Dionysiac delirium to the women.

Here again tragedy restores lost reciprocity, but only partially; it does not dare challenge the dominant feminine role in the origins of the Dionysiac rites. And if the lost sexual difference makes it easier to shunt the responsibility for violence onto the women, it still cannot explain away the necessity for violence. Like the animal and the infant, but to a lesser degree, the woman qualifies for sacrificial status by reason of her weakness and relatively marginal social status. That is why she can be viewed as a quasi-sacred figure, both desired and disdained, alternately elevated and abused. A reading of Greek mythology and tragedy (especially the plays of Euripides) with particular attention to the possible inversion of the sexes would undoubtedly yield some striking results.

ᴏᴄᴋᴜ Chapter Six

From Mimetic Desire to the Monstrous Double

ᴏᴄᴋᴜ IN *THE BACCHAE* the intervention of the god coincides with the loss of generative unanimity and the inevitable slide into reciprocal violence. When the transcendental element descends to the human sphere it is reduced to immanence, transformed back into mimetic fascination. Reciprocal violence now demolishes everything that unanimous violence had erected. And as the institutions and interdictions based on generative unanimity perish, violence roams at will, unchallenged and unchecked. The god who has appeared malleable and complaisant, a willing servant of mankind, always manages to slip away at the last moment, leaving destruction in his wake. Then the men who sought to bend him to their uses turn on one another with murderous intent.

In *Oedipus the King* the tragic conflict still centers, at least in appearance, on specific concerns: the throne of Thebes and the queen who is both mother and wife. In *The Bacchae*, by contrast, Dionysus and Pentheus have nothing concrete to fight over. Their rivalry centers on divinity itself; but behind that divinity there lies only violence. To compete for divinity is to compete for a chimera, because the reality of the divine rests in its transcendental absence. It is not the hysterical rivalry of men that will engender gods—only unanimous violence can accomplish that. Insofar as divinity is real, it cannot serve as a prize to be won in a contest. Insofar as it is regarded as a prize, it is merely a phantom that will invariably escape man's grasp and turn to violence.

Every tragic protagonist is fated to pursue this phantom. And as soon as one individual attempts to incarnate divine violence, rivalries spring up. The violence remains reciprocal; there is no profit to anyone when only blows are traded. The chorus perceives the train of events and scrupulously avoids involving itself in the tragic action.

We must take care not to view the tragic conflict in terms of its immediate goals, even when they are objects of such consequence as a throne or a queen. *The Bacchae* teaches us that we must invert the usual order of things in order to appreciate the import of tragic rivalry. In the traditional view the object comes first, followed by human desires that converge independently on this object. Last of all comes violence, a fortuitous consequence of the convergence. As the sacrificial conflict increases in intensity, so too does the violence. It is no longer the intrinsic value of the object that inspires the struggle; rather, it is the violence itself that bestows value on the objects, which are only pretexts for a conflict. From this point on it is violence that calls the tune. Violence is the divine force that everyone tries to use for his own purposes and that ends by using everyone for its own—the Dionysus of *The Bacchae*.

In the light of this knowledge even the preliminary stages of the sacrificial crisis can be seen to reveal the dominant influence of violence. Certain scenes of *Oedipus the King*, while less explicit in their violence than those of *The Bacchae*, gain intensity and significance when viewed with the lessons of *The Bacchae* in mind. When Oedipus and Laius meet at the crossroads, the father/son and king/subject relationship is not initially in question. Their encounter begins with a stranger's menacing gesture, the older man barring the road to the younger one. Oedipus's reaction is to strike out at the stranger then at his throne, then at his wife; that is, to strike at the objects belonging to the initiator of violence. Only in the end is the aggressor identified as father and king. In other words, it is violence that bestows value on the violent man's possessions. Laius is not violent because he is a father; rather, it is because of his violence that he passes as a father and a king. Is that not what Heraclitus had in mind when he proclaimed that "violence is the father and king of all"?

Nothing, perhaps, could be more banal than the role of violence in awakening desire. Our modern terms for this phenomenon are *sadism* or *masochism*, depending on its manifestations; we regard it as a pathological deviation from the norm. We believe that the normal form of desire is nonviolent and that this nonviolent form is characteristic of the generality of mankind.

But if the sacrificial crisis is a universal phenomenon, this hopeful belief is clearly without foundation. At the very height of the crisis violence becomes simultaneously the instrument, object, and all-inclusive subject of desire. This is why social coexistence would be impossible if no surrogate victim existed, if violence persisted beyond a certain threshold and failed to be transmuted into culture. It is only at this point that the vicious circle of reciprocal violence, wholly destructive in nature, is replaced by the vicious circle of ritual violence, creative and protective in nature.

At the height of the sacrificial crisis man's desires are focused on one thing only: violence. And in one way or another violence is always mingled with desire. The statement that violence is "instinctive" adds nothing to our understanding of this strange and startling relationship; on the contrary, it only clouds the issue. Today we know that animals possess individual braking mechanisms to insure that combats between them seldom result in the actual death of the vanquished. Because such mechanisms tend to assure the perpetuation of the species, it would perhaps be not inappropriate to term them *instinctive*. To use the same term in connection with man's lack of such a braking device, however, would be absurd.

The notion of an instinct (or if one prefers, an impulse) that propels men toward violence or death—Freud's famous "death wish"—is no more than a last surrender to mythological thinking, a final manifestation of that ancient belief that human violence can be attributed to some outside influence—to gods, to Fate, to some force men can hardly be expected to control. Once again, it is a mode of thought that refuses to confront human conflicts squarely. It is an act of evasion, an attempt to "pass the buck" and find an alternate sacrificial solution in a situation which makes such a solution increasingly difficult.

In the midst of the sacrificial crisis there is no point in attaching desire to any one object, no matter how attractive, for desire is wholly directed toward violence itself. This does not mean, however, that we must endow man with an instinctive drive toward death or violence. There is still another approach open to us.

In all the varieties of desire examined by us, we have encountered not only a subject and an object but a third presence as well: the rival. It is the rival who should be accorded the dominant role. We must take care, however, to identify him correctly; not to say, with Freud, that he is the father; or, in the case of the tragedies, that he is the brother. Our first task is to define the rival's position within the system to which he belongs, in relation to both subject and object. The rival desires the same object as the subject, and to assert the primacy of the rival can lead to only one conclusion. Rivalry does not arise because of the fortuitous convergence of two desires on a single object; rather, *the subject desires the object because the rival desires it*. In desiring an object the rival alerts the subject to the desirability of the object. The rival, then, serves as a model for the subject, not only in regard to such secondary matters as style and opinions but also, and more essentially, in regard to desires.

When modern theorists envisage man as a being who knows what he wants, or who at least possesses an "unconscious" that knows for him, they may simply have failed to perceive the domain in which human uncertainty is most extreme. Once his basic needs are satisfied (indeed, sometimes even before), man is subject to intense desires, though he may not know precisely for what. The reason is that he desires *being*, something he himself lacks and which some other person seems to possess. The subject thus looks to that other person to inform him of what he should desire in order to acquire that being. If the model, who is apparently already endowed with superior being, desires some object, that object must surely be capable of conferring an even greater plenitude of being. It is not through words, therefore, but by the example of his own desire that the model conveys to the subject the supreme desirability of the object.

We find ourselves reverting to an ancient notion—mimesis—one whose conflictual implications have always been misunderstood. We must understand that desire itself is essentially mimetic, directed toward an object desired by the model.

The mimetic quality of childhood desire is universally recognized. Adult desire is virtually identical, except that (most strikingly in our own culture) the adult is generally ashamed to imitate others for fear of revealing his lack of being. The adult likes to assert his independence and to offer himself as a model to others; he invariably falls back on the formula, "Imitate me!" in order to conceal his own lack of originality.

Two desires converging on the same object are bound to clash. Thus, mimesis coupled with desire leads automatically to conflict. However, men always seem half blind to this conjunction, unable to perceive it as a cause of rivalry. In human relationships words like *sameness* and *similarity* evoke an image of harmony. If we have the same tastes and like the same things, surely we are bound to get along. But what will happen when we share the same desires? Only the major dramatists and novelists have partly understood and explored this form of rivalry.[1] Even Freud treated it in an indirect and distorted fashion, as we shall see in the next chapter.

By a strange but explicable consequence of their relationship, neither the model nor the disciple is disposed to acknowledge the inevitable rivalry. The model, even when he has openly encouraged imitation, is surprised to find himself engaged in competition. He concludes that the disciple has betrayed his confidence by following in his footsteps. As for the disciple, he feels both rejected and humiliated, judged unworthy by his model of participating in the superior existence the model himself enjoys.

The reason for these misunderstandings is not hard to grasp. The

[1] For a discussion of these works see my *Deceit, Desire, and the Novel* (Baltimore, 1965).

model considers himself too far above the disciple, the disciple considers himself too far below the model, for either of them even fleetingly to entertain the notion that their desires are identical—in short, that they might indeed be rivals. To make the reciprocity complete, we need only add that the disciple can also serve as a model, even to his own model. As for the model, no matter how self-sufficient he may appear, he invariably assumes the role of disciple, either in this context or another. From all indications, only the role of disciple is truly essential—it is this role that must be invoked to define the basic human condition.

The mimetic aspects of desire must correspond to a primary impulse of most living creatures, exacerbated in man to the point where only cultural constraints can channel it in constructive directions. Man cannot respond to that universal human injunction, "Imitate me!" without almost immediately encountering an inexplicable counterorder: "Don't imitate me!" (which really means, "Do not appropriate *my* object"). This second command fills man with despair and turns him into the slave of an involuntary tyrant. Man and his desires thus perpetually transmit contradictory signals to one another. Neither model nor disciple really understands why one constantly thwarts the other because neither perceives that his desire has become the reflection of the other's. Far from being restricted to a limited number of pathological cases, as American theoreticians suggest, the *double bind*—a contradictory double imperative, or rather a whole network of contradictory imperatives—is an extremely common phenomenon. In fact, it is so common that it might be said to form the basis of all human relationships.[2]

Bateson is undoubtedly correct in believing that the effects of the double bind on the child are particularly devastating. All the grown-up voices around him, beginning with those of the father and mother (voices which, in our society at least, speak for the culture with the force of established authority) exclaim in a variety of accents, "Imitate us!" "Imitate me!" "I bear the secret of life, of true being!" The more attentive the child is to these seductive words, and the more earnestly he responds to the suggestions emanating from all sides, the more devastating will be the eventual conflicts. The child possesses no perspective that will allow him to see things as they are. He has no basis for reasoned judgements, no means of foreseeing the metamorphosis of his model into a rival. This model's opposition reverberates in his mind like a terrible condemnation; he can only regard it as an act of excommunication. The future orientation of his desires—that is, the choice of

<hr/>

[2] See Gregory Bateson et al., "Toward a Theory of Schizophrenia," in *Steps to an Ecology of the Mind* (New York, 1972), pp. 201–27.

his future models—will be significantly affected by the dichotomies of his childhood. In fact, these models will determine the shape of his personality.

If desire is allowed to follow its own bent, its mimetic nature will almost always lead it into a double bind. The unchanneled mimetic impulse hurls itself blindly against the obstacle of a conflicting desire. It invites its own rebuffs, and these rebuffs will in turn strengthen the mimetic inclination. We have, then, a self-perpetuating process, constantly increasing in simplicity and fervor. Whenever the disciple borrows from his model what he believes to be the "true" object, he tries to possess that truth by desiring precisely what this model desires. Whenever he sees himself closest to the supreme goal, he comes into violent conflict with a rival. By a mental shortcut that is both eminently logical and self-defeating, he convinces himself that the violence itself is the most distinctive attribute of this supreme goal! Ever afterward, violence and desire will be linked in his mind, and the presence of violence will invariably awaken desire. Perhaps this is why the possessions that serve to symbolize being in *Oedipus the King*—the throne and the queen—are behind the stranger's angry gesture at the crossroads. *Violence is the father and king of everything!* Jocasta affirms this truth in declaring that *Oedipus belongs to whomever speaks to him of "phobou"*—of unhappiness, terror, disasters, nefarious violence of any sort. The oracular pronouncements of Laius, Creon, and Tiresias and the ill tidings of the messengers emanate from that *logos phobou* to which all the characters in the myth belong. The *logos phobou* is ultimately the wordless language by which mimetic desire and violence communicate with one another.

Violent opposition, then, is the signifier of ultimate desire, of divine self-sufficiency, of that "beautiful totality" whose beauty depends on its being inaccessible and impenetrable. The victim of this violence both adores and detests it. He strives to master it by means of a mimetic counterviolence and measures his own stature in proportion to his failure. If by chance, however, he actually succeeds in asserting his mastery over the model, the latter's prestige vanishes. He must then turn to an even greater violence and seek out an obstacle that promises to be truly insurmountable.

Mimetic desire is simply a term more comprehensive than *violence* for religious pollution. As the catalyst for the sacrificial crisis, it would eventually destroy the entire community if the surrogate victim were not at hand to halt the process and the ritualized mimesis were not at hand to keep the conflictual mimesis from beginning afresh. As I have already indicated (a little later on I will formally examine the evidence), there are all sorts of rules and regulations that prevent desire from floating free and attaching itself to the first model that comes along. By channeling its energies into ritual forms and activities sanctioned by ritual, the cultural order prevents multiple desires from converging on the same object. Notably, it protects children from the disastrous effects of the double bind.

AS THE READER MAY RECALL, I have tried to demonstrate that the characters in tragedy are ultimately indistinguishable. The words used to describe any one of them in psychological, sociological, moral, or even religious terms—for example, "hot-tempered," "tyrannical," "hubristic"—are all equally applicable and equally inadequate. If the commentators have failed to remark that these traits are the common property of all the characters in the play, it is because they are not all affected by them at the same time. Anger, for example, is always transitory. It comes in fits, emerging from a background of tranquillity—which is why it is always referred to as sudden and unexpected. Tyranny, too, is essentially unstable. A newcomer can ascend unexpectedly to the very summit of power, only to plummet, while one of his opponents assumes his lost position. In short, there is always a tyrant and always an oppressed, but the roles alternate. There is always one character who is angry; but while one of the enemy brothers rants and rages, the other may temporarily regain his composure.

In tragedy everything alternates. But we must also reckon with the irresistible tendency of the human spirit to suspend this oscillation, to fix attention on one extreme or the other. This tendency is, strictly speaking, mythological in nature. It is responsible for the pseudo-determination of the protagonists, which in turn transforms revolving oppositions into stable differences.

The concept of alternation appears in tragedy, but it figures there deprived of its reciprocity. Paradoxically, it becomes a pseudo-specification; it is presented as the characteristic attitude of a single individual in the play. Oedipus, for instance, proclaims himself the child of Fortune and of Chance. (We moderns would be inclined to use the word *destiny*, which lends an air of solemnity and "individuality" to the situation, and avoids any hint of reciprocity.)

The hold of Fortune (*tukhe*) on Oedipus is manifested in a series of "highs" and "lows." "Fortune was my mother, and the years that tracked my life saw me in turn both great and small." In the final lines of the play the chorus defines the hero's existence in terms of his *peripeteiai*, his reversals of fortune; that is, in terms, once again, of alternation. (It matters little whether these lines were or were not written by Sophocles.)

The definition is correct, but it is no more correct for Oedipus than for any other tragic hero. That is apparent if we turn our attention from a single play to the whole corpus of tragedy. If the tragic heroes are all compared, their distinctive traits vanish, for they all successively assume the same roles. Oedipus is an oppressor in *Oedipus the King* but the oppressed in *Oedipus at Colonus*; Creon is oppressed in *Oedipus the King* but becomes the oppressor in *Antigone*. Nobody, in short, incarnates the true oppressor or the true oppressed; and the modern ideological interpretations seriously misconstrue the tragic spirit. They relegate the plays to the company of romantic melodrama or American Westerns. A static Manichaean confrontation of "good guys" and "bad guys," an unyielding rancor that holds fast to its victims, has replaced the revolving oppositions of real tragedy and completely overshadowed the concept of the tragic peripeteia.

Tragedy is interested in reversal as such; it cares little for the domains these reversals happen to affect. Oedipus's alternating states of anger and serenity, for example, contribute no less to his portrait as a child of Fortune than do his alternating periods of exile and kingship. The different rhythm of these alternations and the disparity between the realms to which they belong are such that we would scarcely think of connecting the two; indeed, as far as I know traditional criticism has never attempted to do so. Yet once our attention has been drawn to the subject we may suspect that every motif in tragedy is governed by an alternating movement, and our suspicion is confirmed by close examination.

It is clear that alternation constitutes a *relationship*. In fact, alternation is a fundamental fact of the tragic relationship—which is why it can scarcely be considered characteristic of any single individual. At first glance the alternation of tragedy may well seem dependent on the object under dispute by the enemy brothers. The object itself seems of such importance that its loss of possession entails a radical reversal of status, a passage from being to nothingness or from nothingness to being. Such is the case for Eteocles and Polyneices, who decide to take turns wielding the power they are incapable of dividing between them. When Eteocles is king, Polyneices is one of his subjects, and vice versa.

However, this alternation of objects has little direct connection with tragic action. The rhythm of the action is faster and more abrupt; it is reflected in the tragic dialogue or *stichomythia*, that is, in the exchange of insults and accusations that corresponds to the exchange of blows between warriors locked in single combat. As we have noticed, the description of the duel between Eteocles and Polyneices in *The*

Phoenician Women takes the place of a tragic dialogue and plays an identical role.

Whether the violence is physical or verbal, an interval of time passes between each blow. And each blow is delivered in the hope that it will bring the duel or dialogue to an end, constitute the *coup de grâce* or final word. The recipient of the blow is thrown momentarily off balance and needs time to pull himself together, to prepare a suitable reply. During this interval his adversary may well believe that the decisive blow has indeed been struck. Victory—or rather, the act of violence that permits no response—thus oscillates between the combatants, without either managing to lay final claim to it. Only an act of collective expulsion can bring this oscillation to a halt and cast violence outside the community.

Desire, as we have seen, is attracted to violence triumphant and strives desperately to incarnate this "irresistible" force. Desire clings to violence and stalks it like a shadow because violence is the signifier of the cherished being, the signifier of divinity.

If unanimous violence alone (that is, violence that spends itself) can properly be regarded as generative, all the implications it makes manifest and all the differences it succeeds in establishing are intimately associated with the back-and-forth antagonism that precedes, with the oscillation of victory from one combatant to another throughout the sacrificial crisis. The fits of vertigo that attend the process stem from this terrible oscillation, and they ultimately engulf all perceived reality. Everything oscillates with a violence that seems to favor first one, then another individual or faction. Whatever an initial act of violence seems to settle is invariably subverted by a second act, which reorders everything anew. As long as violence remains present among men, and as long as men pursue it as an absolute, as a kind of divinity, it will continue its devastating oscillations.

Euripides' *Bacchae* offers the clue. The idea of a contest in which divinity is the prize, passing from one contestant to the other with uniformly disastrous results, is essential to an understanding of all tragic motifs, for the structuring of these motifs is really patterned on the action. The reader may protest that we are dealing with an abstraction, that the idea of a divine stake or prize identical to violence is foreign to *The Bacchae*. This idea may indeed be only suggested here but no one can deny that it is explicit elsewhere and that it is quintessentially Greek. Certainly it is quite explicit in Homer—that is, in a literary text predating the tragedies.

There are several terms in Homer that dramatically illuminate the relationship of violence, desire, and divinity. The most useful, perhaps, in the context of our discussion is the substantive *kudos*. *Kudos* is best defined in terms of semidivine prestige, of mystical election attained by military victory. It was the reward sought by both Greek and Trojan, particularly in single combat.

In his *Dictionary of Indo-European Institutions* Benveniste translates *kudos* as "talisman of supremacy." It is the fascination of superior violence. Violence strikes men as at once seductive and terrifying; never as a simple means to an end, but as an epiphany. Violence tends to generate unanimity, either in its favor or against it. And violence promotes imbalance, tipping the scales of Destiny in one direction or another.

At the least success violence begins to snowball, becoming finally an irresistible avalanche. Those who possess kudos see their strength multiplied a hundredfold; those deprived of it discover that they are hopelessly handicapped. Kudos passes to the man who strikes the hardest— the victor of the moment. It belongs to the man who manages to convince others, and who believes himself, that his violence is completely irresistible. The opposition must then exert itself to break the spell cast by this conviction and to wrest the kudos from the enemy's grasp.

When the rivalry becomes so intense that it destroys or disperses all its objects, it turns upon itself; kudos alone becomes the ultimate object. The word is sometimes translated "glory," but, as Benveniste has remarked, such a translation ignores the magico-religious aspects that are fundamental to the term. Although the modern world lacks a word for this phenomenon, the phenomenon itself is familiar. The spiritual effects of triumphant violence are readily apparent in sexual activity, in games of skill or chance, in athletic matches, and in contests and competitions of all kinds. For the Greeks, the issue of violence carried to its extreme was divinity itself. The epithet *kudros* signifies an attitude of triumphant majesty, a demeanor characteristic of the gods. Man can enjoy this condition only fleetingly, and *always at the expense of other men.* To be a god is to possess kudos forever, to remain forever a master, unchallenged and unchallangeable. That is beyond the reach of mortal man.

It is the gods who confer kudos on men and the gods who take it away. The intermingling of human and divine in human conflicts is so obvious that even Benveniste acknowledges it here; in other cases where this mixture is present he tries to separate the human and the divine, even though their combination might offer a clue to the process of sacralization.

As long as the concept of kudos exists—that is, as long as there exists a prize, eminently desirable and thoroughly abstract, that men strive constantly to wrest from one another—there can be no transcendent force capable of restoring peace. What we are witnessing in this struggle for kudos is the decomposition of the divine, brought about by violent reciprocity. When the tide of battle turns against them, Homer's warriors sometimes justify their retreat with remarks like "Today Zeus has chosen to bestow kudos on our enemies; perhaps tomorrow he will give it to us." This alternation of kudos is identical to the alternations of tragedy. We may even wonder whether the division of the gods into two camps in the *Iliad* is not a late development. The original version may have involved a single god, the personification of kudos, who oscillated from one camp to another depending on the course of battle.

In some Euripidean tragedies the alternation between "high" and "low" is sharply delineated. It is linked to a form of violence that is no longer physical but spiritual, that inverts the relationship between dominating and dominated. In *Andromache*, for instance, Hermione treats the heroine with complete disdain, insisting on the vast gulf that must separate Neoptolemus' lawful wife and queen from his mistress, a captive slave at the mercy of her captors. Presently, however, the tragic peripeteia takes place. Hermione meets her downfall, and becomes in effect the slave of Andromache:

> What god would I invoke? At what shrine offer prayers? Must I slavishly embrace the knees of a slave?

Euripides is less interested in the changes of circumstance brought about by the plot than in Hermione's overreaction to these changes. The nurse remarks:

> My child, I did not hide my disapproval when you gave way to such violent hatred for the Trojan woman; nor do I now approve your giving way to panic.

Overreaction is characteristic of these tragic reversals of fortune. Yet the overreactions that actually serve to alter the power structure in the play are drawn from other sources. Although no decisive action has taken place while Neoptolemus was away in Delphi, a tragic debate has taken place between Hermione's father Menelaus, who is determined to kill Andromache, and the aged Peleus, who stands forth as her champion. Peleus gains the upper hand and emerges with kudos.

The transferal of kudos is not simply a subjective matter, though it is not objective either. It involves a relationship in which the roles of dominating and dominated are constantly reversed. Neither psychological nor sociological interpretations can help us here. There is no point in invoking a master-slave dialectic because the situation affords no stability of any sort, no synthetic resolution.

In the end the kudos means nothing. It is the prize of a temporary victory, an advantage no sooner won than challenged. It might be compared to those sporting trophies that are passed from winner to winner and that are really nothing but a title, an abstraction. To take the metaphor too seriously, however, would only lead to another mythical and ritualistic distortion. Far from subordinating religion to sport or play (as does Huizinga in *Homo Ludens*), we must subordinate play to religion, and in particular to the sacrificial crisis. Play has a religious origin, to be sure, insofar as it reproduces certain aspects of the sacrificial crisis. The arbitrary nature of the prize makes it clear that the contest has no other objective than itself, but this contest is regulated in such a manner that, in principle at least, it can never degenerate into a brutal fight to the finish.

There is no term in any language that is not accompanied by mythological inflections. In the case of *kudos* the reciprocity of the violence is not relinquished, but is muted so as to suggest some joust or tourney. Because we see that the prize is worthless we tend to assume that the contest itself, no matter how perilous, is only a pastime, an event of limited interest to the protagonists, mere "sport."

To correct this impression it suffices to consider some other psychological terms whose mythological inflections are somewhat different. *Thymos*, for instance, means soul, spirit, or anger like "the anger of Oedipus." At first glance *thymos* has nothing in common with kudos— except for one trait, which we would normally consider altogether trivial: its alternating character. When a man possesses *thymos* he possesses an irresistible dynamism. When *thymos* is withdrawn he is plunged into anguish and despair. *Thymos* is derived from the verb *thuein*, which means to make smoke, to offer sacrifices; to act violently, to run wild.

The *thymos* comes and goes at the bidding of the *thuein*. In fact, kudos and *thymos* represent two different and partial aspects of the same problem. It is not some vulgar trophy or second-rate divinity the adversaries are trying to wrest from each other's grasp, but their very souls, their vital force, their being. Each finds this being reflected in the other's violence, because their mimetic desires have converged on one and the same object.

Cyclothymia is the term psychiatrists use to designate the alternating presence and absence of *thymos*. Every case of cyclothymia is characterized by mimetic desire and a strong competitive drive. Psychiatrists make the mistake of regarding cyclothymia as an essentially individual phenomenon; this is a genuinely mythical misconception, identical to the delusion whereby men see all sudden reversals of Destiny, all manifestations of divine anger, as stemming from the action of a single hero (cf. *Oedipus the King*). An individual perspective on cyclothymia yields only half the truth. In all such cases, when one person is high in the favor of fortune, another is low, and vice versa.

Modern psychiatry often fails to perceive the basic antagonism underlying the pathological manifestations of cyclothymia, because all traces of conflict have vanished. The physical violence, even the harsh language of the tragic confrontation no longer manifests itself; the adversary himself has disappeared, or appears in a static form that conceals the reality of the agonistic process. The conflict seems to take place in a domain far removed from the hurly-burly of competition and strife. In our own day literary or artistic creation would qualify as such a domain, for the romantic and modern artist generally claims to draw his creations from the purest inner sources, from a region uncontaminated by imitation. In an age where the tyranny of fashion has never been more absolute, the artist proclaims his independence from all outside influence.

The tragic cyclothymia would engulf an increasing number of individuals if nothing intervened to stop it and would end by plunging the whole community into madness and dissolution. Thus we can easily understand the terrified response of the chorus, its frantic efforts to remain uninvolved and avoid the contamination of mimetic rivalry. The virtues of moderation and "common sense," so dear to ordinary mortals, are openly challenged by the constant shiftings of the tragic situation. This timidity of the chorus offends the Romantic sensibilities of modern-day intellectuals, who are scornful of any reluctance to embrace what is forbidden by custom and law.

Some will attribute the cautiousness of the Greek chorus to a pusillanimous temperament, already at this early date imbued with bourgeois attitudes, or else to an arbitrary and merciless superego. We must be careful to note, however, that it is not the "sinful" act in itself that horrifies the chorus so much as the consequences of this act, which the chorus understands only too well. The vertiginous oscillations of tragedy can shake the firmest foundations and bring the strongest houses crashing to the ground.

Fortunately, even among modern readers there are some who do not hold tragic "conformism" in scorn; certain exceptional individuals who have succeeded, through genius and a good deal of pain, in arriving at a full appreciation of the tragic concept of peripeteia.

At the very portals of madness, Hölderlin paused to question *Antigone* and *Oedipus the King*. Swept up by the same vertiginous movement that seized the heroes of Sophocles, he tried desperately to attain that state of moderate equilibrium celebrated by the chorus. The relationship between tragedy and Hölderlin's madness becomes clear if we accept as literal facts the accounts of his existence set forth in the poet's own poems, novels, essays, and letters. The premises of madness are sometimes neither more nor less than an exceptional encounter with feelings appropriate to Greek tragedy: an increasingly stressful alternation between moments of superhuman exhaltation and hours when only the emptiness and desolation of life holds any illusion of reality. The *god* bestows his presence on the poet only, it seems, to withdraw it. A thin thread of remembrance links these alternating visitations and absences, a thread just strong enough to assure the individual's sense of continuity and to sustain those visions of the past that heighten the intoxication of possession but render even more painful the anguish of loss. A being who thought himself eternally damned finds himself ecstatically involved in his own resurrection; a being who thought himself a god is struck with horror at the revelation of his self-delusion. The god is *other*, and the poet, though still alive, is little better than a corpse, for he has lost all reason for living. He is like a sacrificial lamb, dumbly submitting to the executioner's knife.

Hölderlin's *god* often bears a proper name—sometimes the name of the poet himself, sometimes that of another. Usually that other is at the outset a woman, who later assumes the features of a man—the poet Schiller. Contrary to what Jean Laplanche asserts, there is no essential difference between masculine and feminine attributions.[3] The idolized antagonist undergoes first a feminine incarnation, then a masculine incarnation. As the poet's correspondence makes clear, this substitution is unrelated to any sexual difficulties. On the contrary, amatory success deprives the sexual domain of its value as a *test* between the I and the other.

The constant shifting back and forth from divinity to nothingness in Hölderlin's relationships with others is expressed in poetic, mythic, quasi-religious terms as well as in a perfectly rational form, which is at once the most deceptive and most revealing of all. His letters to Schiller lucidly describe the plight of the disciple who sees his model transformed into an obstacle and rival.

In his "Thalia Fragment," a first draft for the *Hyperion,* Hölderlin writes:

> I imagined that the poverty of our nature would change to abundance when two such wretched creatures [men] could share one heart, a single and indivisible life, as if all the ills of our existence were brought about by the dissolution of some primitive unity.

[3] Jean Laplanche, *Hölderlin et la question du père* (Paris, 1961).

With melancholy rapture (I can still sense it), thinking of naught but how to find someone to accept the gift of my loving smile, of how to give myself to the first passerby. . . . Ah! How often I then believed I had encountered and possessed the Ineffable simply by having dared to delve to the very depths of my love! How often I believed I had been granted direct access to the divine! I called out, called again, and the poor creature put in an appearance; embarrassed, ill at ease, often even slightly aggressive—he wanted only a little pleasure, certainly nothing very demanding!

What a blind imbecile I was! I was seeking pearls from beggars even poorer than myself; so very poor, so sunken in poverty, that they were incapable of judging the extent of their misery and delighted in the rags and tatters which covered their naked bodies. . . .

In fact, when it seemed to me that the last remnants of my lost life were at stake, and when my pride began to revive, I found that I had become a mass of unleashed activity and I discovered in myself the omnipotence of despair. Whenever my wan and languishing spirit happened to imbibe an unexpected draught of happiness I flung myself precipitously into the midst of the crowd, spoke out in inspired tones, and sometimes even felt welling up in my eyes the tears of felicity. Or whenever the thought of image of a hero flashed across the dark firmament of my soul, I rejoiced in my surprise, as if a god had seen fit to visit my forlorn domain. And it seemed to me then that a whole world was about to take shape within me. But the more suddenly these dormant powers were stirred into awakening, the more precipitous was their subsequent decline, and unsatiated nature experienced a redoubling of afflictions.

In a letter to Schiller Hölderlin writes:

I have sufficient courage and judgment to free myself from other masters and critics and to pursue my own path with the tranquil spirit necessary for such an endeavor, but in regard to *you*, my dependence is insurmountable; and because I know the profound effect a single word from you can have on me, I sometimes strive to put you out of my mind so as not to be overcome by anxiety at my work. For I am convinced that such anxiety, such worry is the death or art, and I understand perfectly well why it is more difficult to give proper expression to nature when the artist finds himself surrounded by masterpieces than when he is virtually alone amidst the living world. He finds himself too closely involved with nature, too intimately linked with it, to consider the need for rebelling against its authority or for submitting to it. But this terrible alternation is almost inevitable when the young artist is exposed to the mature genius of a master, which is more forceful and comprehensible than nature, and thus more capable of enslaving him. It is not a case of one child playing with another child—the primitive equilibrium attained between the first artist and his world no longer holds. The child is now dealing with men with whom he will never in all probability be familiar enough to forget their superiority. And if he feels this superiority he must become either rebellious or servile. Or must he? . . .

When differences begin to shift back and forth the cultural order loses its stability; all its elements constantly exchange places. So it is that in tragedy the differences between the antagonists never vanish entirely, but are constantly inverted. In such a system enemy "brothers" can never occupy the same position at the same time. Earlier I defined this system in terms of abolished distinctions, of symmetry and reciprocity. Now I am saying that differences never really disappear. The contradiction between the two definitions is, I trust, a contradiction in appearance only.

In a tragedy the reciprocal relationship between the characters is real, but it is the sum of nonreciprocal moments. The antagonists never occupy the same positions at the same time, to be sure; but they occupy these positions in succession. There is never anything on one side of the system that cannot be found on the other side, provided we wait long enough. The quicker the rhythm of reprisals, the shorter the wait. The faster the blows rain down, the clearer it becomes that there is no difference between those who strike the blows and those who receive them. On both sides everything is equal; not only the desire, the violence, the strategy, but also the alternation of victory and defeat, of exaltation and despair. Everywhere we encounter the same cyclothymia.

My original definition therefore holds, and I trust that the concept of shifting differences serves to refine it. After all, it is not the elimination of differences that lends itself to direct observation, but the successive inversion of differences. In the temporal plan of the system there is not a moment when those involved in the action do not see themselves separated from their rivals by formidable differences. When one of the "brothers" assumes the role of father and king, the other cannot but feel himself to be the disinherited son. That explains why the antagonists only rarely perceive the reciprocal nature of their involvement. Each is too intensely engaged in living out his nonreciprocal moment to grasp the whole picture, to take in several of these moments in a single glance and compare them in such a way as to penetrate the illusory quality of singularity that each moment, observed in isolation, seems to possess—in a universe that otherwise appears commonplace, banal, without interest. The *same* characters who are blind to the phenomenon of reciprocity while they are caught up in it perceive it all too well when they are not involved. That is why, during the sacrificial crisis, all men are endowed with the spirit of prophecy—a vainglorious wisdom that deserts them when they themselves are put to the test.

Because they are essentially outsiders and therefore misread the differences shifting back and forth between the antagonists, Oedipus, Creon, and Tiresias in turn imagine themselves capable of "banishing the plague"—that is, of serving as arbitrator in the conflicts convulsing Thebes. Each thinks that he can make it clear to the antagonists that no difference actually stands between them. And each in turn is drawn into the conflict whose contagiousness he failed to comprehend.

From within the system, only differences are perceived; from without, the antagonists all seem alike. From inside, sameness is not visible; from outside, differences cannot be seen.

Only the outside perspective, which takes into consideration reciprocity and unity and denies the difference, can discern the workings of the violent resolution, the cryptic process by which unanimity is reformed against and around the surrogate victim. When all differences have been eliminated and the similarity between two figures has been achieved, we say that the antagonists are *doubles*. It is their interchangeability that makes possible the act of sacrificial substitution.

My reading of *Oedipus the King* is based on this "outside" perspective, on an objectivity that takes in at a glance the identity of all the antagonists. However, the generative unanimity does not come from outside. It is produced by the antagonists themselves, to whom the objective outlook is utterly alien. The preceding description, then, cannot be sufficient. In order for violent unanimity to become a possibility—in order, that is, for the sacrificial substitution to function—their own identity and reciprocity must somehow impose themselves on the antagonists themselves, and triumph within the confines of the system. Both the outside and inside viewpoints must communicate, yet remain distinct; the misapprehension must remain within the system, for otherwise the polarization of violence onto the surrogate victim could not be effected, and the arbitrary choice of that victim would be too readily evident.

We must be prepared, therefore, to start our analysis afresh, and try to examine from within the mechanism responsible for sacrificial substitution in the crisis-ridden community.

As I have said, the differences that seem to separate the antagonists shift ever faster and more abruptly as the crisis grows in intensity. Beyond a certain point the nonreciprocal moments succeed each other with such speed that their actual passage becomes blurred. They seem to overlap, forming a composite image in which all the previous "highs" and "lows," the extremes that had previously stood out in bold relief, now seem to intersect and mingle. Where formerly he had seen his antagonist and himself as incarnations of unique and separate moments in the temporal scheme of things, the subject now perceives two simultaneous projections of the entire time span—an effect that is almost cinematographic.

Up to this point I have described the system in terms of single, unique difference, the difference between the "god" and the "non-god." This is clearly an oversimplification. The "Dionysiac" state of mind can and, as we have seen, often does erase all manner of differences: familial, cultural, biological, and natural. The entire everyday world is caught up in the whirl, producing a hallucinatory state that is not a synthesis of elements, but a formless and grotesque mixture of things that are normally separate.

It is this monstrosity, this extraordinary strangeness of the world that captures the attention not only of the characters involved but also of latter-day scholars who till the fields of folklore and psychiatry. An attempt is made to classify the monsters; but despite their initial disparities they end by resembling one another; no stable difference really serves to separate them. And there is really nothing very interesting to say about the hallucinatory aspects of an experience that for all practical purposes exists solely to divert attention from the essential fact, which is that the antagonists are truly doubles.

A fundamental principle, often overlooked, is that the double and the monster are one and the same being. The myth, of course, emphasizes only one aspect (usually the monstrous aspect) in order to minimize the other. There is no monster who does not tend to duplicate himself or to "marry" another monster, no double who does not yield a monstrous aspect upon close scrutiny.[4] The duality claims precedence—without, however, eliminating the monstrous; and in the duality of the monster the true structure of the experience is put in relief. The nature of the relationship between monster and double, stubbornly denied by the antagonists, is ultimately imposed on them in the course of the shifting of differences—but it is imposed *in the form of a hallucination.* The unity and reciprocity that the enemy brothers have rejected in the benign form of brotherly love finally impose themselves, both from without and within, in the form of monstrous duality—the most disquieting and grotesque form imaginable.

We can expect little help from literature and even less from medi-

---

[4] The hysterical experience of the four lovers in *A Midsummer Night's Dream* is a powerful description of this process that generates the monsters of the night, notably the "marriage" of Titania, queen of the fairies, with an ass-headed Bottom. See René Girard, "More than Fancy's Images: A reading of *A Midsummer Night's Dream,*" in *Textual Strategies: Perspectives in Post-Structuralist Criticism,* ed. Josue Harari (Ithaca, N.Y., 1979).

cine in our investigation of the double. Doctors not infrequently share their patients' fascination with burgeoning monstrosities. In so doing they neglect the crucial aspects of the experience: its reciprocal character, its affinity with violence. Psychoanalysts and folklorists declare that these hallucinatory phenomena are purely imaginary. They refuse to acknowledge the reality of the symmetry that underlies the fantasy. This transformation of the real into the unreal is part of the process by which man conceals from himself the human origin of his own violence, by attributing it to the gods. To say that the monstrous double is a god or that he is purely imaginary is to say the same thing in different terms. Our abstract skepticism vis-à-vis religion serves admirably to fill the function formerly performed by religion itself.

To my knowledge only Dostoevsky, both in his early novel *The Double* and in the masterpieces of his maturity has set forth in concrete terms the elements of reciprocity at work in the proliferation of monsters.

In the collective experience of the *monstrous double* the differences are not eliminated, but muddied and confused. All the doubles are interchangeable, although their basic similarity is never formally acknowledged. They thus occupy the equivocal middle ground between difference and unity that is indispensable to the process of sacrificial substitution—to the polarization of violence onto a single victim who substitutes for all the others. The monstrous double gives the antagonists, incapable of perceiving that nothing actually stands between them (or their reconciliation), precisely what they need to arrive at the compromise that involves unanimity *minus* the victim of the generative expulsion. The monstrous double, all monstrous doubles in the person of one—the "thousand-headed dragon" of *The Bacchae*—becomes the object of unanimous violence:

> Appear, great bull!
> Come, dragon with a thousand heads!
> O come to us, fire-breathing lion!
> Quick, quick, you smiling Bacchant, and cast your fatal net about this man who dares to hunt you Maenads!

We can now appreciate the atmosphere of terror and hallucination that accompanies the primordial religious experience. When violent hysteria reaches a peak the monstrous double looms up everywhere at once. The decisive act of violence is directed against this awesome vision of evil and at the same time sponsored by it. The turmoil then gives way to calm; hallucinations vanish, and the détente that follows only heightens the mystery of the whole process. In an instant all extremes have met, all differences fused; superhuman exemplars of violence and peace have in that instant coincided. Modern pathological experiences offer no such catharsis; but although religious and pathological experiences cannot be equated, they share certain similarities.

〜✕ MANY LITERARY TEXTS, both ancient and modern, make reference to the double, to duality, to double vision—references that have long been disregarded. In *The Bacchae*, the monstrous double is everywhere. As we have seen, from the opening of the play animal, human, and divine are caught up in a frenetic interchange; beasts are mistaken for men or gods, gods and men mistaken for beasts. Perhaps the most intriguing instance of this confusion occurs during the encounter between Dionysus and Pentheus, shortly before Pentheus is murdered—that is, at the very moment when the enemy brother is due to disappear behind the form of the monstrous double.

And that is exactly what happens. Pentheus has already fallen prey to Dionysiac vertigo; he *sees double*:

> *Pentheus:* I seem to see two suns, two Thebes, with two times seven gates. And you, you are a bull walking before me, with two horns sprouting from your head.
> *Dionysus:* You see what you ought to see.

In this extraordinary exchange the theme of the double appears initially in a form completely exterior to the subject, as a double vision of inanimate objects, an attack of dizziness. Here we are dealing solely with hallucinatory elements; they are undeniably a part of the experience, but only a part, and not the essential one. As the passage unfolds, so too does its meaning. Pentheus associates the double vision with the vision of the monster. Dionysus is at once man, god, and bull. The reference to the bull's horns links the two themes: doubles are always monstrous, and duality is always an attribute of monsters.

Dionysus's words are arresting: *"You see what you ought to see."* By seeing double, by seeing Dionysus himself as a monster bearing the double seal of duality and bestiality, Pentheus conforms to the immutable rules of the game. Master of the game, the god makes sure that events take their course according to his plan. The plan is identical to the process we have just described, with the monstrous double making his appearance at the height of the crisis, just before the unanimous resolution.

These lines become even more intriguing when read in conjunction with the passage that follows. Now we have to reckon not with hallucination or vertigo but with real flesh and blood doubles. The identical nature of the antagonists is explicitly formulated:

Pentheus: Tell me, who do I look like? Like Ino, or like my mother Agauë?
Dionysus: You seem the very image of them both.

Similarities are at the heart of the encounter, but the question is treated ambiguously, in terms of family resemblance—a formulation brought to mind by Pentheus' transvestite masquerade. Yet something more is clearly at stake here. Surely it is the similarity of doubles that is being suggested; that of the surrogate victim and the community that expels it, of the sacrificed and the sacrificer. All differences are abolished. *"You seem the very image of them both"*: once again it is the god himself who confirms the basic principles of a process initiated by him and which, in fact, comes to seem a sign of his presence.

〰️ THE WRITINGS OF ANOTHER ANCIENT AU-thor are equally vital, I believe, to a discussion of the monstrous double. Empedocles' description of the birth of monsters has never been adequately interpreted. However, if the cycles described by the philosopher correspond to a cultural system founded on an act of generative violence, maintained by ritual, and destroyed by a new sacrificial crisis, then we can scarcely doubt that the birth of monsters as described by him is meant to suggest terrible apparition of the monstrous double. The author attributes the cyclical movement to the alternation of two fundamental impulses, Love and Hate. *The birth of monsters come about through the attraction of like for like, under the aegis, not of Love, but of Hate, before the birth of a new world:*

57. Then there began to sprout in profusion heads without necks, and arms without bodies or shoulders swarmed everywhere, and naked eyes floated as planets [in the world of Hate].
58. The dismembered limbs, subservient to the will of Hate, wander about separately, yearning to unite.
59. But as soon as a god draws closer in harmony to another god, the limbs begin to link up at random, and they all rush together;
60. We find creatures with revolving legs and countless hands.
61. Others are born with two faces, two torsos; there are cows with human heads and men with the heads of cows; and hermaphrodites, whose sex is shrouded in mystery.

The interpretation I propose happens to coincide with the recent tendency to reject "physical" interpretations of pre-Socratic thought; interpretations that are, to be sure, always dependent on the belief that the primary purpose of myths is to explain natural phenomena. Although the more recent interpretations are superior to the early ones they still, I believe, underestimate the religious element in the thinking of Empedocles, and indeed in all the pre-Socratics.

My attempt to link the passage from Empedocles with the phenomenon of the monstrous double may seem less far-fetched if we consider this passage in conjunction with another work of Empedocles, *Purifications*. I alluded to this work earlier on, but it seems to take on new significance in this context. "The father takes hold of his son *who has changed form*, and in a fit of madness, sacrifices him; the son cries out, but his pleas fall on deaf ears; the demented father cuts the son's throat, and prepares an abominable feast in his palace. Similarly, the son seizes the father and the children of their mother, kills them all and devours their flesh."

Whether or not we choose to take this passage literally, it underscores the atmosphere of acute sacrificial crisis that was the background for Empedocles' work. The father kills his son *who has changed form*, just as Agauë kills her son *who has changed form*, mistaking him for a lion, and just as Pentheus mistakes Dionysus for a bull. As in *The Bacchae*, we are witnessing the degeneration of a rite into a form of reciprocal violence that is so irrational it conjures up the monstrous double. That is, it harkens back to the very origins of the rite and thus closes the circle of religious compositions and decompositions that preoccupied the pre-Socratics.

THE APPARITION OF THE MONSTROUS DOUble cannot be verified empirically; nor for that matter can the body of phenomena that forms the basis for any primitive religion. Despite the texts cited above the monstrous double remains a hypothetical creation, as do the other phenomena associated with the mechanism that determines the choice of surrogate victim. The validity of the hypothesis is confirmed, however, by the vast number of mythological, ritualistic, philosophical, and literary motifs that it is able to explain, as well as by the quality of the explanations, by the coherence it imposes on phenomena that until now appeared isolated and obscure.

My hypothesis permits me to essay an explanation of two sets of phenomena that are among the most puzzling in all human culture: possession and the ritual use of masks.

Under the heading *monstrous double* we shall group all the hallucinatory phenomena provoked at the height of the crisis by unrecognized reciprocity. The monstrous double is also to be found wherever we encounter an "I" and an "Other" caught up in a constant interchange of differences. The same set of images is projected almost simultaneously in two symmetrical locations. In *The Bacchae* we discover two types of phenomena that are capable of rapid interchange.

The subject of the action, Pentheus, at first sees the two series of images as exterior to himself; this is the phenomenon of "double vision." A moment later one of the two series is perceived as "not me," and the other as "me." It is this second experience we are referring to when we use the term *double*. It is a direct extension of the previous stages, and it retains the concept of an antagonist exterior to the subject—a concept crucial to an understanding of possession.

The subject watches the monstrosity that takes shape within him and outside him simultaneously. In his efforts to explain what is happening to him, he attributes the origin of the apparition to some exterior cause. Surely, he thinks, this vision is too bizarre to emanate from the familiar country within, too foreign in fact to derive from the world of men. The whole interpretation of the experience is dominated by the sense that the monster is alien to himself.

The subject feels that the most intimate regions of his being have been invaded by a supernatural creature who also besieges him without. Horrified, he finds himself the victim of a double assault to which he cannot respond. Indeed, how can one defend oneself against an enemy who blithely ignores all barriers between inside and outside? This extraordinary freedom of movement permits the god—or spirit or demon—to seize souls at will. The condition called "possession" is in fact but one particular interpretation of the monstrous double.

It is hardly surprising that possession should often take the form of a hysterical mimesis. The subject seems to be responding to some outside influence; he has the jerky movements of a marionette. Some presence seems to be acting *through* him—a god, a monster, or whatever creature is in the process of investing his body. He is caught in the double bind of the model-obstacle that condemns both partners to a continual heightening of violence. The monstrous double now takes the place of those objects that held the attention of the antagonists at a less advanced stage of the crisis, replacing those things that each had sought to assimilate and destroy, to incarnate and expel. Possession, then, is an extreme form of alienation in which the subject totally absorbs the desires of another.

The possessed subject bellows like Dionysus the bull; like a lion he is ready to devour anyone who ventures within sight. He can even impersonate inanimate objects. He is at the same time one and many beings as he reenacts the hysterical trance and the crazy mixture of differences that immediately precedes the collective expulsion. There exist entire sects devoted to possession, with their own group sessions. It is interesting to note that in colonial countries or oppressed societies it is often the representatives of the dominant power—the governor-general or the sentry at the barracks gate—who serve as models.

Possession, like everything pertaining to primordial religious experience, tends to acquire a ritual character. The existence of a ritual form of possession implies that something in the nature of an intense case of collective possession took place *initially*; for it is of course that spontaneous occurrence that the ritual is striving to reproduce. Ritual possession seems inseparable at first from the sacrificial rites that serve as its culmination. In principle, the religious practices follow the order of the cycle of violence they are attempting to imitate. Such is the case with the Dinka, in those occasional instances in which possession precedes the immolation of the victim. As soon as the excitement aroused by the chants, dances, and mock combats has reached a certain pitch of intensity, the ritual imprecations pass over into signs of possession. As Lienhardt recounts it,[5] first young men, then adult men and women are overcome. They stagger about among their companions, then fall to the ground in convulsions, moaning or emitting piercing cries.

In some sects possession is regarded as beneficial, in others as harmful. And there are still others that consider possession beneficial or harmful, depending on the circumstances. Behind these diverse attitudes lies a problem of interpretation similar to the one we have discussed in connection with ritual incest and with festivals. In dealing with liberating violence religion can choose either faithfully to reenact the all too characteristic phenomena of the crisis or systematically to ignore them. The phenomenon of possession, therefore, can appear as sickness, cure, or both at once.

As the rites disintegrate some of the elements that formed them tend to disappear. Others assume new identities, divorced from their past context. Possessions, like many other aspects of primordial experience, can become the chief object of religious preoccupation. In such cases "possession cults" arise. The group sessions of the cult find their climax in an act of sacrificial slaughter.[6] At a later stage of the cult the sacrifice disappears from the rites. The shamans then try to utilize possession for magico-medical purposes. They become "specialists" in the practice of possession.

STILL ANOTHER RITUAL PRACTICE acquires fresh significance in the light of investigations into the monstrous double: the ritual use of masks.

Masks are among the necessary tools of many primitive sects, but we cannot answer with certainty the questions raised by their presence. What do they represent? What is their purpose? How did they originate? Surely there must be some unifying factor, some criterion for

---

[5] Godfrey Lienhardt, *Divinity and Experience*, pp. 136–37, 274, et passim.
[6] Cf. Jeanmaire's description of the *Zar* and *Bori* (*Dionysos*, pp. 119–31.)

masks, among the great variety of forms and styles, something we can recognize if not define. After all, whenever we encounter a mask we do not hesitate to identify it as such. The unity of the mask cannot be extrinsic; it exists in societies remote from each other in space and culture, and it cannot be traced to a single geographical locus. The almost universal use of masks is often said to answer some deep-seated "esthetic need." Primitive people, we are told, are obsessed with "disguises"; they also have a compulsion to "create forms."

This kind of art criticism offers no real answer to the problem of masks. Primitive art, after all, is fundamentally religious. And masks will undoubtedly, therefore, serve a religious function. They are certainly not "pure inventions"; their models vary greatly from culture to culture, but certain traits remain constant. Although it would not be correct to say that masks invariably represent the human face, they are almost always associated with it: designed to cover the face, to replace it, or in some way to substitute for it.

The problem of the unity and diversity of masks is the same as that of the unity and diversity of myths and rituals. It undoubtedly originates in some real experience, common to a large portion of humanity but now lost to us.

Like the festival in which it often plays an important role, the mask displays combinations of forms and colors incompatible with a differentiated order that is not primarily that of nature but of the culture itself. The mask mixes man and beast, god and inanimate object. Victor Turner makes reference to a *ndembu* mask that represents at once a human face and a meadow.[7] Masks juxtapose beings and objects separated by differences. They are beyond differences; they do not merely defy differences or efface them, but they incorporate and rearrange them in original fashion. In short, they are another aspect of the monstrous double.

The ritual ceremonies that require the use of masks are reenactments of the original experience. In many cases the celebrants (at least, those who play the most important role in the ceremony) don masks at the climax of the rite, just before the sacrifice. These rites permit the participants to play out all the roles performed by their ancestors during the original crisis. They are enemies first, engaging in mock combats and symmetrical dances; then they put on their masks and change into monstrous doubles. The mask is no apparition drawn from the thin air; it is a transformation of the antagonists' normal features. The different modes of its ritual use, the structure within which the masks operate, are in most cases more revealing than any terms their

[7] Victor Turner, *The Forest of Symbols: Aspects of Ndembu Ritual* (Ithaca, N.Y., 1970), p. 105.

wearers may use to describe them. If the mask is intended to conceal human faces at a fixed point in the ritual, that is because this is what happened to human faces *the first time*. Masks, then, serve as an interpretation and concrete representation of phenomena that we described previously in purely theoretical terms.

There is no point in trying to determine whether masks represent human or supernatural beings. An inquiry of that kind is relevant only to later developments of the ritual, brought about by a further accentuation of differences, a deepening misapprehension of the phenomena that the ritualistic use of masks allows the wearers to reenact. Masks stand at that equivocal frontier between the human and the "divine," between a differentiated order in the process of disintegration and its final undifferentiated state—the point where all differences, all monstrosities are concentrated, and from which a new order will emerge. There is no point in trying to determine the "nature" of masks, because it is in their nature not to have a nature but to encompass all natures.

Greek tragedy, like the festival and indeed all other rites, is primarily a representation of the sacrificial crisis and the generative violence. The use of masks in the Greek theater requires, therefore, no special explanation; the masks serve the same role as they do elsewhere. Masks disappear when the monsters once again assume human form, when tragedy completely forgets its ritual origins. That is not to say, of course, that tragedy ceases to play a sacrificial role in the broad sense. On the contrary; it has taken over the role of ritual.

Chapter Seven

Freud and the Oedipus Complex

ᐊᑕᕐᑲ WE CAN OBSERVE both similarities and differences between the mimetic desire described in the previous chapter and Freud's Oedipus complex. Mimetism is a source of continual conflict. By making one man's desire into a replica of another man's desire, it invariably leads to rivalry; and rivalry in turn transforms desire into violence. Although Freud may appear on first glance to have ignored this mechanism, he in fact came very close to apprehending it. A rigorous examination of this text will make it clear why he ultimately failed to do so.

The mimetic nature of desire plays an important role in Freud's work—not important enough, however, to dominate and revolutionize his thinking. His mimetic intuitions are incompletely formulated; they constitute a dimension of his text that is only half visible and tends to disappear in transmission. There is nothing surprising about the refusal of present-day psychoanalysts to turn their attention to this subject. Factions of psychoanalytic thought, bitterly opposed in other respects, are here at one. The mimetic aspect of desire has been ignored at once by those whose main concern is the elimination of inconsistencies in Freud's work in favor of a unified whole and by that other group who, while orthodox Freudians in name, quietly reject some of the most lucid and cogent of Freud's analyses on the grounds that they are tainted with "psychologism."

Although traces of the mimetic conception are scattered through Freud's work, this conception never assumes a dominant role. It runs counter to the Freudian insistence on a desire that is fundamentally directed toward an object; that is, sexual desire for the mother. When the tension between these opposing tendencies becomes too great, both Freud and his disciples seem to resolve it in favor of the object-desire.

The mimetic intuition of Freud gives rise to a series of concepts ambiguous in definition, obscure in status, and vague in function. Among the offshoots of this ill-defined mimetic desire are certain concepts that come under the heading *identification*. Among the categories of Freudian identification, one that nowadays receives little attention is the first one discussed in the chapter entitled "Identification," in *Group Psychology and the Analysis of the Ego*. This category has to do with the father: "A little boy will exhibit a special interest in his father; he would like to grow like and be like him, and take his place everywhere. We may say simply that he takes his father as his ideal. This behavior has nothing to do with a passive or feminine attitude towards his father (and towards males in general); it is on the contrary typically masculine. It fits in very well with the Oedipus complex, for which it helps to prepare the way."[1]

There is a clear resemblance between identification with the father and mimetic desire; both involve the choice of a model. The choice is not really determined by parentage, for the child can select as model any man who happens to fill the role that our society normally assigns to the natural father.

As we have pointed out in the previous chapter, the mimetic model directs the disciple's desire to a particular object by desiring it himself. That is why we can say that mimetic desire is rooted neither in the subject nor in the object, but in a third party whose desire is imitated by the subject. Granted, the passage quoted above is hardly explicit on this point. But its implications are clear and conform to our definition of mimetic desire. Freud asserts that the identification has nothing passive or feminine about it; a passive or feminine identification would mean that the son wanted to become the object of his father's desire. How, then, will the active and "typically masculine" identification realize itself? Either it is wholly imaginary, or it finds concrete form in the desire for some particular object. The identification is a desire *to be* the model that seeks fulfillment, naturally enough, by means of appropriation; that is, by taking over the things that belong to his father. As Freud says, the son seeks to take the father's place everywhere; he thus seeks to assume his desires, to desire what the father desires. The proof that we are not distorting Freud's intention is supplied by the last sentence of the passage: "[The identification] fits very well with the Oedipus complex, for which it helps to prepare the way."

What can this sentence mean, if not that identification directs desire toward those objects desired by the father? We have here an undeniable instance of filial desire undergoing the influence of mimesis. Con-

[1] Sigmund Freud, *The Standard Edition of the Complete Psychological Works of Sigmund Freud*, ed. and trans. James Strachey, 24 vols. (London, 1953–66), vol. 18, *Group Psychology and the Analysis of the Ego*, p. 105.

sequently, there already exists in Freud's thought, at this stage, a latent conflict between this mimetic process of paternal identification and the autonomous establishment of a particular object as a basis for desire—the sexual cathexis toward the mother.

This conflict is all the more apparent because identification with the father is presented as fundamental to the boy's development, *anterior to any choice of object*. Freud emphasizes this point in the opening sentences of an analysis that will eventually unfold into an overall description of the Oedipus complex and that is to be found in the chapter on identification previously referred to.[2] After identification with the father comes the sexual cathexis toward the mother, which, according to Freud, first appears and develops independently. The object-choice of the mother appears to have its origins in two factors: first, the identification with the father, the mimesis; second, the fixation of the libido on the mother. These two forces act together and reinforce one another, as Freud makes clear a few lines further on. After having subsisted "side by side for a time without any mutual influence or interference," the two "come together at last," and the libidinal drive is thereby strengthened. This is a wholly natural and logical turn of events if we choose to regard this identification as the mimesis of paternal desire. Indeed, once we have seen matters in this light all other explanations seem irrelevant.

I am not trying to put words in Freud's mouth. In fact, it is my contention that Freud saw the path of mimetic desire stretching out before him and deliberately turned aside. One need only examine his definition of the Oedipus complex, which follows a few lines further on, to see how he evades the issue: "The little boy notices that his father stands in his way with his mother. His identification with his father takes on a hostile colouring and becomes identical with the wish to replace his father in regard to his mother as well. Identification, in fact, is ambivalent from the very first. . . ."[3]

The passage contains at least one point well worth noting. When, as Freud explains, the son discovers that his father is becoming an obstacle to him, his identification fuses with his desire "to replace his father in regard to his mother as well." That "as well" rivets the attention. Freud has earlier defined identification as the desire to re-place the father, and he now repeats that formula. Must we therefore conclude that the mother was initially excluded, implicitly or explic-itly, from the program? On examining the definition we see nothing that suggests such an exclusion; quite the contrary. As Freud has put

[2] Ibid.
[3] Ibid.

it: "The little boy will exhibit a special interest in his father; he would like to grow like and be like him, and *take his place everywhere* [italics added]."

The casual reader may well assume that the "as well" in the phrase "in regard to the mother as well" is merely a slip of the pen; after all, if the son wants to replace his father "everywhere," it follows that he would want to replace him in regard to the mother. But this apparent triviality in phrasing conceals an important point. As we have seen, it is impossible to elucidate Freud's theory of identification without encountering a mimetic mechanism that makes the father into the desire-model. It is the father who directs the son's attention to desirable objects by desiring them himself; thus, the boy's desires are inevitably directed toward his own mother. This much is clearly implied by Freud's text, yet these conclusions are never made explicit. Of course, it is possible that they never took shape in his mind, though they must surely have hovered there in some form when he was writing the opening passages of chapter 7, "Identification." Having first implied a mimetic interpretation, Freud then rejected it, also by implication, with the phrase "his mother as well." Such is the hidden meaning of that "as well." The two words retrospectively neutralize any mimetic interpretation of identification, at least in regard to the object of primary importance—the mother.

Freud's eagerness to dispell the mimetic elements that were impinging on his Oedipus theory can readily be discerned in his later work. Here, for instance, is his definition of the Oedipus complex as stated in *The Ego and the Id* (1923):

> At a very early age the little boy develops an object-cathexis for his mother . . . ; the boy deals with his father by identifying himself with him. For a time these two relationships proceed side by side, until the boy's sexual wishes in regard to his mother become more intense and his father is perceived as an obstacle to them; from this the Oedipus complex originates. His identification with his father then takes on a hostile colouring and changes into a wish to get rid of his father in order to take his place with his mother. Henceforward his relation to his father is ambivalent; it seems as if the ambivalence inherent in the identification from the beginning had become manifest.[4]

At first glance this looks like a faithful resume of the concepts set forth in *Group Psychology and the Analysis of the Ego.* A further examination reveals certain differences that, though apparently minor, are in reality very important. My previous analysis dealt specifically with the mimetic elements to be found in the earlier text. It is precisely

[4] Freud, *Standard Edition*, vol. 19, *The Ego and the Id*, pp. 31–32.

those elements, relegated to the shadows in that earlier description of the Oedipus complex, that are banished entirely from this later definition.

In the earlier text Freud insists on the anteriority of the identification with the father. In the later text he does not explicitly repudiate this doctrine, but he gives first mention to the son's sexual attraction to the mother. In short, he discourages us from thinking that one and the same impulse—the wish to take the father's place *everywhere*—stimulates identification with the model and directs desire toward the mother.

That this inversion of the original order is not a matter of chance becomes abundantly clear when the process is repeated a little further on. In the second text, we find that the formulation of the "complex" is preceded by the reinforcement of the sexual wish; but instead of presenting this reinforcement as a consequence of the boy's first identification with the father, Freud inverts the order of the phenomena, thereby formally rejecting the cause-and-effect relationship suggested initially. This reinforcement of the libido is now totally lacking in motivation. The effect is retained, but because it now precedes the cause, neither cause nor effect seems to make much sense. As we can see, in *The Ego and the Id* Freud makes a clean sweep of all mimetic effects, but in so doing he sacrifices some of the most trenchant insights of *Group Psychology and the Analysis of the Ego* and some of his coherence as well.

Why did Freud banish mimesis from his later work? The best way to reply to this question is to continue along the path abandoned by him, to discover where he might have gone had he chosen to be guided by those mimetic effects that abounded in his earlier analyses but that were swept away as if by magic the instant they were found to cast doubt on his Oedipus complex. We must, in short, return to that phrase that is surreptitiously contradicted and canceled out by "the mother as well." To identify with the father, Freud informed us, is first of all to want to replace him: the little boy "would like to grow like and be like him, and *take his place everywhere* [italics added]."

In order to exclude the mother from this "everywhere," it is necessary to assume that the son is already conscious of the "law" and that he conforms to it without any prior instruction; for in principle it is the father who is supposed to teach him. But to exclude the mother is in actuality to assert that the Oedipus complex is already in operation; if that is not true the mother should be included, and that is what Freud has done—initially. The comprehensiveness of the statement that the son wishes to take his father's place "everywhere" is wholly appropriate, for the son cannot have a clear and distinct impression of his father's objects—including the mother—insofar as they are indeed his father's. In short, if the son turns toward his father's objects it is because he is following the example of his model, and this model necessarily turns toward his *own* objects—those that are already in his possession or that he hopes to acquire. The disciple's movement toward the objects of his model, including the mother, is already accounted for by the concept of identification as defined by Freud. Far from discouraging such an interpretation, Freud seems initially to have encouraged it.

Because disciple and model are converging on the same object, a clash between them is inevitable. The resulting rivalry appears "Oedipal," but it takes on a wholly different meaning. Because it is predetermined by the model's choice, there is nothing fortuitous about it; nor is it, strictly speaking, a question of one person's usurping what belongs to the other. The disciple's attraction to the model's object is wholly "innocent"; in seeking to take his father's place with his "mother as well," the son is simply responding in all candor to a command issued by the culture in which he lives and by the model himself. If we pause to consider closely the model-disciple relationship, it should become clear that the so-called Oedipal rivalry, reinterpreted in terms of a radically mimetic situation, must logically result in consequences that are at once similar to and quite different from those attributed by Freud to his "complex."

Earlier on I defined the effects of mimetic rivalry and affirmed that they invariably end in reciprocal violence. This reciprocity is the result of a process. If there is a stage in human existence at which reciprocity is not yet in operation and at which reprisals are impossible, that stage is surely early childhood. That is why children are so vulnerable. The adult is quick to sense a violent situation and answer violence with violence; the child, on the other hand, never having been exposed to violence, reaches out for his model's objects with unsuspecting innocence. Only an adult could interpret the child's actions in terms of usurpation. Such an interpretation comes from the depths of a cultural system to which the child does not yet belong, one that is based on cultural concepts of which the child has not the remotest notion.

The model-disciple relationship precludes by its very nature that sense of equality that would permit the disciple to see himself as a possible rival to the model. The disciple's position is like that of a worshiper before his god; he imitates the other's desires but is incapable of recognizing any connection between them and his own desires. In short, the disciple fails to grasp that he can indeed enter into competition with his model and even become a menace to him. If this is true for adults, how much truer it must be for the child experiencing his first encounter with mimetic desire!

The model's very first no—however softly spoken or cautiously phrased—can easily be mistaken by the disciple for an irrevocable act of excommunication, a banishment to the realms of outer darkness. Because the child is incapable of meeting violence with violence and has in fact had no real experience with violence, his first encounter with the mimetic double bind may well leave an indelible impression. The "father" projects into the future the first tentative movements of his son and sees that they lead straight to the mother or the throne. The incest wish, the patricide wish, do not belong to the child but spring from the mind of the adult, the model. In the Oedipus myth it is the oracle that puts such ideas into Laius's head, long before Oedipus himself was capable of entertaining any ideas at all. Freud reinvokes the same ideas, which are no more valid than Laius's. The son is always the last to learn that what he desires is incest and patricide, and it is the hypocritical adults who undertake to enlighten him in this matter.

The first intervention by the model between the disciple and the object is a traumatic experience, because the disciple is incapable of performing the intellectual operation assigned him by the adult, and in particular by Freud himself. He fails to see the model as a rival and therefore has no desire to usurp his place. Even the adult disciple is unable to grasp that conflict with the model is indeed rivalry, is unable to perceive the symmetry of their situation or acknowledge their basic equality. Faced with the model's anger, the disciple feels compelled to make some sort of choice between himself and the model; and it is perfectly clear that he will choose in favor of the model. The idol's wrath must be justified, and it can only be justified by some failure on the part of the disciple, some hidden weakness that obliges the god to forbid access to the holy of holies, to slam shut the gates of paradise. Far from reducing the divinity's prestige, this new attitude of vengeful spite serves to increase it. The disciple feels guilty—though of what, he cannot be sure—and unworthy of the object of his desire, which now appears more alluring than ever. Desire has now been redirected toward those particular objects protected by the *other's* violence. The link between desire and violence has been forged, and in all likelihood it will never be broken.

Freud, too, wants to show that an indelible impression is made on the child when he first discovers his own desires overlapping those of his parents. But because he eventually rejected the mimetic elements that had initially intrigued him, he takes a different approach. To appreciate this difference, let us look again at that crucial passage in *Group Psychology and the Analysis of the Ego*: "The little boy notices that his father stands in his way with his mother. His identification with his father then takes on a hostile colouring and becomes identical with the wish to replace his father in regard to his mother as well."

If we are to believe Freud, the little boy has no difficulty recognizing his father as a rival—a rival in the old-fashioned theatrical sense, a nuisance, a hindrance, a *terzo incommodo*. But even if this rivalry were provoked by something other than a desire to imitate the father's desires, a child would be unaware of this. We have only to look at the numerous everyday displays of envy and jealousy to realize that even adults never attribute their mutual antagonisms to that simple phenomenon. Freud is thus conferring on the child powers of discernment not equal but superior to those of most grown-ups.

Let me make myself clear. I am not objecting to certain basic Freudian assumptions, such as the attribution to the child of libidinal desires similar to those of adults, but rather to the bold and surely untenable assertion, which stands at the very center of his system, that the child is fully aware of the existing rivalry, of "the hostile colouring."

Undoubtedly I am flying in the face of psychoanalytical orthodoxy, denying the alleged evidence of "clinical findings"; and before the doctor's scientific mystique the layman can only bow. But the texts we have been examining are based on no specific "clinical findings." Their speculative character is obvious, and there is no more reason to treat them as holy writ (as some have done) than to try to sweep them under the carpet. In either case we would be depriving ourselves of some valuable insights (even if the object of these insights is not always what Freud takes it to be) and depriving ourselves as well of the fascinating spectacle of Freud's intellect at work, of the gradual and halting evolution of Freudian doctrine.

Undoubtedly "clinical findings" can be turned to almost any account, but we can hardly expect them to serve as evidence for a consciousness, no matter how transitory, of patricidal or incestuous desire. After all, it is precisely because this consciousness refuses to yield to clinical observation that Freud is obliged to devise such unwieldy and dubious concepts as those of the "unconscious" or "suppression."

And here we arrive at my principal complaint against Freud. The mythical element of Freudianism has nothing to do—despite traditional assertions to the contrary—with the nonconscious nature of those basic impulses that determine the individual's psychological make-up. If my complaint were a reiteration of that well-worn theme, it would undoubtedly be classified among the "reactionary" criticism of Freudianism. In the final analysis, what I object to most is Freud's obstinate attachment—despite all appearances—to a philosophy of consciousness.

The mythical aspect of Freudianism is founded on the conscious knowledge of patricidal and incestuous desire; only a brief flash of consciousness, to be sure, a bright wedge of light between the darkness of the first identifications and the unconscious—but consciousness all the same. Freud's stubborn attachment to this consciousness compels him to abandon both logic and credibility. He first assumes this consciousness and then gets rid of it in a kind of safe-deposit box, the unconscious. In effect he is saying: ego can suppress all consciousness of a patricidal and incestuous desire only if at one time ego truly experienced it. *Ergo sum.*

The most remarkable aspect of this moment of unobstructed consciousness, which Freud posits as the basis for man's psychic existence, is its sheer uselessness. Only by stripping it away do we uncover Freud's essential point: the crucial and potentially catastrophic nature of the first contacts between child and parent or, in other terms, between the disciple's desire and the model's desire. This moment of consciousness not only offers us nothing of importance but also serves to obscure the mimetic process, which in both form and context possesses many advantages over the Freudian "complex."

Further discussion along these lines might distract us from our main subject of inquiry, so I shall only say in passing that I believe that a radically mimetic conception of desire offers a novel approach to psychiatric theory, one as far removed from the Freudian unconscious as it is from any philosophy of consciousness camouflaged as an existential psychoanalysis. Specifically, this new approach succeeds in circumventing the fetish of "adjustment" without plunging into the inverse fetish of "perversion" that is typical of so much of modern theory. The individual who "adjusts" has managed to relegate the two contradictory injunctions of the double bind—to imitate and not to imitate—to two different domains of application. That is, he divides reality in such a way as to neutralize the double bind. This is precisely the procedure of primitive cultures. At the origin of any individual or collective "adjustment" lies concealed a certain arbitrary violence. The well-adjusted person is thus one who conceals his violent impulses and condones the collective's concealment of them. The "maladjusted" individual cannot tolerate this concealment. "Mental illness"[5] and rebellion, like the sacrificial crisis they resemble, commit the individual to falsehoods and to forms of violence that are certainly more damaging *to him* than the disguised violence channeled through sacrificial rites but that bring him closer to the heart of the enigma. Many psychic

[5] Because the very notion of "mental illness" has been, up to a point, correctly challenged in the writings of some contemporary physicians, I put the term in quotation marks.

catastrophes misunderstood by the psychoanalyst result from an in-choate, obstinate reaction against the violence and falsehood found in any human society.

A psychoanalytic system that no longer oscillated between the rigid conformism of social adjustment and the false scandal arising from the assumption of a mythical patricide-incest drive in the child would not result in mere tepid idealism. Rather, such a system would bring us face to face with some traditional concepts that are troubling, to say the least. For example, in Greek tragedy, as in the Old Testament, the "good" son cannot generally be distinguished from the "bad" son; the "good" son is Jacob rather than Esau, the prodigal son rather than the faithful son, Oedipus. . . . For the good son imitates the father with such passion that father and son become each other's chief stumbling block—a situation the indifferent son more easily avoids.

It may appear, at this point, that all these concerns are foreign to the Freudian mode of thought and that the mimetic double bind has noth-ing to do with Freudian theory. "Act like your model/do not act like your model"—the contradictory double imperative we see as funda-mental—may be thought to lead us far from the realms of psycho-analysis.

In reality it does not, and this shows that Freud's work is too pre-cious to be left to the psychoanalysts. The mimetic approach preserves and enhances Freud's most acute insights. In *The Ego and the Id* Freud explains that the relation between the ego and the superego "is not exhausted by the precept: 'You ought to be like this (like your fa-ther).' It also comprises the prohibition: 'You *may not be* like this (like your father)—that is, you may not do all that he does; some things are his prerogative. . . .' "[6]

Who, after reading this passage, can deny Freud's proximity to my mimetic double bind? Not only was he familiar with its operation, but the context in which he placed it can help us realize its full potential. Freud's definition of the superego presupposes something quite differ-ent from a mythical consciousness of rivalry; he seems to have based it on the model's identification with the obstacle, an identification unper-ceived by the disciple. The superego is in fact nothing more than a resumption of identification with the father, now appearing chrono-logically *after* the Oedipus complex rather than *before* it. As we have seen, Freud did not actually suppress this previous identification, per-haps because he balked at contradicting himself; but he cunningly relegated it to secondary status by eliminating its primordial character.

[6] Freud, *The Ego and the Id*, p. 32.

In any case, the identification with the father now operates chiefly after the complex has taken hold; it has become the superego.

If we reflect on the definition of the superego offered by Freud two facts become clear. In the first place, the definition accords with the concept of the double bind. In the second place, it fails to harmonize with Freud's picture of a "sublimated" Oedipus complex; that is, a patricide-incest desire that has been transposed from the conscious to the unconscious.

To appreciate in full the predicament brought about by the super-ego's contradictory commands, issued as they are in the atmosphere of ignorance and uncertainty implied by Freud's definition, we must try to imagine the son's initial act of imitation. It is performed with fervor and devotion and rewarded by sudden, stupefying disgrace. The positive injunction, "Be like your father," had seemed to cover the entire range of paternal activities. Nothing in this first command anticipates, much less helps the son to understand, the contradictory command that follows: "You may not be like your father." And this command too seems to brook no exceptions.

All the son's efforts to differentiate between the commands and to formulate distinctions end in failure, and his bewilderment gives rise to terror. He wonders what he has done wrong and struggles to find separate areas of application for the two commands. He finds it difficult to see where he is at fault—certainly he has broken no law yet known to him—so he applies himself to discovering some new law that will allow him to define his conduct as illegal.

What conclusions must be drawn from this definition of the super-ego? Why did Freud again toy with the mimetic effects that he had rejected at the Oedipal stage? There seems only one possible answer: he had no intention of renouncing the mimetic effects resulting from identification. For he reverts to them when he takes up the concept of the superego. Yet the definition of the superego follows almost immediately on the definition of the Oedipus complex previously quoted, a definition purged of the mimetic elements that had characterized Freud's earlier definition in *Group Psychology and the Analysis of the Ego*.

It seems possible, then, to follow the evolution of Freud's thought from *Group Psychology* in 1921 to *The Ego and the Id* in 1923. In the earlier work Freud believed it possible to reconcile the mimetic effect with his main thesis, the Oedipus complex; that is why observations on the mimetic phenomenon are sprinkled throughout this work. But in the very course of composition, it seems, Freud began to sense the incompatibility of the two themes. And this incompatibility quickly becomes all too clear. The mimetic process detaches desire from any predetermined object, whereas the Oedipus complex fixes desire on the maternal object. The mimetic concept eliminates all conscious knowledge of patricide-incest, and even all desire for it as such; the Freudian proposition, by contrast, is based entirely on a consciousness of this desire.

Freud evidently decided to permit himself the luxury of his Oedipus complex. When he had to choose between the mimetic concept and a full-blown patricide-incest drive, he opted firmly for the latter. This is not to say that he renounced exploring the promising possibilities of mimesis; the admirable thing about Freud is his refusal ever to renounce anything. In suppressing the effects of mimesis he was simply trying to prevent mimesis from subverting his own cherished version of the Oedipus myth. He wanted to get hold of the "Oedipus complex" once and for all so as to be free to return to the mimesis question. Once he had the complex behind him, he could take mimesis up where he had left it before the burgeoning of the idea of the complex.

In short, Freud attempted initially to develop the Oedipus complex on the basis of a desire that is both object-oriented (cathectic) and yet originates in mimesis—whence comes the strange duality of the identification with the father and the lubidinous attraction for the mother in the first, and even the second, version of the complex. The failure of this attempt at compromise compelled Freud to base his complex on a purely cathectic desire and to reserve the mimetic effect for another psychic structure, the superego.

The duality of Freud's position stems from his effort to separate two poles of his thinking on desire: cathectic and Oedipal at one extreme, mimetic at the other. But any attempt to sever the link between the two will end in failure, as did the attempt at synthesis that preceded it.

It is hopeless to attempt to isolate the three elements of mimetic desire: identification, choice of object, and rivalry. That Freud's thought was never free of the influence of mimetic preoccupations can be proved by the irresistible conjunction of these three elements; whenever any one of them appears, the other two are sure to follow. It was only with the greatest effort and at the expense of much of his credibility that Freud managed to rid his Oedipus complex of all traces of mimesis. Conversely, in the case of the superego, where in principle nothing interferes with the son's paternal identification, we witness once again an upsurge of rivalry for the mother object. When the superego proclaims, "You may not be like this (your father) . . . some things are his prerogative," Freud is clearly referring to the mother. That is why he adds: "This double aspect of the ego ideal derives from the fact that the ego ideal had the task of repressing the Oedipus complex; indeed it is to that revolutionary event that it owes its existence."[7]

This superego, simultaneously repressing and repressed, which only exists thanks to "that revolutionary event," poses a formidable problem. It knows too much, even in a negative sense. The truth is that the reactivating of the father-identification, which gives the superego its meaning, automatically reactivates the Oedipal triangle. As I have remarked, Freud cannot evoke one of the three elements of the mimetic configuration without the other two's putting in an appearance. The reappearance of the Oedipal triangle was not in his program. The Oedipus complex, the capital that served to launch the entire psychoanalytic enterprise, is supposed to be firmly locked away in the unconscious, deposited deep in the vaults of the psyche.

This inopportune reappearance of the Oedipal triangle compelled Freud to admit that the son might experience certain difficulties in repressing his Oedipus complex! In fact, it is Freud himself who was having trouble disposing of the mimetic triangle. Haunted by the mimetic rivalry, he repeatedly sketched out triangular formations he believed to represent his complex, whereas in fact they depict a constantly thwarted mimesis—an interplay of model and obstacle that lingers at the edge of his thought but that he never succeeds in articulating fully.

I limited myself to examining two or three passages whose comparison seems particularly revealing; other passages could have been chosen that would have suited my purposes equally well, including some from the so-called clinical cases. In my chosen passages a term fundamental to Freudian speculation—*ambivalence*—reappears at frequent intervals. It seems to me that this term testifies to the existence of the mimetic pattern in Freud's mind and to his inability to express correctly the relationship among the three elements of the structure: the model, the disciple, and the object that is disputed by both because the model's desire has made the object desirable to the disciple. The object represents a desire shared by both, and such sharing leads not to harmony, as one might suppose, but to bitter conflict.

The term *ambivalence* appears toward the close of the two definitions of the Oedipus complex previously quoted. Here are the passages again:

> His [the boy's] identification with the father takes on a hostile colouring and becomes identical with the wish to replace the father in regard to his mother as well. Identification, in fact, is ambivalent from the very first.

[7] Ibid.

His identification with his father takes on a hostile colouring and changes into a wish to get rid of his father in order to take his place with his mother. Henceforward his relation to his father is ambivalent; it seems as if the ambivalence inherent in the identification from the beginning had become manifest.

When we recall how the identification with the father is initially presented—"This behavior has nothing to do with a passive or feminine attitude towards his father . . ."—we seem to be dealing with a unified relationship, free of ambiguity. Why then does Freud, a few lines later and seemingly as an afterthought, attribute an underlying ambiguity to this identification? Simply because he now senses (and his intuition does not betray him) that the positive feelings resulting from the first identification—imitation, admiration, veneration—are fated to change into negative sentiments: despair, guilt, resentment. But Freud does not realize *why* such things must happen. He does not realize because he cannot accept a concept of desire based on mimesis; he cannot openly acknowledge the model in the identification to be a model of the desire itself, and thus a powerful force of opposition.

Whenever he encounters the effects inherent in mimetic desire and finds himself struggling vainly to formulate its mechanism of rivalry, Freud takes refuge in the idea of ambivalence. To label these effects as ambivalent is to confine them to a solipsistic context, a traditional philosophic subject, instead of identifying them as a fundamental trait of all human relations, the universal double bind of imitated desires. If we try to grasp these effects of mimetic desire as individual pathology or psychology, they become utterly incomprehensible; in consequence, we ascribe them to "physical" causes. Freud himself conveys this impression and managed to persuade himself that in using the term *ambivalence* he had made a daring plunge into the dark regions where the psychic and the somatic meet. In reality, he was simply refusing to decipher a perfectly decipherable message. And because the "physical" is by nature mute, no rebuttal is possible. Today everyone imagines himself tuned in to the "physical," able to decode the body's messages after the example of Freud. Yet in all Freud's work there is not a single example of "ambivalence" that does not have its origins in the obstacle-model.

To attribute the conflict to the "body" is to give up on the logic of mimetic desire that can account most intelligibly and economically for all phenomena. With Freud, the "physical" aspect of the subject, the corporeal regions of the psyche, are endowed with a more or less organic propensity to run head on into the obstacle of the model-desire. Ambivalence becomes the main virtue of physicality insofar as it nourishes the psyche; it becomes the *virtus dormitiva* of modern scholasticism in the face of desire. Thanks to this idea and a number of others, psychoanalysis has been able to grant a reprieve—even apparently to grant new life—to the myth of the individual, by reasserting the claims of physicality. Yet this is the very myth it should be trying to demolish.

Freud's use of the term *ambivalence* reveals a genuine, if very limited, recognition of mimetic desire—which is more than can be said for many of his followers. The interesting question is how Freud managed repeatedly to misconstrue such a simple mechanism. In a sense its very simplicity served to camouflage its presence; but there is something else at work here as well.

That something else is not difficult to identify; we have encountered it at every turn in the course of our inquiry. It is, of course, the hard core of the Oedipus complex: that brief interval of consciousness when the patricide-incest desire is felt to become a formal expression of the child's intentions. It is clear that this Freudian view makes Freud's full discovery of mimetic desire impossible. To persuade himself that the patricide-incest desire actually exists, Freud was obliged to disregard the model, insofar as it is responsible for awakening the desire and designating the object. Freud was forced to perpetuate a traditional, retrogressive concept of the desire. The drift of his thought in the direction of mimesis was perpetually checked by his strange loyalty to the patricide-incest motif.

As an interpretative tool the concept of mimetic rivalry is far more serviceable than the Freudian complex. By eliminating the conscious patricide-incest desire it does away with the cumbersome necessity of the desire's subsequent repression. In fact, it does away with the unconscious. The concept explains the Oedipus myth and does so with an economy and precision lacking in the Freudian approach. Why then, we may well ask, did Freud renounce the superior utility of mimetic desire to lavish his attention on the poor substitute of patricide-incest?

Even if I am mistaken—even if I am blind to the virtues of the Oedipus myth as a universal model for the human psyche—still my question remains valid. It seems unlikely that Freud ever formally rejected the interpretation I am proposing here as a substitute for his complex; in all likelihood, it never came to his attention. Had it done so, Freud would surely have taken it under consideration, if only to reject it. My reading brings together a number of clues that seem to play little part in Freud's texts; the obstacle of the patricide-incest motif once removed, we can bring together elements that remain disconnected in Freud's own work. Freud was dazzled by what he took to be his crucial discovery. Loyalty to this discovery kept him from forging ahead on the path of mimesis. Had he done so he would have come to realize the mythic nature of the patricide-incest motif, as it appears in the Oedipus myth and in psychoanalysis as well.

The whole of psychoanalysis seems to be summed up in the patricide-incest theme. It is this theme that has won psychoanalysis its glory and its notoriety, that has provoked the incomprehension, hostility, and extraordinary devotion we have come to associate with the discipline. It is this theme that is invariably invoked whenever any rebellious spirit dares to cast doubt on the efficacy of psychoanalytic doctrine.

Freud's intimations of mimetic desire never crystallized into a theory. The founder of psychoanalysis brooded over the same themes throughout his lifetime, and his unending struggle to reorganize the elements of desire never produced truly satisfactory results, because he refused to abandon his object desire, his "cathectic" viewpoint. The various structures and examples of Freudianism, theoretical concepts such as the castration complex, the Oedipus complex, the superego, the unconscious, repression, ambivalence—all these are nothing more than defensive positions in his eternal battle to resolve the problem of desire.

Freudian analysis should not be regarded as a fully articulated system, but as a series of experiments dealing almost invariably with the same subject. The superego, for instance, is only a recasting of the Oedipus complex; the more I examine the origins of the two concepts, the more convinced I become that their differences are purely illusory.

Freud at his best is no more "Freudian" than Marx at his best is "Marxist." Nevertheless, uncomprehending critics did on occasion provoke him to adopt a dogmatic line of argument that his followers blindly accepted and his opponents as blindly rejected, therefore making it difficult for any of us to approach these texts with an open mind.

Post-Freudian psychoanalysis has clearly perceived what must be done to systematize Freudianism—or rather, to sever it from its living roots. To assure the autonomy of desire it is only necessary to erase the last traces of mimesis from the Oedipus complex. Thus, the identification with the father must be dropped. Freud had already pointed the way, after all, in *The Ego and the Id*. Inversely, to establish the supremacy of the superego on a firm basis, one need only eliminate all those elements that tend to implicate the object and the subject of rivalry in its definition. In short, the post-Freudian psychoanalyst reasserts a system, an order of things based on "common sense," such as only Freud himself ever challenged. In the case of the Oedipus complex the father becomes a disgraced rival; thus there is no question of his being a venerated model. Reciprocally, in the case of the superego, the father is the venerated model, with no trace of the disgraced rival about him. Ambivalence, it would appear, is good for patients, but of no use to psychoanalysts.

We are presented, therefore, with a rivalry devoid of preliminary identification (the Oedipus complex) followed by an identification without subsequent rivalry (the superego). In one of his earliest articles, "Aggression in Psychoanalysis," Jacques Lacan noted the bewildering character of this sequence: "The structural effect of the identification with the rival does not follow naturally, except perhaps in mythic thinking."[8] But let us leave the myth aside; we will presently see that it can take care of itself. Moreover, the effect noted by Lacan makes perfect sense in terms of the mimetic nature of desire, which Lacan, too, failed to discover, forced as he was by his linguistic fetishism to reinforce the more rigid and "structural" aspects of Freudian thinking.

The interest of Freudian analysis does not lie in its results, in its pretentious accumulation of psychic agencies; nor does it lie in the spectacle of Freudian apprentices clambering up and down the precarious scaffolding of Freudian doctrine with an agility as remarkable as it is futile. It lies, paradoxically enough, in the ultimate inadequacies of the whole system. Freud never succeeded in establishing the precise relationship of the model, the disciple, and their common object, although he never entirely abandoned the effort. Whenever he attempted to manipulate any two of the terms, the third raised its head like a mocking jack-in-the-box, which his disciples made haste to cram back in its box in the belief that they were doing something useful. In fact, it is hard to imagine a more effective method of "castrating" the Master!

SINCE FREUD'S TIME it has often been disputed whether the Oedipus complex is a phenomenon exclusive to the Occidental world or whether it is also to be found in primitive societies. Malinowski's *The Father in Primitive Society* has been cited in this context.

Malinowski begins by asserting that the Trobrianders are happier than Occidentals. Yet these savages, while free of the conflicts and tensions of civilization, are beset by conflicts and tensions of their own. In Trobriander society the maternal uncle performs some of the functions that in our society are allotted to the father. It is from the uncle rather than the father that the children inherit their worldly goods; it is the uncle who is responsible for their tribal education. We should not be surprised, therefore, to observe that conflicts and tensions arise between children and uncle rather than between children and father

[8] Jacques Lacan, *Ecrits* (Paris, 1966), p. 117.

and that in time of stress the father functions as a source of comfort and protection, as an indulgent and well-disposed comrade.[9]

Malinowski himself presents his observations in the context of a dialogue with Freud. The impression they leave is unclear. The author begins by contradicting Freud's assertion that the Oedipus complex is universal. His reflections on the status of the uncle follow, seeming to cast a more favorable light on psychoanalytic theory. Malinowski no longer appears to be questioning Freud, but rather to be filling out his theories. The uncle's position in Trobriander society is analogous to the father's position in Western society, and in this sense the Oedipus complex could be said to partake of a certain universality.

Psychoanalysts have accorded Malinowski's work a warm reception. They see it as a refutation of the anthropologists who have accused psychoanalysis of parochialism, but they fail to notice that Malinowski, whose Freudianism is rather superficial, refers only to an explicit and fully conscious conflict between children and their Trobriander uncles. There is nothing here, on the psychoanalytic level, that allows us to declare these conflicts to be rooted in an unconscious drama whose protagonist is the uncle himself. It is scarcely likely that this omission would have gone unnoticed had the work been unfavorable to psychoanalysis.

Some of Malinowski's observations seem vital to the present discussion. They address themselves directly to relationships that are of particular interest to us and that are the only real aspect of the Oedipus complex. Without fully appreciating the significance of his own remarks, Malinowski demonstrates that primitive societies (or at any rate, Trobriander society) employ methods for combating mimetic rivalry and the double bind that are totally foreign to our own culture. The essential factor here is not the father's indulgence or the uncle's severity, not the displacement of authority from one masculine image to another; rather, it is the cleavage made between father and son, the fact that the father, and paternal culture in general, *does not serve as a model.*

Father and son do not belong to the same lineage. The father never commands the son: "Do as I do!"

> The child . . . learns that the place where his *kada* (mother's brother) resides is also his, the child's, "own village"; that there he has his property and his other rights of citizenship; that there are his future prospects, there reside his natural allies and associates. He may even be taunted in the village of his birth with being an "outsider". . . . Thus the life of a Trobriander runs under a twofold influence—a duality which must not be imagined only as a mere surface play of custom. It enters deeply into

[9] Malinowski, *The Father in Primitive Society,* pp. 17–18.

the existence of individual men, it produces strange complications of usage, it creates frequent tensions and difficulties. . . .[10]

The sons live with a man—their father—who does not incorporate their ideal in the Freudian sense of the "ideal ego" or the "superego." Such an ideal is indeed provided by the culture in the form of the closest adult relative in the maternal line, but the children do not live with this model. To begin with, the maternal uncle intervenes rather late in the childrens' existence, and even then his presence is only intermittent, for he usually lives in another village. Moreover, and most importantly, there is a very strict taboo denying him any contact with his sister, the mother of the children. So in Freudian terms, as well as in those of the double bind, the displacement toward the uncle is illusory. The avuncular Oedipus complex, then, turns out to be little more than a whimsy. In fact, the tensions that exist between uncle and nephew are the more explicit because the child is not torn by contradictory feelings; for him, the obstacle cannot become the model nor the model the obstacle. The mimesis is channeled in such a way that desire will not take its own obstacle as an object.

The study of other primitive systems would probably reveal that, in those instances where the cultural model is incarnated in a specific individual, the model's sphere of activity never impinges on that of the disciple so as to produce a convergence of their two desires. In fact, the two spheres of activity only touch at those points and at those predetermined moments that are necessary to ensure the disciple's initiation into the culture.

Malinowski's observations give us reason to believe that primitive societies cope with the double bind more effectively than does Western society. Indeed, how can we define Western society in terms relevant to the Trobrianders? In our society, ever since the time of the ancient patriarchs, a plurality of functions, which among the Trobrianders are divided between father and uncle, have been assigned to one man alone. Our patriarchal system is less differentiated than the Trobriander system, and even though it can and must appear to us, from the point of view of the modern family, as the extreme of arbitrary structuralization, from the perspective of primitive societies it would be regarded as the opposite.

Surely we should abandon the use of the "Oedipus complex," a seemingly inexhaustible source of confusion. We could then bring into conjunction with conflictual mimesis those entirely genuine phenomena that psychoanalysis has explained by its "Oedipus complex." These phenomena would gain in coherence; moreover, it would become pos-

[10] Ibid., pp. 18–19.

sible to incorporate them into a diachronic plan, to situate historically not only the phenomena themselves but also the theories that have been proposed to explain them—beginning, of course, with psycho-analysis itself.

A theoretical concept such as the Oedipus complex can only be applied to a society in which reciprocal mimesis has already been established and the model-obstacle mechanism set in motion, but its violent effects not yet generally felt. In addition, this mechanism must usually be triggered by the father. If the double bind originates with the father, the mimetic attraction will preserve its paternal coloring as long as the victim lives. With the individual as with groups, mimetic attraction always becomes more and more acute, it always tends to reproduce its initial forms; in other terms, it always seeks new models—and new obstacles—that resemble the original one. If this original model is the father, the subject will choose models that resemble him.

In Western society, the father had already become the model by the patriarchal era. In order for the double bind to operate, he had also to become the obstacle. And the father can only become an obstacle when the diminution of his paternal authority has brought him into a direct confrontation with his son, obliging him to occupy the same sphere. The Oedipus complex appears most plausible in a society in which the father's authority has been greatly weakened but not completely destroyed; that is, in Western society during the course of recent centuries. Here the father has functioned as the original model and the original obstacle in a world where the dissolution of differences encourages the proliferation of the double bind.

This state of affairs requires an explanation. If the history of modern society is marked by the dissolution of differences, that clearly has something to do with the sacrificial crisis to which we have repeatedly referred. Indeed, the phrase "modern world" seems almost like a synonym for "sacrificial crisis." It should be noted, however, that the modern world manages to retain its balance, precarious though it may be; and the methods it employs to do so, though extreme, are not so extreme as to destroy the fabric of the society. As my previous chapters indicated, primitive societies are unable to withstand such pressures; violence would quickly get out of hand and trigger the mechanism of generative unanimity, thus restoring a social system based on multiple and sharply pronounced differences. In the modern Western world nothing of this kind takes place. The wearing away of differences proceeds at a slow but steady pace, and the results are absorbed more or less gracefully by a community that is slowly but steadily coming to encompass the entire globe.

It is not law, in any conceivable form, that is responsible for the tensions and alienation besetting modern man; rather, it is the increasing lack of law. The perpetual denunciation of the law arises from a typically modern sense of resentment—a feedback of desire that purports to be directed against the law but one that is actually aimed at the model-obstacle whose dominant position the subject stubbornly refuses to acknowledge. The more frenzied the mimetic process becomes, caught up in the confusion of constantly changing forms, the more unwilling men are to recognize that they have made an obstacle of the model and a model of the obstacle. Here we encounter a true "unconscious," and one that can obviously assume many forms.

Freud is of little use as a guide over this terrain. So, for that matter, is Nietzsche, who reserves his resentment for the "weak" while trying vainly to establish a distinction between this resentment and a truly "spontaneous" desire, a will to power that he can claim as wholly his own but that is in reality nothing more than the ultimate expression of cumulative resentment. No, our best guide is perhaps Kafka, one of the few to perceive that the absence of law is in fact identical with law run wild and that this identity constitutes the chief burden of mankind. Once more our best guide turns out to be one of those writers of fiction whose insights have been studiously ignored by psychological researchers. When the father is no longer an overbearing patriarch the son looks everywhere for the law—and finds no lawgiver.

If the patriarchal system, when compared to primitive systems, seems to represent a "lesser" degree of structuralization, then Western civilization since the decline of the patriarchal system can be said to have been governed by a principle of decreasing structuralization or destructralization during the whole of its historical course—a tendency that can almost be seen as an ultimate aim. A dynamic force seems to be drawing first Western society, then the rest of the world, toward a state of relative indifferentiation never before known on earth, a strange kind of nonculture or anticulture we call modern.

The advent of psychoanalysis has been historically determined by the advent of the "modern." Most of the phenomena associated with the Oedipus complex reveal a true unity and intelligibility when seen in the light of the mimetic process—and this remains true even if the main body of belief is purely mythical. The Oedipus complex might seem to be a satisfactory theory during the early stages of mimetic propagation in a historical situation characterized by the limited survival, at least for a while, of family structures derived from the patriarchal system. We can witness here the same process of disintegration that takes place in primitive societies during the sacrificial crisis, but in this case the process is gradual, kept more or less in rein, with no catastrophic outbursts of violence and no resolution of any kind taking place. The astonishing flexibility of the "modern," along with its extraordinary functionalism, is here on view. Equally visible are the ever-increasing tensions that beset modern times.

The Oedipus complex is a Western and modern phenomenon, as are the relative neutralization and sterilization of a mimetic desire that, though in the process of freeing itself, is still oriented toward the father and therefore inclined toward certain forms of order and stability. Psychoanalysis at this particular moment in history seems at once to announce and to prepare the way for something it cannot itself describe: an advanced stage of indifferentiation, or "decoding," which involves the complete effacement of the paternal function.

Like all forms of mythical thought, psychoanalysis is a closed system that can never be refuted. If there is no conflict between father and son, it is because the unconscious aspect of the complex has come into play; and if there is a conflict, that too is a result of the complex. In short, the complex is bound to appear, and if it does not, that circumstance only confirms its existence.

Not only can the teachings of psychoanalysis always be confirmed, but they seem increasingly to the point as mimesis spreads and grows more acute, as destructuralization becomes more widespread and the double bind proliferates. The Oedipus complex waxes as the father wanes. It has become routine to ascribe all sorts of psychic disorders to an Oedipus whose Laius remains obstinately out of sight. The need to trace the complex to some flesh-and-blood father, or uncle, or any one individual at all, is now said to be illusory; as indeed it is. Psychoanalysis vanquishes all challengers. It is everywhere—and nowhere. It finally dissolves into the banality of multisided familial and nonfamilial rivalries in a more and more competitive world.

☙ IF THE OEDIPUS COMPLEX constitutes an erroneous reading of the double bind, then we can say that those desires that the world at large, and the father in particular, regard as emanating from the son's own patricide-incest drive actually derive from the father himself in his role as model.

The Freudian myth is still so influential today, even among skeptics that the foregoing statement may well seem like sheer perversity. I feel constrained, therefore, to seek support from a reputable author whose authority in these matters is generally acknowledged: Sophocles. We could, of course, turn once more to *Oedipus the King*, but that play has been used so often and for so many purposes that its value as an example has worn thin. Let us rather consider a less familiar play: *The Women of Trachis*.

In the last episode, Heracles, the protagonist, has put on his poisoned tunic and lies writhing in agony on the ground. His son Hyllos stands by, respectfully awaiting his father's last orders. Heracles orders his son to light a great fire and place him, still living, on the pyre; thus Heracles will be free of his pain. Hyllos cries out in protest; his father is making a patricide of him! Heracles insists in such a manner as to make himself responsible for the act, responsible for perpetrating a ruthless double bind:

Heracles: Do as I say, for this must be done. Or else, cease to call yourself my son.
Hyllos: Oh father, what are you asking of me? To be your murderer, to assume the guilt of your death!

What follows is even more extraordinary. Heracles has a second favor, less important than the first, to ask of his son—and at this point the play takes on a distinctly comic air, at any rate for modern ears attuned to Freudian motifs. Because his death leaves his young wife Iole (acquired in the course of the last labor) without a protector, Heracles makes a proposal to his son:

Heracles: When I am dead, if you wish to show your piety and stand by the vows made to your father, make her [Iole] your wife. Do not deny me this. She has slept at my side, and it is my wish that no one but you possess her. Go, take her to your bed. What good is it if you carry out my greater commands, and neglect the lesser ones like this?
Hyllos: Ah, it is wrong to lose one's temper at a sick man, yet how hard it is to put up with him when he has such ideas!

After this exchange, not unworthy of a post-Freudian Molière, the dialogue continues to gain in interest. Hyllos offers as his reason for refusing Iole the role she has played—though only as passive spectator —in the family tragedy that is now drawing to a close. In fact, it is the true relationship between the father's desire and the son's desire that is being challenged; an identification that appears as impious rebellion to the world at large, although it is in fact an absolute submission to the paternal command, to the insidious and imperious suggestion by the paternal model that the son desire what the father desires.

Hyllos: Father, have pity on me, I am the most wretched of men!
Heracles: Because you refuse to obey your father.
Hyllos: But when you preach impiety to your son!
Heracles: There can be no impiety in your pleasing me.
Hyllos: Then these are your final orders?
Heracles: They are; and the gods are my witnesses.

Hyllos: Then I will obey. For the gods know it is your will; and surely a son does no wrong in obeying his father.

Heracles: Then all is well . . .

As we can see, the ancient drama is more knowledgeable in the ways of fathers and sons than is modern psychoanalytic theory. It provides modern theorists with a lesson in humility. For Sophocles, speaking over the span of twenty-five centuries, can help us to cast off that most burdensome of all mythologies: the myth of the Oedipus complex.[11]

---

[11] This is perhaps the place to call attention to the signal perceptiveness of other purely "literary" works that touch upon the same subject. On the question of paternal incitement to patricide, Calderon's remarkable *La Vida es sueno* merits special attention. See also Cesareo Bandera's highly original study *Mimesis conflictiva* (Madrid: Gredos, 1975). This study reveals Calderon as an author who goes one step beyond Freud in dealing with the question of desire and the obstacle that masquerades as the "law."

Chapter Eight

Totem and Taboo and the Incest Prohibition

◆◆◆ CONTEMPORARY CRITICISM is almost unanimous in finding unacceptable the theories set forth in *Totem and Taboo*. Freud assumes at the outset the very propositions his book is supposed to explore: Darwin's primal horde is a caricature of the family, and the sexual monopoly of the dominant male coincides with future prohibitions regarding incest. As Lévi-Strauss remarks in *The Elementary Structures of Kinship*, we have here "a vicious circle deriving the social state from events which presuppose it."[1]

This objection has validity if one considers the work only in its broad outlines. Still, there are aspects of *Totem and Taboo* that elude categorization. And although one might assume that the theory of collective murder, for example, presented in the work has been amply clarified by the critics, such is not the case. To be sure, the subject of collective murder invariably crops up in connection with the book; indeed, it seems to constitute the main attraction of this work, this bizarre edifice through which we are guided by glib commentators who seem, one and all, to have the same story to tell; *Totem and Taboo*, they assure us, is an example of the aberrations to which genius is prone! These commentators see the work either as an anomaly or as an unwitting farce—something like the novels of Victor Hugo's old age.

A reexamination of the work in question confirms our uneasiness. The murder motif is conspicuous, but it serves no apparent purpose. If the subject of the book is the genesis of sexual prohibitions, then this motif hinders Freud's argument rather than helps it. Without the murder motif, we could pass easily from the sexual privations inflicted on the young by a primordial father to the strictly cultural prohibitions. But the murder breaks the circuit, and while Freud tries dutifully to

---

[1] Claude Lévi-Strauss, *The Elementary Structures of Kinship*, trans. James Harle Bell, John Richard von Sturmer, and Rodney Needham (Boston, 1969), p. 491.

restore the connection, he does so without conviction. Ultimately his ideas on the subject of sexual prohibitions are both more confused and less simplistic than has been generally acknowledged.

Far from serving to "put things in order," the murder motif seems to throw everything into disarray. The theory that attributes the prohibitions to the father's sexual monopoly is not Freud's invention, as Freud himself makes plain:

> Atkinson (1903) seems to have been the first to realize that the practical consequence of the conditions obtaining in Darwin's primal horde might be exogamy for the young males. Each of them might, after being driven out, establish a similar horde, in which the same prohibition upon sexual intercourse would rule owing to its leader's jealousy. In course of time this would produce what grew into a conscious law: "No sexual relations between those who share a common home." After the establishment of totemism this regulation would assume another form and would run: "No sexual relations within the totem."[2]

The concept of collective murder, however, undoubtedly originates with Freud. Its apparent superfluousness and incongruity has prompted critics to wonder why Freud included it at all, and French psychoanalysts have responded to the question in their customary fashion by attributing the concept to the author's unconscious. In *Totem and Taboo*, they inform us, Freud treats his readers to a particularly spectacular revelation of his own repressed desires. And although this is the sort of response we have learned to expect from Freud's followers, it is slightly disconcerting to find it applied to the master himself. Of all Freud's works, *Totem and Taboo* is the only one thus singled out for therapeutic treatment, the only one for which such a treatment is not only permitted, but apparently encouraged.

Freudians are generally prompt to pay obeisance to the least utterance of their oracle and to denounce in violent terms the most tentative questioning of his conclusions.[3] A summary condemnation of *Totem and Taboo* must make a strong impression on the lay observer, who can only conclude that this particular work must have been very badly botched indeed.

Modern ethnologists, although generally kinder to amateurs than are their colleagues in the field of psychoanalysis, have shown themselves equally severe toward *Totem and Taboo*. The work was published in 1913, when ethnology was still a fledgling science. The theories drawn on by Freud—Frazer's, and in particular Robertson Smith's—have long

[2] Freud, *Standard Edition*, vol. 13, *Totem and Taboo*, p. 126.
[3] The author has in mind primarily the modern French school of Freudian psychoanalysis.—Trans.

been superseded. The concept of totemism is virtually obsolete; and above all, Freud's main thesis is patently false.

In short, there are so many excellent reasons for condemning *Totem and Taboo* that the work has never received serious critical examination. Yet if it is true that Freud lost his head in the writing of this essay, surely it is worthwhile to determine how, why, and to what extent he went astray. The greater one's esteem for Freud's genius, the more valid such an inquiry appears. The accusations leveled at *Totem and Taboo* must cast doubt on Freud's other theories as well—at any rate, until the Freudians succeed in localizing the difficulty and correcting it. But this is precisely what certain neo-Freudians fail—indeed refuse—to undertake. The antireferential prejudice is so strong that it has become second nature.

True scientific inquiry is always open to disquieting speculations, to theories that flatly contradict the beliefs of the moment or challenge their most cherished conventions. But perhaps it is misleading to speak of "disquieting" theories; we should rather refer to theories of varying degrees of credibility. Before accusing Freud of succumbing to his illusions—as if he were a mere fiction-maker—a Shakespeare or a Sophocles or a Euripides—let us at least give him a hearing. It is strange that the very people who claim to represent the living spirit of psychoanalysis dismiss Freud the most flippantly.

Everyone seems intent on covering *Totem and Taboo* with obloquy and condemning it to oblivion. My own attitude toward the book is obviously quite different. Freud's concept of collective murder and the arguments he uses to present it are too close to the themes of my own work for me to pass over the book in silence.

It is important to bear in mind that an ethnological theory can be justly criticized, even conclusively refuted, without invalidating the evidence collected in its defence. Although totemism has been shown to be only one facet of a far broader form of activity—that of classification—it does not necessarily follow that the religious phenomena that were previously explained by totemism are now to be considered null and void. These phenomena must simply be considered in a broader context; our concern should now be directed to the relationship between religion and the overall question of classification. That distinctions should exist or that these distinctions should remain stable cannot be taken for granted from the standpoint of primitive societies. Totemism may indeed be illusory, but this illusion served to focus attention on the enigma of religious belief.

Freud was fully aware of the risks involved in selecting totemism as the rallying point for his arguments. Far from placing a blind trust in the concept, he scrutinized his results with a critical eye and concluded that "everything connected with totemism seems to be puzzling."[4] He found none of the proposed solutions to his liking, including the one he qualified as "nominalism," which, when carried to its logical conclusions, has led to the contemporary refutation of the entire concept: "The [nominalist] theories I have so far discussed . . . might perhaps explain the fact that primitive peoples adopt animal names for their clans, but they could never explain the importance that has become attached to this nomenclature—namely, the totemic system.[5]

What is important here is not the reference to the totem or to any other system, but the religious presence, which must not be casually and fraudulently dismissed as something that "goes without saying." It is no part of the role of science to deprive the spirit of the justifiable sense of wonderment that is occasioned by certain human acts. Freud rejected all those "too rational" points of view that "fail to take into account the affective side of things."

Freud's attention was caught by the same kinds of acts—in some instances actually by the identical acts—that I have presented in the preceding chapters. He observed that in primitive religion extreme opposites coincide: good and evil, sadness and joy, accepted and forbidden practices. The festival, for example, is "a permitted, or rather an obligatory, excess, a solemn breach of a prohibition."[6] The coincidence of the permitted and the prohibited brings to mind the sacrificial process: "when the deed is done, the slaughtered animal is lamented and bewailed. . . ." This is hardly surprising, because sacrifice and festival are one and the same rite. "There is no gathering of a clan without an animal sacrifice, nor—and this now becomes significant— any slaughter of an animal except on these ceremonial occasions."[7]

The same mingling of the permitted and the prohibited is found in the treatment of certain animals, even when the sacrificial element is not formally present: "A totem animal that is found dead is mourned and buried like a dead kinsman. If it is necessary to kill a totem animal, this is done according to a prescribed ritual of apologies and ceremonies of expiation."[8]

Freud discerns this strange duality of sacrificial custom in all aspects of primitive religion. The rite is invariably presented in the form of a murder, a transgression both culpable and obligatory whose virtue lies ultimately in its very impiety.

Robertson Smith clearly perceived the unifying factors in those

[4] Freud, *Totem and Taboo*, p. 108.
[5] Ibid., p. 111.
[6] Ibid., p. 140.
[7] Ibid., p. 135.
[8] Ibid., p. 104.

practices that, broadly speaking, correspond to our "sacrificial rites" and that he chose to group under the heading "totemism." The term had a great vogue among ethnologists who shared a particular body of knowledge, as well as certain intellectual attitudes that no longer seem valid. But if we do not always agree with their concepts, we approve of their quest: to fathom the hidden meaning of primitive religions and to establish their essential unity.

It is this quest for unity that led Robertson Smith, and later Freud, to propose totemism as the origin of all religious manifestations. These so-called totemic beliefs serve to direct our attention to some extraordinary manifestations of religious belief, customs at once paradoxical and enigmatic that seem to demand a full interpretation and that are, therefore, the most likely to lead us toward the truth. It was in the aspects of totemism that dealt specifically with religion that Freud found, far more conspicuously than elsewhere, that coincidence of opposites that serves to define the overall process of religion. Religious totemism is connected with the operation in which violence, caught up in its own paroxysm, produces an inversion by means of an actual act of collective murder. Freud astutely surmised the necessity for this act, but because the mechanism of the surrogate victim eluded him, he failed to grasp its *modus operandi.*

This mechanism provides the only feasible explanation of how a sacrificial murder, originally regarded as a crime, can literally be transformed into an act of piety. There seems to be a very close connection, if not an essential similarity, between this transformation and the clans' individual attitudes toward their totems. In many instances the pursuit of the totem, its slaughter and devouring, are expressly restricted to those solemn festivals that seem to involve a somewhat equivocal inversion of custom—for during those festivals the entire clan is obliged to commit all the acts forbidden throughout the rest of the year.

The urge to duplicate the operation of the surrogate victim is even more apparent in the case of totemic belief than in the "classic" sacrifice. Clearly the truth we are seeking is close at hand, and although Freud failed to grasp it, he was surely on the right track when he concentrated his attention on totemism. His intuition did not play him false in suggesting a connection between the enigmas of religion and an actual act of murder. But for want of a mechanism that would make this connection, Freud was unable to translate his discovery into any kind of plausible formulation. He never advanced beyond the idea of a single act of murder, in principle at least, committed in prehistoric times—an idea that, if taken literally, lends a note of fantasy to his theory.

Before we assert that Freud dreamed of murdering his own father or wrote his book under dictation from his unconscious, it might be worth while to review the arguments so forcefully advanced in *Totem and Taboo*. Freud insists (as I have also done) on the need for unanimous participation in the rites. If these rites were not performed by the entire group acting in unison they would be nothing more than criminal acts of destructive intent. Freud fails to perceive the functional dimension of unanimity, but he is nonetheless aware that the sanctity of the proceedings depends on their indivisibility. In many cultures, moreover, the man/animal or totemic monster assumes the guise of judge, mentor, and *ancestor*, without relinquishing his role as victim slaughtered by his fellows and peers, the first being cut down by a community which, while mythic, is nonetheless a double of real society.

We have here a series of clues well worth pursuing, and it is a sad commentary on our present intellectual scene that we cannot draw the logical conclusion from them—namely, a theory of collective murder —without provoking an automatic rejection from critics who like to think of themselves as the practitioners of impartial scientific inquiry!

A careful comparison of sacrificial rites and totemic beliefs will bring out certain dominant strains that have a direct bearing on the subject of collective murder. All the signs seem to suggest that the gods, along with the community itself, owe their origin to internal and unanimous violence and to a victim who is a member of the community:

"A life [Freud quotes Robertson Smith] which no single tribesman is allowed to invade, and which can be sacrificed only by the consent and common action of the kin, stands on the same footing with the life of the fellowtribesmen." The rule that every participant at the sacrificial meal must eat a share of the flesh of the victim has the same meaning as the provision that the execution of a guilty tribesman must be carried out by the tribe as a whole. In other words, the sacrificial animal was treated as a member of the tribe; *the sacrificing community, the god and the sacrificial animal were of the same blood and members of the same clan*. (Freud's italics)[9]

As we can see, the problematic aspects of the totemic theory do not affect Freud's basic conclusions. Indeed, totemism plays no part here. The dynamism of *Totem and Taboo* is directed toward a general theory of sacrifice. Robertson Smith had already pointed the way, but Freud managed to push the inquiry further—largely because he was indifferent to the theoretical debates then raging among anthropologists. The enormous mass of collaborative information obviously de-

[9] Ibid., p. 133.

manded a single, all-embracing explanation, a general theory that was first and foremost related to the subject of sacrifice: "Robertson Smith explains that sacrifice at the altar was the essential feature in the ritual of ancient religions. It plays the same part in all religions, so that its origin must be traced back to very general causes, operating everywhere in the same manner."[10]

Freud's archetypal sacrificial rite was practiced by a tribe of the Sinai desert. It is described by St. Nilus in the fourth century, and cited by Robertson Smith, who himself found it highly significant:

> The victim of the sacrifice, a camel, [Freud quoting Robertson Smith] "is bound upon a rude altar of stones piled together, and when the leader of the band has thrice led the worshippers round the altar in a solemn procession accompanied with chants, he inflicts the first wound . . . and in all haste drinks the blood that gushes forth. Forthwith the whole company fall on the victim with their swords, hacking off pieces of the quivering flesh and devouring them raw with such wild haste, that in the short interval between the rise of the day star [to which the sacrifice was offered] . . . and the disappearance of its rays before the rising sun, the entire camel, body, bones, skin, blood and entrails, is wholly devoured."[11]

In my opinion the so-called totemic survivals that Robertson Smith thought he had detected in the sacrifice can be attributed, here as elsewhere, to an incomplete grasp of the part played by the surrogate victim. And Freud's interest in these "totemic survivals" sprang from their relationship to his own concept of collective murder. Given the Sinai sacrifice and the context in which it appears, we can hardly blame Freud from drawing the conclusions that he did in favor of his murder theory. Indeed, is it really so obvious that Freud has abandoned the principles of sound scientific practice in this work and that his whole theory is based on a personal illusion that is psychological in origin?

Faithful to his sources, Freud limits his discussion almost exclusively to the camel sacrifice. One cannot help wondering what conclusions he would have drawn had he taken into account similar practices over a broad spectrum of independent cultures and submitted them to a systematic comparison.

In the Sinai sacrifice the camel is bound like a criminal and the crowd is armed; in the Dionysiac *diasparagmos* the victim is not bound and the attackers have no weapons. But two constants remain: the crowd and the mad rush at the victim. In some instances the victim is encouraged to flee; in others, it is the participants who take flight. *In every instance a mob murder is being reenacted, although the scenes*

---

[10] Ibid.
[11] Ibid., p. 138.

will vary in details. These divergences should not be attributed to any lapse of the ritual memory, for the forms of collective murder differ somewhat from one religion to another. These differences, though slight, are revealing, for they evoke the realism of the model and therefore discourage any attempt at purely formalist interpretation. These differences may have led to Freud's intuitive grasp of the situation, even though they are only implicit in *Totem and Taboo*. Indeed, it would have been impossible for Freud to consider them explicitly, for his theory of a single, unique act of murder could neither accommodate nor explain them.

An investigation into the nature of ritual resembles the sort of criminal investigation—no less valid for figuring so frequently in detective fiction—in which the solution of the mystery depends on a reenactment of the crime. No matter how clever the criminal, no matter how careful he may be to eliminate all traces of his presence, he is unable to extend his activities or repeat his past successes without laying down a trail for his pursuers. A seemingly insignificant detail, passed over in haste during the investigation of the first crime, suddenly assumes importance when it reappears in a slightly different guise. In the same way the successive proofs of an engraving allow us to discern patterns or images that might well pass unnoticed when looking at one print in isolation. These differences constitute the ethnological equivalent of *Abschattungen*, those partial and always shifting perceptions that end by establishing, in terms of Husserlian phenomenology, the stable and indubitable element of a given object. Once the law of their variations has been apprehended, the true object is correctly perceived. Doubt is then no longer possible; the image remains indelible, and any additional information can only serve to consolidate and reinforce the now correctly identified object.

Freud was not dreaming when he wrote *Totem and Taboo*, and he assumed that the participants in sacrificial rites were not dreaming either. He could well have turned the rites into a dream; this would have been a possible line of defense for a formalist hard pressed by the massed body of ethnological evidence. But Freud did not take that path. Efforts have been made to prove him a formalist; but in this case, at least, he clearly perceived that any attempt to structure the dream would be as futile as trying to structure the wind. To declare sacrifice a psychoanalytical fantasy would mean to lay aside an impressive body of rigorously determined facts and observations that cry out for attention. To dissolve these phenomena in dreams would be to deny the rites any status as a social institution; it would be to deny, in effect, social unity itself.

The sacrificial act is too rich in concrete details to be only a simulation of something that never actually occurred. This assertion can be made without contradicting my previous statement that the act is a simulated performance designed to offer a substitute satisfaction. Sacrifice takes the place of an act that nobody under normal cultural conditions would dare or even desire to commit; it is this aspect that Freud, wholly intent on the *origins* of sacrifice, paradoxically failed to perceive. I qualify his failure as paradoxical because *Totem and Taboo* lacks the one form of truth that appears, though sometimes in distorted form, in the rest of his work. Freud understands that sacrifice must be traced back to an event of a quite different type from ritual itself; yet his intuition of origins, because he did not follow it to the end, caused him to lose all sense of the *function* of the rite. If sacrifice is accorded a particular role in the rite, this is because it was at one time something else and because it retains that "something else" as a model. In order to reconcile function with origin and illuminate one by means of the other, Freud needed a tool that he failed to unearth: the surrogate victim.

Nevertheless, Freud made an important discovery. He was the first to maintain that all ritual practices, all mythical implications, have their origins in an actual murder. Freud was unable to exploit the boundless implications of this proposition; in fact, he seemed unaware of the truly vertiginous scope of this idea. After his death, his discovery was summarily dismissed. On the basis of secondary considerations *Totem and Taboo* was written off as misleading or trivial. This attitude can be partially explained by the primary concern of Freud's followers to consolidate the terrain conquered in the previous generation by Freud and others; they found their efforts severely challenged by the implications of *Totem and Taboo*, and so the work was thrust aside. Freud's momentous discovery was ignored as if it had never taken place.

Far from handling his ethnological material like a clumsy amateur, Freud accomplished such a feat of systematization that he himself was thrown off balance. He was unable to formulate the hypothesis that would do justice to his discovery, and no one after him had the vision to perceive that such a thing was even possible. As an advance scout Freud was all too daring, and he found himself cut off from his own line. Freud has been called a victim of naïve historicism; the opposite is true. His general orientation and his methods of research freed him from the fragmentary theories of origin and the antistructural associations that his contemporaries were prone to; at the same time he stayed clear of the opposite excesses, which plague our own era. His mind was not closed to questions of origin; nor did his failures awaken in him any formalistic or antigenetic prejudices. Freud swiftly perceived that a firm grasp of synchronic totalities should result in new concepts regarding the problem of origins, concepts that had previously been wholly unimaginable.

ONE PASSAGE in *Totem and Taboo* is of particular relevance to our inquiry. Freud is discussing tragedy, the tragic mode as it is practiced all over the world:

> A company of individuals, named and dressed alike, surrounded a single figure, all hanging upon his words and deeds; they were the Chorus and the impersonator of the Hero. He was originally the only actor. Later, a second and third actor were added, to play as counterpart to the Hero and as characters split off from him; but the character of the Hero himself and his relation to the Chorus remained unaltered. The Hero of tragedy must suffer; to this day that remains the essence of a tragedy. He has to bear the burden of what was known as "tragic guilt"; the basis of that guilt is not always easy to find, for in the light of our everyday life it is often no guilt at all. As a rule it lay in rebellion against some divine or human authority; and the Chorus accompanied the Hero with feelings of sympathy, sought to hold him back, to warn him and to sober him, and mourned over him when he had met with what was felt as the merited punishment for his rash undertaking.
>
> But why had the Hero of tragedy to suffer? And what was the meaning of this "tragic guilt"? I will cut the discussion short and give a quick reply. He had to suffer because he was the primal father, the Hero of the great primaeval tragedy which was being re-enacted with a tendentious twist; and the tragic guilt was the guilt which he had to take on himself in order to relieve the Chorus from theirs. The scene upon the stage was derived from the historical scene through a process of systematic distortion—one might even say, as the product of a refined hypocrisy. In the remote reality it had actually been the members of the Chorus who caused the Hero's suffering; now, however, they exhausted themselves with sympathy and regret and it was the Hero himself who was responsible for his own sufferings. The crime which was thrown on to his shoulders, presumptuousness and rebelliousness against a great authority, was precisely the crime for which the members of the Chorus, the company of brothers, were responsible. Thus the tragic Hero became, though it might be against his will, the redeemer of the Chorus.[12]

In many respects this passage brings us closer to the concept of the surrogate victim and the mythical structuration effected through it than anything we have yet encountered in Freud. Whole sentences address themselves directly to our discussion. The hero represents the

12 Ibid., p. 155–56.

victim of a momentous and unexpected tragedy. The tragic flaw attributed to him is shared by the whole community, but he alone must bear its burden in order for the city to be saved. The hero thus assumes the role of surrogate victim; and in the very next paragraph Freud alludes to "the divine goat, Dionysus." Tragedy is thus defined as a tendentious reenactment, a mythic inversion of an event that actually took place: "The scene upon the stage was derived from the historical scene through a process of systematic distortion—one might even say, as the product of a refined hypocrisy."

Let me again call attention to what is undoubtedly an essential point: the collective violence directed against the solitary hero takes place amidst that dissolution of distinctions I discussed earlier on. The sons of the primitive clan, henceforth deprived of fathers, have all become "enemy brothers." Their resemblance is such that they do not possess identities of their own. We are left with a group of people *all bearing the same name, identically dressed.*

I must take care, however, not to exaggerate the similarities between Freud's theories and my own. The outlooks are ultimately different; and the difference bears on the genesis of difference. According to Freud, the crowd of doubles stands in opposition to the absolute specificity of the hero. The hero monopolizes innocence; the mob monopolizes guilt. The flaw attributed to the hero is not his, but belongs exclusively to the crowd. The hero, then, is a victim pure and simple, charged with a crime he did not commit. This concept of a simple one-way projection of guilt seems to me inadequate. Sophocles is wiser; he makes it clear (and Dostoevsky was to do the same in *The Brothers Karamazov*) that the surrogate victim, even when falsely accused, may be as guilty as the others. For the traditional concept of the "flaw" (perpetuated as "sin" by theologically minded critics) should be substituted that of violence—violence in the past, the future, and above all in the present, violence equally shared by all. After all, Oedipus himself joined in the manhunt.

The Freudian interpretation is thoroughly modern in its inversion of the mythical content. Thanks to the innocent victim, with whose fate one can easily identify, it becomes possible to inculpate all the false innocents. This is precisely what Voltaire did in his *Oedipe*, and what the contemporary antitheater is striving to do in an atmosphere of ever-increasing confusion and hysteria. Our neighbor's "values" are forever being inverted, to be used as a weapon against him. In the final analysis, however, each and every one of us is implicated in the effort to perpetuate the structures of the myth whose very imbalance is designed to stimulate our own aggression.

Differences seem to have vanished, only to reappear in inverted form, thereby perpetuating themselves. It is these differences that Heidegger refers to in relation to all of philosophy from Plato to Nietzsche; there the identical inversion occurs. Philosophical concepts serve to shield from sight the tragic conflict of human antagonisms. What Freud fails to perceive is that his own thought is influenced by these same patterns and that even his interpretation of tragedy forms part of the conflict and never succeeds in rising above it. Moreover, the fixed nature of his reading corresponds precisely to the concept of the single murder, the murder of a true father, a true hero, which took place at a single moment in time.

The father figure is viewed as an oppressive monster during his life but is transformed at death into a persecuted hero. This operation is effected by the mechanism of the sacred—a mechanism Freud does not uncover, since he remains its victim. In order to escape once and for all from the domination of a certain kind of morality (even meta-morphosed into antimorality) and a certain kind of metaphysic (even disguised as antimetaphysics), we must renounce the gambit of "good" and "bad"—even in its inverted form. We must acknowledge that misapprehensions abound, that violence is to be found everywhere, and that our partial understanding of violence by no means assures us victory over it. The first step must be the hero's reintegration into the chorus, his assumption of the chorus' characteristic lack of characteristics.

It might be argued that Freud adheres more closely to the structure of tragedy in his interpretation than I do, and in one sense this is correct. In the tragic form inherited from myth and ritual the solitary figure of the hero does indeed occupy the dominant central position assigned him by Freud. But that is only the beginning of the analysis; the matter must be pressed to its conclusion, and the tragic form itself, along with the myth, must be scrupulously dismantled. Thus we will learn that Sophocles, while not following through to the end, succeeded nonetheless in advancing farther than Freud along the path of demystification. Sophocles treats the essential elusiveness of the heroic difference with relentless irony, making it plain that the most conspicuous examples of "individuality" are put in doubt at the very moment when they seem strongest and most valid—when, in short, they are brought into violent opposition with another individual who turns out to be almost identical.

My approach incorporates all Freud's observations; it also takes into account those elements that escaped his, but not Sophocles', attention. Finally, it deals with those elements that escaped even Sophocles' notice—with the configurations that give rise to myth and the different perspectives (including the psychoanalytic and the tragic) from which the subject can be viewed. In short, my innovation is to introduce the mechanism of the surrogate victim.

Freud's comments on Greek tragedy are undoubtedly the most profound of all modern pronouncements on the subject. And yet they remain inconclusive.

Strictly speaking, it is not incorrect to qualify tragedy as tendentious, for the tragic element always springs up amidst the ruins of a mythic framework. However, tragedy is the least tendentious of all mythic forms. As we have seen, the aim of tragic inspiration is to reestablish the reciprocity of reprisals, to restore the symmetry of violence; in short, to correct the tendentious aspect. And Freud's approach takes the same line. It reestablishes certain elements of reciprocity, but it does not go so far as tragedy itself goes. The Freudian approach is even more tendentious than tragedy is, because Freud shares the modern inclination to shift all blame for violence onto others. Thus Freud finds himself caught up in the give-and-take of reprisals, in the dual role of model and obstacle, and in the vicious cycle of mimetic desire. That is the fallacy of the modern mind—which, even when it is either too evolved or too knowledgeable to claim immunity from all violent impulses, invariably resorts to an ideal of nonviolence, completely foreign to the Greek mind, as a covertly violent criterion for all judgments and critical evaluations.

Like all biased pronouncements, Freud's strictures on Greek tragedy ultimately turn against their author. Ultimately it is Freud himself who appears guilty of "refined hypocrisy." And the modern critic in his concerted effort to undermine the structure of all religious, moral, and cultural distinctions ultimately brings these distinctions crashing down on his own head. He sets himself up as the prophet of new insights and new ideas, as the sole possessor of an infallible system of analysis—and finds himself condemned to recapitulate all the age-old distinctions of difference: Tiresias *redivivus*!

The quality of tendentiousness is representative of the sacred difference that each faction strives to wrest from the other and that shifts from one side to the other with ever-increasing speed as the rival insights come into contact. It is a quality that perhaps applies to interpretation itself, whether it is an analysis of *Oedipus the King* or a quarrel over psychoanalysis and other modern methodologies. Ostensibly the sole object in dispute is the culture-in-crisis, of which each antagonist flatters himself he is the true champion. Everybody is intent on diagnosing the illness in order to find a cure. But in fact the illness is the *other*, the other with his false diagnoses and poisonous prescriptions. When real responsibilities vanish, the game remains unchanged;

in fact it is all the better for being played without stakes, with each contestant striving to outshine his neighbor rather than trying to shed real light on the supposed object of their concern.

All in all the modern crisis, like all sacrificial crises, can be defined as the elimination of differences. The interplay of antagonisms actually does the eliminating, without ever being recognized for what it truly is: the increasingly feeble, increasingly tragic intervention of an en-feebled difference. This difference appears to be always growing, but it fades away whenever someone tries to appropriate it. Each faction is mystified by the isolated restructurings, increasingly fragile and transi-tory, which lend their support to each of the antagonists in turn. The final degradation of the mythic element takes the form of a prolifera-tion of rival and mutually destructive forms whose relationship to the myth itself is highly ambiguous. These forms are demystifying as well as mythic; that is, they are mythic in the very nature of their demystifi-cation, which is never illusory, to be sure, but is always restricted to the *other* myth. The myths of demystification cling to the great col-lective myth and draw nourishment from it, rather like worms feeding on a corpse.

Greek tragedy, which acknowledges the influence of this process, clearly has more to say about it than does psychoanalysis, which claims immunity from it. Only by studiously ignoring those texts that threaten to undermine their system do psychoanalysts maintain their complacency. Although they concede that artistic beauty is worthy of reverence and awe, they scornfully dismiss the actual work as fanciful, effete, narcotic—the antithesis of hard scientific truth. Critics consider the work of art a passive object that will yield its secrets on command to all adherents of the latest form of absolute knowledge, whatever that form may be.

As far as I can see, this process of mystifying demystification has been fully comprehended by artists, but never by psychoanalysts or sociologists. What is most remarkable is the role played by literary critics. Not infrequently they inveigh against the scientists for what-ever hard-headed insights they may actually have contributed to an understanding of the creative process. Yet at the same time they echo the scientists' belief that "literature" is basically innocuous and ulti-mately meaningless and seem to share their a priori conviction that no work of literature has any direct relation to reality.

We have on occasion observed Sophocles demystifying psycho-analysis, but we shall never see psychoanalysis demystifying Sophocles. In fact, psychoanalytic thought has never really come to grips with Sophocles. Only at his best, as in the case discussed above, does Freud manage to move even parallel to him.

To examine a work of art from the perspective of the surrogate victim and its attendant mechanism is to consider it in terms of collective violence and to attempt to discover what the work omits as much —if not more—as what it includes. That is surely an essential first step in any critical venture. Yet at first glance the task may seem futile; any practical application to literature seems destined to end in broad generalities and esoteric abstractions.

Returning to the text of Freud, however, we find that such is not the case. Here we encounter an omission that is conspicuous, not to say astonishing, if we take the context into account.

In any general discussion of Greek tragedy there is a tendency to refer either implicitly or explicitly to one particular work that exemplifies the genre. This practice was initiated by Aristotle and is still in force today. And when one's name is Sigmund Freud, one has every reason to adhere to the convention.

And yet Freud did not do so. It is, of course, *Oedipus the King* that springs to mind in connection with Freud, and we have ourselves already had recourse to the play; but Freud does not make the slightest allusion to it—neither in the passage I have cited nor in the pages preceding and following it. There are references to Attis, Adonis, Tammuz, Mithra, the Titans, Dionysus, Christianity—in the name of demystification, of course!—but there is no mention of Oedipus as a tragic hero nor any reference to the play about him.

It can be objected that *Oedipus the King* is, after all, only one tragedy among many; nothing obliges Freud to make any specific reference to it. The fact that it is not specifically referred to does not mean that Freud has specifically excluded it. One can just as well conclude that he has simply incorporated this particular tragedy into his total picture of tragedy and thus taken it into consideration.

However, this line of argument is not valid. Once our attention has been drawn to the absence of the archetypal tragedy, details come to mind that suggest that its absence is due neither to chance nor to accident.

On rereading Freud's definition of *tragic guilt*, we realize that it cannot be made applicable to *Oedipus the King*. The hero "has to bear the burden of what was known as 'tragic guilt'; the basis of that guilt is not always easy to find, for in the light of our everyday life it is often no guilt at all." This definition applies to some tragedies—but not to *Oedipus the King*. There is nothing vague or indefinite about the source of Oedipus' guilt, at least not in the eyes of Freud and his followers.

Can it be that Freud did not think of Oedipus at this juncture, that he simply forgot about him—that Oedipus slipped his mind? It is easy to imagine what that voracious pack of neopsychoanalytic blood-hounds, hot on the trail of *Totem and Taboo*, will deduce from such a lapse or "slip." Far from seeing in *Totem and Taboo* a classic example, in conformity with the usual diagnostic pattern, of the return of a repressed subject, they will undoubtedly recognize here the ultimate example of extreme repression—Oedipus's surprising and momentous journey to the innermost recesses of the Freudian unconscious.

The Freud of *Totem and Taboo*, then, is in such a state that he has repressed all references to Oedipus. Such a proposition is truly mind-boggling!

Fortunately, another possibility presents itself. In the passage just quoted there occurs a modest qualifier that may be of importance. "In the light of our everyday life," Freud cautions us, tragic guilt "is often no guilt at all." The word "often" serves to warn us that the assertion is not invariably valid; it admits the possibility of exceptional tragedies, or at the very least of one exceptional tragedy. That admission seems relevant here. In at least one tragedy, Freud is saying, there is a case of tragic guilt that would be readily accepted as such in everyday existence: it involves patricide and incest. This modifying "often" is explicit; it cannot be interpreted as ignoring Oedipus. In fact, there is reason to believe that it was inserted specifically with Oedipus in mind.

Throughout *Totem and Taboo* Oedipus is conspicuous by his absence. The omission is not a natural or an unconscious one; it is wholly conscious and deliberate. We do not have to do with Freud's complexes here, but with his conscious motives—which, it should be said, are a good deal more varied and interesting than his complexes. We must ask ourselves why Freud has suddenly made Oedipus the object of a systematic act of exclusion.

If we examine this exclusion not only in its immediate context but in that of the work itself, it seems even more troubling. For what after all is the subject of *Totem and Taboo*? Is Freud not dealing with the father, the father of the primitive tribe who was destined to be murdered? Freud's subject is patricide—the very crime Freud believed he had discovered at the heart of Greek tragedy, a crime projected by the criminals onto their victims. Certainly, it is the very crime that first Tiresias and then all of Thebes attributed to the unfortunate Oedipus. It would be hard to imagine a more economical and more telling argument in favor of the theory of tragedy advanced in *Totem and Taboo* than a simple comparison of this theory with the content of *Oedipus the King*. And yet Freud says not a word about the play. It is all we can do to keep from tugging at the sleeve of the celebrated inventor of the *Oedipuskomplex*, to remind him that there exists a tragedy that deals precisely with the subject of patricide.

Why did Freud choose to dispense with this striking example? There is only one answer: he could not use *Oedipus the King* in an interpretation that linked tragedy to an actual case of patricide without undermining his other, standard interpretation, the official psychoanalytic interpretation, which presents *Oedipus the King* as a simple reflection of unconscious desires that formally excludes any execution of these desires. Oedipus here appears in a strange relationship to his own complex. As a primordial father-figure, he has no father of his own and thus can scarcely be said to have any complexes regarding his paternity.

On a broader and more general plane, we cannot view Oedipus's crimes in their true light, observe patricide and incest in a context that includes phenomena of the "scapegoat" variety, no matter how dimly they may appear, without giving rise to questions that challenge the very basis of psychoanalytic thought.

A question mark cropped up in Freud's work, and because he had no answer at hand he chose to ignore it. A more prudent author would have simply suppressed all the passages in *Totem and Taboo* relating to tragedy. Fortunately, prudence was not one of Freud's characteristics. It is the richness of his ideas, their intuitive interest that Freud savored; he therefore decided to preserve them all, while carefully sidestepping any embarrassing allusions to *Oedipus the King*.

Freud's censorship of the Oedipus references was not exercised in any psychoanalytic sense, but as an act of censorship pure and simple. That is not to say, however, that his intention was to deceive. Freud was fully confident that given time he would be able to answer all questions without violating the basic premises of psychoanalysis; but, as always, he was in a hurry. He therefore put the question aside for future consideration, without realizing that the answer would never be forthcoming.

If Freud had attempted to resolve the contradiction he would probably have realized that neither his first nor his second reading of *Oedipus the King* had succeeded in coming to grips either with the Oedipus myth or with tragedy as a whole. Neither repressed desire nor an actual act of patricide are really satisfactory answers, and the obstinate duality of Freud's theories, both here and throughout his work, suggests that a certain distortion has taken place. In avoiding the true problem Freud turned away from what was potentially the most profitable line of inquiry, one that might finally have led him to the surrogate victim. Behind Freud's exclusion of Oedipus from *Totem and Taboo*, an initial act that constitutes a deliberate tactical maneuver, it is possible to perceive a second, inadvertent and unconscious act of exclusion that in fact determines the structure of the whole work. Here again psychoanalysis offers no explanation. And there is no point in asking psychoanalysis to explain an exclusion which, among other things, lays the groundwork for psychoanalysis itself.

The parentheses around *Oedipus the King* constitute a sort of critical hiatus, a protective barrier surrounding the theory of psychoanalysis. Earlier we had a glimpse of the same process operating in connection with mimetic desire; there too it was a question of defending the Oedipus complex from possible attack. In the hierarchy of Freudian themes this complex maintains a priveleged position that defines Freud's historical limitations as a thinker. It represents the point beyond which deconstruction of the myth cannot go.

We find, too, the same contrast between Freud and his successors as we did in the case of mimetic desire. Freud attempted to isolate and neutralize the insights that threatened to contaminate the purity of his doctrine, but he was too gifted and too vital to reject them entirely, and he had too great a love for intellectual exploration to suppress his most adventurous observations. His followers, however, did not share this boldness. They set out to eliminate all incongruities from his work, and their censorship extended to the vital issue of mimetic desire on the one hand, and on the other, to all of *Totem and Taboo*. The passages on tragedy seem never to have exerted any influence; even the most devoutly Freudian of literary critics has failed to make use of them. And yet it is these passages alone that contain Freud's most striking literary insight.

If the great advance of *Totem and Taboo* is also a kind of detour and the work seems to end in an impasse, this is due to the heavy burden of psychoanalytic dogma with which the author approaches his text. Naturally he is unwilling to relinquish this burden, which he has come to regard as his most precious possession. The major obstacle is the theme of the father. By transforming the crucial revelation of collective murder into an act of patricide, the paternal theme provides Freud's psychoanalytic adversaries, and others, with the very arguments they need to discredit his theory. It is the paternal theme that skews Freud's interpretation of tragedy, preventing him from settling the problem of incest interdiction in a wholly satisfactory manner.

As we have seen, the intrusion of the collective murder into *Totem and Taboo* fails to answer the problems raised by the incest interdictions and can even be said to stand in the way of their solution. It breaks the continuity between the sexual monopoly of the awesome father figure and the historical strength of the interdictions. In an initial effort to restore this continuity Freud resorts to a piece of juggling which, however, fails of its effect:

> What up to then had been prevented by his [the father's] actual existence was thenceforward prohibited by the sons themselves, in accordance with the psychological procedure so familiar to us in psycho-analysis under the name of "deferred obedience." They revoked their deed by forbidding the killing of the totem, the substitute for their father; and they renounced its fruits by resigning their claim to the women who had now been set free. They thus created out of their filial sense of guilt the two fundamental taboos of totemism, which for that very reason inevitably corresponded to the two repressed wishes of the Oedipus complex.[13]

Freud shows that he recognizes the fragility of this argument by immediately introducing a supplementary proof. As is so often the case with this ingenious but hasty thinker, these new arguments are not only additional supports for the old ones, but they constitute a wholly fresh theory that surreptitiously challenges certain fundamental assumptions of psychoanalysis:

> The prohibition of incest . . . has a powerful practical basis as well. Sexual desires do not unite men but divide them. Though the brothers had banded together in order to overcome their father, they were all one another's rivals in regard to the women. Each of them would have wished, like his father, to have all the women to himself. The new organization would have collapsed in a struggle of all against all, for none of them was of such overmastering strength as to be able to take on his father's part with success. Thus the brothers had no alternative, if they were to live together, but—not, perhaps, until they had passed through many dangerous crises—to institute the law against incest, by which they all alike renounced the women whom they desired and who had been their chief motive for dispatching their father.[14]

In the first quotation the father has been dead only a short time and his memory pervades everything. In the second his death has receded in time; we might almost say that it is repeated afresh, this time in Freud's imagination. Freud sees himself following the avatars of the clan, *after* the act of collective murder, proceeding through time step by step. In fact he is gradually disengaging himself from the confines of modern family life that have held him prisoner. All family relation-

13 Ibid., p. 143.
14 Ibid., p. 144.

ships blur and fade away. For instance, it is no longer possible to determine the degree of concupiscence by the closeness of the blood tie. All the women are now on the same level: "Each of them would have wished, like his father, to have all the women to himself." "Mothers" and "sisters" become a cause of rivalry not because they are intrinsically more desirable but simply because they happen to be at hand. Desire no longer seeks out a priveleged object.

Although this rivalry is initially sexual, it eventually attains a scope and intensity that is hardly justified by sexual appetite alone. Freud himself makes that clear. No one can hope to emulate the great feats of the father, "for none of them was of such overmastering strength as to be able to take on his father's part with success." There are a thousand pretexts for such a rivalry, because in the last analysis its sole object is the attainment of sovereign violence. On one side there are only the women, and on the other the men, who are unable to divide the women among themselves. The situation described by Freud has supposedly arisen because of the death of the dominant father, but now everything takes place *as if the father had never existed.* The emphasis has shifted to the *enemy brothers*, who are virtually indistinguishable from one another; and we now find ourselves caught up in the familiar process of reciprocal violence, confronting the symmetrical patterns of the sacrificial crisis.

Freud here approaches the ultimate cause of the incest taboo, as he moves away from his habitual psychoanalytical themes. That is the way of tragedy itself, the way of indifferentiation that Freud, as we have seen, brings into *Totem and Taboo* with his description of the chorus of enemy brothers: "A crowd of people all with the same name and similarly attired."

The interdiction is no longer presented as a consequence of a "psychological procedure so familiar to us in psychoanalysis," but of the urgent necessity of preventing a "struggle of all against all" that would bring about the collapse of the society. We are now dealing with a concrete fact: "Sexual desires do not unite men, but divide them."

Freud does not make the slightest allusion to his initial theory. Without seeming even to realize it, he is clearing the scene of complexes and fantasies to make way for *real functions*, which will now provide the basis for the interdictions. Freud, who contributed to so much of the confusion and misunderstanding concerning the nature of religion, became in *Totem and Taboo* the first to proclaim the true function of incest interdictions. And he was also the first to turn his back on his own revelations.

THE SECOND THEORY is superior to the first in its explanation of the function of the prohibitions. In discussing the origin of these prohibitions, it asserts that the brothers eventually come to an amicable agreement concerning their mutual renunciation of the women.

However, the absolute character of the prohibition excludes the possibility that it might originate in a negotiated peace. If the men were indeed capable of arriving at some sort of mutual agreement, it is certain that all the women would not have fallen under the same irrevocable taboo. Some sort of division of the goods would surely have been arranged.

Freud suspected that in such circumstances violence was bound to triumph. That was why he referred to the "serious dissensions" that would inevitably precede the final agreement and the forceful arguments that were meant to bring home to the warring brothers the gravity of their situation. If violence is unleashed, prohibitions become indispensable, for without them human society would vanish. Yet is there any reason why human society should not vanish? Freud says nothing that makes a reconciliation necessary, or even possible—a reconciliation that must be brought about by means of a prohibition as "irrational" and "affective" (to use Freud's terms) as the prohibition concerning incest. An antiincestuous social contract is hardly a convincing proposition, and the theory that had such a promising beginning falters at its conclusion.

Although Freud's second theory marks an advance on the first in its explanation of the function of prohibitions, it is less satisfactory than the first in regard to origins. The true outcome was to have eluded the brothers; it eluded Freud instead.

I have attempted to follow step by step the path that led from the first theory to the second. In so doing I have focused on the dynamics of a line of thought that is ridding itself, little by little, of all cultural and family ties. It is now clear that this line of thought never achieves its goal. The second incest theory follows the same pattern as the passages on tragedy. Both brothers and women are reduced to the anonymity of complete equality, but the father retains his separateness. Because he is dead, he is immune from the operation of indifferentiation. He is the only one who does not relinquish his family role in the course of the proceedings; and unfortunately his is the crucial role. Freud manages to "defilialize" the sons, but he goes no further. The line of thought that breaks off here needs to be drawn out to its conclusion: the father has to be "depaternalized."

To pursue Freud's train of thought to a conclusion does not involve rejecting the role of the murder, whose importance is confirmed by ample ethnological evidence. Rather, it involves rejecting the role of the father, transcending the family framework and the dogma of psychoanalysis.

The overbearing presence of the father figure intervenes constantly, concealing the mechanism of religion and preventing Freud from articulating the true character of the sacrificial rites, festivals, and all the other evidence. Every sentence that begins, "Psychoanalysis demonstrates . . ." or "Psychoanalysis has revealed . . ." invariably evades the true explanation. "Psychoanalysis has revealed that the totem animal is in reality a substitute for the father; and this tallies with the contradictory fact that, though the killing of the animal is as a rule forbidden, yet its killing is a festive occasion—with the fact that it is killed and not mourned."[15]

In fact the father explains nothing. If we hope to get to the root of the matter we must put the father out of our minds and concentrate on the fact that the enormous impression made on the community by the collective murder is not due to the victim's identity per se, but to his role as unifying agent. In other words, this impression derives from the wave of unanimity reestablished by the victim's presence and directed against the victim. It is this conjunction of "by" and "against" that explains the apparent contradictions of the religious practices, the constant need to repeat the killing even though the victim is divine—indeed, *because* it is divine.

It is not the theme of collective murder that constitutes the weakness of *Totem and Taboo*, but the mass of psychoanalytical material that obscures that theme. If only Freud had shifted his attention away from the arguments that precede the murder and that he hoped would provide a motivation for it; if only he had been willing to jettison his psychoanalytic explanations, then he would have seen that the violence occurs without reason, that the murder has no meaning outside itself.

Once the murder has been stripped of its associations with the father figure the reason for its tremendous impact on the community becomes plain, as does the secret of its success, of its ritual repetitions and the double judgment that invariably accompanies it. To understand all this is to realize that the conclusion to the second theory, which the enemy brothers are vainly trying to reach, has already been found by Freud, and indeed constitutes his main theme: anything that prevents the act of murder from becoming merely an unalloyed operation of the surrogate victim also prevents it from taking place at its truly appropriate time, at the end—not the beginning—of the sacrificial crisis.

[15] Ibid., p. 141.

Only the surrogate victim is capable of bringing the inconclusive second theory to a conclusion; only its intervention can put an end to the violence and effect a union of the two incest theories. Instead of serving as a futile and even obstructive prologue to the crisis of the brothers, the murder can play a crucial role at the end, providing the resolution to the crisis outlined by Freud himself and a point of departure for the cultural order. Indeed, that murder must be the ultimate source of all incest prohibitions.

~✑✍ UP TO THIS POINT I have limited my examination of incest prohibitions to the context of *Totem and Taboo*. My reading of the work has led me to suppose that the roots of these prohibitions, as of many other facets of the cultural order, are embedded in generative violence. Freud was the first to link the problem of prohibitions to that of sacrifice and the first who sought to resolve the two problems by means of the collective murder. If Freud's explanation of sacrifice must be adjusted in favor of the surrogate victim, then we must assume that the same will apply to his account of incest prohibitions. But before I embark on this question I would like to make it clear that even though this adjustment may favor my own line of enquiry, it does no violence to the basic premises of Freud's study. It introduces no elements not already contained therein and, in fact, owes its origins to the inherent dynamism and suggestiveness of Freud's work.

Let us briefly recall the role played by the primitive horde in *Totem and Taboo*. Darwin's hypothesis offers a clear-cut explanation of the incest prohibitions, and it is obvious that Freud's initial attraction to the hypothesis stems from this fact. The hypothesis appears in the course of an initial discussion of exogamy. The second important hypothesis of *Totem and Taboo*—this one wholly Freud's—concerns collective murder and must have been formulated somewhat later as a result of Freud's readings in ethnology. Initially, then, the two hypotheses are independent of one another. Darwin makes no mention of the collective murder; on the other hand, there is nothing relating to Darwin's theory of the primitive horde in the ethnological material that suggested the theme of the collective murder.

Freud attempted to wed the two theories, and the result was a mixture of history and prehistory whose arbitrary quality has frequently been noted. Equally dubious is Freud's claim to have extracted from cultural documents of relatively recent date material pertaining to an event supposedly unique and situated in a fabulous and distant past.

Freud's argument not only fails to carry conviction but also contributes nothing to the insights that form the true substance of the work. If Freud took up the primitive horde theory because of the possibilities it offered for dealing with the problem of prohibitions, it is hard to see why he did not renounce it once the murder concept, by breaking the link between the sexual privilege of the primordial father and the prohibitions, had for all practical purposes eliminated these possibilities.

Again, if Freud meant to develop his murder theory he had no reason to cling to the horde, which is hindered rather than helped by the concept of the murder. Ultimately the two theories are incompatible, and one must choose between them. Because the best part of *Totem and Taboo* is devoted to a presentation of the murder theory and a demonstration that the murder is the consequence of all the religious and ethnological· data at our disposal, it is natural to assume that ultimately Freud would have opted for the murder theory. Moreover, the horde is irrelevant here; its initial usefulness seems to have been dissipated.

However, Freud made no such choice. He kept the murder and declined to renounce the horde, never realizing that the horde had now lost its raison d'être. The reason for this lapsus is clear: the horde theory refers the collective murder to the sphere of the father figure. Consequently, the precious axioms of psychoanalysis are preserved. The primitive horde is a perfect materialization of the psychoanalystic myth. Once again we brush against invisible barriers beyond which Freud's logic never ventures.

Here again Freud's successors seem to emphasize the regressive aspect of his thought. The "murdered father" theory of *Totem and Taboo* is clearly indefensible, but the vulnerable element is not the "murder" but the "father." And although the arguments of Freud's successors have some merit if taken literally, we cannot respect their rejection of the work as a whole. While purporting to attack the weaknesses of Freud's concept they are in fact seeking to suppress its strengths. It is at once paradoxical and highly significant that Freud's heirs—his sons, so to speak—should draw on one of their "father's" principal weaknesses, that timidity that they themselves share, in order to purge his doctrine of all elements that are foreign to their own way of thinking. Yet it is precisely those elements that constitute the truly important and innovative aspect of *Totem and Taboo*. When the effort is made to separate true from false, the false is invariably paraded as the true. The error lies in the concept of the father and the application of psychoanalysis; the truth lies in the concept of the collective murder and, strange as it may seem, in Freud's ethnology. A fresh and constructive reading of the work should lead us to reject almost all the elements that psychoanalysts recognize as valid and to acknowledge the validity of those very elements that psychoanalysts reject.

In the course of this investigation it has become clear that *Totem and Taboo* is more compatible with the theory of the surrogate victim as the foundation of culture than is any other modern work. Thus, in spite of the manifold difficulties created by the impossibilities in the Freudian theory—impossibilities that had hitherto discredited it—we were able to acknowledge a great insight in *Totem and Taboo*.

The overlapping of theories in Freud's work, their profusion and multiplicity, can only be interpreted as a sign of failure. As soon as the surrogate victim is introduced into the picture, the scattered fragments of Freud's speculations come together like pieces in a puzzle. In their fragmentary state the Freudian analyses have little to tell us, but when once they have been drawn together by means of the surrogate victim their impact appears momentous, and it can hardly be claimed that this new unity was imposed from the outside. We have only to cease regarding Freud's thought in terms of infallible dogma to see that he was always fundamentally concerned with the operation of the surrogate victim, and was constantly, though hesitatingly, attempting to come to terms with that question.

I could easily extend my demonstration to other works of Freud. These works should be analyzed in the same manner as we analyze rites. For any cultural interpretation is ultimately only another form of rite; as such, it stems from the operation of the surrogate victim and can be fully systematized and analyzed only in its light.

The comparative approach should yield the common denominator of those works of Freud that complement without ever quite repeating or duplicating each other. The many different elements that make up these related texts obscure their fundamental unity; yet that unity lies near at hand.

Freud's *Moses and Monotheism* seems to complement *Totem and Taboo* in many respects. Just as in *Totem and Taboo* we encounter, prior to the murder, a father and son—that is, a family—so in *Moses and Monotheism* we encounter, prior to the murder, the story of Moses and the Mosaic religion—that is, society. Moses plays a role similar to that of the primordial father. And the Hebrew people, deprived of their prophet by Moses' death, resemble the group of brothers deprived of their father after the murder described in *Totem and Taboo*.

Once again, all the possible implications of the act of collective violence can be set forth in advance. If we deduct all those that pertain exclusively to *Totem and Taboo* on the one hand, and on the other, all those with relevance only to *Moses and Monotheism* (that is, the implications for the family in the former work, and for the people, the nation and the Jewish religion in the latter work), we find that we are

left with a single common denominator: the metamorphosis of reciprocal violence into generative violence by means of the murder of
somebody, no matter whom—a figure chosen, as it were, at random.

Similarly, in order to bring about a synthesis of the two Freudian
theories on the origin of incest prohibitions, the collective murder
must be taken out of the familial framework of the first theory and
incorporated into the societal framework of the second theory.

My own theories are based upon this operation of double synthesis.
In fact, their primary concern is that point where all the Freudian
interpretations examined here begin to converge. No sooner does the
generative violence make its appearance, caught up in the Freudian
dynamics, than we begin to anticipate the slight modifications that
permit it to assume its function as a universal bond—a function that in
turn derives from its role as a universal structural support.

We are not indulging in impressionistic literary criticism, but in
objective research. The fact that we can proceed further than Freud
down a path of his own choosing offers us valuable insight into his
work. It becomes possible to finish phrases left dangling by the author,
to determine why and when his thought went astray; in short, to place
him precisely. In his *Essay on Psychoanalysis* Freud comes as close to
the concept of mimetic desire as he does to that of generative violence
in *Totem and Taboo* and *Moses and Monotheism*. In each instance the
distance from the objective is the same, as is the margin of error; the
basic standpoint remains unchanged.

Desire, for most modern thinkers, is anchored in an object. In order
to perceive the implications of an infinitely mobile mimesis we must
realize that the boundless potentiality of violence can only be contained by the operation of the surrogate victim. After all, we cannot
postulate the existence in man of a desire radically disruptive of human
relations without simultaneously postulating the means of keeping this
desire in check. To free ourselves forever from the illusions of humanism there is only one requirement, which happens to be the very one
that modern men refuse to meet: we must acknowledge mankind's
thorough dependence on religion. This, it is plain, Freud was not inclined to do. He was not alone in his subservience to an increasingly
enfeebled humanist ideal; he had no notion of the intellectual revolution for which he was paving the way.

HOW ARE WE TO IMAGINE the birth of cultural
prohibitions? It must be thought of concurrently with all other cultural births. The divine epiphany, the universal upsurge of the monstrous double engulfs the community and simultaneously makes its
presence felt at all points of conflict. It passes between the "enemy

brothers," who fall back thunderstruck. Whatever the pretext for the conflict may have been—food, weapons, land, women—the antagonists suspend their struggle, now and forever. Henceforth everything touched by the sacred violence belongs to the gods; as such, it becomes the object of a most solemn prohibition.

The antagonists have been sobered and thoroughly frightened. From now on they will do everything possible to keep from relapsing into reciprocal violence. Moreover, divine anger has taught them that preventive measures are necessary. Wherever violence occurs, a prohibition is proclaimed.

The sentence weighs on all the women who figured as prizes in the rivalry; that is, on all women who live within a group—not because they are intrinsically more desirable, but because they are near at hand and therefore likely objects of rivalry. The prohibition always covers the closest instances of consanguinity, but its outer limits are not necessarily confined to blood relations.

Both the principle of prohibition and the forms it takes are not without their practical uses. It would be untrue to say that they were designed to deal with an imaginary situation; on the contrary, they serve to prevent people from being caught up in violent mimesis. As we saw in the previous chapter, the prohibitions of primitive peoples display a knowledge of violence and its ways that surpasses our modern comprehension. The reason is clear: the prohibitions were dictated by violence itself, by the violent manifestations of a previous crisis, and they are fixed in place as a bulwark against similar outbursts. If the prohibitions seem evenly matched with the violence they are directed against, that is because in the final analysis the two are one and the same. That explains why in times of crisis the prohibitions ultimately contribute to the very violence they are designed to suppress. Like any other form of sacrificial prophylaxis, prohibitions can on occasion turn against their users.

All the evidence seems to confirm the proposal, set forth at the outset of this work, that sexuality is part of the larger problem of violence and the sacred. Sexual prohibitions, like all other prohibitions, are sacrificial in nature; and all legitimate sexuality is sacrificial. Strictly speaking, between members of the same community, legitimate sexuality exists no more than legitimate violence in the community. The prohibitions involving incest and those directed against murder or ritual killing among members of the same community have a common origin and function. That is why they resemble one another and why in many cases, as Robertson Smith has pointed out, they cover exactly the same ground.

Like blood sacrifice, legitimate sexuality (that of matrimonial unions) never chooses its "victims" among those who live together. The regulations governing marriage resemble the regulations governing the choice of sacrificial victims. All these regulations serve to endow both sexuality and violence with the same centrifugal force. In many instances the sacrificial deviations of sexuality and violence are virtually indistinguishable. Marriage vows can be duly attended by ritualized violence, analogous to other forms of ritual warfare. This systematized violence resembles the endless cycle of revenge that might well rage inside if there were no substitute for it outside the community, and the reciprocal exchange of violence with outsiders is one with the exchange of women that provides men with sexual objects from outside the community. The problem is always the same: violence is both the disease (inside) and the cure (outside). Violence, like sexual desire, must be forbidden wherever its presence is incompatible with communal existence.

Even today, legitimized sexuality in the West reveals traces of its sacrificial character. The sexual relation of husband and wife is the central and fundamental issue of family life. After all, it is the origin of family life—and yet it is kept out of sight and plays no part, strictly speaking, in family life. As far as the closest relatives, particularly the children, are concerned, the sexual relation of husband and wife does not exist. It is sometimes as thoroughly hidden as that most secret sort of violence, generative violence itself. Psychoanalysis is wrong I believe to attribute to young children a knowledge of parental sexuality.

Surrounding this legitimized sexuality is a vast expanse of forbidden territory defined by the whole gamut of sexual prohibitions. Within this territory all sexual activity, sexual allusions, and erotic stimulants are forbidden. So within the immediate environs of the temple, and in the area surrounding the place of sacrifice, any form of violence is strictly forbidden. Beneficial and life-giving, but also dangerous, regulated sexual violence (like ritual murder) is surrounded by a veritable buffer zone. If it were granted free rein to propagate itself within the community, it would become evil and destructive.

Primitive societies are generally more hemmed in by prohibitions than Western society has ever been. However, many of them are unfamiliar with some of our own particular prohibitions. We must take care not to interpret the relative liberty of these primitive peoples as presenting an ideological contrast, as standing in direct opposition to the "repression" characteristic of our own society, especially and most notoriously in the sexual realm. The vast importance attributed to sexuality by humanists and naturalists is, after all, a modern and Western phenomenon. In primitive societies wherever sexual activity is neither legitimized (that is, seen as ritual either in a strict or a broad sense) nor prohibited, it seems to be regarded as a matter of little or no importance; in other words, it is too trivial to provoke internal violence. This is the case in certain societies with regard to the sexual activities of children and unmarried adolescents, or with regard to sexual dealings with foreigners as well as, naturally, the sexual activities among foreigners.

Prohibitions serve a basic function. They maintain a sort of sanctuary at the heart of the community, an area where that minimum of nonviolence essential to the survival of the children and the community's cultural heritage—essential, in short, to everything that sustains man's humanity—is jealously preserved. If prohibitions capable of performing this function actually exist, one can hardly attribute them to the beneficence of Nature (that good angel of complacent humanism, the last relic of those optimistic theologies engendered by the deterioration of historical Christianity). It should now be apparent that humanity's very existence is due primarily to the operation of the surrogate victim. We know that animals possess individual braking mechanisms against violence; animals of the same species never fight to the death, but the victor spares the life of the vanquished. Mankind lacks this protection. Our substitution for the biological mechanism of the animals is the collective, cultural mechanism of the surrogate victim. There is no society without religion because without religion society cannot exist.

Ethnologists should long since have drawn on their cumulative evidence to explain the function of these prohibitions and even to discover their origins. The act of violence performed in the course of a rite or a festival points the way clearly enough, for it hinges on sacrificial practices or on "totemic" ceremonies. And if we also examine the disastrous, or merely disturbing, consequences attributed to nonritualized violations, we see that they always boil down to half-mythical, half-real manifestations of the sacrificial crisis. Thus what motivates prohibition is the fear of violence. Just because this violence can be disguised behind a contagious illness, a drought, or a flood, we do not have the right to dismiss this fear as "superstition." Modern philosophers invariably choose as representative the most "irrational" and bizarre (at any rate to modern eyes) aspects of religious prohibitions. Thus they manage to convince themselves that religion has no connection with reality.

This misconception cannot prevail much longer. The real function of prohibition was brought to light by Freud; and although it was almost immediately discarded by him, it has recently been reformulated with great precision by Georges Bataille. To be sure, Bataille is primarily inclined to treat violence in terms of some rare and precious condiment, the only spice still capable of stimulating the jaded appetite of modern man. Yet on occasion Bataille is able to transcend the decadent estheticism he has so fervently espoused, and explain quite simply that "the prohibition eliminates violence, and our violent impulses (including those resulting from our sexual drives) destroy our inner calm, without which human consciousness cannot exist."[16]

[16] Georges Bataille, *L'Erotisme* (Paris, 1965), p. 43.

ᏜᎧᎦᎶᏜ Chapter Nine

Lévi-Strauss, Structuralism, and Marriage Laws

ᏜᎧᎦᎶᏜ THE UNIT OF STRUCTURE from which a kinship system is built up is the group which I call an "elementary family," consisting of a man and his wife with their child or children. The existence of the elementary family creates three special kinds of social relationships: that between parent and child, that between children of the same parents (siblings), and that between husband and wife as parents of the same child or children. . . . The three relationships that exist within the elementary family constitute what I call the first order. Relationships of the second order are those which depend on the connection of two elementary families through a common member, and are such as father's father, mother's brother, wife's sister, and so on. In the third order are such as father's brother's son and mother's brother's wife. Thus we can trace, if we have the genealogical information, relationships of the fourth, fifth or nth order.[1]

In outlining the basic premises of his own research, A. R. Radcliffe-Brown sets forth the principles that prevailed in the study of kinship before Lévi-Strauss arrived on the scene. In an article entitled "Structural Analysis in Linguistics and in Anthropology,"[2] Lévi-Strauss quotes the above passage as the counter position to his own methodology, which was to set the pattern for structuralist studies of kinship.

According to Lévi-Strauss, the elementary family is based on marriage and is therefore not an irreducible unit. Far from being elementary, it is by definition composite. It is to be regarded as an end point rather than a point of departure, the result of an exchange between two groups that share no biological affiliations. "Kinship is allowed to establish and perpetuate itself only through specific forms of marriage. In other words, the relationships which Radcliffe-Brown calls 'relation-

---

[1] A. R. Radcliffe-Brown, "The Study of Kinship Systems," *Journal of the Royal Anthropological Institute* 71 (1941):2.
[2] Claude Lévi-Strauss, *Structural Anthropology*, trans. Claire Jacobson and Brooke Grundfest (New York, 1963), 1–54.

ships of the first order' are a function of, and depend on, those which he considers secondary and derived. The essence of human kinship is to require the establishment of relations among what Radcliffe-Brown calls 'elementary families.' Thus, it is not the families (isolated terms) which are truly 'elementary,' but, rather, the relations between those terms."[3]

We must be wary of "common sense," which never loses sight of the actual biological relationship linking Radcliffe-Brown's "elementary family" and which refuses to regard the system as a system: "Of course, the biological family is ubiquitous in human society. But what confers upon kinship its socio-cultural character is not what it retains from nature, but, rather, the essential way in which it diverges from nature. A kinship system does not consist in the objective ties of descent or consanguinity between individuals. It exists only in human consciousness; it is an arbitrary system of representations, not the spontaneous development of a real situation."[4]

The arbitrary element is assimilated to what has been called here the "symbolic" character of the system. Two entities—in this case, two individuals—are brought together not by necessity, but by symbolic thought; two cross-cousins, let us say, are joined in marriage, and the circumstances that "necessitated" the marriage can be attributed to social convention rather than to any real need. The fact that a type of marriage permitted or even required in one society is formally forbidden in another makes this point clear.

Are we therefore to conclude that kinship systems in general are essentially unnatural? As the last quotation from Lévi-Strauss demonstrates, his pronouncements on this question are more cautious and more finely shaded than some of his critics have led us to believe. After explaining that the kinship system is not "the spontaneous development of a real situation," he remarks that "this certainly does not mean that the real situation is automatically contradicted, or that it is to be simply ignored. Radcliffe-Brown has shown, in studies that are now classic, that even systems which are apparently extremely rigid and artificial, such as the Australian systems of marriage-classes, take biological parenthood carefully into account."[5]

The point seems clear enough in this context. Yet it is the very point that could be misinterpreted in different circumstances through a hasty or overzealous application of Lévi-Strauss's own discoveries.

Lévi-Strauss's homage to Radcliffe-Brown, whose views he had convincingly refuted a few lines further back, is no mere formality.

[3] Ibid., p. 50.
[4] Ibid.
[5] Ibid.

But there is reason to question whether Lévi-Strauss's acknowledgment deals adequately with the issue. Kinship systems, we are informed, even those "which are apparently extremely rigid and artificial . . . take biological parenthood carefully into account." That is certainly true— as far as it goes. There is, however, a good deal more to be said.

Men can "take into account" only those concepts that are already accessible to their understanding. The phrase implies that the concept of biological kinship exists outside the kinship system; that is, outside culture. This notion strikes me as inconceivable. We must take care not to confuse two distinct realities: (1) the *fact* of biological kinship, the actual process of human reproduction; and (2) an *understanding* of these same procedures, a recognition of the functioning of generation and consanguinity. It is obvious that men must always behave according to the first reality, insofar as they cannot reproduce themselves by any other means than those prescribed by the laws of biology. This is as true for men living within a "culture" as for those who might live in a "state of nature," where promiscuity would be the rule. As for the second reality, however, that is a very different matter, for if sexual promiscuity prevailed, the conditions would not exist that make possible the discovery of biological laws.

It might be objected that I am drifting into abstractions. On the contrary; my purpose is to expose a speculative assumption, tacitly accepted and wholly without basis, that is part and parcel of the modern naturalist myth—the belief that a particular affinity exists between the "state of nature" and biological truth or even scientific truth in general.

There is, then, no difference between nature and culture in regard to the mere biological facts of human reproduction. In regard to the understanding of these facts, however, a difference assuredly exists, and it is to the detriment of nature. In order to appreciate the truth of this statement we need only consider what happens to a litter of cats left to breed at random. The result inevitably is a hopelessly tangled network of marriage alliances, blood relationships, and inlaw relationships that would confound even the most assiduous student of "elementary" (or, as we would say, "nuclear") families.

No matter how bewildering such a spectacle might be, it would not rid us of the conviction that the three types of family relationships described by Radcliffe-Brown are indeed distinct and do exist. Even our most advanced thinkers cannot persuade us that the distinction between father and son, brother and sister, and mother and daughter are mere figments of our deluded senses or the products of some deep-rooted obsession fostered in our imaginations by a repressive cultural order. Once the facts regarding reproduction have been established, it is impossible to understand how they could ever have been misunderstood.

It should now be apparent that the establishment of basic biological facts requires the *formal* recognition of the three distinct relationships —marriage, direct descent, and consanguinity—defined by Radcliffe-Brown; and that this formal recognition is dependent on a real separation—that is, it is based on incest prohibitions and kinship systems.

Kinship systems, then, are essential to the ordering of biological data. There is no kinship system, no matter how rigid and artificial, that will not serve this function. As Lévi-Strauss has observed, the common basis of all kinship systems is the recognition of a firm distinction between marriage and consanguinity.

Although kinship systems vary greatly in scope, their premises remain the same: marriage is always forbidden between parents and children and between brothers and sisters. The exceptions to this pattern are so rare and so special (usually having to do with ritual) that for all practical purposes they can be regarded as exceptions that prove the rule. No matter how harsh and excessive certain marriage ordinances may appear, no matter how arbitrary and extreme their accompanying prohibitions (the reverse aspect of these rules) may seem, the basis of the system remains stable and comprehensible. Every kinship system defines the licit and the illicit in sexual matters so as to exclude from the reproductive process those sharing a parent-child or brother-sister relationship. Therefore, all those who submit to its governance are obliged to acknowledge the basic facts of human reproduction.

There is reason to believe that in the state of natural promiscuity the connection between the sexual act and the birth of children (or even, perhaps, the very idea of conception) would go unrecognized. Only through the establishment of incest prohibitions could man hope to obtain the quasi-experimental conditions necessary to the recognition of the reproductive process. Only through incest prohibitions could man introduce into his sexual life the stabilizing elements and systematic exclusions without which the relevant linkages and comparisons could not be made. Prohibitions, then, serve as a necessary controlling factor, permitting man to recognize the results of sexual activity through comparison with the sterility of abstinence.

Of course it is impossible to reconstruct the historical chain of events. But that is not my concern here. My sole purpose is to carry the Lévi-Straussian critique of the nuclear family a little further than Lévi-Strauss himself has chosen to do. The three types of relationships that constitute the nuclear family are the very ones that must be isolated and made explicit in order to establish the basic biological premises, and these relationships are in fact isolated and made explicit in all kinship systems. The very concept of the nuclear family would be inconceivable without kinship systems; however, it is always possible to deduce this concept, at least in theory, from any imaginable kinship system, because the distinctions that define the concept are an integral part of such systems. It thus becomes clear that the nuclear family is the product rather than the constituent of the kinship system, and to a far greater extent than ethnologists have hitherto suspected. That is why it is not sufficient to say that kinship systems, even the most complex and artificial of them, take biological kinship "into account"; such systems are responsible for the discovery of biological kinship, and their existence conditions all understanding of it.

In short, the system itself has priority over the relationships it establishes. If everything must be seen in connection with the system, that is because the system truly comes first, even as regards biology, and not because the system could theoretically flout biological laws. In fact the system never flouts biology, at least as long as it adheres to the strict separation of marriage and consanguinity. One must not think of the system as stemming from its results, for the system alone makes these results possible. The refusal to regard biology as a starting point is made not because biology belongs in the realm of nature but because, on the contrary, it belongs entirely to culture and is deduced from systems of which the nuclear family is the smallest common denominator. The system is all of a piece and must be viewed as such. We must take care not to be distracted by its multiple variations, which in no way affect its essence.

The three types of relationship that compose the nuclear family all have real biological counterparts, yet they depend for their definition on incest prohibitions. In other words, if there were no incest prohibitions there would be no biological laws. But the purpose of the system is clearly not to uncover biological truths. Such truths are not the only ones set forth by the system; they are only part of a vaster statement. For that reason, they must not be taken as the point of departure.

The proposition developed here takes no particular stand on the controversial question, Are there cultures that are ignorant of the biology of human reproduction? I would venture to say, however, that in its handling of native testimony our theory can accomodate the skeptical approach of contemporary researchers as well as the positive approach of their predecessors. The possibility does indeed exist that certain cultures, despite incest prohibitions, have never discovered the connection between the sexual act and childbirth. Such a theory has been proposed by a number of ethnologists, including Malinowski; it is based on long and intimate contact with native life, and there is reason to doubt whether the contemporary reaction against it is justified. We are asked to believe that these ethnologists were hoodwinked by their informants, who were simply pretending ignorance on the subject of conception.

This skeptical approach is ostensibly based on a new esteem for the intellectual capacities of primitive man; but it may well stem from yet another and still more insidious form of ethnocentrism. There is something vaguely demagogic about an appeal to common sense couched in these terms: "Look here, you surely don't believe that there are men so stupid that they can't see the connection between sex and procreation! It's just cultural provincialism that makes us assume that sort of thing whenever we encounter someone a bit different from ourselves!"

As I have already said, the field of inquiry of this book does not extend to this particular question; nor would its answer affect my argument. I only wish to point out that modern attacks on the previous generation of anthropologists are inspired by intellectual attitudes that can only perpetuate an old tendency to remove basic biological truths from the domain of culture and reattribute them to nature. The appeal to "common sense," the use of such daunting phraseology as "it is self-evident that . . ." fits all too well with the misguided belief that kinship systems take biological facts into account independently of their other concerns. More generally, we encounter here a still mythic view of nature, one that sees nature as more receptive than culture to scientific verities. In fact there is no truth, no matter how elementary, that is not mediated by culture. The "great book of Nature" is an enigma one can only approach obliquely.

⟨ornament⟩ THE SIGNS OF HESITANCY and equivocation that we detect in Lévi-Strauss's efforts to situate a knowledge of true biological relationships within the framework of the kinship system clearly stem from an inclination (almost automatic today) to exclude scientific concepts from the company of myths, rituals, and kinship systems. We are less concerned here with the particular doctrine (which, moreover, displays certain inconsistencies) set forth by Lévi-Strauss in the article cited above than with the implicit principles that govern his thinking—and that are, in fact, almost universal suppositions. The object of our own search remains our intellectual attitude toward the nuclear family, which remains an obstacle, even after Lévi-Strauss, if we now treat our own privileged treatment of it as nothing but an arbitrary prejudice.

That kinship systems do not ignore or contradict biological kinship, but rather take them "carefully into account," is not self-evident to present-day thinkers. It is difficult to admit that our own knowledge of the basic facts of biology issues from the same thought process that produced the most arbitrary and artificial distinctions of kinship systems. Yet in both instances we have to do with the same type of intellectual operation, the same process of symbolic thought: the gathering of, and distinguishing between, entities whose union and separation are not made obvious in nature. Nonetheless, it is clear that all the products of symbolic thought cannot be considered equivalent. There is such a thing as *false* symbolic thought (for example, the assumption that childbirth is the result of a woman's possession by spirits) as well as *true* symbolic thought (for example, the assumption that childbirth is the result of the sexual union of man and woman).

There is no thought that is not *symbolic* in the structuralist sense of the word. Nevertheless, it is no more appropriate for us to employ the term today as a synonym for *false* than it was appropriate in the past to employ it as a synonym for *true*. Lévi-Strauss was the first to emphasize that all cultures contain an enormous store of knowledge that is useful because it is grounded in the truth. If this were not the case, these cultures would not have survived.

Whatever their differences, then, kinship systems are such that they cannot disregard the basic biological facts, though in primitive cultures these facts are somewhat lost in a maze of other distinctions.

All these distinctions are of a piece; that is, they make up a system. Our tendency to grant prime consideration to biological matters lead us to misunderstand the systematic aspect of the system. To yield to this tendency is to produce elements that do not adhere, inexplicable aberrations and exceptions that betray our inability to read the system correctly. The structuralists are surely right in urging their ethnologist colleagues to check their compulsion to take biological facts as a point of departure.

Why has this compulsion become second nature to us? Because our own system corresponds exactly to that of the nuclear family. It reduces the principle of exogamy to its simplest form and requires in consequence only the minimum number of prohibitions necessary to bring out the basic facts of generation.

This coincidence must be kept in mind when we consider the basic differences between our society and primitive societies. Nowadays it is often said that the concept of the modern family is just as arbitrary as the assumptions of other kinship systems. That is both true and false. A phenomenon can be arbitrary in relation to something and not arbitrary in relation to something else. As far as the facts of procreation are concerned, it is true that our system is as arbitrary as any other. For as far as real biological functioning is concerned, it scarcely matters whether a system forbids a man to marry either (1) his mother, his sisters, his daughters, and any of the women of tribe X; or (2) his mother, his sisters, and his daughters only. The biological machinery works neither better nor worse in the first case than in the second, and it might work just as well (*pace* Westermarck) if there were no restrictions whatsoever. In regard to the true facts of generation, then, the verdict is plain: all kinship systems are equally arbitrary.

Differences do exist, however, between the nuclear family system and all other systems. If it is true that all systems have a certain didactic value in regard to biological knowledge, our system is certainly preeminent in this regard. There are no longer any prohibitions in it that do not bring a basic relationship to light, and there is no basic biological relationship that is not revealed by a prohibition.

This difference between our own and other systems may appear slight. Our extreme reduction of prohibitions may serve to underline certain determined facts and bring them into sharper relief, but it discloses nothing that more complex systems could not also disclose. The biological example thus can suggest the relative singularity of our own system but cannot demonstrate it.

I began by emphasizing the biological question in order to dispose of an important stumbling block at the outset; namely, the confusion between fact and knowledge. It was necessary to select the simplest, most accessible example by which to demonstrate the ability of symbolic thought, even at its most mythic, to uncover scientifically significant relationships and differences—an ability that would remain unperceived by cultural relativism. But biology is too rudimentary an example to continue with. Let us turn our attention to another realm, that of the cultural sciences, and try to demonstrate that my approach provides ethnology with a new and fertile field of activity.

For Lévi-Strauss, the language of kinship is a system of rules that establishes a circuit of exchange between exogamic groups. Each time a group transfers one of its women to another group, the beneficiary group will respond by transferring one of its own women either to the first group or to a third group, depending on the requirements of the system. This response constitutes a new appeal, which will be answered accordingly. The circle may be large or small, but it always closes itself. The questions and responses emanating from the system always follow the same order, at least in principle. Although this constitutes a language in the structuralist sense, it fails to meet Chomsky's criteria. For him, an essential trait is missing: the infinite creativity of a true language, the constant potential for inventing new phrases and expressing things never before expressed.

Thus we should bear in mind that the language of kinship is incomplete and also that it is no longer spoken in certain societies, most particularly our own. A system that restricts its prohibitions to a bare minimum, as does ours, suppresses all positive rules. In other terms, it reduces the language of matrimonial exchange to nothing. Wherever modern society is found, marriages are no longer confined to a determined matrimonial circuit. That does not mean, of course, that exogamy has vanished. Not only does it still exist, but it manages to bring together the most disparate groups, even transcending the formidable barriers of racial, economic, and national prejudice. If sufficient information were available, we could evaluate the mediative role of such cultural manifestations as clothing styles, entertainment, and so forth in determining marriage alliances. From the viewpoint of scientific determinism, exogamy is certainly a determined factor, but it is no longer determined by the mediation of socio-religious prescriptions to which everyone can and must refer. The factors influencing these unions no longer possess a purely matrimonial significance. Kinship no longer possesses a language of its own. And there is no code of conduct telling people how to behave toward others and what behavior to expect in return, for expectations assume the form of statistics and no longer apply to individual cases. The linguistic metaphor must not be allowed to distract us from these essential differences.

Imperfect as it may be, the assimilation of the system to a language is a precious tool, even in the case of primitive systems, as long as we remain within the framework of these systems. It can help us to understand the difference between all these systems and our own relative lack of system. As everyone knows, the main obstacle to learning a foreign language is one's mother tongue. Our command of our native idiom is probably less firm than its command of us; and it displays a certain jealous possessiveness by making it difficult for us to acquire any other language. Children's capacity to assimilate languages depends on their ability to forget. And the greatest linguists often have no tongue they can any longer call their own.

The fact that we have eliminated the last vestiges of a matrimonial language undoubtedly has something to do with our particular interest in those who continue to speak such languages, as well as with our exceptional ability to decipher and classify them. Our society can learn to speak all the kinship languages because it speaks none of them. Not only do we read all those systems that actually exist, but we even invent those that do not. We can produce an infinite number of systems because we have the matrix of all exogamic languages in our grasp. Between each of the systems and the system of systems, between the kinship "languages" and Lévi-Strauss's own language in *The Elementary Structures of Kinship*, the same differences exist as between the traditional structuralist concept of language and Chomsky's concept.

From this we can only conclude that our ethnological essence must be in some way related to our vocations as ethnologists, linguists, and more generally, fieldworkers in the realm of culture. Clearly our kinship system alone is not responsible for our ethnological inclinations; rather, the two phenomena are parallel. The only society that has given itself over to the pursuit of ethnological knowledge happens to be one that has confined its system of prohibitions to the nuclear family. We cannot regard this fact as simple coincidence.

In order to speak the language of scholarly research we must first lay aside the language of rites and kinship, passing through the intermediary dialects of "cultural activities" in their broadest sense. One stage follows the other without a break, and at no point do the elements of "sacrificial" misapprehension wholly disappear. Nonetheless, the elements of comprehension increase in number, value, and coherence.

If ethnology is to become a true science it must reflect on its own principles, and that reflection must transcend the limits of ethnology to take in the sort of society that produces ethnologists—along with other types of men, such as romantic heroes. In ethnological literature the society that gives rise to ethnologists is always treated, as it were, in parentheses. The reasons for this treatment can be traced back to the assumption that this society has nothing in common with primitive societies. Today, when it is boldly asserted that our own society is only one among many, differing from other societies only in the way that all societies differ, this attitude has not vanished, but has become implicit rather than explicit. This modern view is demonstrably false. And if we seek more from ethnology than a means by which to quell the arrogance of our fellow Westerners, we will have to face the fact that our kinship system cannot be put on the same level as the systems of aboriginal Australians or the Crow-Omahas. In our system there is nothing arbitrary in the forms of knowledge to which we feel ourselves bound. We must not succumb to an antiethnocentrism which, because it diverts us from essentials, has a somewhat sacrificial character. Antiethnocentrism is the final and parodoxical, but ultimately logical, maneuver of ethnocentrism itself.

∾⊱⊰ CONTEMPORARY THINKERS have drawn attention to the largely arbitrary character of cultural systems. Most of the propositions that form these systems are neither true symbolic thought or false symbolic thought (in the sense of the two examples offered on page 229), but generally belong to a third category: they have no reality ouside the cultures that give rise to them. An example is the proposition that cross-cousins have a particular affinity for matrimony.

This body of arbitrary elements is the "original sin" of human thought, and it seems to increase as our skill in uncovering and interpreting these elements improves. We cannot blame the researchers for minimizing or even disregarding the elements of truth that lie hidden amidst the arbitrary. "Symbolic thought" in general is equated to mythic thought and thus occupies a position some thinkers believe is privileged, but one that proves in the long run both deceptive and unproductive, for it has lost all link with reality. The cultural heritage of humanity is regarded with suspicion. Its only interest lies in its "demystification"—that is, in providing the "demystifier" with a chance to display his forensic skills.

Humanity, we are told, has fallen victim to a vast mystification unrecognized until now. This is cultural nihilism, and it is often associated with a fetishistic cult of science. Because we have discovered the "original sin" of human thought, we think ourselves free of it. What is now needed is a radically different mode of thought, a new science that will allow us to appreciate the absurdity of all previous thinking. And because this lie was until recently immune from detection, the new scientific approach must be altogether unconnected with the past. Inevitably, it will take the shape of a unique discovery by some inspired being who has little in common with ordinary mortals, or even with his own past. In severing the cord that attached us to the matrix of all mythic thought, this liberator of humanity will have delivered us from dark ancestral falsehood and led us into the luminous world of truth. Our hard and pure science is to be the result of a *coupure épistémologique*, an epistemological revolution that is totally unexpected and for which we are entirely unprepared.

This scientific angelism springs from a deep-rooted reluctance, philosophical and even religious in origin, to admit that truth can coexist with the arbitrary and perhaps even derive from it. Certainly such an idea runs counter to our habitual modes of thought. And the proposition that true thought and so-called mythic thought are one and the same seems nothing short of scandalous. Perhaps it is because there are so few certain truths in the domain of culture that we are so eager to have the origins clear, easily understood, and accessible to reason.

The dualism of science and nonscience dates from the beginning of the scientific era and has assumed a great variety of forms. It grows more acute when we approach a foreign culture and are unable to grasp it. It is undoubtedly what prompted Lévi-Strauss to express mild astonishment that even the most artificial of kinship systems "carefully took into account" biological facts. In *The Savage Mind* Lévi-Strauss attempted to formulate this dualism, in highly attenuated and nuanced form, under the categories of "savage thought" and "*bricolage*"[6] on the one hand, and "the thought of the engineers" on the other.

We find in the work of Lévi-Strauss a strong tendency to relegate truth either to the domain of "natural" thought or the domain of "engineering"; or else to a loosely defined combination of the two that he designates as "naturalist thought." In his article on structural analysis, for instance, Lévi-Strauss asserts that the study of kinship systems obliges us to renounce "naturalistic thought"—as if it were not "symbolic," too—not because this mode of thought is intrinsically false, but because, on the contrary, it adheres too closely to the truth and is thus incapable of taking into account the fantasies of "symbolic thought." Structural ethnology thereby assumes a transitional and transitory quality; it is seen as a detour that uses savage thought against itself in order to "dissolve" it, to banish the hallucinations of our culture and clear the way for the union of nature and science.

All these questions converge on a fundamental question: the origin of symbolic thought. And if symbolic systems are never "the spontaneous development of an actual situation," if there is a rupture between nature and culture, then the question becomes pressing. Lévi-Strauss and the structuralists in general acknowledge this problem of origins only in an abstract fashion. The passage from nature to culture, they say, is assured by "the permanent traits of human nature"; the problem is a false one, falling outside the domain of science. The myths, which falsely dramatize this passage by means of imaginary catastrophes, only serve to conceal its true nature. *Totem and Taboo* is seen in this view as another origin myth, with little to offer beyond a certain curiosity value. The work should, in short, be treated like any other myth.

It might be well to return to the closing lines of "Structural Analysis in Linguistics and in Anthropology," because of what they say, and fail to say, about the viewpoints we are trying to assess here; and also because of the curious note of hesitancy they reveal. Most untypically,

---

[6] The French term *bricolage*, as employed here by Lévi-Strauss, has no English equivalent. The best we can do is to refer to Lévi-Strauss's own discussion of the term in *The Savage Mind* (Chicago, 1966): "There still exists among ourselves an activity which on the technical plane gives us quite a good understanding of what a science we prefer to call 'prior' rather than 'primitive', could have been on the plane of speculation. This is what is commonly called 'bricolage' in French. In its old sense the verb 'bricoler' applied to ball games and billiards, to hunting, shooting and riding. It was however always used with reference to some extraneous movement: a ball rebounding, a dog straying or a horse swerving from its direct course to avoid an obstacle. And in our own time the 'bricoleur' is still someone who works with his hands and uses devious means compared with those of a craftsman. . . . It might be said that the engineer questions the universe, while the 'bricoleur' addresses himself to a collection of oddments left over from human endeavors, that is, only a sub-set of the culture.'" (pp. 16–17, 19).—Trans.

the problem raised by the advent of symbolic thought is here viewed as a real problem, though we cannot be sure whether the problem has already been resolved: "Although it may be legitimate or even inevitable to fall back upon a naturalistic interpretation in order to understand the emergence of symbolic thinking, once the latter is given, the nature of the explanation must change as radically as the newly appeared phenomenon differs from those which have preceded and prepared it."[7]

If symbolic thinking is a "given," is this because we grasp its emergence or, on the contrary, because we do not? Does its emergence pass unnoticed? Does it take the form of a silent mutation, as many previous references either assert or imply; or is it a real, discernible event? The preceding passage seems to lean toward the second possibility, permitting us to view the symbolic advent as a legitimate and even inevitable subject of inquiry. But what are those phenomena that "preceded and prepared" this event? How must we envision a line of inquiry apparently committed to the "naturalist interpretation"?

Lévi-Strauss is the first to raise the essential question, even though he does so indirectly and, one might almost say, inadvertently. The reader knows my response to the question. My task now is to show, or at least to suggest, that this is the only approach capable of exposing the deficiency of a contemporary mode of thought that circles around the problem of origins without ever coming to grips with it—that in fact foregoes the opportunity to come to grips with it in favor of pure formalism.

The origin of symbolic thought lies in the mechanism of the surrogate victim; such has been the burden of my argument, particularly in my analyses of the myths of Oedipus and Dionysus. It is a fundamental instance of "arbitration" that gives rise to the dual presence of the *arbitrary* and the *true* in all symbolic systems.

Collective murder restores calm, in dramatic contrast to the hysterical paroxysms that preceded it. The conditions favorable to thought coincide with the death of the surrogate victim. Men's minds turn back to the miracle in order to perpetuate or renew it; and in order to accomplish this they need to reflect upon that miracle, to rethink it. Myths, rituals, and kinship systems are the first fruits of this endeavor.

To refer to the origin of symbolic thought is to speak as well of the origin of language. If the mechanism of the surrogate victim gives birth to language and imposes itself as the first object of language, it is easy to see why language should first state the conjunction of best and worst, the divine epiphany, the rite that commemorates this epiphany

[7] Ibid., p. 51.

and the myth that recalls it. For a long time language remains imbued with the sacred; thus there is good reason why it should long appear as a vassal of the sacred, obedient to its every command.

Cultural significations naturally include an arbitrary element, for they establish differences where formerly the symmetry of the doubles prevailed and substitute the stability of fixed meanings for the vertiginous alternation of violent reciprocity. For example, they relegate "plague" to one category, and "patricide" and "incest" to another. The machinery of discrimination plays us false as long as it applies itself to those whom nothing distinguishes. Indeed, it must play us false in order to work effectively, in order to bring about the differentiated unity of the whole community. In the midst of a living culture men are incapable of recognizing the arbitrary nature of the significations produced by this mysterious mechanism.

The processes of discrimination, exclusion, and conjunction are the products of the generative process. They are applied first to this same process, and this application gives rise to religious thought. But they do not confine themselves to religious thought alone; they are the mechanism for all orders of thought. And we cannot afford the luxury of rejecting or even denigrating them, for the truth is that they do their work well. When applied to something other than the original process, they bring to light veritable differences, analyze real phenomena, and encompass data of a nonrelative variety—for instance, the data of human generation. It is not correct to say that these data have recently become "verifiable" under modern laboratory conditions that have transformed them into scientific truths. They are scientific truths today because they have always been scientific truths. Basic discoveries may result from *bricolage*.

In the realm of religion, to be sure, error prevails. But even here we are not dealing with anything imaginary or gratuitous, as the modern rationalists arrogantly assume. Primitive religion is not given over to the phantoms, fantasies, and aberrant impulses that modern man thinks he alone has discarded. Rather, and quite simply, religion fails to grasp the mechanism of the surrogate victim, just as we still fail to grasp it. This perpetuation of the same error is what links our own thought to primitive thought and what, paradoxically, compels us to regard the latter as very different from our own, even though the two modes of thought are very similar. This condescending attitude toward the primitive is nothing more than an extension of a primitive attitude— that is, an indefinite prolongation of misunderstanding of the role of the surrogate victim.

The generative process plays a major role in primitive culture but passes unnoticed in ours. This fact has dictated enormous changes in many aspects of our life and in our range of knowledge, but it alters nothing in regard to the basic misapprehension that continues to govern us and to shield us from our own violence and from awareness of this violence. It is this chronic primitivism that prompts us to dismiss as mere illusion anything that draws our attention to the true state of things; and it is this same primitivism that prevents us from recognizing that falsehood in religious thought is something quite different from mere error; that falsehood has protected mankind from self-destruction.

Men may be even more dependent on the surrogate victim than we have indicated. It is the surrogate victim who provides men with the will to conquer reality and the weapons for all victorious intellectual campaigns—having first secured society against violence. The myths of symbolic thought can be compared to a larva's cocoon: without this shelter no development could take place.

To explain the preponderance of the arbitrary in primitive culture, we must understand that these societies are closer to the generative act of arbitration than we are, and we must realize that this proximity informs every aspect of their historical reality. We can envision this original arbitrary act as overflowing its limits and engendering a super-abundance of differences; historical societies may well offer a weakened image of this process when, after a period of chaos and turmoil, they do a volte-face and adopt a rigid, hierarchic, and highly compartmentalized mode of existence. Without making too much of the analogy, I might say that certain highly subdivided cultures, confined to the languages of ritual and kinship, are closer both temporally and temperamentally to the original impact of the generative violence than are the more mobile and flexible societies whose systems of social structure are less in evidence. The omnipresent and inflexible difference may well assure stability, but it will certainly discourage intellectual speculation, especially speculation regarding the origins of culture.

In order for men to make discoveries about their own culture, codified rituals must give way to an agile mode of thinking that uses the same mechanisms as religion with a virtuosity that religion never approached. The cultural order itself must have begun to disintegrate, and the overflow of differences must have subsided—not so much, however, as to provoke a new outbreak of violence, which would in turn generate new differences. For reasons unknown to us, primitive societies never meet these conditions. When the cycle of violence begins, it also comes to an end with such rapidity that the opportunity for making major self-discoveries hardly exists.

Modern Western society, however, can be described in terms of an exceptionally far-ranging and drawn-out critical cycle. The very essence of modern society might be said to be its ability to sustain the possibility for new discoveries in the midst of an ever-worsening sacrificial crisis—not, to be sure, without many signs of anxiety and stress. There is room for discovery in the natural sciences, in the field of cultural significations, and finally, on the specific subject of the arbitrary generative act.

The extreme poverty of our kinship system in comparison with those of primitive societies seems a sign of crisis in itself. The Western world is in a perpetual state of crisis, and the crisis is always spreading. As its ethnological basis falls away, its specific nonspecificity becomes more pronounced. The Western world has always had a penchant for anthropology. And that penchant becomes more urgent as the situation around us worsens.

The present crisis affects all aspects of scholarship, its polemical characteristics as well as its rate of progress. Our anthropological vocation stems from the general nature of Western society and increases in intensity to keep step with the crisis; just so Oedipus' investigation kept pace with the accelerating rhythm of the tragic crisis. The crisis could determine as well the overall pattern of our researches and successive discoveries and the order in which the theoretical premises keep changing. All scholarly priorities are historically determined, whether or not research in the strict sense is involved.

Like all cultures, our culture wears away from the periphery toward the center. The newly emerging social sciences exploit this deterioration in a rational, systematic fashion. The debris of the process serves as the object of objective knowledge; thus the positive regulations of kinship (as opposed to the prohibitions) and, more generally, its systems of expression become in structural ethnology the object of positive knowledge.

The essential characteristic of structuralism is that it puts the emphasis on positive regulations. If the prohibition and the regulation constitute two opposite poles of the same object, there is good reason to inquire which is the essential one. Lévi-Strauss poses this very question, and resolves it in favor of the regulation: "Exogamy has a value less negative than positive. . . . It asserts the social value of other people, and . . . it prohibits endogamous marriage only in order to introduce, and to prescribe, marriage with a group other than the biological family, certainly not because a biological danger is attached to consanguineous marriage, but because exogamous marriage results in social benefit."[8]

[8] Lévi-Strauss, *The Elementary Structures of Kinship*, p. 480.

We could easily cite fifteen or twenty such declarations, all perfectly explicit, which prove that Lévi-Strauss's work, far from displaying a "passion for incest," is remarkable for its dispassionate approach:

> They do not conceive of the prohibition as such, i.e., in its negative aspect; the prohibition is merely the reverse or counterpart of a positive obligation, which alone is present and active in the consciousness. . . .
>
> Marriage prohibitions . . . are prohibitions only secondarily and derivatively. Rather than a prohibition on a certain category of persons, they are a prescription directed towards another category. In this regard, how much more penetrating is native theory than are so many modern commentaries! There is nothing in the sister, mother or daughter which disqualifies them as such. Incest is socially absurd before it is morally culpable.
>
> The prohibition of incest is less a rule prohibiting marriage with the mother, sister or daughter, than a rule obliging the mother, sister or daughter to be given to others.[9]

I have already broached the problem of priorities and adopted a point of view diametrically opposed to that of Lévi-Strauss: for me, prohibitions come first. This perspective is necessitated by my overall approach. Positive exchanges are merely the reverse of prohibitions, the results of a series of maneuvers or avoidance taboos designed to ward off outbreaks of rivalry among the males. Terrified by the fearful consequences of endogamous reciprocity, men have created the beneficial reciprocity of exogamic exchange. It is only natural that in a smoothly functioning system, positive regulations should move to the forefront as the awareness of danger grows dim. At the outset, however, the matrimonial rules are like those perfectly choreographed gestures unwittingly executed by characters in classic comedy and inspired by sentiments wholly foreign to the dance, such as jealousy or fear.

Lévi-Strauss is undoubtedly correct to minimize the fascination for incest as such; insofar as it is a cultural phenomenon, it constituted a manifestation of the sacrificial crisis. But this does not mean that prohibitions do not come first. If they did not, it would be virtually impossible to situate our own society within the universal ethnological pattern.

If rules are to be considered the cornerstone of a society, then we are faced with something of a problem in regard to our own society, which is deficient in positive regulations and has, in fact, discarded everything except the basic exogamic prohibition. The structuralists hasten to assure us that there is nothing unique about our society. Yet in placing their emphasis on regulations they make it appear very unique indeed. Any attempt to minimize the singularity of our society

[9] Ibid., pp. 485, 481.

only serves, by a process of self-denigration that still has its roots in religion, to raise it to the top once more. If we wish to situate ourselves in relation to other cultures we must refine the current view of our ethnocentrism and resign ourselves to the *relative* uniqueness of our society.

Contemporary thought is in chaos, as it must be when progress is real. Where it still survives, it displays pathological symptoms. Thought, in fact, is caught up in a circle, the very circle drawn for us by Euripidean tragedy. In striving to escape from the circle, thought only enters more deeply into it, and as the radius of the circle shrinks, thought moves ever faster, spinning itself into an obsession. However, there is no such thing as an obsession pure and simple, as the legion of timorous anti-intellectuals would have us believe; and it is not by breaking out of the circle that thought will ultimately free itself, but by penetrating to its very center, while somehow managing to avoid the pitfall of madness.

Nothing now exists to interfere with a full revelation of violence—not even violence itself, which men and its own extraordinary growth have combined to deprive of that freedom of moment that formerly assured the efficiency of the generative mechanism and the repression of the truth. The trap that the Western Oedipus has set for himself will snap closed at the precise moment when the quest is finished, for trap and quest, here again, are one and the same thing.

Today the reign of violence is made manifest. It assumes the awesome and horrific form of technological weaponry. These weapons, as the "experts" blandly inform us, are what is keeping the whole world more or less in line. The idea of "limitless" violence, long scorned by sophisticated Westerners, suddenly looms up before us. Absolute vengeance, formerly the prerogative of the gods, now returns, precisely weighed and calibrated, on the wings of science. And it is this force, we are told, that prevents the first planetary society, the society that already encompasses or will soon encompass the whole of humanity, from destroying itself.

It seems increasingly clear that the pressure of violence or the insistence of truth (for whom man acts as a kind of torchbearer) has forced modern man to come face to face with this same violence or truth. For the first time he is confronted with a perfectly straightforward and even scientifically calculable choice between total destruction and the total renunciation of violence.

It is something more than mere chance that has led to the coincidence of these remarkable events, linking the indubitably real progress of the so-called human sciences with the slow but steady progress of knowledge toward an understanding of the surrogate victim and of the violent origins of all human culture.

꼭꼭 ETHNOLOGICAL STRUCTURALISM works at uncovering differences everywhere. Superficially, it might be said to be the simple antithesis of an older ethnological approach, that of Lévy-Bruhl, which refused to see differences anywhere. Lévy-Bruhl thought that he had located the "primitive mind" in certain aspects of myth and religion, and he postulated a permanent inability on the part of primitive peoples (the Australian aborigines, for example) to discern differences. He went so far as to suggest that these aborigines could hardly distinguish between men and kangaroos. The structuralists have replied that as far as kangaroos are concerned, the aborigines have a thing or two to teach the ethnologists.

It sometimes seems as if the variations of twentieth century ethnology run parallel to the variations in esthetics and to intellectual fads in general. Lévy-Bruhl's primitive man, lost in the mists of his mythic stupor, is succeeded by the structuralist chess player, elaborating intricate systems with imperturbable ease. We are constantly shuttling between these extremes, which serve to create an illusion of change by means of increasingly bizarre constructs, but which in reality change very little.

Lévy-Bruhl and the structuralists cannot be put on the same level, because differentiated structures have a definite autonomy, a textual reality that the sacred never possesses or possesses only in appearance. Structural analysis cannot deal with everything, but within its limits it is highly satisfactory.

The sacred concerns itself above all with the destruction of differences, and this nondifference cannot appear as such in the structure. It can only appear (as we saw in Chapter 2) in the guise of a new and somewhat equivocal kind of difference—a double, multiple, monstrous, fantastic difference, but one that is nonetheless meaningful. In *Mythologiques*, monsters are ranked alongside tapirs and peccaries as if they constituted real zoological species. And in a sense they do. For in myths the role of violence in destroying and producing significations is muted and disguised, and those aspects of the myth that refer to its own origins are woven into a tissue of enigmatic allusions. Structuralism cannot penetrate this enigma because it deals only with differential systems; because, strictly speaking, only differential systems are directly observable.

As long as meaning is healthy, the sacred is absent. It remains outside the structure, untouched by structural ethnology, banished by structuralism. In a sense this elimination of the sacred constitutes real progress, for it is finally accomplished in a thorough and systematic manner. And though accompanied by ideological prejudices, it is not dependent on them for its efficacy. Structuralism constitutes a negative but indispensable stage in the discovery of the sacred, for it does away with the confusion that has previously prevailed. Thanks to structuralism, it is possible to distinguish the finite quality of sense—of structure —from the infinite quality of the sacred, that inexhaustible reservoir from which all differences flow and into which they all converge.

We now know that the sacred reigns supreme wherever a cultural order has not yet taken hold, has only begun to take hold, or has lost its hold entirely. The sacred also reigns over structure: engenders, organizes, observes, and perpetuates it or, on the contrary, mishandles, dissolves, transforms, and on a whim destroys it. But the sacred is not actually present in structure in the sense that it is present everywhere else.

Structuralism makes this relationship clear, but it is incapable of expressing it directly, for structuralism is itself locked into the structure, a prisoner of the synchronic, unable to perceive a change in terms of violence or fear of violence. Structuralism has its limits, and it is precisely these limits that make the disappearance of the sacred seem natural to the structuralists. Yet they can no more reply to the question, "Where did the sacred disappear?" than they can reply to the accusation of overemphasizing binary oppositions. Their proper reply to this latter charge should be that binary oppositions are predominant because there are never more than two antagonists or two sides in any conflict, and as soon as a third adversary appears, the two others either join forces in opposing him or he elects to join one or the other side.

To pass beyond the limits of structuralism we must first pause to consider the doubtful significations, those that imply both too little and too much: twins, illnesses, all forms of contaminations and contagions, inexplicable reversals of meaning, unexpected growths and shrinkages, strange excrescences and deformations, and all forms of the monstrous and the bizarre. Nor, of course, should we overlook sexual and other transgressions, acts of violence, or behavior that is in any way exceptional, especially when such behavior seems to be in defiance of an explicit gesture of communal unanimity.

The opening pages of Lévi-Strauss's *The Raw and the Cooked* seem to abound in signs relating to mythic birth: incest, vengeance, betrayal by either a brother or brother-in-law, collective metamorphoses or destructions as preambles to acts of foundation and creation—and all of them attributed to culture heroes whose antagonisms have somehow been aroused.

In a Bororo myth the sun commands the inhabitants of a village to cross a river by means of a footbridge, which collapses under their combined weight. All the villagers perish with the exception of the culture hero, who "could only walk slowly because his legs were deformed," and therefore lagged behind the rest.[10] The hero brings the drowned villagers back to life under different forms: "The hair of those who were sucked into the whirlpools turned wavy or curly; the hair of those who drowned in calm waters was fine and smooth."[11] They return in separate groups and on a selective basis. In a Tenetehara myth the culture hero, Tupan, is furious at learning that his godchild had been mistreated by the relatives in whose care he had placed the boy, and he orders the child

> to gather all the feathers he could find and to spread them around the edge of the village. Then Tupan set fire to the feathers, and the entire village was surrounded by walls of flame. The inhabitants ran from side to side, but they were unable to escape. Little by little their cries became lower until they were transformed into the grunts of pigs; at the same time the people began to take on the form of peccaries and wild pigs. A few of them escaped into the dense forest, and the wild pigs that inhabit the forest today are their descendants. Tupan made his godchild, Marana ywa, the owner of the wild pigs.[12]

In an interesting variant, the culture hero "puffed clouds of [tobacco] smoke into the interior. The occupants became dizzy, and when the demiurge cried out to them, 'Eat your food!' they thought he was ordering them to copulate. They proceeded to have coitus and made the usual grunting sounds while doing so. They were all changed into wild pigs."[13]

This passage offers a clear indication of the "mystical" role played by tobacco and drugs in chamanistic and other practices. Tobacco contributes to the sense of dizziness induced by the sacrificial crisis. The reciprocal violence expressed by the inhabitants running "from side to side" in the first version is reinforced by the sexual promiscuity in the second, the result of an explitit loss of significations.

Although Lévi-Strauss if not referring specifically to a sacrificial crisis, he is clearly referring to the birth, if not the rebirth, of significations: "It is clear that the myths I am comparing all offer an original solution to the problem of the change-over from continuous quantity to discrete quantity."[14] Thus we are indeed dealing with significance-

---

[10] Claude Lévi-Strauss, *The Raw and the Cooked*, trans. John Weightman and Doreen Weightman (New York, 1969), p. 51.
[11] Ibid.
[12] Ibid., p. 84.
[13] Ibid., p. 85.
[14] Ibid., p. 53.

producing mechanisms, for "in any field a system of significances can be constructed only on the basis of discrete quantities."

However, Lévi-Strauss always views the production of sense as a purely logical problem, an act of symbolic mediation. The role of violence remains hidden. In exposing this role to view, we are not merely evoking the "affective" aspects of the myth—its ability to inspire mystery and terror—but calling attention to the violence that dominates all aspects of myth, including its logic and meanings. Violence is behind all mythic themes, and only an understanding of its role is capable of bestowing a coherence on these themes; for without sacrificing structure, we can recover its lost origins and confer on myth an essential function.

ᕦᕤ THE ANALYTICAL METHOD applied in previous chapters to Greek tragedy has been primarily employed to decipher the myths of which the tragedies themselves constitute the first efforts at decipherment. In concluding the present chapter I will try to show that this method loses none of its validity when applied outside the realm of Greek tragedy and mythology.

Because the last two chapters have been largely devoted to incest prohibitions and marriage regulations, it might be interesting to examine a myth that attributes the same origin to both of them and lends support to our theory as a whole. The myth in question comes from the Tsimshian Indians who inhabit the Pacific coast of Canada.[15]

A chieftain's son falls in love with the daughter of his mother's brother—that is, his cross-cousin. The girl, out of sheer perversity, demands that the young man prove his love by disfiguring himself. The young man therefore scars first his left cheek, then his right; and the girl, horrified by his ugliness, banishes him from her sight. The brokenhearted young man flees the country, intent only on death. Finally he arrives in the land of Chief Pestilence, Master of Deformities. A crowd of tribesmen surround their leader, all of them mutilated and crippled. They are dangerous, for anyone who responds to their advances comes to resemble them. The young man is careful to ignore them, and the chief agrees to restore his features, in fact to make him handsomer than before. The young man is boiled in a magic pot, from which the chief's daughter extracts his stripped and whitened bones. He is then brought back to life, resplendent with beauty.

Now it is the girl's turn to fall in love with her cousin, and her cousin's turn to demand the same proof of love she had asked of him.

---

[15] Franz Boas, "Tsimshian Mythology," *Report of the Bureau of American Ethnology* 31, 185, No. 25. See also Stith Thompson, ed., *Tales of the North American Indians* (Bloomington, Ind., 1968), pp. 178–186.

The girl scars both sides of her face and is scornfully rejected by the young man. Frantic to have her lost beauty restored, she too repairs to the court of Chief Pestilence; but unlike the young man, she accepts the tribesmen's invitation to join them. Thereupon they make the unfortunate young woman one of their own, crippling and mutilating her and then casting her out to die.

The reader will have recognized in this tale a number of familiar themes. All the people in the myth either disfigure others, demand that others disfigure themselves, try in vain to disfigure others, or actually disfigure themselves—all of which amounts ultimately to the same thing. One cannot exert violence without submitting to it: that is the law of reciprocity. Everybody in the myth comes to resemble everybody else. The danger threatening newcomers at the hands of Chief Pestilence's tribesmen is in fact visited by both cousins on each other. Pestilence and mutilation signify one and the same reality: the sacrificial crisis.

In the relationship between the two cousins the woman initially has the upper hand. She incarnates beauty, the man ugliness; she is free of desire, while he is caught in its thrall. The relationship is then reversed. Differences cancel each other out; a symmetry is constantly generated, invisible in each synchronic moment taken separately but visible in the accumulation of successive moments. This is what constitutes the non-difference of the sacrificial crisis, a truth forever inaccessible to the two partners who live out the relationship in the form of alternating differences. The symmetry of the overall picture is reflected in the two sides of the face, each scarred in turn. The same details are reiterated throughout the story (until the conclusion), but never simultaneously.

Between the two cousins and Chief Pestilence's tribesmen there is the same relationship as that between the protagonists of *Oedipus the King* and the Theban plague victims. The only way to avoid contagion is to turn a deaf ear to the appeals of the enemy brothers. On the level of the tribesmen—that is, the collectivity—the myth speaks objectively. It does what we ourselves did in our opening chapters: it "short-circuits" the alternating differences. It does so with good reason, for this difference only ends in similarity. The reciprocal mutilation takes the direct form of a loss of differences, a "becoming the same" at the hands of those whom violence has already made identical. When we note that this process consists of turning men into doubles as well as into monsters, it is clear that we are dealing here with a sacrificial crisis.

Mutilation symbolizes the working of the crisis in dramatic fashion. Clearly, it must be viewed both as the creation of fearfully deformed beings and as the elimination of all distinguishing characteristics, all the salient features of these beings. The process imposes uniformity and eliminates differences, but it never succeeds in establishing harmony. In the image of monstrous mutilation the procedures of reciprocal violence are expressed in such powerfully condensed form that they appear bizarre, indecipherable, and "mythic."

Lévi-Strauss mentions this Tsimshian myth in one of his essays; he calls it a "horrific little fiction."[16] We prefer to describe it as a remarkable fiction about the horrific human relationships occasioned by reciprocal violence. In any case, the term "fiction" is hardly worth retaining. Although the myth itself is foreign to our Western mode of thought, the relationship between the cousins introduces an element that our classic theater traditionally treats in terms of tragic conflict or comic misunderstanding and that also bears a striking resemblance to the sentiment of love-jealousy found in the novels of Stendhal, Proust, and Dostoevsky.

The prince and princess claim and obtain from each other the same violent loss of difference that Chief Pestilence's tribesmen inflict on those who are mad enough to join their ranks. All differences dissolve and disappear, yet in a sense they remain inviolate and whole. We are never told in the myth that the differences between the tribesmen and the two cousins, and more importantly between the two cousins themselves, have been eliminated; and the destruction of the symmetry between the cousins at the conclusion forcefully affirms the primacy of differences.

There is nothing in the relationship between the cousins to justify this loss of symmetry, except for the fact that the Indian girl, like Oedipus, initiated the whole action. This identifying of the origin with an instance of impure violence is not wholly satisfactory. Once again we find ourselves confronted by the basic contradiction that underlies *Oedipus the King* and *The Bacchae*. While the course of the relationships reveal a constant erosion of all the differences, and while the mythic action tends toward the perfect symmetry of the undifferentiated relationships, the outcome of the myth arbitrarily reverses the process. The asymmetry of the message is here again in direct contrast to the burgeoning symmetry apparent on every other level. Everything leads us to suspect that this contradiction must be linked to a specific event that lies buried in the myth's conclusion—the murder of the girl, who to all appearances performs the role of surrogate victim. Once again the unanimity-minus-one of collective violence recreates mythic differences, which are themselves the issues of a violent undifferentiation taking place throughout the narrative.

[16] Claude Lévi-Strauss, "La Geste d'Asdiwal," *Annuaire de l'école pratique des hautes études* 6 (1958–59).

The violence to which the young woman is subjected at the hands of Chief Pestilence's tribesmen resembles the violence that preceded it in every way but one: its finality. The act serves definitively to stabilize a difference that otherwise would have continued to alternate between the two protagonists. It is the whole mob of tribesmen, the whole community, which falls upon the girl and tears her limb for limb with their naked hands. Once again we recognize a Dionysiac *sparagmos*. And once again we recognize the generative, because unanimous, act of mob murder.

The return to differentiated harmony is based on the arbitrary expulsion of the surrogate victim. The metamorphosis of the chieftain's son is also based on this generative violence, even though it happens to precede it in the mythic sequence and is integrated in part to the reciprocal interplay. It is the other face of the generative violence, the return to beneficence following the paroxysm of malevolence. That is why this metamorphosis also abounds in elements that designate and disguise the mechanism of the surrogate victim. The strange technique of the happy metamorphosis resembles a shamanistic initiatory dream, of which there are many examples in American Indian folklore—dreams about dead men who are revived when their body or bones have been trampled on.[17] This technique can perhaps be compared to a sacrificial practice, referred to earlier (see p. 100), in which the crowd stamps on the victim himself or on his burial place. It should also be noted, however, that the final metamorphosis occurs with stripped and whitened bones—that is, with human remains that are free from all taint of corruption or decay. The metamorphosis of the chieftain's son thus constitutes a return from the dead. It is the happy result of an act of supreme violence, perpetrated by restored unanimity. The reconquest of beauty coincides with the renovation of the cultural order. And Chief Pestilence himself incarnates all the successive aspects of violence; master of deformities and metamorphoses, sole arbiter of the ultimate game, he plays the same role as Dionysus in *The Bacchae*.

All the significant differentiations of the myth—the difference between the protagonists and Chief Pestilence's tribesmen, then the sexual difference between the protagonists, together with the fact that they are cross-cousins—all these can be traced back to the act of generative violence. The mythic action, the process of violent undifferentiation, cannot fail to upset the norm established at the myth's outset: the difference, which is now normative as well as significant, enjoining these two cross-cousins of different sex to marry. An unstable combination of undifferentiation and difference, the myth is inevitably pre-

[17] Cf. Thompson, ed., *Tales of the North American Indians* (Bloomington, 1968), p. 261 n. 3.

sented in terms of the violation of a rule established by itself. This is the way it was originally told to Franz Boas by his native informant. Ever since the girl in the myth met her unhappy fate, he was told, young girls have been married off to their cousins regardless of their personal preferences.

It is interesting to compare our myth with the rites performed at the marriage of cross-cousins of a princely family of the Tsimshian people: "When the prince and the princess have been joined together, the tribesmen of the young man's uncle begin to shake; then the tribesmen of the girl's uncle begin to shake, and a combat breaks out between the two groups. Stones are thrown, and many heads are battered. The scars and wounds . . . [serve] as proof of the wedding contract."[18]

Up to this point the presence of the sacrificial crisis behind the myth was only a hypothesis, prompted by the belief that the mutilation image was based on a real occurrence. The matrimonial myth confirms this hypothesis by incorporating the violence in question; ritual violence, to be sure, but perfectly real and clearly linked to the theme of mutilation in the myth: "Stones are thrown and man heads battered." It is easy to imagine a twentieth-century Cervantes or Molière planting in the midst of those flying stones a devotee of the self-referential text in order to prove to him that some metaphors are more striking than others. The Indians had no doubts on this subject: "The scars and wounds . . . [serve] as proof of the wedding contract." The sacrificial nature of this violence is further confirmed by an additional fact communicated to Boas by another native informant. Among the Niquas, whose marriage customs are similar to those of the Tsimshians, the battle between the two groups can reach such a pitch of intensity that one of the slaves on the fiancé's side is killed. The sacrificial aspect of this action is implicit, but obvious. It is known in advance to what side the victim will belong and that he will be a slave and not a free man—that is, somebody wholly apart from the community, whose death will not risk unleashing a *real* crisis. Although foreseen, the death retains a problematical quality that recalls the unforeseeable advent of the surrogate victim, for a man is not killed on every such occasion. When a man is killed, his death is looked upon as a good omen, a sign that the couple will never separate.

The diverse mutilations described in the Tsimshian myth and ritual will undoubtedly prompt the psychoanalytically inclined to see the whole affair in terms of "castration." The loss of difference is a more comprehensive interpretation. The theme of violent undifferentiation

[18] Boas, "Tsimshian Mythology."

includes that of castration, whereas the castration theme cannot possibly include all the elements covered by violent undifferentiation.

Ritual violence is intended to reproduce an original act of violence. There is nothing mythic about this original violence, but its ritual imitation necessarily includes mythic elements. The original violence certainly did not bring into conflict two such neatly differentiated groups as those of the two uncles. It can be stated as a principle that violence precedes either the division of an original group into two exogamous moieties, or the association of two groups of strangers, gathered together to effect matrimonial exchanges. The original violence took place within a single, solitary group, which the mechanism of the surrogate victim compelled either to split in separate groups or to seek an association with other groups. Ritual violence invariably takes place between already constituted groups.

Ritual violence is always less internal than the original violence. In assuming a mythico-ritual character, violence tends toward the exterior, and this tendency in turn assumes certain sacrificial characteristics; it conceals the site of the original violence, thereby shielding from this violence, and from the very knowledge of this violence, the elementary group whose very survival depends on the absolute triumph of peace. The ritual violence that accompanies the exchange of women serves a sacrificial purpose for each group. In sum, the groups agree never to be completely at peace, so that their members may find it easier to be at peace among themselves. We see here the principle behind all "foreign" wars: aggressive tendencies that are potentially fatal to the cohesion of the group are redirected from within the community to outside it. Inversely, there is reason to believe that the wars described as "foreign wars" in the mythic narratives were in fact formerly civil strifes. There are many tales that tell of two warring cities or nations, in principle independent of one another—Thebes and Argos, Rome and Alba, Hellas and Troy—whose conflicts bring to the surface so many elements pertaining directly to the sacrificial crisis and to its violent resolution that it is hard not to view these stories as mythic elaborations of this same crisis, presented in terms of a "fictive" foreign threat.

≈⊗⋈ *Chapter Ten*

The Gods, the Dead, the Sacred, and Sacrificial Substitution

≈⊗⋈ EVERY GOD, HERO, AND MYTHIC CREATURE
so far encountered, from the sacred African king to Chief
Pestilence of the Tsimshians, embodies the interplay of violence projected by an act of generative unanimity.

Oedipus, our first example, seemed at the outset of his career to
incarnate an almost exclusively maleficent form of violence. It was
only later, in *Oedipus at Colonus*, that he assumed an actively beneficent role. As we know, unanimous violence is generative of a religious
order and the man charged with the crime of patricide and incest is
credited with the act of generation. Thus Oedipus's transformation
into an object of public reverence is not hard to understand.

The two Oedipus tragedies permit us to study in isolation two
conflicting and successive moments of the hero's sacralization. In *The
Bacchae*, as we have observed, these same two moments serve to define
the dual personality of Dionysus, his beneficent and maleficent aspects.
In the Euripidean drama the moments are so telescoped and juxtaposed
that it would be almost impossible to recognize their point of origin or
appreciate their historical development if we did not have Sophocles'
Oedipus plays to guide us. The religious formulation of the Oedipus
myth is considerably easier to grasp because it is less transmuted, more
directly based on the mechanism of the surrogate victim.

In *The Bacchae* Dionysus plays the role not of victim, but of
executioner. This difference, which may at first seem crucial, is in fact
of no consequence for the religious implications of the work. As we
have already remarked, the mythic or divine creature who appears as
the incarnation of violence is not restricted to the role of surrogate
victim. The metamorphosis of the maleficent into the beneficent is the
major aspect of his mission, the aspect that elicits public veneration;
but he is equally capable of effecting the reverse transformation. He
can intervene at any stage and assume all roles, either simultaneously or
in succession. Thus, there are moments in Dionysus' career when he

relinquishes the role of executioner to assume that of victim of the *diasparagmos*. In one episode of his myth, for instance, he is torn limb for limb by a raging mob of Titans: a mythic creature (Zagreus or Dionysus) is sacrificed by other mythic creatures. The burden of the story is identical to that of the origin myths referred to earlier.

We have seen that in the course of the Incwala rites the King of the Swazi becomes simultaneously executioner and victim. Similarly, the Aztec god Xipe-Totec demonstrates the ability of the incarnation of the sacred to assume different roles within the system. Sometimes this god is killed and flayed in the person of a victim offered as substitute for him; at other times the god becomes the executioner, flaying victims in order to don their skin. Evidently religious thought perceives all those who participate in this violent interplay, whether actively or passively, as doubles. Xipe-Totec can be translated "our flayed lord and master"—a name that suggests that the basic role remains that of surrogate victim.

The theory of a violence that is sometimes reciprocal, sometimes unanimous and generative, is the first truly to take into account the double nature of all primitive divinities, the blending of beneficent and maleficent that characterizes all mythical figures who involve themselves in mortal affairs. Dionysus is at one and the same time the "most terrible" and the "most gentle" of the gods. There is a Zeus who hurls thunderbolts and a Zeus "as sweet as honey." In fact, there is no ancient divinity who does not have a double face. If the Roman Janus turns to his worshippers a countenance alternately warlike and peaceful, that is because he too reflects the same alternation; and if he comes in time to symbolize foreign war, that is because foreign war is merely another form of sacrificial violence.

If we understand the interplay of violence in primitive societies, the origins and structure of all mythical and supernatural beings becomes clear. As we have seen, the surrogate victim meets his death in the guise of the monstrous double. All sacred creatures partake of monstrosity, whether overtly or covertly; this aspect of their nature can be traced to the monstrous double. The marriage of beneficent and maleficent constitutes, of course, the original and fundamental monstrosity, the superhuman creature's absorption of the difference between "good" and "bad" difference, that basic difference that dominates all others.

There is no essential difference between the monstrous aspects of Oedipus and the monstrous aspects of Dionysus. Dionysus is simultaneously god, man, and bull; Oedipus is simultaneously son, husband, father, and brother of the same human beings. Both have incorporated into themselves differences normally considered irreconcilable. Religious thinking puts all differences at the same level; it assimilates family and cultural differences to natural differences. When we are dealing with mythology, therefore, we must make do without any clear distinction between physical monstrosity and moral monstrosity. Religious thought makes no distinction between biological twins and twins of violence engendered by the disintegration of the cultural order.

All the episodes of the Oedipus myth are repetitions of one another. Once we recognize this fact it becomes apparent that all the figures in the various episodes are monsters and that their resemblance is far closer than appearance alone might suggest. Oedipus, naturally, is a monster, but Tiresias is a monster, too: as a hermaphrodite he incorporates the difference between the two sexes. The sphinx is a monster, a veritable conglomerate of differences, with its woman's head, lion's body, serpent's tail, and eagle's wings. On first glance there is a radical difference between this imaginary creature and the human protagonists, but this difference vanishes on closer inspection. The sphinx plays the same role in relation to Oedipus as do all the human figures. The sphinx bars Oedipus's way; it becomes an object of fascination and a secret model; it is the bearer of the *logos phobou*, the oracle of doom. Like Laius, like the drunken Corinthian earlier in the story and Creon and Tiresias later, the sphinx dogs Oedipus's tracks—whenever, that is, Oedipus is not dogging the sphinx's tracks. Like the others, the sphinx catches Oedipus in an oracular trap; in short, the episode of the sphinx recapitulates the other episodes. The sphinx appears as the incarnation of maleficent violence, as Oedipus himself will appear later on. The sphinx has been sent by Hera to punish Thebes, just as the plague is visited upon the city by order of Apollo. Like the plague, the sphinx's appetite for victims increases steadily until it is vanquished by Oedipus, who thereby restores the city. The episode of the sphinx shows Oedipus in the role of monster-killer or executioner. Later, a monster himself, he will assume the role of surrogate victim. Like all incarnations of sacred violence, Oedipus can and does play every part in succession.

The sacred king is also a monster. He is simultaneously god, man, and savage beast. Royal titles like "the Lion" or "the Leopard" may degenerate into mere formulas, but they have their origin in memories of the monstrous double and generative unanimity. Moral and physical monstrosity are thus blended and confused. Like Oedipus, the king is at once stranger and son, the most intimate of insiders and the most bizarre of outsiders; he is an exemplar of enormous tenderness and frightful savagery. As an incestuous criminal, he stands above and beyond all the rules he promulgates and enforces. He is the wisest and the most lunatic, the blindest and the most lucid of men. This monopolizing of differences, which makes of the king a *sacred monster* in every possible sense of the term, finds vivid expression in ritual chants:

> The chieftain is neither this nor that.
> The chieftain is neither good nor bad.
> He is at once guest, foreigner, and host villager.
> He is the wise man and the fool.[1]

It should be no cause for surprise, then, that the august inhabitants of Olympus have been charged with a fair number of rapes, murders, parricides, and incestuous acts, as well as innumerable incidents of savagery and madness. Nor should we be surprised to discover that these divine personages seem to be made up of bits and pieces taken from every order of reality—human, animal, inorganic, cosmic. Nothing is more futile than to seek stable distinctions among these monsters, unless it is the attempt to derive psychological insights from their stories, insights pertaining either to individuals or to the "collective consciousness." Of all learned pursuits undertaken in the course of Western history, that one is surely the most foolhardy. The pseudo-rational treatment of monsters, the classification of monster stories into "archetypes," can only serve as a humorless revision of Ovid's subtle and exhaustive *Metamorphoses*; it can only serve further to elaborate the mythological process. To pontificate on the subject of monsters is in effect to take them seriously, to enter into their game; it is to be duped by their appearance instead of recognizing the human being who lurks behind the monstrous form.

The variations among various types of mythological creatures only become interesting if we relate these variations to their common origin in generative violence. We then realize that the differences reside not in the objects themselves but in the indeterminate nature of the hallucinated indifferentiation they embody, an indifferentiation that is made determinate retrospectively by the generative violence.

Some religious differences clearly reflect the violence that engendered them: the ritual incest of the African monarchs, for instance, or such sacrificial practices as the Dionysiac *sparagmos*. In many mythologies the gods, spirits, or mythic creatures are divided into two distinct camps, one of "serious" and one of "comic" personalities. The Greek Hermes and the Roman Mercury are examples of comic gods. Some societies harbor sacred clowns or fools. The North Americans have their "tricksters"; there are royal fools, and kings of fools, and any number of temporary sovereigns, both comic and tragic, who are ceremonially sacrificed at the predetermined end of their brief reign. These figures are incarnations of sacred violence as surely as the Afri-

---

[1] Theuws, "Naître et mourir dans le rituel Luba," p. 172.

can king, but on a somewhat different level. In each case we are dealing with collective violence, and more specifically with a certain mode of collective violence. In addition to the "serious" expulsion, there must always have been an act of expulsion based at least in part on ridicule. In the modern world our everyday, much diluted forms of social ostracism are generally based on ridicule; much of contemporary literature is explicitly or implicitly concerned with this phenomenon. We need only think of those social categories and individuals that provide the victims in scapegoat rites—vagabonds, beggars, cripples—to recognize that derision of one form or another plays a large part in the negative feelings that find expression in the course of the ritual sacrifice and that are finally purified and purged by it.

We have here a body of material that calls out for detailed analysis. But because the relevance of this material to my general thesis presents, at least in principle, no real problem, let us pass on to other forms of religion and consider how they can fit my scheme. Let us turn first to a religious practice that may appear very different from those previously examined but one that is in actuality closely related: ancestor worship or, more simply, the worship of the dead.

In certain cultures the gods are either absent or insignificant. In such cases mythic ancestors, or the dead, take the place of the missing divinities and are seen as the founders, guardians and, if need be, disrupters of the cultural order. When incest, adultery, and other social ills begin to proliferate, when family relationships begin to crumble, the dead are displeased and visit their displeasure on the living. They bring nightmares, madness, contagious diseases; they provoke discord among relatives and neighbors and instigate all sorts of perversions.

The crisis assumes the form of a loss of difference between the living and the dead, a casting down of all barriers between two normally separate realms. We have here the proof that the dead incarnate violence; exterior and transcendent violence when order reigns, immanent violence when things turn bad and maleficent reciprocity walks abroad. The dead do not want the total destruction of an order that is after all basically their own. After they have brought about a paroxysm of sorts in the community they are willing once more to accept the homage of their descendants; they cease to haunt the living and withdraw to their usual retreats. If they do not go into exile of their own accord, they allow themselves to be led into exile by the community's ritual observances. The difference between the living and the dead is thereby restored.

This troubling confusion between living and dead is sometimes regarded as the consequence of the crisis and sometimes as its cause. The punishments that the dead inflict upon the living are indistinguishable from the consequences of wrongdoing. In a small community hubris spreads rapidly, with, as we know, dire results. Thus the vengeance of the dead, like the vengeance of the gods, is both real and implacable. It is, in fact, violence's own revenge on those who wield it.

In this instance the dead have clearly replaced the gods, and the beliefs relating to the dead lead us back to our discussion of Oedipus, Dionysus, and the rest. Yet a question remains: How can the dead incarnate violence as authoritatively as do the gods?

Death is the ultimate violence that can be inflicted on a living being. It is therefore the extreme of maleficence. With death a contagious sort of violence is let loose on the community, and the living must take steps to protect themselves against it. So they quarantine death, creating a *cordon sanitaire* all around it. Above all, they have recourse to funeral rites, which (like all other rites) are dedicated to the purgation and expulsion of maleficent violence.

Whatever the cause and circumstances of his death, the dying man finds himself in a situation similar to that of the surrogate victim vis-à-vis the community. The grief of the mourner is a curious mixture of terror and hope—a mixture conducive to resolutions of good conduct in the future. The death of the individual has something of the quality of a tribute levied for the continued existence of the collectivity. A human being dies, and the solidarity of the survivors is enhanced by his death.

The surrogate victim dies so that the entire community, threatened by the same fate, can be reborn in a new or renewed cultural order. Having sown the seeds of death, the god, ancestor, or mythic hero then dies himself or selects a victim to die in his stead. In so doing he bestows a new life on men. Understanding this process, we can also understand why death should be regarded as the elder sister, not to say the mother and ultimate source, of life itself.

Belief in a union between life and death has long been ascribed to the cycle of the seasons, the annual rebirths and deaths in the plant kingdom. Such a theory simply involves heaping one myth on top of another; it refuses to acknowledge the violence that permeates all human relationships. The theme of death and resurrection flourishes in regions where seasonal change is nonexistent or very slight. And even where analogies do exist or when the religious imagination has put them to use, we are not justified in regarding nature as the source of this belief. The periodicity of the seasons serves as a rhythmic accompaniment to the changes that occur in human relationships and have as their pivot the death of a sacrificial victim.

Death, then, contains the germ of life. There is no life on the communal level that does not originate in death. Death can appear as the

true godhead, the confluence of the most beneficent and most maleficent forms of violence. This may well have been what Heraclitus
meant when he declared: "Dionysus and Hades are the same." Surely
he is not merely making reference to Dionysus' anecdotal link to the
Underworld, but rather is directing attention to death, community
harmony, and the genesis of the gods.

A duality of "good" and "bad" may be found even in the material
aspects of death. As long as the process of decomposition takes its
course, the cadaver is an impure element. Like the violent disintegration of a society, the physiological decomposition of the corpse leads
gradually from a very complex system of differentials to undifferentiated dust. The forms of the living revert to formlessness. And language itself falters in describing the "remains." The rotting corpse
becomes, in the words of Bossuet, "cet objet qui n'a de nom dans
aucune langue."

However, once the process has been completed and the terrible
dynamism of decomposition is over, the impure status of the "nameless
object" is generally terminated as well. In certain societies the dry and
whitened bones of the deceased are thought to possess beneficial properties, to be conducive to fertility.[2]

Every death tends to become ritualized after the model of the generative expulsion, to make allusion to the underlying mystery of
violence. In return, the generative expulsion may be memorialized in
the form of death. This is precisely what takes place when the dead
exercise functions that are elsewhere the prerogative of the gods. All
aspects of violence are assimilated to an individual ancestor or to the
entire legion of the dead. The monstrous character of the original
ancestor, the fact that he is frequently the incarnation of an animal,
can be seen as proof that the "monstrous double" still holds sway at the
origin of the cult. The worship of the dead, like the worship of the
gods, represents an interpretation of the role of violence in the destiny
of a community. In fact, it is the most transparent of all such interpretations, the closest to what actually occurred *the first time*—except, of
course, that it has misconstrued, as always, the mechanism of recovered
unanimity. This interpretation states explicitly that the origin of any
cultural order involves a human death and that the decisive death is
that of a member of the community.

    I BEGAN BY TRACING the course of violence
through those beings who appear to incarnate it: mythic heroes, sacred
kings, gods, and deified ancestors. Those various incarnations enrich

[2] See Chapter 9, p. 247.

our understanding of the many roles of violence and clarify the function of the surrogate victim and the preeminent importance of violent unanimity.

These incarnations are invariably illusory in one sense. Violence belongs to all men, and thus to none in particular. All the actors have the same role, with the exception of the surrogate victim. But anybody can play the part of surrogate victim. It is futile to look for the secret of the redemptive process in distinctions between the surrogate victim and the other members of the community. The crucial fact is that the choice of the victim is arbitrary. The religious interpretations we have considered so far are at fault precisely because they attribute the beneficial results of the sacrifice to the superhuman nature of the victim or of the other participants, insofar as any of these appears to incarnate the supreme violence.

In addition to such "personalized" interpretations, there is an impersonal approach. It corresponds to the full range of the term *sacred*, or rather, of the Latin *sacer*, which is sometimes translated "sacred," sometimes "accursed," for it encompasses the maleficent as well as the beneficent. Analogous words can be found in many languages; the famous *mana* of the Melanesians, for example, or the *wakan* of the Sioux and the *orenda* of the Iroquois.

In one respect at least the structure of the *sacer* is the least deceptive, the least mythic of all; it postulates no single master of ceremonies, no intervention by a privileged party, even a superhuman one. The fact that the *sacer* can be understood in terms that require no anthropomorphic presence demonstrates that religion should not be defined as animism or anthropomorphism. If religion consisted of "humanizing" the nonhuman or bestowing "souls" wherever they were felt to be lacking, an impersonal apprehension of the sacred would not be possible.

My effort to group all the subjects considered in this study under a general heading has resulted in the title *Violence and the Sacred*. This impersonal designation is fundamental to our discussion. In Africa, as in many other parts of the world, there is only a single term to denote the two faces of the sacred—the interplay of order and disorder, of difference lost and retrieved, as enacted in the immutable drama of the sacrifice of the incestuous king. This term serves to describe all the royal transgressions, all forbidden as well as all permitted sexual practices, all forms of violence and brutality; unclean things, decaying matter, monstrosities, disputes between relatives and neighbors, outbursts of spite, envy, and jealousy. In addition, the same term embraces the creative impulse and the urge for order, for peace, calm, and stability. All these varied significations appear under the aegis of royalty.

Royalty is an incarnation of the sacred. But these same manifestations of the sacred can also exist apart from royalty; we must have recourse to the sacred in order to understand the institution of royalty, but the reverse does not hold true.

Sacrifice too can be defined solely in terms of the sacred, without reference to any particular divinity; that is, it can be defined in terms of maleficent violence polarized by the victim and metamorphosed by his death (or expulsion from the community, which amounts to the same thing) into beneficent violence. Although the sacred is "bad" when it is inside the community, it is "good" when it returns to the exterior. The language of pure sacredness retains whatever is most fundamental to myth and religion; it detaches violence from man to make it a separate, impersonal entity, a sort of fluid substance that flows everywhere and impregnates on contact. The concept of contagion is obviously a by-product of this way of envisaging the sacred. As a concept contagion makes empirical sense in many cases, but it is mythic insofar as it ignores the reciprocal aspect of violence; it literally reifies the violence that is active in human relationships by transforming it into a pseudo-substance. Though generally *less* mythic than the language of divinity, the language of pure sacredness is *more* mythic in that it eliminates the final traces of the real victims, thereby concealing the fact that the sacred cannot function without surrogate victims.

I have used the phrase "violence *and* the sacred"; I might as well have said "violence *or* the sacred." For the operations of violence and the sacred are ultimately the same process. Although ethnologists are generally disposed to acknowledge that violence exists at the heart of the sacred, they also hasten to add that the sacred includes another, more important and directly contradictory element. The sacred, as they see it, involves order as well as disorder, peace as well as war, creation as well as destruction. In fact, the sacred seems so heterogeneous that the specialists have despaired of ever sorting it out. Yet the theory of generative violence permits us to define the sacred in simple, concrete terms that emphasize its underlying unity without overlooking its complexity; it enables us to bring together all the disparate elements of the sacred into an intelligible whole.

Once we have recognized the role of generative violence, it becomes clear why the sacred is able to include within itself so many opposites. Sometimes it rallies the whole community around itself in order to save mankind and restore culture, sometimes it seems intent on destroying its own creations. Men do not worship violence as such. Primitive religion is no "cult of violence" in the contemporary sense of the phrase. Violence is venerated insofar as it offers men what little peace they can ever expect. Nonviolence appears as the gratuitous gift of violence; and there is some truth in this equation, for men are only capable of reconciling their differences at the expense of a third party. The best men can hope for in their quest for nonviolence is the unanimity-minus-one of the surrogate victim.

If primitive religious thought is mistaken in deifying violence, it is correct in its refusal to attribute to mankind the principle of social unity. To date, Western society has escaped the most catastrophic form of basic violence, the violence that is capable of annihilating society. This privilege, however, has not been obtained through the kind of *dépassement* advanced by the idealist philosophers, who cannot conceive either of the nature of this privilege or the reason behind it, and indeed hardly realize their good fortune. That is why modern philosophers attribute the origin of society to a "social contract," either implicit or explicit, rooted in "reason," "good sense," "mutual self-interest," and so forth. They are incapable of grasping the essence of religion and attributing to it a real function. This incapacity is mythic in character, since it perpetuates the religion's own misapprehensions in regard to violence. It evades the problem of human violence and mistakes the nature of the threat this violence poses for human society.

Even the crudest of religious viewpoints acknowledges a truth ignored by even the most lucid nonreligious system. The religious believer knows that the establishment of a human society is no simple matter and that the credit for its accomplishment cannot go to man. The relationship between modern thought and primitive religion is somewhat different from what it appears at first glance. Although modern and primitive man share a fundamental misunderstanding of the nature of violence, primitive man retains certain insights into this nature, insights that are perfectly real and that wholly escape our grasp.

Religion instructs men as to what they must and must not do to prevent a recurrence of destructive violence. When they neglect rites and violate prohibitions they call down upon themselves transcendent violence, which assumes the role of the demonic temptor—an illusion for which men will continue to fight, spiritually as well as physically, to the point of total annihilation. The surrogate victim alone can save them; almighty violence may judge the "guilty" parties to have been sufficiently "punished" and may condescend to become its transcendence once more, to withdraw far enough away to observe mankind from the exterior of the community, yet not so far away that it ceases to inspire the dreadful awe that is essential to man's salvation.

We, the spoiled children of privilege, consider the god's anger as something illusory. In fact it is a terrible reality. Its justice is implacable, its impartiality truly divine. Anger shows no distinctions in its dealings with men; it is at one with reciprocity, with the irresistible tendency of violence to turn against the unfortunate beings who have sought to shape it exclusively to their own uses.

Because of their large-scale and sophisticated organization, modern Western societies have appeared largely immune to violence's law of retribution. In consequence, modern thinkers assume that this law is, and has always been, mere illusion and that those modes of thinking that treat it as real are sheer fantasies. To be sure, these modes of thinking must be considered mythic insofar as they attribute the enforcement of the law to an authority extrinsic to man. But the law of retribution itself is very real; it has its origins in the reality of human relationships. If we are still strangers to this law it is not because we have managed to transcend it, but because its application to the modern world has been indefinitely postponed, for reasons unknown to us. That, perhaps, is what contemporary history is making clear.

EACH OF THE PHENOMENA discussed in this study can be explained by the identity of violence and the sacred. This identity explains the dual influence for good and evil of blood in general and menstrual blood in particular; it also explains the structure of Greek tragedy and Freud's *Totem and Taboo*. The union of the sacred with violence may seem fanciful or incredible; it may jar our habitual way of thinking. But the more we look about us the more intelligible this union appears.

To the examples previously adduced I should like to add one that seems particularly appropriate at this stage of the discussion. It can be phrased as a question: Why is the production of metal, particularly in Africa, accompanied by strict regulations, and the metal workers themselves endowed with sacred qualities? The application of my general theory should yield a ready answer to this small enigma, which forms part of the larger enigma of the sacred.

Metal is the source of inestimable benefits. It facilitates domestic tasks and helps the community defend itself against outside enemies. But these advantages are not without a reverse side; all weapons, after all, are double-edged. The existence of metal increases the danger that would result from an internal conflict; its potentiality for good is balanced by its potentiality for evil. The dual tendency of human relations—toward discord and conflict as well as toward cohesion and harmony—is complemented by the nature of metals.

For better or for worse, the metal worker is the master of a potent form of violence. That is why he is "sacred" in the dual sense of the word. He enjoys certain privileges but is considered a slightly sinister figure. He is someone to be avoided; and his forge is relegated to the outskirts of the community.

Some modern discussion of this phenomenon conveys the impression, at least implicitly, that the prestige of the metal worker arises from the natives' vague sense that he is somehow infringing on domains reserved for "superior civilizations"—especially the most superior civilization of all, our very own. In this interpretation it is not the dangers inherent in the production of metal, or the uses to which men put metal, that inspire fear, but rather the fact that metalworking is the prerogative of the white man. In short, the cult of the metal worker would be related directly or indirectly to a single real object—ourselves. Such a theory bears witness to the monumental fatuousness of a technological culture that has been so dulled by its long and mysterious immunity from attack that it no longer has any consciousness of hubris, or even a word to describe that concept.

Men who have mastered the techniques of metalworking have no reason to regard the process with fear since, after all, they themselves have mastered it. The sacredness of the forge does not emanate from us; we have no monopoly on the technique and exert no influence, Promethean or otherwise, on its practitioners. The specters of nuclear warfare and industrial pollution that menace our own society constitute only one illustration—admittedly a dramatic one—of a law that primitive people regard as real even if they do not entirely understand it but that we dismiss as fictitious: whoever uses violence will in turn be used by it.

The community that sponsors a forge on its outer boundaries is not very different from our own. As long as some profit can be derived from them, the metal workers, or magicians, are left in peace. But as soon as the community becomes aware of some backlash of violence it will shift the responsibility to those who led the community into temptation, the manipulators of sacred violence. They will be accused of having betrayed a community to which they only half belong, of having used against this community a power that had always been mistrusted. The village may be visited by a calamity that has nothing to do with metal or metal production; nevertheless, the metal worker's life will be in jeopardy. In time of trouble he is the one who takes all the blame.

As soon as the sacred—that is, violence—has found its way to the interior of the community, the motif of the surrogate victim will start to emerge. The position of the metal worker, even in time of peace, reveals his connection not only to the magician but also to the sacred king. In certain societies the metal worker, without ceasing to be a kind of pariah, assumes the role of supreme arbiter. In the event of an irresolvable struggle he is called upon to "differentiate" the irreconcilable antagonists, thus proving that he incarnates the sacred violence that is sometimes maleficent, sometimes beneficent. If the metal worker or magician should happen to die at the hands of the community, and the community's hysteria be thereby appeased, the intimate connection between the victim and the sacred seems confirmed. Like all systems of thought founded on sacrifice, the reasoning that endows the metal worker with sacred qualities forms a virtually closed system; it can never be refuted.

The violent death of a metal worker, a sorcerer, a magician, and in general of anybody who seems to share a particular affinity with the sacred, might be seen as a half-way point between spontaneous collective violence and ritual sacrifice. There is a perfect continuity from one to the other. To grasp the nature of this ambiguity is to move closer to an understanding of generative violence and ritual sacrifice, and the relationship between these two phenomena.

THE FAILURE OF MODERN MAN to grasp the nature of religion has served to perpetuate its effects. Our lack of belief serves the same function in our society that religion serves in societies more directly exposed to essential violence. We persist in disregarding the power of violence in human societies; that is why we are reluctant to admit that violence and the sacred are one and the same thing. It is important to insist on this identity; and the field of lexicography provides ample supporting evidence.

Many languages, most notably Greek, contain terms that reveal the nondifference between violence and the sacred. And it is easily demonstrable that cultural evolution in general, and lexicographers in particular, have a tendency to put asunder that which primitive language has joined; that it, to suppress the scandalous conjunction of violence and the sacred.

We will take our examples from a work of great stature whose very mistakes carry weight: Emile Benveniste's *Le Vocabulaire des institutions indo-européennes*. The use of the term *hieros* to qualify instruments of violence and warfare is so regular that scholars sometimes translate the word as "strong," "active," "excited," etc. The Greek *hieros* is related to the Vedic *isirah*, which is generally translated as "vital force." This is itself a compromise that conceals the conjunction of the most maleficent and most beneficent forces in the nucleus of the term. It is the sort of compromise that modern scholars frequently resort to when defining terms that have to do with the sacred.

Benveniste asserts that *hieros* has nothing to do with violence and should always be translated as "sacred." He makes no mention of the fact that even in French the word *sacré* retains an ambiguous sense, perhaps inherited from the Latin *sacer*. To the linguist, the fact that *hieros* is frequently associated with terms implying violence is of no importance. The use of this term seems to him justified not by the word it directly modifies but by the appearance in the text of some god or some specifically religious motif he regards as wholly foreign to the idea of violence.

In order to eliminate from words relating to the sacred a duality he finds both dubious and inconvenient, Benveniste has recourse to two procedures. The first, as we have just seen, is to suppress altogether whichever of the two meanings has been most weakened in the course of the historical evolution of the word. In those rare cases where historical evolution has had no effect on the word's duality, or where two opposite meanings both carry equal weight, Benveniste unhesitatingly affirms that we are really dealing with two different terms, accidentally grouped together under the same signifier. This second procedure is illustrated by Benveniste's treatment of *kratos* and its derived adjective *krateros*. *Kratos* is generally translated as "divine force." *Krateros* is sometimes used of a god, in which case it is translated as "divinely strong," "supernaturally powerful," and so forth. At other times it qualifies things that seem so foreign to *our notion* of the gods that the lexicographer flatly refuses the Greeks permission to consider them divine:

> When from *kratos* we turn to *krateros* we expect the adjective to convey the same sense as the substantive. *Kratos* always denotes a quality pertaining to heroes, warriors and leaders; it is reasonable to assume that the adjective *krateros* has a eulogistic connotation, and such is indeed the case. However, this makes it all the more surprising to encounter *krateros* being used to describe qualities which are very far from praiseworthy and which incur blame or reproach. When Hecuba, Priam's wife, calls the Achilles who has just killed her son Hector an *aner krateros* (*Iliad* XXIV. 212) she clearly intends no compliment on his martial virtue. Paul Mazon translates the phrase as "brutal hero." And to appreciate the application of the adjective to Ares (II. 515) we must consider it in the context of some of the god's other epithets: *miaiphonos* (homicide), *androphones* (killer of men), *brotoloigos* (fatal to mortals), *aidelos* (destroyer) . . . none of which present him in a favorable light.
>
> The discrepancy goes even deeper. Whereas *kratos* applies exclusively to gods and men, *krateros* can refer to animals and objects, and its sense in those cases is always "hard, cruel, violent. . . ."

In Hesiod, who uses some of the same vocabulary, we find the two meanings we have ascribed to the Homeric *krateros:* favorable when it accompanies the word *amumon*, "without reproach" (*Theog.* 1013), unfavorable when it describes Ares the killer of men (*Scutum* 92, 101) or a dragon (*Theog.* 328), or the Erinyes. . . .[3]

The basis for the semantic partitioning of the word is its "eulogistic connotation," the fact that it sheds favorable light, the fact of its *beneficence*. Benveniste does not entertain the notion of a union of the beneficent and maleficent within the context of sacred violence. *Krateros* can apply equally to a savage beast tearing apart its prey and to the iron blade of a sword; to the hardness of a breastplate, to terrible illnesses, to the most barbarous acts, to strife, and to vehement conflicts. Were we to quote every example offered by Benveniste, virtually all the elements of the sacrificial crisis would pass in parade before our eyes. Thus we are dealing with a term that admirably displays the conjunction of good and bad violence within the sacred. Because the two meanings of the word are too widely distributed for either of them to be suppressed, Benveniste concludes that the lexicographical grouping around *kratos* reveals "a very unusual semantic situation." This grouping, he asserts, is a unity in appearance only; in reality the two conflicting meanings should be attached to "two Indo-European roots of distinctly different origins, though related if not actually similar in form."[4]

The sole basis for this theory is a refusal to admit the union of violence and the divine that is made manifest by the various usages of *krateros*. The good *krateros* of gods and heroes is the same as the bad *krateros* of monsters, plagues, and savage beasts. An example cited by Benveniste himself—*Ares krateros*—shows the futility of his division. Here, Benveniste asserts, is an instance of the bad *krateros*. That may be, but Ares is no less divine for being cruel and brutal. And Ares is the god of war. It may be that the deification of war is a far more significant matter than the bombastic odes dedicated to the military glory of an Augustus or a Louis XIV might suggest.

In the rationalist's dictionary the sacred is defined either as a concept that is still lacking in specificity or as a fully developed concept that has become confused with other concepts. The lexicographer takes it upon himself to make a clean sweep of all "ambiguities," "confusions," and "uncertainties" and to replace them with a perfectly coherent set of significations. In fact, this tendency is not confined to lexicography alone. As we have seen, religious interpretations of the sacrificial crisis have always been inclined to categorize its accompanying phenomena as either "good" or "bad." The farther one progresses, the more pronounced becomes the tendency to make separate and distinct entities

[3] Emile Benveniste, *La Vocabulaire des institutions indo-européennes*, 2 vols. (Paris 1969), 2:78–79.
[4] Ibid., p. 80.

of the two aspects of the sacred. In Latin, for example, *sacer* has retained its original double connotation, but the need to isolate the beneficent aspects of the word has resulted in an offshoot, *sanctus*. So it is that modern lexicography is caught up in the continuing mythological evolution that is little by little effacing the last signs of the generative experience and making the true role of violence ever more difficult to ascertain.

Some, however, have resisted this impulse. Here, for example, is Henri Jeanmaire's remarkable commentary on the word *thysias*, which signifies a priestess of Bacchus or one of the bacchantes. The word is derived from the verb *thyiein*, which we discussed earlier on in connection with another derivative, *thymos*:

> The probable etymology of the word suggests that it is connected to a verb whose sense remains somewhat ambiguous; it signifies to make a sacrifice, on the one hand, and on the other to hurl oneself impetuously or to whirl around like something caught up in a tempest, or to swirl about like the waters of a river or sea, or bubble up like spilled blood, like anger, like mad rage. There is no need to split these two sets of usages, as is sometimes done today; no need to divide them into two signifiers with different roots, especially if we are willing to agree that this tempestuous whirling motion corresponds to one of the methods by which a bacchante attains her characteristic state of trance, and that a sacrifice, a *sparagmos* or otherwise, is the normal accompaniment of this sort of state; or even that certain archaic forms of sacrifice provided the occasion for ecstatic exercises. In addition, some modern observers have remarked that the death throes of the sacrificial victim and the convulsive gestures of the possessed person are both seen as manifestations of divine intervention, and that the analogy between them is appreciated and explicitly expressed.[5]

THE FORMAL IDENTIFICATION of violence with the sacred, as brought about by the mechanism of the surrogate victim, will now permit us to complete that theory of sacrifice whose basic tenets were set forth in the earlier chapters of this study. I have already rejected the traditional interpretation of sacrifice as an offering made to the gods, often in the form of food, that provides "nourishment" for the transcendent being. This traditional interpretation is certainly mythic, but should not for that reason be regarded as simply imaginary. It is worth noting that religious discourse is closer to the truth on this point than all the theories that modern scholars have sought to put in its place.

Polarized by the sacrificial killing, violence is appeased. It subsides.

[5] Jeanmaire, *Dionysos*, p. 158.

We might say that it is expelled from the community and becomes part of the divine substance, from which it is completely indistinguishable, for each successive sacrifice evokes in diminishing degree the immense calm produced by the act of generative unanimity, by the initial appearance of the god. Just as the human body is a machine for transforming food into flesh and blood, generative unanimity is a process for changing bad violence into stability and fecundity. On the other hand, by the very fact of its occurrence, this unanimity has set up a mechanism that will repeat its operation indefinitely in the attenuated form of ritual sacrifice. If the god is nothing more nor less than the massive violence that was expelled by the original act of generative unanimity, then ritual sacrifice can indeed be said to offer him portions of his own substance. Every time the sacrifice accompanies its desired effect, and bad violence is converted into good stability, the god is said to have accepted the offering of violence and consumed it. It is not surprising, then, that all theological systems place sacrificial operations under the jurisdiction of the divinity. Successful sacrifice prevents violence from reverting to a state of immanence and reciprocity; that is, it reinforces the status of violence as an exterior influence, transcendent and beneficent. Sacrifice accords the god all that he needs to assure his continued growth and vigor. And it is the god himself who "digests" the bad immanence, transforming it into good transcendence, that is, into his own substance. The alimentary metaphor is confirmed by the fact that in most cases the sacrificial victim is an animal that man uses for food. Behind this metaphor it is easy to discern violence at work and to catch a glimpse of its metamorphoses. Although religious explanations of sacrifice are wholly false from the viewpoint of strict scientific truth, they are perfectly true from the only viewpoint of any interest to religion—that of protecting human beings from violence. For if we neglect to feed the god, he will waste away; or else, maddened by hunger, he will descend among men and lay claim to his nourishment with unexampled cruelty and ferocity.

The surrogate victim is generally destroyed, and always expelled from the community. As the violence subsides it is thought to have departed with the victim, to have somehow been projected outside the community. The community itself is felt to be free of infection—so long, that is, as the cultural order within it is respected.

Once the outer limits of the community have been crossed we enter the domain of savage sacredness, which recognizes neither boundaries nor limits. This is the realm not only of gods and supernatural creatures, of monsters and the dead, but also of nature itself (insofar as it remains untouched by culture), of the cosmos and of all the rest of humanity.

We are wont to say that primitive peoples are imbued with the sacred. The truth is that these peoples assume, just as we ourselves do, that they have freed themselves, up to a point, from subjection to the sacred. They alone adhere to the rules, promulgated by the sacred itself, that allow them to maintain a precarious independence from divine intervention. Foreigners are considered something less and more than human because they fail to follow these rules. They may appear very maleficent or very beneficent, but in either case they are deeply imbued with the sacred.

Each community sees itself as a lonely vessel adrift in a fast ocean whose seas are sometimes calm and friendly, sometimes rough and menacing. The first requirement for staying afloat is to obey the rules of navigation dictated by the ocean itself. But the most diligent attention to these rules is no guarantee of permanent safety. The ship is far from watertight; ceaselessly, insidiously, it takes in water. Only a constant repetition of rites seems to keep it from sinking.

If it is true that the community has everything to fear from the sacred, it is equally true that the community owes its every existence to the sacred. For in perceiving itself as uniquely situated outside the sphere of the sacred, the community assumes that it has been engendered by it; the act of generative violence that created the community is attributed not to men, but to the sacred itself. Having brought the community into existence, the sacred brings about its own expulsion and withdraws from the scene, thereby releasing the community from its direct contact.

The more men reflect on the apparent supremacy of the sacred, on the vast disproportion between it and the community, the clearer it becomes that the initiative in all domains, on all levels, belongs to the sacred. The birth of the community is first and foremost an act of separation. That is why metaphors of severance permeate the generative act. For instance, the royal rites of the Incwala involve a cutting, biting, and slicing of the New Year. In other words, the new temporal cycle is inaugurated by a break with the sacred, which is invariably "bad" when it has infiltrated the community. Whether we refer to catharsis or purification, purgation or exorcism, it is actually the idea of evacuation and separation that is foremost. Modern thinkers view the sacred solely as a mediating force, because they try to interpret primitive reality in terms of a religion that has been purged of its maleficent qualities. But as we have seen, any mingling of the community and the sacred, whether due to the intervention of gods, mythic heroes, or the dead, produces exclusively maleficent results. Every supernatural visitation is prompted by the spirit of revenge. Benefits accrue only after the divinity has departed.

This is not to say that the mediative element has been eliminated. A total separation of the community and the sacred would be fully as dangerous as a fusion of the two. Too great a separation can result in a massive onslaught of the sacred, a fatal backlash; then, too, there is always the risk that men will neglect or even forget how to implement the preventive measures taught them by the sacred itself as a defense against its own violence. Human existence thus remains under the constant tutelage of the sacred and is observed, regulated, and promoted by it.

The outcome of this relationship is as follows: although men cannot live in the midst of violence, neither can they survive very long by ignoring its existence or by deluding themselves into the belief that violence, despite the ritual prohibitions attendant on it, can somehow be put to work as the mere tool or servant of mankind. The complex and delicate nature of the community's dealings with the sacred, the ceaseless effort to arrive at the ordered and uninterrupted accord essential to the well-being of the community, can only be expressed, for want of the naked truth, in terms of optimum *distance*. If the community comes too near the sacred it risks being devoured by it; if, on the other hand, the community drifts too far away, out of range of the sacred's therapeutic threats and warnings, the effects of its fecund presence are lost.

This spatial interpretation is clearly seen in societies in which the sacred assumes the form of a special personage—the African sacred king, for example. The presence in the midst of the community of a figure deeply imbued with the sacred poses extraordinary problems. In certain cases the king is forbidden to touch the ground for fear of contaminating it and thereby causing the death of his subjects. Sometimes, too, the king is forbidden to feed himself; the simple fact of his having touched food makes it unsuitable fare for ordinary mortals. And there are cultures where the sacred monster is carefully hidden from view, not for his own protection but for that of his subjects, who would be struck dead by a single glance from him.

Such precautions are designed to prevent direct contact. They do not mean to imply that it is bad to shelter such an extraordinary being; quite the contrary. As we have seen, the king is both very "bad" and extremely "good"; the *historical* alternation of violence and peace is transferred from time to space. The results have a faint analogy to modern theories of the transformation of energy—perhaps because religious thought habitually draws its models from nature.

The king's subjects may feel ill at ease in his presence, awed by his sheer superabundance of power, his *silwane*. Nevertheless, they would be terrified if they were deprived of his presence. Our "timidity" and "respect" are diluted forms of these same phenomena. There is an optimum distance from which to confront a divine incarnation; it permits the reception of beneficent effects without giving access to maleficent ones. The absolute can be likened to fire: too near and one gets burned, too far away and one gets nothing. Between these two extremes is a zone where one is warmed and heartened by the welcome light.

ALL SACRIFICIAL RITES are based on two substitutions. The first is provided by generative violence, which substitutes a single victim for all the members of the community. The second, the only strictly ritualistic substitution, is that of a victim for the surrogate victim. As we know, it is essential that the victim be drawn from outside the community. The surrogate victim, by contrast, is a member of the community. Ritual sacrifice is defined as an inexact imitation of the generative act. Why, we may ask, does sacrifice systematically exclude those who seem the most appropriate victims, who bear the closest resemblance to the original: the members of the community?

The need for some distinction between the original victim and the ritual victims can readily be explained. If the sacrificial victim belonged to the community (as does the surrogate victim), then his death would promote further violence instead of dispelling it. Far from reiterating the effects of generative violence, the sacrifice would inaugurate a new crisis. But because certain conditions must be met, an organization capable of meeting them does not inevitably have to come into being. If we think it does, we succumb to the functionalist illusion. The second sacrificial substitution still poses a problem that must be resolved.

We may wonder if the difference between the original and the copy, between the primordial and the ritual victim, does not have its basis in human reason. A kind of basic good sense would effect the shift from within to without the community. The functional discrepancy between the two types of victim could easily be taken for the "humane" (in the sense of modern humanism) aspect of the sacrifice. What was referred to earlier as sacrificial trickery would in fact be the sacrificers' trickery; they would choose to overlook some of the demands of ritual mimesis. And their casual atittude toward the god's command would stem from an attitude they share with us moderns: deep within themselves, they would sense the futility of these, and indeed of all, rites.

It is tempting to suppose that the second sacrificial substitution shows that fanaticism has already given way to a primitive skepticism that foreshadows our own. Unfortunately, this theory will not stand up. First of all, there are many societies in which the victims are human beings: prisoners of war, slaves, children, even (in the case of the sacred king and related sacrifices) members of the community. In these instances there seems to be no second, sacrificial substitution. This is why the connection between the original violence that had the surrogate victim for object and the ritual imitations that succeeded it is particularly striking in the case of the sacred king. In Chapter 4, when I was attempting to clarify the relationship between the surrogate victim and the rite, the sacred king served as a convenient example of the proximity of the original victim to the ritual victim.

This is not to say that the second sacrificial substitution has been entirely omitted in the case of the sacred king. While an exact repetition of the generative violence is impossible, the very fact that the future victim has been drawn from the community and is designated to replace the surrogate victim sets him apart from the other members of the community and makes normal relations between himself and these other members impossible. He now belongs to a category that can contain only one member at a time, but it is one that nevertheless qualifies as "sacrificeable" to almost the same degree as the categories of cattle and sheep in other societies.

If the sole fact of being selected as a future victim is sufficient to metamorphose the chosen object, to make a sacred personage out of him, then it is not hard to uncover the reasoning behind the different choices of original victim and ritual victims. When a victim has been killed he belongs to the sacred; it is the sacred itself that permits its own expulsion or is expelled in the victim's person. The surrogate victim thus appears as a monster. He is no longer regarded in the same way as the other members of the community.

If the sacrificeable categories are generally made up of creatures who do not and have never belonged to the community, that is because the surrogate victim belongs first and foremost to the sacred. The community, by contrast, has emerged from the sacred and separated itself from it. Members of the community, then, are less suitable as ritual victims than are nonmembers. That is why ritual victims are chosen from outside the community, from creatures (like animals and strangers) that normally dwell amidst sacred things and are themselves imbued with sacredness.

From our vantage point as objective observers the other members of the community seem closer to the original victim and consequently far more suitable, in accordance with the theory of imitation, as sacrificial objects. But the viewpoint of the primordial religious experience is determined by the generative violence. From that perspective the surrogate victim is completely transformed. It is this transformation that serves to protect the community from violence, that prevents the faithful from choosing one of their own number as a replacement for the original victim, and that consequently helps prevent any new outbreak of reciprocal violence. If the ritual victim is drawn from outside the community—if the very fact of choosing a victim bestows on him an aura of exteriority—the reason is that the surrogate victim is not perceived as he really was—namely, as a member of the community like all the others.

This choice should not, then, be attributed to a kind of primitive skepticism. The centrifugal dynamism of the second substitution has its origins in religion itself, in protective misapprehension. It has nothing to do with a primitive effort to escape the tyranny of religion. And if the community is spared, it is not because it has violated the law of exact imitation but because it has rigorously observed it. Whatever deception is involved in the sacrificial act must be attributed to the scapegoat mechanism, not to its beneficiaries.

We should not conclude, however, that the surrogate victim is simply foreign to the community. Rather, he is seen as a "monstrous double." He partakes of all possible differences within the community, particularly the difference between within and without; for he passes freely from the interior to the exterior and back again. Thus, the surrogate victim constitutes both a link and a barrier between the community and the sacred. To even so much as represent this extraordinary victim the ritual victim must belong both to the community and to the sacred.

It should now be clear why ritual victims tend to be drawn from categories that are neither outside nor inside the community, but marginal to it: slaves, children, livestock. This marginal quality is crucial to the proper functioning of the sacrifice.

If the victim is to polarize the aggressive tendencies of the community and effect their transfer to himself, continuity must be maintained. There must be a "metonymic" relationship between members of the community and ritual victims. There must also be discontinuity. The victim must be neither too familiar to the community nor too foreign to it. We have previously noted that this ambiguity is essential to the cathartic functioning of the sacrifice. But we could not explain how it was put into practice, nor even imagine how an institution as subtle and complex as that of sacrifice could function without its inventors (who are also its operators) being aware of the secret of its operation. Now we see that there is nothing surprising in this fact, at least on the level that concerns us here. Ritual requires the sacrifice of a victim as similar as possible to the "monstrous double." The marginal categories from which these victims are generally drawn barely fulfill this requirement, but they provide the least unsatisfactory compromise. Situated as they are between the inside and the outside, they can perhaps be said to belong to both the interior and the exterior of the community.

Ritualistic thought does not limit itself to seeking out those categories that are the least unsuited for supplying ritual victims. Once the victims have been obtained, it strives in various ways to make them conform to its own image of the original victim and simultaneously to increase their quotient of cathartic potential. We consider that anything involving this kind of intervention is *sacrificial preparation*; that is, our use of the term goes beyond the usual definition of *sacrificial preparation* as the ritual actions that immediately precede a sacrificial killing.

The victim should belong both to the inside and the outside of the community. As there is no category that perfectly meets this requirement, any creature chosen for sacrifice must fall short in one or another of the contradictory qualities required of it. It will be deficient in its exterior or its interior connections, but never in both at the same time. The goal is to make the victim wholly sacrificeable. In its broadest sense, then, sacrificial preparation employs two very different approaches. The first seeks to make appear more foreign a victim who is too much a part of the community. The second approach seeks to reintegrate into the community a victim who is too foreign to it.

The sacred king illustrates the first sort of preparation. His choice as king is not sufficient to transform this future sacrificial victim into the "monstrous double" he must reincarnate. In order to eliminate his lingering and superfluous humanity, in order to cut him off from the community, he is required to commit an act of incest, thereby absorbing an enormous charge of maleficent sacredness. At the end of the period of preparation the king has taken on both the interior and the exterior qualities that are required to transform him into a sacred monster.

The procedure must be inverted for a victim who sins by an excess of exterior qualities. The sacrifice of cattle in the Dinka ceremonies, described by Godfrey Lienhardt in *Divinity and Experience*, illustrates this second type of sacrificial preparation.[6] The Dinka never sacrifice an animal fresh from the herd. First it undergoes a period of isolation from its fellow cattle, being sheltered in a special place adjacent to human habitations. The halter it wears is reserved for sacrificial beasts.

[6] Cf. Chapter 4, pp. 97–99.

Invocations are pronounced, destined to bring it closer to the community and link it to the human members. We have already discussed the similar invocations that treat the victim as a human being.[7]

In summary, it is apparent that the intimate relationship that normally exists between the Dinka and their cattle, remarkable though this relationship may be, is still not sufficient for sacrificial purposes. The identification between man and beast must be such that the latter assumes the role of the original outcast and draws all the reciprocal hostilities of the community to itself. Every member of the community must be able to consider the beast, before its metamorphosis into a "very sacred object," as the logical target for his anger.

Sacrificial preparations involve many actions that may seem contradictory, but all are perfectly adapted to their goals. With persistent foresight the religious mind pursues its ends and without realizing it fulfills all the conditions for catharsis. Its only interest is to imitate the generative violence as faithfully as possible. It strives to procure, and if need be to invent, a sacrificial victim as similar as possible to its ambiguous vision of the original victim. The model it imitates is not the true model, but a model transfigured by the mechanism of the "monstrous double." This transfiguration, this primordial difference, directs all religious thought toward victims that, thanks to their nature and sacrificial preparation, are neither divisive nor trivial victims, thus assuring for the ritual performance a cathartic value beneficial to the community that enacts it.

We encounter once again a remarkable fact: religious misapprehension figures largely in the very real protection offered society by ritual sacrifice, and indeed by religion in general.

---

[7] Cf. Chapter 1, p. 13.

ᴏᴈᴚᴚ| *Chapter Eleven*

The Unity of All Rites

ᴏᴈᴚᴚ| WE MAY NOW TURN our attention to certain ritual forms that, because of their frankly disagreeable nature, are often regarded as aberrations. In fact they are neither more nor less explicable than any other rites when viewed without reference to generative violence, and they become perfectly intelligible when seen in that context. Our discussion of the second type of sacrificial preparation—the integration into the community of a victim of foreign origin—leads directly into a consideration of the most notorious example of cannibalistic ritual, as practiced by the Tupinamba Indians of northwest Brazil.[1]

The Tupinamba occupy a prominent place in the intellectual history of modern Europe. The two Indians whom Montaigne met in Rouen and referred to in his *Essays* were members of this tribe. They thus served as models for the most famous pre-eighteenth-century portrait of the "noble savage," who was shortly to play a great role in the history of Western humanism.

War was endemic among this people, who made it a practice to devour all the enemies they could lay their hands on. However, their cannibalism assumed two distinct forms. An enemy killed in the course of battle was eaten on the spot without further ado. Outside the community and its laws there was no place for ritual; undifferentiated violence held sway.

The ritual form of cannibalism was reserved for enemies who were brought alive to the village. These prisoners lived for months and sometimes years on intimate terms with the men who would one day devour them. They participated in their captors' daily activities and married into their families; much the same relationship existed for a while between themselves and their sacrificers (for, as we shall see, we are dealing with sacrifice here) as their sacrificers maintained among themselves.

The prisoner was subjected to two apparently contradictory modes

---

[1] I will discuss only those aspects of the Tupinamba rituals that bear directly on my argument. For further information on these practices, see Alfred Métraux, *Religions et magies indiennes d'Amérique du Sud* (Paris 1967), pp. 43–79.

of treatment. Sometimes his sexual favors were sought after, and he was treated with respect and even veneration. At other times he was the object of abuse, showered with insults and blows.

Shortly before the date of his execution, the prisoner's "escape" was ritually staged. Invariably, of course, he was quickly recaptured and—for the first time—bound with a heavy rope around his ankles. His master now stopped giving him food, and he was forced to resort to stealing. One of the early travelers cited by Métraux reports that the prisoner was "permitted during this period to lay about him with his fists, to steal fowl and geese and other things, and to do his utmost to avenge his coming death." In short, the future victim was encouraged to violate the laws. Most modern observers agree that the purpose of these indulgences was to transform the prisoner into a "scapegoat." Francis Huxley remarks:

> It is the fate of the prisoner to act out a number of contradictory roles and incarnate them in himself. He is an enemy who is adopted; he takes the place of the man in whose honour he will be killed; he is an in-law and an outcast; he is honoured and reviled, a scapegoat and a hero; he is intimidated but, if he shows fear, is thought unworthy of the death that awaits him. By acting out these primarily social roles, he becomes a complete human being, exemplifying the contradictions that society creates: an impossible situation, which can only end in his death. The impossibility is exaggerated when he is charged, by ritual, with the powers and attributes of the culture-hero: he becomes the representative of the other world living in the centre of this one, a Janus figure too sacred to live with.[2]

This is an admirable summary, although it should be added that the recipient of society's contradictory drives does not in the end appear as a paragon of humanity, but as a "monstrous double" and a god. As Huxley points out, it is the true relationship between society and human nature that is laid forth here; and because this truth is intolerable, it must somehow be expelled. This is where generative violence plays its role; its basic function is to get rid of the truth, to transpose it beyond the realm of human activity.

In order to understand this operation we must realize that the surrogate victim actually brings about communal cohesion. Indeed, ritual cannibalism remains inaccessible to the intellect unless some basis in social reality can be found for it. And as long as we insist on interpreting the "scapegoat" in purely psychological terms we can only assume that cannibals are seeking some sort of moral justification for their acts of violence. It is true that the more misdeeds the prisoner commits, the

---

[2] Francis Huxley, *Affable Savages* (New York, 1966), p. 254.

more legitimate the sanctions imposed on him might appear. But the primary purpose of the rites has nothing to do with satisfying some neurosis or putting to rest some guilt complex. They are meant to bring about solid, concrete results. If the modern mind fails to recognize the strongly functional nature of the scapegoat operation and all its sacrificial surrogates, the most basic phenomena of human culture will remain misunderstood and unresolved.

The mechanism of the surrogate victim is redemptive twice over: by promoting unanimity it quells violence on all fronts, and by preventing an outbreak of bloodshed within the community it keeps the truth about men from becoming known. The mechanism transposes this truth to the realm of the divine, in the form of an inscrutable god.

The prisoner drew to his person all the community's inner tensions, all its accumulated bitterness and hatred. Through his death he was expected to transform maleficent violence into sacred beneficence, to reinvigorate a depleted cultural order. Ritual cannibalism is a rite that functions like any of the other rites I have discussed. The Tupinamba were following a model—or rather, their ritual system was following a model. They were trying to reproduce an original event that actually took place, to recover the unanimity that occurred and recurred around the person of the surrogate victim. If the prisoner was treated in two contradictory ways, if he was sometimes vilified and sometimes honored, it was because he represented the primordial victim. He was hated insofar as he polarized the as yet untransformed violence; he was revered insofar as he transformed the violence and set in motion the unifying mechanism of the surrogate victim. The more detestable the victim was made to appear and the more passion he aroused, the more effectively the machinery functioned.

The role of the Tupinamba prisoner is, therefore, similar to that of the African king. Consecrated by his future death, his person represents—not successively, but simultaneously—two aspects of the sacred. He takes upon himself the totality of violence during his lifetime and bears his burden for eternity, beyond reach of time.

It seems likely that the prisoner was intended to reincarnate a mythical hero who, in certain versions of Tupinamba legend, appeared as a prisoner who was about to be executed and eaten. Thus, from the perspective of the practitioners, ritual cannibalism was designed to reproduce a primordial event.

The cannibalism of the Tupinambas, like the incestuous practices of certain African monarchies, inflames our imagination and tends to distract attention from the essential intent of the ritual, the basic trait that it shares with all other rituals: its sacrificial aspect. We are perhaps more distracted by incest than by cannibalism, but only because cannibalism has not yet found its Freud and been promoted to the status of a major contemporary myth. Some modern film makers have tried, to be sure, to bring cannibalism into fashion, but their efforts to date have been less than successful.

Mircea Eliade makes the acute observation that the sacred precedes cannibalism, that cannibalism may be said not to exist in a "natural" state.[3] In other words, the victim is not killed to be eaten, but eaten because he has been killed. The same is true of animal victims that are afterward eaten. The cannibalistic element, then, requires no special explanation. Moreover, it serves to help explain other, far more mysterious rites. The eating of sacrificial flesh, whether animal or human, can be seen in the light of mimetic desire as a veritable cannibalism of the human spirit in which the violence of others is ritually devoured. Mimetic desire, once frustrated, seeks at once to destroy and to absorb the violence incarnated with the model-obstacle. This explains why cannibals are always eager for their victim to demonstrate by a show of courage that he is the incarnation of supreme violence. And, of course, the victim is eaten only after he has been killed, after the maleficent violence has been completely transformed into a beneficent substance, a source of peace, strength, and fecundity.

Once we have recognized that ritual cannibalism is simply another form of sacrificial rite, the prisoner's preliminary adoption and partial assimilation into the tribe that is going to eat him no longer presents a mystery. Because the victim comes from outside the community, from the realm of the undifferentiated sacred, he is too foreign to be immediately eligible as a proper sacrificial offering. If he is to become a true representative of the original victim he must first establish some sort of relationship with the group and be made to appear like an "insider"—without, however, surrendering that sacred exteriority that remains his essential characteristic.

Through the process of sacrificial preparation the victim acquires a sufficient resemblance to the "natural," direct target of violence—that is, the other members of the community—to ensure the transference of their aggressions and to make him an attractive sacrificial object. At the same time, he remains sufficiently foreign for his death not to risk plunging the community into a cycle of revenge. The only person able, and perhaps to some extent required, to espouse the victim's cause is his wife. But she must not be too insistent in her protests, or she too (along with her children, if she has any) will be summarily executed.

It is now clear how a scrupulous imitation of the surrogate victim, though necessarily affected by the transformation of the first victim,

3 Mircea Eliade, *The Sacred and the Profane* (New York, 1961), p. 103.

establishes a system of ritual practices that conforms to the needs of the community. These practices ensure the "purgation" of violence, its transference to victims whose relationship to the community is neither too close nor too distant; who are, in short, suitable figures for relieving the community of its burden of violence and effecting its "purification." It is equally clear that this system (including the sacrificial preparation that contributes to the "efficiency" of the total operation) can arise purely and simply from an effort to imitate the original murder, the act that either established or reestablished communal unity.

The prisoner's adoption by the community should be regarded as belonging to the second type of sacrificial preparation referred to above. Ritual cannibalism resembles African kingship in that the future victim is consecrated during his lifetime. To discern the relationship between the two rites we might think in terms of Jean Genet's *Deathwatch*, which deals with a condemned prisoner whose favors are sought by a pair of petty criminals—"enemy brothers," so to speak—who are fascinated by the prospect of his imminent execution.

The relationship between the African kingship system and the cannibalism of the Tupinambas is somewhat blurred because in the former case the victim is drawn from within the community, in the latter from without. The process of sacrificial preparation functions in a contradictory manner to achieve the same results in both cases. By integrating the prisoner within the community the Tupinamba are pursuing the same goal as the Dinka, who separate their sacrificial beast from the herd and shelter it among the villagers. Among the Tupinamba the practical application of the principle is carried to far greater lengths. And the tribe's extraordinary adoption of the prisoner seems to support my theory that the surrogate victim is fundamentally a member of the community, a neighbor of those destined to kill him. The Tupinamba seem to have been particularly conscious of the "nearness" of the original victim, and in order to reproduce this quality without compromising the sacrificial effectiveness of the rite, they devised a system of implacable logic and rare ingenuity.

AS IN THE CASE of the Tsimshians (see Chapter 9), violence among the Tupinamba is shifted from the interior of the community to the exterior. This displacement is sacrificial in character and is by no means limited to mere verbiage; the communities actually go to war with one another and devour their respective members. Here again it can be said that the tribes have come to an agreement never to agree; that a permanent state of war is maintained for the express purpose of providing victims for ritual cannibalism. The number of captives on either side should be more or less equal in order to constitute a more or less reciprocal exchange; and this exchange would seem somehow to be linked to the exchange of women, which is also (again, as in the case of the Tsimshians) accompanied by violence. But whether it is a question of prisoners or women, the exchange ritualized into warfare and the warfare ritualized into exchange are both variants of the same sacrificial shift from the interior of the community to the exterior. Both are equally beneficial in that they keep violence from exploding precisely where it would do the most damage, in the midst of the elementary group. Thus, the interminable vengeance engulfing two rival tribes may be read as an obscure metaphor for vengeance that has been effectively shifted from the interior of the community. This displacement is not, of course, mere shadow play. The system works precisely because the intimate rivalry between the groups is very real. Moreover, it is evident that this sort of warfare cannot always be confined within reasonable limits.

The various meanings of the word *tobajara* seem to define the parameters of the type of ritual cannibalism practiced by the Tupinambas. In its primary sense it designates the symmetrical posture assumed by the subject in regard to the opposition, the hostile confrontation. The word is related to a verb meaning "to be face to face, to be opposite."[4]

It is worth noting, with regard to *tobajara*, that the prisoner's murder is carried out in a manner that resembles as closely as possible the structure of single combat. The victim is tied with a rope but given enough free play to allow him to defend himself, for a limited time, against the attack of his solitary adversary, his own personal *tobajara*.

It is not surprising that the word *tobajara* refers specifically to the victim of cannibalism. But the word also has a third meaning: "brother-in-law." The brother-in-law is the substitute for the brother, the most natural adversary. In exchange for one of his women, the brother-in-law is ceded a woman "too close" to the giver, a woman who would inevitably become the object of fraternal rivalry if the men of the elementary community reserved their women for their own use. The brother-in-law, then, becomes the sacrificial substitute for the brother as hostile object. The entire structure of the sacrificial system is implicit in the triple semantic thrust of *tobajara*. And this structure reminds us once more of Greek tragedy, which abounds in enemy brothers and enemy brothers-in-law, for example, Eteocles and Polyneices, Oedipus and Creon.

The ideology of ritual cannibalism brings to mind the nationalistic

[4] Huxley, *Affable Savages*, p. 242.

myths of our own modern world. Of course it is conceivable that the observers have distorted the natives' own explanations, but even if this were the case, the distortions would not effect the general outline of my interpretation. A sacrificial cult based on war and the reciprocal murder of prisoners is not substantially different from nineteenth-century nationalistic myths with their concept of an "hereditary enemy." To insist on the differences between two myths of this type is in effect to succumb to the mystique of the myths themselves, to turn away from the identical reality residing at the center of each. In both instances the basic function of foreign wars, and of the more or less spectacular rites that generally accompany them, is to avert the threat of internal dissension by adopting a form of violence that can be openly endorsed and fervently acted upon by all.

In his novel *1984* George Orwell portrays the dictators of two superstates as cynically resolved to perpetuate their struggle in order to maintain permanent control over their mesmerized subjects. The institution of ritual cannibalism, based on the principle of permanent war and designed to perpetuate domestic tranquillity, reminds us that the modern world has no monopoly on such stratagems. It also demonstrates that the concept of permanent warfare is not particular to sophisticated and unscrupulous tyrants but can be put into practice by the primitive communities.

⟡⟡ IT IS NOT DIFFICULT to see the relationship between Tupinamba cannibalism and a theory of ritual based on the concept of the surrogate victim. In fact, this relationship serves to illuminate aspects of the Tupinamba practice that have hitherto seemed obscure; reciprocally, the Tupinamba customs bring into relief certain aspects of the theory that my examination of other rites neglected or ignored.

Limited though they are in number, the ritual practices I have mentioned differ greatly in character as well as in geographical location. Yet in spite of their diversity they all seem to support my claim that the surrogate victim is the basis for all religious systems. It might be prudent, however, to examine still another type of ritual, one that may serve to invalidate this line of argument.

The rites I have discussed up to this point might be said to perpetuate or reinforce certain domestic or religious systems. Their purpose is the maintenance of the status quo, and this purpose explains why they all center around that exemplary guarantor of cultural stability, the unanimous act of violence directed against the surrogate victim.

These rites may be defined as rites of stability or stasis. However, there also exists a body of rites generally referred to as rites of passage. I have not yet considered such rites in the light of my theory; I will not attempt to demonstrate that the surrogate victim lies at the heart of these rites as well.

Rites of passage have to do with the acquisition of a new status. For example, there are initiation rites that confer on adolescents full admission to the community. In our own society the passage from one status to another presents—at least in theory—only minor problems of adaptation, which are limited to those individuals directly involved in the process, those who are actually making the passage. Although this belief has been somewhat shaken in recent times, it continues to exert a strong influence on our thought and conduct.

In primitive societies, however, the slightest change in the status of an isolated individual is treated as if it carried the potential to create a major crisis. What to us appear to be perfectly normal and predictable transitions, essential to the preservation of the social unit, are regarded by primitive man as portents of apocalyptic upheaval.

Arnold Van Gennep's *Rites of Passage* (the work that introduced the term into ethnological parlance) distinguishes two distinct stages in a primitive's change of status. In the first stage he loses his previous status, and in the second he acquires his new one. To attribute this observation to a typically French predilection for neat Cartesian categories would be somewhat unfair, for Van Gennep's analysis does conform to the processes of religious thought. Religious thought does indeed distinguish between these stages, perceiving them as quite independent of one another, separated by a gap that could well become a terrible abyss swallowing up the entire cultural structure.

Van Gennep's observations serve to underline the critical aspect of the process. When he focuses on the initial loss of status, he calls to mind that loss of difference I described earlier; suddenly we find ourselves on familiar terrain. For if all violence involves a loss of difference, all losses of difference also involve violence; and this violence is contagious. Thus we are dealing with the sort of dilemma we encountered in the case of twins. Religious thought makes no distinctions between natural and cultural differences. Perfectly innocent phenomena can provoke fear, but that fear cannot for that reason be dismissed as mere fantasy: there is nothing fantastical about its impact or its results.

The individual who is "in passage" is regarded in the same light as a criminal or as the victim of an epidemic: his mere physical presence increases the risk of violence. The slightest loss of difference, no matter how isolated the case may be, is capable of plunging the entire community into a sacrificial crisis. The slightest tear in the social fabric can spoil the whole garment if not promptly attended to.

Clearly, the first measure in such a situation is to isolate the victim, to forbid all contact between him and the healthy members of the community; he must be placed in quarantine. All suspected victims are included in this proscription. They are kept on the periphery of the community or sometimes even exiled to the forest, jungle, or desert. There undifferentiated violence reigns; there is the sacred realm inhabited by beings devoid of those stable differences, of that fixed status, possessed by men who have freed themselves from the power of the sacred.

Because the modern mind conceives contagion solely in terms of microbiology, it sees no reason why any particular loss of status cannot be restricted to its specific case. Primitive societies view the matter differently. For them, any change in individual status threatens to become universal. It is the nature of such changes to spread like a disease; the individual becomes the first victim and prime carrier of his own infection. In some societies the individual in passage is stripped of his name, his history, and his family connections; he is reduced to an amorphous state of anonymity. In collective initiations, where adolescents of the same age participate together in rites of passage, total equality and unrestricted promiscuity is the rule.

As we have seen, differences disappear in the domain of the sacred only because they are indiscriminately mixed together and become indistinguishable in the confusion. To be associated with the sacred is to share in this monstrosity; to be lacking in differences or over-equipped with them comes to the same thing. That is why the initiate can appear both as a hermaphroditic aberration and as a creature with no sexual identity at all.

The rite of passage is always an awesome experience, because it is impossible to predict at the outset what its course will be. Although the initiate knows what he is losing, he has no idea what he will be taking on. Violence will determine the final result of this monstrous mixture of differences, and the less one has to do with that, the better. In short, structure and change don't go together. And even when change looks predictable to us, religious man fears that it might become uncontrollable. The idea of a nature subservient to social laws, or even to natural laws, is utterly foreign to primitive religion.

"Conservative" is a word too weak to describe the rigidity of spirit and terror of change that characterizes those societies in which the sacred holds sway. The imposition of a socio-religious order appears as an enormous boon, an unhoped-for act of grace that could at any moment be withdrawn. There is no question of subjecting the order to critical evaluation or comparison, of trying to alter and improve it in any way. The primitive mind would regard such endeavors as at once impious and insane, guaranteed to provoke the violent retribution of the gods. The proper posture for man is watchfulness and immobility. A single careless gesture could unleash a holocaust in which society would be utterly destroyed.

Although the prospect of the passage may appear terrifying to the primitive mind, it also offers hope. After all, it was by way of a general outbreak of violence and universal loss of difference—that is, by way of sacrificial crisis—that the community achieved a differentiated order in former times. And it can be hoped that this crisis will achieve the same results. Differences will be restored or established; specifically, the neophyte will gain his coveted new status. A happy outcome must depend on the good will of supreme violence, but the community believes that it can influence this outcome by channeling the "bad" energy into prearranged outlets. In order for the final results to match those of the original action, however, every possible precaution must be taken to follow the original model. The neophytes must adhere to the rules laid down by tradition; they must try to shape the new event in the mold of the old one. For only if the ritual reiterates the original crisis is there hope that the outcome will be the same.

Such is the reasoning behind these rites of passage. We can now readily understand that some of the most bizarre aspects of the rites, variations that have previously been dismissed as "morbid" or "perverse," are simply the logical outcome of certain basic religious views. Instead of avoiding the crisis, the neophyte must advance to meet it, as his ancestors did before him. Instead of fleeing the most painful and terrifying aspects of reciprocal violence, he must submit to each and every one of them in the proper sequence. The postulant must endure hardship, hunger, even torture, because these ordeals were part of the original experience. In some instances it is not enough to submit to violence; one must also inflict violence. This double obligation corresponds to the "bad" reciprocity associated with the sacrificial crisis. It also reminds us that the celebrants in certain festivals are required to perform a number of actions that are normally forbidden: real or symbolic acts of sexual aggression, stealing, the eating of proscribed foods. In some societies cannibalism, prohibited at all other times, forms the essence of the initiation rites. For the Tupinamba the murder of a prisoner constitutes the rite. Indeed, in many societies the ultimate act of initiation is the killing of an animal or a human being.

Any man deprived of his status is transformed into a "monstrous double." For the initiate, this transformation is exteriorized. Sometimes he assumes the role of an animal, threatening to pounce on and devour anyone who comes near him. Like Dionysus or the sacred king, he becomes a lion or a leopard for the duration of the initiatory crisis, expressing himself solely in growls and roars. In some rites, normally marking the culmination of the crisis, he exhibits all the characteristics of violent possession. The successive stages of the rites allow us to trace the real or supposed evolution of the crisis.

Other rites offer additional proof that the entire course of the ceremony is modeled on the original crisis. In addition to rites specifically designed to simulate the crisis itself, we encounter details that reproduce the unanimous violence directed against the surrogate victim and that clearly serve to bring the whole ritualistic process to a close. The introduction of masks at the supreme moment of the process can be taken as a direct allusion to the monstrous double, whose presence had already been suggested by the "metamorphoses" of the neophytes. The forms of the ceremonies may vary widely, but they all bear witness to the violent resolution of the crisis and the subsequent return to order: that is, to the neophytes' assumption of their new and definitive status.

The purpose of rites of passage, then, is to graft onto the model of the original crisis any burgeoning crisis brought into being by a sudden outbreak of undifferentiation; in other words, to change into certainty that awful uncertainty that accompanies contagious violence. With regular repetition and a pattern of success, these rites are gradually transformed into simple tests or trials, becoming increasingly "symbolic" and formalistic. The sacrificial nature of the rites tends to become obscured with the passage of time until finally it is hard to say what the symbols are intended to symbolize.

AS WE HAVE SEEN, there is no real difference between rites of passage and rites intended to maintain the status quo. In both cases the model is the same. The sole purpose of ritual is to ensure total immobility, or failing that, a minimum of disturbance. If the door is opened to admit change, there is always the risk that violence and chaos will force an entry. Some change, of course, is inevitable; men cannot be prevented from growing up, marrying, falling sick, and dying. But primitive societies have found procedures to direct the dangerous flow of energy generated by these events into channels prepared by the cultural order. Some societies even have rituals to cope with the change of seasons. Wherever there is a potential for dangerous change, the remedy lies in ritual; and the rites invariably entail a repetition of the original solution, a rebirth of differences. The model for cultural stability is identical with the model for noncatastrophic change. In the final analysis, then, rites of passage have the same function and the same origin as all other rites.

That is not to say that rites of passage do not have distinctive characteristics. Their most spectacular elements are modeled on the crisis itself (rather than on the resolution of the crisis, as is true of most other rites), and this emphasis gives them their particular initiatory quality. This is also why these rites tend to linger on during periods of general decadence, maintaining their hold even when the most fundamental ritualistic practices have fallen into neglect or disappeared completely. As we have already observed, the generative conclusion is the first thing to disappear. This disappearance cuts the umbilical cord, so to speak, that links all rites to generative violence. The rites then appear to exist on their own, although this is pure illusion.

With the passage of time the terror inspired by the original crisis fades from memory. The younger generation no longer respects the prohibitions laid down by the religious system or watches jealously over its preservation. The younger men have no personal acquaintance with maleficent violence. In subjecting them to rites of passage the culture is trying to induce a state of mind favorable to the perpetuation of a differentiated system. It attempts to recreate the atmosphere of sacred terror and veneration characteristic of its ancestral period, when rites and prohibitions were scrupulously observed.

The structure of the sacrificial crisis and of generative violence permits us to understand the means by which violence is deflected and diffused in human society, and this in turn explains why rites of passage can fulfill a function only as long as they maintain their character as impressive, painful, and at times almost unendurable ordeals. As always, it is a question of keeping the sacrificial crisis in check; in this instance, the concern is directed at the inexperienced neophyte whose youthful impetuosity could well unleash a new crisis.

Rites of passage give the young person a foretaste of what lies in store for anyone rash enough to neglect or transgress prescribed religious rituals. Thanks to these rites, successive generations acquire a healthy respect for the awesomeness of the sacred and learn to perform their religious obligations in such a way as to assure the stability of the cultural order. Physical hardships speak louder than intellectual arguments; it is these hardships that make the establishment of the socioreligious order appear an extraordinary blessing.

Rites of passage thus constitute a vitally important force in the conservation of institutions. They assure the dominance of generations long gone over generations yet to come. It would be wrong, however, to regard them as a conscious political device for keeping the young in their place, a scheme directed by the haves against the have-nots. As with all the rites discussed previously, the mechanisms set in motion by rites of passage can never be fully anticipated. In fact, their effectiveness seems to depend on their not being viewed in the context of strict social utility. Their efficacy is a consequence of the religious attitude in general, which precludes all those forms of conscious social engineering that modern man likes to think he can detect in the socially efficient traditional organizations.

ᐧᐁᐧᐊ THE PATTERN RECURS in all forms of initiation— initiation into adulthood, into secret societies, into a religious order, or, into a shamanistic fraternity. The shaman's initiation, for instance, differs from the others only in the dramatic and rigorous quality of the hardships the initiate must endure and in the explicit identification with a divinity or spirit whose awesome and fantastic adventures recall the mechanism of the surrogate victim.

The shaman claims mastery over supernatural forces. If he wishes to acquire the means of ridding men of illnesses, the apprentice shaman must first expose himself to the full fury of these illnesses—that is, expose himself to maleficent violence. He emerges triumphant from an ordeal that would have killed an ordinary mortal, thus demonstrating that he not only enjoys the protection of Supreme Violence but also shares in its power and can even, to some extent, effect the transformation of "bad" into "good" violence.

Even the most fantastic details of the shaman's initiation faithfully reflect a ritualistic viewpoint on generative violence. In isolated cultures as far apart as Australia and Asia the initiation culminates in a vision of dismemberment, after which the neophyte awakens or, rather, is reborn as a full-fledged shaman. This final vision calls to mind the collective ritual dismemberment of the Dionysiac rites, the *diasparagmos*, and many similar rituals of diverse provenance. Dismemberment is emblematic of triumph and resurrection; it reflects the operation of the surrogate victim, the transformation of maleficent violence into beneficent violence. The neophyte experiences the same metamorphosis as the mythical creatures whose help he will later require in the exercise of his shamanistic functions. And if he manages to secure their aid, it will be because he is able to approach them on equal terms, as someone who has shared their experiences.

Shamanism is like a theatrical performance in which one actor plays all the roles at once. The lead role, however, is clearly that of commander in chief of the forces of Good, which finally rout the forces of Evil. This final expulsion is frequently associated with some kind of symbolic object; for example, the healer may hold up a twig or a bit of cotton that he claims to have extracted from the body of the patient and that supposedly caused the illness.

The Greek term for an evil object extracted by means of a similar ritual is *katharma*. This term was also used as a variant of pharmakos to designate a sacrificial human victim.

In the ritual context of crisis and victimization, interpreted as an expulsion of evil, the extraction of a shamanistic *katharma* becomes intelligible. The illness is equated to the crisis; it can lead either to death or to a cure, invariably seen as the expulsion of "impurities"— spiritual impurities in the form of evil spirits or physical impurities in the form of the shamanistic object. Once again, the process is based on a repetition of a successful scapegoat effect. The patient is induced to give birth to his own cure, just as the entire community at one time gave birth, in the midst of collective violence, to a new order. The extracted object had no place in the human organism and no right to be there. It was something brought in by outside forces. It plays the part of the actual surrogate victim, whereas the human organism, fully mobilized against the invader, takes the part of the collectivity. If, as has long been assumed, primitive medicine is indeed ritualistic in nature, then it is not surprising that its primary purpose is to reproduce the generative process.

The word *katharsis* refers primarily to the mysterious benefits that accrue to the community upon the death of a human *katharma* or *pharmakos*. The process is generally seen as a religious purification and takes the form of cleansing or draining away impurities. Shortly before his execution the *pharmakos* is paraded ceremonially through the streets of the village. It is believed that he will absorb all the noxious influences that may be abroad and that his death will transpose them outside the community. This is a mythical representation of what does in fact *almost* take place. The communal violence is indeed drawn to the person of the surrogate victim, but the final resolution cannot be described as the expulsion of some substance. The interpretation thus approaches the truth but fails to attain it because it fails to perceive three essential facts: the mimetic nature of reciprocal violence, the arbitrary choice of the victim, and the unanimous polarization of hostility that produces the reconciliation. To view violence as an impurity or blemish that is located in a physical substance is to materialize violence once again. When the shaman draws forth from his patient an object he identifies as the sickness itself he is transferring and transforming this mythical interpretation into yet another form—that of a small, insignificant object.

In addition to its religious sense and its particular meaning in the context of shamanism, the word *katharsis* has a specific use in medical language. A cathartic medicine is a powerful drug that induces the evacuation of humors or other substances judged to be noxious. The illness and its cure are often seen as one; or at least, the medicine is considered capable of aggravating the symptoms, bringing about a salutary crisis that will lead to recovery. In other words, the crisis is provoked by a supplementary dosage of the affliction resulting in the expulsion of the pathogenetic agents along with itself. The operation is the same as that of the human *katharma*, although in medicine the act of purgation is not mythic but real.

The mutations of meaning from the human *katharma* to the medical katharsis are paralleled by those of the human pharmakos to the medical *pharmakon*, which signifies at once "poison" and "remedy." In both cases we pass from the surrogate victim—or rather, his representative—to a drug that possesses a simultaneous potential for good and for bad, one that serves as a physical transposition of sacred duality. Plutarch's use of the expression *kathartikon pharmakon* seems meaningfully redundant in this context.

The "translation" of this violent process into terms of expulsion, evacuation, and surgical operations is made in the most diverse cultures. For example, the Swazi Incwala involves ritual acts whose literal meanings denote the biting, cutting, and slicing of the new year. These words belong to a semantic grouping that includes a variety of highly significant operations, from the consummation of the king's first marriage to decisive victory in an armed conflict. The common denominator appears to be acute suffering destined to assure recovery from an illness or designed to bring about the natural or artificial resolution of a potential crisis. The same grouping designates the therapeutic action of certain substances. In the course of the Incwala rites the king spits out magic medicinal potions, first toward the east, then toward the west. The term *Incwala* is apparently connected with the notion of cleanliness, the process of cleansing by evacuation. As has been mentioned (see above, Chapter 4) the ceremony concludes with a great fire that consumes the accumulated refuse of the past year. Max Gluckman describes the general effect of the rites in terms of "Aristotelian catharsis."

Katharma and katharsis are derived from *katharos*. If we wished to group together all the themes associated with these terms, we would find ourselves with a veritable catalog of the subjects discussed here under the double heading of violence and the sacred. *Katharma* is not limited to the victim or the surrogate object; it also refers to the supreme efforts of a mythic or tragic hero. Plutarch speaks of the *pontia katharmata*, expulsions that purified the seas, with reference to the labors of Heracles. *Kathairo* means, among other things, "to purge the land of monsters." Its secondary meaning, "to whip," may appear puzzling in this context, until we recall the practice of whipping the pharmakos on the genitals.

It is worth noting that *katharsis* is used in connection with purification ceremonies that form part of the "mysteries" initiation rites;

the word is also sometimes used to designate menstruation. Such usages make it clear that we are not dealing here with a heterogeneous collection of references, but rather with a unified system, to which the surrogate victim holds the key.

Whenever we describe the generative process or its products in terms of expulsion, purgation, or purification, we are attributing natural causes to phenomena that are not in the least natural, because they derive from violence. Expulsions, evacuations, and purgations are found in nature; the natural model does indeed exist. But its reality should not distract us from the extraordinary role that this model has played in the history of the human imagination, from primitive religious rituals and shamanistic medicine down to the present day. The pattern outlined in Chapter 8 should provide the perspective. Violence furnishes the initial impetus for the discovery of the model, which is applied in mythic fashion to violence itself, in nonmythic fashion to natural phenomena. The miracle of restored unanimity prompts the conception of the model, which is seen as a combination of natural and cultural influences. The human imagination has regularly reverted to it on many and diverse occasions. Even today we have not succeeded in sorting the arbitrary from the nonarbitrary elements, the useful from the useless, the significant from the insignificant. This failure has been particularly striking in the field of psychopathology.

The obsessive concern during the seventeenth century with clysters and bleedings, with assuring the efficient evacuation of peccant humors, shows plainly that the medical practices of that age were based on the principle of expulsion and purification. These practices constitute, in fact, a slightly refined variant of the shaman's approach with its emphasis on the extraction of the physical *katharma*.

It is easy to laugh, with Molière, at quack doctors and their gargantuan clysters, but physical purging, for better or for worse, is a real process. And what about the modern practice of immunization and inoculation? The model is the same in both cases; clearly, its technique and theory can be applied to pseudo-discoveries as well as to real ones. The patient's defenses, according to modern theory, must be reinforced so that he can repulse a microbiotic invasion by his own means. The beneficent process is still conceived in terms of an invasion repulsed, a harmful intruder chased from the premises. There is no question of mockery here, because the process is scientifically sound. The physician inoculates the patient with a minute amount of the disease, just as, in the course of the rites, the community is injected with a minute amount of violence, enabling it to ward off an attack of fullfledged violence. The analogies abound. "Booster shots," for instance, correspond to the repetition of sacrificial rites. And of course, in all varieties of "sacrificial" protection there is always the danger of a catastrophic inversion; a too virulent vaccine, a too powerful *pharmakon*, can promote the illness it was supposed to prevent. In the first chapter I used vaccination as a metaphor to illustrate certain aspects of sacrifice. Now we can see that vaccination, like so many other human institutions, really amounts to a metaphorical displacement of sacrifice.

ONCE AGAIN WE ENCOUNTER a relic of the primitive mind in modern scientific thinking, a reflection of the imaginative impulse set in motion by generative violence. We discover that a technological tool of undisputed utility is not unrelated to the crudest sort of ritualistic medicine. Certainly we cannot claim that primitive practices stem from a mode of thought that is entirely different from our own. Of course there are differences; certain substitutions take place, and there is a constant shifting of position as one mode of thought merges with another. However, there is no reason to regard the various results of these operations as separate entities, for the process, after all, consists by definition of a series of displacements analogous to those that went before and those that are due to follow (or due not to follow); in other words, to a series of metaphorical substitutions that owe their variety to the fact that none of them ever wholly succeeds in reproducing the essence of a single, unique process.

If we wish to complete our picture of the various meanings of katharsis we must return, once more, to Greek tragedy. As yet I have made no specific reference to Aristotle's use of the term in his *Poetics*. It scarcely seems necessary to do so at this point, for I have already established that tragedy springs from mythic and ritual forms. As for the function of tragedy, Aristotle has already defined it for us. In describing the tragic effect in terms of katharsis he asserts that tragedy can and should assume at least some of the functions assigned to ritual in a world where ritual has almost disappeared.

As we have seen, the tragic figure of Oedipus becomes the original *katharma*. Once upon a time a temple and an altar on which the victim was sacrificed were substituted for the original act of collective violence; now there is an amphitheater and a stage on which the fate of the *katharma*, played out by an actor, will purge the spectators of their passions and provoke a new katharsis, both individual and collective. This katharsis will restore the health and well-being of the community.

"The unity of a given ritual," says Victor Turner in *The Drums of Affliction*, "is a dramatic unity. It is in this sense a work of art."[5] If we

---

[5] Victor Turner, *The Drums of Affliction* (Oxford: Clarendon Press, 1968), p. 269.

agree with this opinion—and it would be difficult to disagree—the reverse should be true as well: a given dramatic performance constitutes a sort of rite, the shadowy similitude of the religious experience.

The Aristotelian use of *katharsis* has provoked endless discussion and will doubtless continue to do so. Modern theorists seek to establish the precise sense that the word had for the philosopher. They brush aside its religious implications because, as they claim, these implications were no longer current in Aristotle's time—were, indeed, hardly less obscure then than they are today. The modern inability to grasp the nature of these implications makes it even harder to come to terms with Aristotle's use of the word.

Yet in order for the term *katharsis* to assume a sacrificial character in the *Poetics* it was not necessary for Aristotle to be aware of the original operation. Indeed, his ignorance of that operation was almost a requirement. If tragedy was to function as a sort of ritual, something similar to a sacrificial killing had to be concealed in the dramatic and literary use of *katharsis*, just as it was concealed in the religious and medical use of the term. It is precisely because Aristotle failed to penetrate the secret of sacrificial rites that his tragic katharsis ultimately constitutes only another sacrificial displacement. It takes its rightful place among all the other displacements, gravitating around the generative violence that owes its enduring efficacy to its elusiveness.

On closer inspection, Aristotle's text is something of a manual of sacrificial practices, for the qualities that make a "good" tragic hero are precisely those required of the sacrificial victim. If the latter is to polarize and purge the emotions of the community, he must at once resemble the members of the community and differ from them; he must be at once insider and outsider, both "double" and incarnation of the "sacred difference." He must be neither wholly good nor wholly bad. A certain degree of goodness is required in the tragic hero in order to establish sympathy between him and the audience; yet a certain degree of weakness, a "tragic flaw" is needed, to neutralize the goodness and permit the audience to tolerate the hero's downfall and death. Freud touches upon this situation in *Totem and Taboo*, but he leaves the matter unresolved. Having accompanied the hero part of the way, the audience suddenly perceives him as wholly "other" and abandons him to his fate, his superhuman ignominy and glory. The spectator may shudder with "pity and fear," but he must also feel a deep sense of gratitude for his own orderly and relatively secure existence. Every true work of art might be said to partake of the initiatory process in that it forces itself upon the emotions, offers intimations of violence, and instills a respect for the power of violence; that is, it promotes prudence and discourages hubris.

Aristotle is discretely vague about which emotions tragedy is meant to purge. But if we see tragedy in terms of a fire used to combat fire, it is clear that its purpose is to protect the community against its own violence. The philosopher asserts that the only violence appropriate to tragic action is violence between close relatives.

If tragedy were a *direct* adaptation of rites, as some erudite theoreticians have claimed, it would itself constitute a work of erudition, and its esthetic and kathartic potential would be in no way superior to that of the Cambridge Ritualists. If tragedy is, or once was, rich in katharsis, that can only be attributed to the antiritualistic aspects of its original inspiration. Tragedy advances toward the truth in the face of reciprocal violence and while assuming the guise of reciprocal violence. But it invariably draws back at the last minute. As soon as mythical and ritualistic differences are seriously challenged, they are replaced by "cultural" and "esthetic" differences. Tragedy thus shares a fundamental experience with ritual. Both have advanced to the very brink of that terrible abyss wherein all differences disappear. Both have been permanently marked by the ordeal.

If tragedy has a sacrificial character, then it must possess a maleficent aspect—a Dionysiac aspect, as Nietzsche would put it—as well as a beneficent, regulatory, Apollonian cultural role. (A parenthetic remark on Nietszche: although his classifications are manifestly superior to the approaches of most critics, they fail to perceive, or at most perceive only dimly, that each and every divinity corresponds to both aspects at once.)

The fundamental duality of tragedy led to the opposing formulations of Aristotle and Plato. Given his time and place, Aristotle was correct to define tragedy in terms of its cathartic qualities. But then, Aristotle is always "correct." That is why he is so great, and so one-sided in his greatness. Aristotle is above and beyond the crisis of tragedy. He incorporates into his theory all the meanings and reasons that pertain to the misunderstanding of this crisis. In choosing Aristotle as their mentor the formalistic literary critics could not have done better, for Aristotle views tragedy solely from the perspective of order. In his view the art of tragedy affirms, consolidates, and preserves everything that deserves to be affirmed, consolidated, and preserved.

Plato, by contrast, is closer in time and spirit to the crisis. It is not the stately affirmation of great cultural rites that he discerns in *Oedipus the King*, but rather the undermining of differences. Plato's attention is caught by tragic reciprocity, by those very aspects that are always eliminated by a formalistic or structuralist reading of the drama; by all those aspects, in short, that William Arrowsmith refers to as constituting the play's tragic "turbulence."[6]

Paradoxically, it was Plato's own acute insight into the nature of tragic inspiration that provoked his hostility to drama. He saw tragedy as opening a window onto the dark and dangerous origins of social values, as somehow posing a challenge to the very concept of civic order. In *Oedipus the King* the public's attention is insidiously diverted from the community's efforts to rid itself of the *pharmakos* to the *pharmakos* itself, with whom the poet and poetry tend to side. The poet, like many a modern intellectual, reveals an ambiguous attitude toward those beings whom the stricken city has driven from its precincts in an effort to regain its lost unity. Even when he is not actually espousing suspect causes, the poet retells ancient, time-honored legends in a new way, giving them a slightly impious and seditious ring. The city, says Plato, must protect itself from subversion; therefore it must rid itself of subversive elements. Sophocles must join Oedipus on the road to exile; the poet too must become a pharmakos.

This situation goes unperceived by rationalist and humanist critics. Their pursuit of what one might perhaps call the "meaning of meanings" leads them away from the source of tragic inspiration and away from undifferentiated violence. By reinforcing and consolidating all the differences, they effectively close the interstices through which violence and the sacred can pass. They succeed so well that they manage to do away with any cathartic value the work might possess. We are left with platitudinous reflections on the work's "cultural values," or with pure erudition, pure classification. Such critics do not seem to realize that by divorcing tragedy from the essential drama of mankind, from the conflict of war and peace and love and hate, they are emptying the work of its tragic substance and preparing a new swing of the pendulum back to tragedy. Nowhere in their works do we encounter an adequate response to the genuine terror of such a work as *The Bacchae*.[7]

[6] William Arrowsmith, "The Criticism of Greek Tragedy," *Tulane Drama Review* 3 no. 3 (1959).

[7] The methods whereby the humanistic tradition, both ancient and modern, has managed to minimize and at times suppress the more horrific aspects of archaic and classical Greek culture surely deserve close study. As Henri Jeanmaire has observed (*Dionysos*, pp. 228–30):

The fact that this horrific aspect is only rarely alluded to by ancient authors is not wholly fortuitous. It is to the great glory of the Greeks that their particular concept of religion and the gods, as manifested primarily in their literature, art, and philosophy, served as a bulwark against that ancient fund of cruelty inherent in most religions whose origins are sunk deep in the past. Those many myths that pertain all too clearly to human sacrifice (myths

Any great writer puts critical platitudes to nought and reveals all pronouncements about literature as shot through with ambiguities. In the preface to *Samson Agonistes* Milton lays emphasis on the paradoxical aspect of katharsis that, though implicit in Aristotle's theory, is rather muted. The poet comments that a sickness and its cure are one and the same, thanks to the kindly intervention of nature. But on closer inspection nature's model reveals, as well as conceals, the warring doubles of tragedy, who can be discerned in the works of Milton and, to some extent, in all true dramatic poets:

> Tragedy, as it was anciently compos'd, hath been ever held the gravest, moralest and most profitable of all other Poems: therefore said by *Aristotle* to be of power by raising pity and fear, or terror, to purge the mind of those and such like passions, that is to temper and reduce them to just measure with a kind of delight, stirr'd up by reading or

---

generally involving children or young girls) suffice to remind us of the hard reality of these barbarous antecedents. But there is no concealing the fact that, as soon as one strays some slight distance from the main cultural centers, traces of these practices could be found, usually in the form of local customs or traditional rituals. Sheer familiarity, a lingering sense of shame, ignorance of what was going on in other regions, and a reluctance to refer to matters that contradicted the accepted ideal of Hellenism all combined to cast these events into shadow. The brutal treatment accorded the *pharmakoi*, poor creatures used as scapegoats, had been greatly reduced in ferocity by the time of Pericles and Socrates and transformed into a sort of old popular custom. Nonetheless, it could be assumed that things had once been quite different, and on the frontiers of Hellenism, at Marseilles or Abdera, one could still hear tell of *pharmakoi* being hurled into the sea or stoned to death.

Trustworthy witnesses testify that as late as the fourth century religious ceremonies on Mount Lyceum in Arcadia included acts of ritual cannibalism involving the eating of an infant's flesh.

Such considerations can hardly do more than touch upon what is, after all, a very complex problem, but they should serve as a warning not to take too lightly the information contained in certain Christian tracts, even though these accounts were written long after the event and derived from the writings of local scholars who, like the later Christian polemicists, were also voicing their aversion to blood sacrifice. The accounts agree that human sacrifices were made to Dionysus. . . . Human sacrifices to Zeus were made at Lyctos. And it is interesting to note that Themistocles, on the eve of Salamis, is said to have sacrificed two young Persians to Dionysus at an inland site on the urging of a soothsayer. The authenticity of this account is questionable because it is recorded so late; and Herodotus' silence hardly adds to its credibility. Yet the author of this story was well placed to inform himself on local history, and Herodotus' reticence may in this case have been deliberate.

It is not the least paradoxical aspect of our subject—the traces of archaism in the various cults of Dionysus—that even so abbreviated a treatment as the one offered here can provide a useful introduction to the circumstances that earned our god (who had already acquired so many attributes and assumed so many different forms, although some of them are more closely connected than has sometimes been thought) the great good fortune of becoming the patron god of the Athenian theater and subsequently, during the Hellenistic period, of the theater as a whole.

seeing those passions well imitated. Nor is Nature wanting in her own effects to make good his assertion; for so in Physic things of melancholic hue and quality are us'd against melancholy, sowr against sowr, salt to remove salt humours.

It is, of course, essential that we refrain from forcing all arguments of the Plato-versus-Aristotle type into the uniform mold of moralistic modernism; we must resist that dangerous craving for differences that prompts us rigidly to grade and categorize art, philosophy, politics.

On the other hand, we must not forget that any significant attitude can be transmuted into a ritual. The Plato-versus-Aristotle conflict is no exception; we have only to recall those neighboring communities whose ritual systems reflected antithetical solutions to identical problems—those communities, for example, in which incest is regarded with horror and loathing, and those in which it is an accepted ritualistic practice. We can compare Plato's attitude to those ritual systems that regard the evil aspects of nature as inexorably evil and do their best to eliminate all trace of them from the community. Plato found it impossible to believe that tragic discord or tragic violence could ever become synonyms for harmony and peace. That is why he rejects with horror those patricidal and incestuous impulses to which Aristotle (and Western culture in general, not excluding the psychoanalysts) assigned a certain "cultural value." In our own day the Dionysiac orgy is simply another form of academicism. The most daring provocations and the most shocking scandals have lost all power to provoke and shock. That does not mean that violence is no longer a threat; quite the contrary. The sacrificial system is virtually worn out, and that is why its inner workings are now exposed to view.

〰️ WHENEVER WE THINK that a stable opposition or a stable difference has been established, we discover that the situation has simply been inverted. The Platonic rejection of tragic violence is itself violent, for it finds expression in a new expulsion—that of the poet. Through his very castigation of the poet Plato reveals himself the poet's "enemy brother," his "double," who, like all true doubles, is oblivious to the relationship. As regards Socrates, whom the community—unwilling to soil its hands by contact with an impious creature—asked to do away with himself, Plato's sympathy is every bit as suspect as Sophocles' sympathy for his pharmakos-hero. Whenever a people has embarked on a tragic course (and this was as true for classical Greece as it is for us today), no heroes arise; only antiheroes. The community, to which everyone in turn adheres in opposition to the enemy of the moment, is betrayed by all, just as Thebes was betrayed by Oedipus and Tiresias. Ultimately it is this antagonism that causes the community's death, even (or rather, especially) when its defense or its so-called best interests serve to disguise and excuse the unleashed violence.

Tragedy holds up a mirror to mankind, and what men saw reflected in it—the inexorable decay of the polis—prompted them to smash it, useless and vain though that gesture might be. Staring back at these double images, we can appreciate the context in which tragedy took place. After all, the same mocking images glitter before our own eyes today.

Philosophy, like tragedy, can at certain levels serve as an attempt at expulsion, an attempt perpetually renewed because never wholly successful. This point, I think, has been brilliantly demonstrated by Jacques Derrida in his essay "La Pharmacie de Platon."[8] He sets out to analyze Plato's use of the term *pharmakon*. The Platonic *pharmakon* functions like the human pharmakos and leads to similar results. The word is a pivot point between sophistic deception and sound philosophy, even though its role is no more justified or justifiable than the violence inflicted on the human scapegoat led through the streets of fair Athens just prior to his execution. When Plato applies *pharmakon* to the Sophists, he generally uses it in its maleficent sense of "poison." When it is applied to Socrates or any Socratic activity, however, it means "remedy." Although Derrida refuses to do away with all differences or to treat these differences as null and void, he demonstrates that between Socrates and the Sophists, the structure of the opposition belies not the difference that Plato would like to establish but rather the reciprocity that is suggested by the recourse to one and the same word. All difference in doctrines and attitudes is dissolved in violent reciprocity, is secretly undermined by the symmetry of the facts and by the strangely revealing, even somewhat naive use of *pharmakon*. This use polarizes the maleficent violence on a double, who is arbitrarily expelled from the philosophic community. From Plato right down to Nietzsche (who took a contrary stand), the philosophic tradition has piously reaffirmed this absolute difference. With Nietzsche the difference was inverted and began to shift back and forth—in preparation, perhaps, for its predestined elimination.

Plato's *pharmakon* is like Aristotle's *katharsis*. And whatever their philosophic intentions may have been, it was their literary intuition that led these two men to select terms that seem suggestive but the full pertinence of which may have escaped them. In both cases the metaphor is used "innocently," in the sense that the misapprehension that

---

[8] Jacques Derrida, "La Pharmacie de Platon," in *La Dissémination* (Paris, 1972), pp. 71–197.

characterizes all sacrificial ceremonies is innocent. In discovering, as we believe we have done, that these metaphors and their respective objects conceal the same process, we have in effect discovered that the metaphoric displacement ultimately alters nothing. Behind the various metaphors a scapegoat effect can always be discerned.

Derrida's analysis demonstrates in striking fashion a certain arbitrary violence of the philosophic process as it occurs in Plato, through the mediation of a word that is indeed appropriate since it really designates an earlier, more brutal variant of the same arbitrary violence. The long line of sacrificial forms, each derived from the other, contains no "right" form from the point of view of philosophy, sociology, or psychoanalysis. But it does contain one genuine, unique event whose essence is invariably betrayed, to one degree or another, by all the translations and metaphoric derivations that Western thought has produced.

Derrida proves that translations of Plato in modern languages manage to obliterate still further the final traces of the generative operation. For the translations destroy the unity of the term *pharmakon*; they use entirely different words to render *pharmakon*-remedy and *pharmakon*-poison. This same process of obliteration was discussed in connection with Benveniste's *Dictionnaire des institutions indo-européennes*.

IN THE COURSE of this work I have tried to demonstrate that generative violence penetrates all forms of mythology and ritual. Yet by Chapter 8, which discussed Freud's *Totem and Taboo*, it was clear that the scope of this inquiry would have to be extended. For if the mechanism of the surrogate victim is simply another aspect of the original mechanism of the symbolic process, then there can be nothing in the whole range of human culture that is not rooted in violent unanimity—nothing that does not find its source in the surrogate victim. That realization led me to turn my attention to various cultural activities derived from ritual. It is now time to enlarge the theory in response to the previous findings.

We are now moving toward an expanded concept of sacrifice in which the sacrificial act in the narrow sense plays only a minor part. If I wish to show that this enlargement of my theory is not arbitrary, I must demonstrate that in those localities where ritual killing no longer occurs, or where there is no evidence of its ever having occurred, its place has been taken by another institution also directly linked to generative violence. I have in mind a society like our own or one belonging to late antiquity.

In Chapter 1, I suggested that there was a direct correlation between the elimination of sacrificial practices and the establishment of a judicial system. That discussion, however, preceded the discovery of the surrogate victim. Consequently, it was not firmly rooted in generative unanimity and now appears inconclusive.

We must endeavor to fill this breach. For if it cannot be proven that the penal system owes its origins to generative violence, it might well be maintained that the judicial system is based on rational agreement, on a sort of social contract, and that men are indeed able to master their social environment in the direct and explicit way that rationalists conceive. Such a conclusion would flatly contradict my line of argument.

Louis Gernet takes up the subject of capital punishment in his *Anthropologie de la Grèce antique.* In his discussion the link between punishment and the surrogate victim can be readily discerned. Capital punishment takes two seemingly separate forms, the first purely religious and the second purely secular. In the first instance:

> The death penalty is a means of eliminating pollution. . . . It purifies the affected group, who are often partly or wholly absolved of responsibility for the newly spilt blood (this is true, at any rate, in the case of lapidation). The violent expulsion, the expulsion unto death of the unworthy or accursed individual, has an ancillary sense: that of *devotio.* Indeed, the killing seems in one sense to be an act of piety. It makes us think of those ancient ordinances which declare that the murder of an outlaw does not cause pollution, or of that prescription of Germanic law that makes such killing a civic duty. . . . Then, too, the victim himself fills a true religious function, a function parallel to the priest-kings who are also put to death. The religious function can be seen in the Latin term for these victims: *homo sacer*; as well as in the Greek term *pharmakos.*[9]

There is no doubt that the death penalty is portrayed here as a direct extension of generative violence.

Gernet also makes reference to another form of punishment, the public exposure of criminals. The exposure was sometimes accompanied by a procession through the streets of the community. Gernet cites Georges Glotz, who compares this procession to *katharma* rites and links it to Plato's suggestion that in his model state "criminals should be publically displayed . . . at the frontiers of the country" (*Laws* 855c). Glotz considers this mention of frontiers significant; his reasons lead us back to our own preoccupation with the surrogate victim and its by-products: "One of the tendencies that manifests itself in religious approaches to punishment is that of elimination, and more

9 Louis Gernet, "Sur l'exécution capitale," in *Anthropologie de la Grèce antique* (Paris, 1968), pp. 326–27.

particularly—for the word must be taken in its etymological sense—of expulsion beyond the frontiers. The bones of the sacrilegious dead are cast out of the community, and—this is a well-known religious practice mentioned by Plato—the inanimate object that caused a man's death, or the corpse of an animal that killed a person, is also subject to expulsion."[10]

The second type of capital punishment was accomplished with the minimum of formalities and is devoid of religious connotations. It is an *apagoge*; its rough and ready character might remind us of the frontier "justice" of American Westerns. According to Gernet, it was usually visited on criminals who had been caught in the act, and it was always ratified by the common accord of the community. However, says Gernet, the public nature of these acts would not have been enough to make the execution of the criminals possible if these criminals had not usually been foreigners; that is, individuals whose death entailed no risk of endless revenge within the community.

The second type of capital punishment is very different from the first in form—or rather, in lack of form. Nevertheless, the two are related. If we acknowledge the role of the surrogate victim in the genesis of religious forms, we cannot regard them as independent institutions. Generative unanimity operates in both cases. In the first type it perpetrates capital punishment by means of ritual; in the second type generative unanimity makes an actual appearance—admittedly in diluted and degenerate form (otherwise its appearance would not be possible), but savagely and spontaneously nonetheless. This latter mode of unanimity gradually evolves into what can perhaps be described as an institutionalized and legalized form of mob violence.

In neither case can the concept of legal punishment be divorced from its original impulse. The concept can be traced back to spontaneous unanimity, to the irresistible conviction that compels an entire community to vent its fury on a single individual. Legal punishment thus has an aleatory character readily recognizable in the numerous intermediary forms between the religious and judicial spheres, notably in the case of the "ordeal" (by fire, water, single combat, etc.).

AS WE BRING TOGETHER the various elements of our discussion, only one conclusion seems possible. There is a unity that underlies not only all mythologies and rituals but the whole of human culture, and this unity of unities depends on a single mechanism, continually functioning because perpetually misunderstood—

---

[10]G. Glotz, "Solidarité de la famille dans le droit criminel," p. 25. Cited in Gernet, "Quelques rapports entre la pénalité et la religion dans la Grèce ancienne," *Anthropologie de la Grèce antique*, pp. 289–90.

the mechanism that assures the community's spontaneous and unanimous outburst of opposition to the surrogate victim.

Such a conclusion may strike some as extreme, not to say extravagant. It might well be useful at this point to review the analytical approach on which it is based. We need one more example—an example that will demonstrate the unity of all sacrificial rites as well as the continuity from these rites to other cultural phenomena that seem, at first glance, utterly alien to them. I have attempted to choose an example that appears essential to the structure of human society: the institution of monarchy—monarchy as it pertains to sovereigns as well as to political power in general and to the whole idea of central authority.

The discussion of African monarchies has already shown that isolating ritual incest, the most "sensational aspect of those monarchies, can only lead us astray. We cannot treat ritual incest as an independent phenomenon but must keep our sights fixed on the sacrifice, even if the sacrificial rites seem dull and ordinary in comparison with ritual incest.

Sacrifice is the most crucial and fundamental of rites; it is also the most commonplace, and that is why it sometimes changes form or disappears in the course of the evolution of any given ceremony. So ritual forms are mutilated even before they reach those modern interpreters usually eager to further minimize, disregard, and efface the last traces of generative violence.

The more peculiar a cultural element appears and the more distinctive its character, the more it tends to distract us from essentials, unless we take care to place it in its proper context. It is the commonplace that truly deserves our attention, for the most frequently encountered cultural elements are the ones most likely to lead us to the truth.

We have already seen how two variants of the same ritual can stand in opposition; for example, the festival and what I have called the antifestival, or the requiring and prohibition of royal incest. Such oppositions stem from different interpretations of the sacrificial crisis. Even if the rite takes into account the basic connection between maleficent and beneficent violence, it still attempts to establish differences between them for practical purposes—differences that can never be anything but arbitrary, since the beneficial reversal only occurs as a result of the maleficent paroxysm and is in a sense produced by it.

We have also observed that the striking variation among rites in any given geographical area is far less important than it seems at first glance. One has no right to find great significance in one tribe's prescription of royal incest and a neighboring tribe's proscription of it, or to conclude from this difference that one tribe is more timid and fearful, the other more daring and "liberated."

The same principle holds true for broad categories of rites; their autonomy is only an illusion. The inability of religious thought to understand correctly the violent mechanism of its own genesis gives rise to countless interpretations that can all be different from each other because they are all erroneous; these interpretations are the rituals and myths of all human societies the world over.

It does not seem to have occurred to modern theorists, bound as they are to their own methodologies, to draw together such disparate institutions as the African monarchies, the cannibalistic rites of the Tupinamba, and the sacrificial ceremonies of the Aztecs. However, each of these institutions casts light on the other.

In the Aztec rites a certain time elapses between the election of the victim and his execution. During this time every effort is made to gratify his desires. The people prostrate themselves before him, fight for the privilege of touching his garments. He is treated like a king, almost like a god. Yet this reverential treatment ends in brutal murder.

The Tupinamba prisoner shares certain similarities with the Aztec victim and the African king. In each case the victim's situation combines grandeur and misery, veneration and ignominy. There is the same combination of positive and negative elements, though in somewhat different proportions.

These analogies are too limited and vague, however, to constitute a solid basis for comparison. For instance, the ephemeral honors accorded the Aztec victim cannot really be compared to the solid political power enjoyed by the African king. As for the Tupinamba prisoner, it would be stretching a point to call his position "regal." Our attempt to bring these three cases together may seem all the more audacious when one considers that their similarities, even when clearly distinguishable, have nothing to do with the most conspicuous features of each institution: ritual incest for the African kings, cannibalism for the Tupinamba, human sacrifice for the Aztecs. These are notable ethnological landmarks, and my treatment of them might well seem sheer willfulness and impressionism, a reversion to the methods of Frazer or Robertson Smith—even though, in this instance, the synchronic groupings established by modern scholars working in the field have been taken into consideration.

At this point the prudent ethnographer might think it is advisable to hold fast the doctrine that a king is a king and a victim is a victim, in the same way that a cat is indubitably a cat. That some kings are sacrificed and some victims are treated like kings is interesting, but nothing more; an amusing paradox that can be exploited by literary folk but that has nothing to do with science.

So prudent an attitude may not be very satisfying, but in the absence of any unifying theory it remains unavoidable. However, everything changes once we begin to realize that the various "scapegoat" phenomena are not the reflection of some ill-articulated guilt complex, but rather the very basis of cultural unification, the source of all rituals and religion. Seen in this light, the differences between these three ritual institutions do not appear so great; they should not be assimilated to the sort of difference that separates carbon monoxide and sodium sulfate. The differences are due to the three different ways in which three societies look at the same process: the loss and subsequent recovery of social unity. We can now furnish explanations for the strange privileges accorded the Tupinamba prisoner and the ephemeral adoration offered the Aztec victim; and we can also glimpse the meaning of the shape of these rites and reaffirm their fundamental unity.

If my analysis still leaves the reader skeptical, if he is still troubled by the differences between the three rituals, we can show that many intermediary ritual forms exist that cast doubt upon the apparent specificity of the forms most distant from each other. Many societies have kings, but it is no longer the king who is the sacrificial victim. Nor is it an animal. The victim is a human being who stands in for the king; he is often chosen from a category of criminals, social misfits, or classless creatures like the Greek pharmakos. Before replacing the real king on the sacrificial altar, the mock king replaces him briefly on the throne. The brevity of the reign, its lack of any real power, recalls the Aztec rite, but the general context is that of true monarchy. At this point the difference between the African king and the Aztec victim begins to blur, for we have here a victim who belongs as much to one rite as to the other, a victim who is exactly situated between the two.

On the other hand, it should be noted that the mock king reigns over a festival that is brought to a proper sacrificial conclusion by his own death. The theme of festival and the theme of sacrifice of a true or simulated king are closely associated—for instance, in the Swazi Incwala—and this is hardly surprising, for the festival is nothing more than a reenactment of the sacrificial crisis, or rather of its resolution by means of the surrogate victim. Whenever the restoration of unity is personally attributed to the surrogate victim, he is seen as "divine," "royal," "sovereign." The words used to designate him—*king, sovereign, divinity, scapegoat*—are nothing more than metaphors used in conjunction with other metaphors. Their purpose is to recapture the original act of generative unanimity, and they are all different because they never entirely succeed.

In any ritual interpretation of the primordial event there is always one dominant element that overshadows the others and finally obscures them as the memory of the generative violence fades from the collective consciousness. In the festival this dominant element is the joyous celebration of a partially transformed sacrificial crisis. In time, as we have seen, the concluding sacrifice is eliminated, as are the rites of exorcism that accompany the sacrifice or replace it. When all vestiges of the generative violence have been removed, we are left with a "festival" in the modern sense. This is the only kind of festival familiar to the cultural historian and recognizable by him, yet he must understand its ritual origins in order to understand its evolution.

The greater vitality these rites possess and the closer they are to their common origin, the more futile becomes any attempt at classification. Of course, difference pervaded these rites from the beginning, for the principal function of the surrogate victim is to restore and solidify difference; but at the outset, differentiation remains circumscribed and limited; it has not yet begun to proliferate.

The rite constitutes the original interpretation of the generative violence. It sets up an initial imbalance between the reciprocal aspects of the sacred, between the maleficent and beneficent elements. With the passage of time this imbalance becomes greater and greater; the feature that was originally given prominence relegates all the other features to the background and finally banishes them altogether. At this point the rational viewer might well conclude that any connection between the maleficent and the beneficent elements is a logical contradiction and, therefore, unworthy of consideration. A choice, it seems, must be made between the "accented" and "unaccented" elements; the continued impoverishment of the latter prompts the rational observer to dismiss them as superfluous appendages introduced into the rite by mistake. Wherever contradictions still exist, reason insists that we do away with them. The moment comes when we find ourselves confronting two institutions that appear wholly unrelated. The whole thrust of Western thought, with its insistence on differences, prevents us from perceiving their fundamental unity. So firmly entrenched is this habit of thought that this effort to uncover the common origins of all rites will be misunderstood by many people as my own inability to differentiate between them.

Royal incest is not truly essential to the African concept of monarchy, either from the point of view of origins, in which it is subordinated to sacrifice, or from the point of view of evolution, of passage into the "monarchal institution." What is essential is the granting of authority during his lifetime to someone who is designated as a future victim and who draws his power and prestige retroactively from the reconciling power of the original scapegoat. With the passage of time the substitute victim's authority becomes more durable, more stable; the factors opposing it lose their importance, and another victim, human or animal, is substituted for the king. Everything that has to do with the reverse side of supreme authority—wrongdoing and humiliation, maleficent violence and sacrificial punishment—becomes merely "symbolic" and soon disappears from view. The vestiges of ritual are like traces of chrysalis clinging to an insect; they are soon discarded. Sacred royalty is transformed into royalty pure and simple, into political power.

When we consider the monarchy of the Ancien Régime in France or any other traditional monarchic system, we cannot help wondering whether it would not be more profitable to consider these institutions in the light of sacred kingship than in the light of modern ideas about monarchy. The concept of Divine Right is not just a fiction made up on the spur of the moment to keep the king's subjects in line. The life and death of the monarchic concept in France—its sacred rites, its fools, its cure of scrofula through the royal touch, the grand finale of the guillotine—all this is clearly structured by the influence of sacred violence. The sacred character of the king—that is, his identity with the victim—regains its potency as it is obscured from view and even held up to ridicule. It is in fact then that the king is most threatened.

The master of these paradoxes, the most daringly perspicacious interpreter of the monarchic principle in a world not so far removed from our own, is Shakespeare. He bridges the gap between the most primitive concepts of kingship and the most modern; he seems to have been better acquainted with both than we are with either.

The dethronement scene in *Richard II* can be seen as a sort of coronation performed in reverse. Walter Pater described it as an inverted rite,[11] but all rites demand that moment of inversion. The king acts as his own sacrificer, transforming himself by quasi-religious means into a double of all his enemies and their surrogate victims as well. He is himself a traitor, in no way different from those who do him violence:

Mine eyes are full of tears, I cannot see;

. . . .

But they can see a sort of traitors here.
Nay, if I turn mine eyes upon myself,
I find myself a traitor with the rest;
For I have given here my soul's consent
T'undeck the pompous body of a king.... (5.1.244)

[11] Walter Pater, *Appreciations* (London, 1957), p. 205.

In his study of the duality of the king's person as portrayed in legal documents of the Middle Ages, *The King's Two Bodies*, Ernst Kantorowicz undertakes an analysis of *Richard II*. Although he does not touch directly upon the question of the surrogate victim, he gives an excellent description of the dual nature of the Shakespearean monarch:

> The duplications, all one, and all simultaneously active, in Richard— *Thus play I in one person many people* (5.5. 31)—are those potentially present in the King, the Fool and the God. They dissolve, perforce, in the Mirror. Those three prototypes of "twin-birth" intersect and overlap and interfere with each other continuously. Yet, it may be felt that the "King" dominates in the scene on the Coast of Wales (3.11), the "Fool" at Flint Castle (3.111), and the "God" in the Westminster scene (4.1) with Man's wretchedness as a perpetual companion and antithesis at every stage. Moreover, in each one of those three scenes we encounter the same cascading: from divine kingship to kingship's "Name" and from the name to the naked misery of man.[12]

We may go a little further and ask ourselves whether this description does not transcend the subject of monarchy strictly conceived to embrace broader concepts of sovereignty and, indeed, all forms of central power that owe their existence to the surrogate victim. There are perhaps two fundamental types of society, which overlap to some extent: those having a central authority essentially monarchal in character and those having no such authority, disclosing no trace of generative violence in their political institutions—the so-called dual systems. The first group, for reasons unknown to us, tends to cluster around a single representative of the original victim, an individual whose status is more or less permanent, who concentrates political as well as religious power in himself. Even if this power is subsequently fragmented, the tendency toward centralism persists.

It is worth noting that structuralist ethnology shows little interest in those societies that no longer reveal any significant opposition between dual forces. In this instance the opposition between the two "extremes" has been interiorized. It can indeed find exterior expression— in the conflict between king and fool, for example—but this always seems like an afterthought, a development of secondary importance.

The unstable character of "historical" societies is perhaps reflected in this "royal" interiorization in each one of us, this play of differences, undifferentiation, and scapegoating in each one of us, which encourages tragedians to treat the surrogate king like the prototype of human

12 Ernst Kantorowicz, *The King's Two Bodies* (Princeton, 1957), p. 27.

beings caught up in a constant state of crisis and plagued by an unending vacillation of differences.

୧୦୫ ALL RELIGIOUS RITUALS SPRING from the surro-
gate victim, and all the great institutions of mankind, both secular and
religious, spring from ritual. Such is the case, as we have seen, with
political power, legal institutions, medicine, the theater, philosophy
and anthropology itself. It could hardly be otherwise, for the working
basis of human thought, the process of "symbolization," is rooted in
the surrogate victim. Even if no example taken alone offers conclusive
proof of my theory, their cumulative effect is overwhelming; all the
more so because they coincide with archetypal myths that tell, in
apparently "naive" fashion, how all man's religious, familial, economic,
and social institutions grew out of the body of an original victim.
The surrogate victim, as founder of the rite, appears as the ideal educa-
tor of humanity, in the etymological sense of *e-ducatio*, a leading out.
The rite gradually leads men away from the sacred; it permits them
to escape their own violence, removes them from violence, and bestows on them all the institutions and beliefs that define their humanity.
In the great Indian texts dealing with sacrifice we discover the same
content, though in slightly different form, as in the origin myths:

> In the beginning the gods sacrificed a man; when he was killed, his
> ritualistic virtues deserted him. They entered a horse; the gods sacrificed
> the horse; when it was killed, its ritualistic virtues deserted it. They
> entered a cow; the gods sacrificed the cow; when it was killed, its
> ritualistic virtues deserted it. They entered a sheep; the gods sacrificed
> the sheep; when it was killed, its ritualistic virtues deserted it. They
> entered a goat; the gods sacrificed the goat. When it was killed, its
> ritualistic virtues deserted it and entered the earth. The gods dug for
> them, and found them in the form of rice and barley. And that is why
> today we still dig the earth to procure rice and barley.[13]

Durkheim asserts that society is of a piece, and that the primary
unifying factor is religion. His statement is not a truism, nor does it
dissolve religion in social institutions. Durkheim believes that men are
shaped culturally by an e-ducational process that belongs to the sphere
of religion. Even concepts of space and time, he says stem from religion. Durkheim never fully articulated his insight, for he never realized what a formidable obstacle violence presents and what a positive
resource it becomes when it is transfigured and reconverted through
the mediation of scapegoat effects.
Human society does not begin with the fear of the "slave" for the

[13] Gatapatha-Brahmana, 1, 2, 3, 6–7, in Sylvain Lévi, *La Doctrine du sacrifice
dans les Brahmanas* (Paris, 1966), pp. 136–37.

"master," as Hegel claims, but—as Durkheim maintains—with religion. To carry Durkheim's insight to its conclusion, I will add that religion is simply another term for the surrogate victim, who reconciles mimetic oppositions and assigns a sacrificial goal to the mimetic impulse. At the moment when differentiated unity is urgently needed and apparently impossible to obtain—that is, during an outburst of reciprocal violence—the surrogate victim comes to the rescue.

The role of the surrogate victim can be ascertained, I believe, even on a spatial plane. There is good reason to think that it has imposed its image on the very structures of some communities, at those special locations forming the center of the community, sites generally dedicated to the spirit of collective unity and whose true nature is sometimes brought to light through archaeological investigation.

In Greece these sites include the tombs of heroes, the omphalos, the stone of the agora and, finally, that perfect symbol of the polis, Hestia, the common hearth. Louis Gernet's essay on these sites leaves this reader at least with the overwhelming conviction that these are places where the surrogate victim met his death or where he was believed to have died.

The traditions attached to these localities and the ritualistic functions associated with them lend credence to the theory that sacred mob violence formed the origin of the polis. This mob violence can take the form of the Bouphonia, which we have referred to on several occasions; or it can take the form of the public exposure of criminals, or other punishments that recall the pharmakos. Further research along the lines of the surrogate victim would undoubtedly turn up even more conclusive evidence.

There is reason to believe that these symbolic sites of unification gave birth to all religious forms; it was there that the various cults were established, spatial relationships fixed, the clock of history set in motion, and the beginnings of a social life plotted out precisely as Durkheim envisioned it. There everything begins; from there everything emanates; there everything returns when discord breaks out. Surely that is the point of the only direct quotation we have of Anaximander, "the earliest voice of Western thought." I would like to repeat those astonishing words here, to show that such a claim is not unbelievable.

In the evolution from ritual to secular institutions men gradually draw away from violence and eventually lose sight of it; but an actual break with violence never takes place. That is why violence can always stage a stunning, catastrophic comeback. The possibility of such an occurrence conforms to the dire predictions of divine vengeance that are to be found in every religious system. His rejection of this apocalyptic message explains why Heidegger has rejected the traditional translation of Anaximander's words. But it seems to me that he has missed the point completely; for the vengeance Anaximander alludes to is wholly human, not divine; in other words, not mythic. I shall revert, therefore, to the more traditional translation of Anaximander, which Heidegger went out of his way to criticize but which seems to me marvelously apposite:

> Where things are born, there too must they perish; for each in turn metes out punishment and expiation for its wickedness, each in the allotted time.[14]

[14] Cf. Heidegger, "The Anaximander Fragment," in *Early Greek Thinking*, trans. David Farrell Krell and Frank A. Capuzzi (New York, 1975).

Conclusion

A THEORY OF THE NATURE of primitive religion has emerged from the foregoing inquiry into the origins of myth and ritual. No attempt will be made here to consider the Judaeo-Christian texts in the light of this theory, or vice versa; that must be left to a future study. However, I hope to have suggested here the course that such a project might take.

My theory depends on a number of basic premises. Even if innumerable intermediary stages exist between the spontaneous outbursts of violence and its religious imitations, even if it is only these imitations that come to our notice, I want to stress that these imitations had their origin in a real event. The actuality of this event, over and above its existence in rite and record, must be kept in mind. We must also take care not to restrict this event to any one context, any one dominant intellectual framework, whether semantic or symbolic, which lacks a firm basis in reality. The event should be viewed as an absolute beginning, signifying the passage from nonhuman to human, as well as a relative beginning for the societies in question.

The theory of the surrogate victim is paradoxical in that it is based on facts whose empirical characteristics are not directly accessible. These facts can be drawn exclusively from texts that invariably offer distorted, fragmentary, or indirect testimony. We can only gain access to the generative event through constant reference to these enigmatic sources, which constitute at once the foreground in which our theory situates itself and the background against which its accuracy must be tested.

The theory of evolution depends on the comparison and linkage of evidence—the fossil remains of living creatures—corresponding, in the case of my hypothesis, to religious and cultural texts. No single anatomical fact studied in isolation can lead to the concept of evolution. No direct observation is possible, no form of empirical verification even conceivable, because evolution occurred over a span of time entirely out of scale with the span of human existence.

In the same way no single text—mythic, religious, or tragic—will yield the operating procedures of violent unanimity. Here, too, the comparative method is the only one possible. If this method has not been successful to date, that is because there are so many variables at work; it is hard to locate the single underlying scheme that controls them all. The theory of evolution, too, constitutes a hypothesis.

The surrogate victim theory presents, as a theory, a distinct superiority over the theory of evolution. The inaccessible character of the generative event is not merely an obstacle unrelated to the theory, an aspect that contributes nothing of positive value; rather, it is an essential part of that theory, something we cannot do without. In order to retain its structuring influence the generative violence must remain hidden; misapprehension is indispensable to all religious or postreligious structuring. And the hidden nature of the event corresponds to the researchers' inability to attribute a satisfactory function to religious practices. My theory is the first to offer an explanation of the primordial role that religion plays in primitive societies, as well as of man's ignorance of this role.

This hidden nature is much less problematic than a notion like the unconscious of Freud. A comparison of certain myths and rituals, viewed in the light of Greek tragedy, leads to the theory of the surrogate victim and violent unanimity through a path much more direct than that of "verbal slips" to such psychoanalytic concepts as suppressed desires and the unconscious. Surely such slips can be attributed to many different causes. But the surrogate victim theory is the only hypothesis that accounts for all features of the cultural phenomena presented here. Unlike the psychoanalytical explanations, it leaves no areas in shadow and neglects no major aspects.

Although generative violence is invisible, it can logically be deduced from myths and rituals once their real structures have been perceived. The further one advances along this path and the more transparent the true nature of religious thought appears, the clearer it becomes that there is nothing here to suppress or to hide. There is no justification for the idea that religious thought either represses or deliberately refuses to acknowledge a threatening self-awareness. Such awareness does not yet present any threat to religion. It is we who are threatened by it, we who flee from it.

If religious misapprehensions were to be regarded in the same light as psychoanalysis regards its material, we should require some religious equivalent to the Freudian repression of the patricide/incest desire; something that must be hidden and kept hidden. Yet such is hardly the case. To be sure, there are many details of the generative event that have dropped out, many elements that have become so warped, misshapen, and transfigured as to be unrecognizable when reproduced in mythical or ritualistic form. Yet no matter how gaping the lacunae may appear, no matter how grotesque the deformations, they are not ultimately indispensable to the religious attitude, the religious misapprehension. Even if it were brought face to face with the inner workings of the mechanism, the religious mind would be unable to conceive of the transformation of bad into good, of violence into culture, as a spontaneous phenomenon calling for a positive approach.

It is natural to assume that the best-concealed aspect of the generative mechanism will be the most crucial element, the one most likely to render the sacrificial system nonfunctional if it becomes known. This aspect will be the arbitrary selection of the victim, its essential insignificance, which contradicts the meaning accumulated upon its head by the scapegoat projections.

Close examination will reveal that even this aspect is not really hidden; it can be readily detected once we know what we must look for. Frequently the rituals themselves are engineered so that they include an element of chance in the choice of the victim, but mythologists have never taken this into account.

Although we have already called attention to those rites designed to give a role to chance in the selection of the victim, it may be that we have not put sufficient stress on this essential aspect.

Sporting contests and games of chance appear to modern man most incongruous as ritual practices. The Uitoto Indians, for example, incorporate a balloon game into their ritual; and the Kayans of Borneo use a top in the course of their religious ceremonies.

Even more remarkable, apparently even more incongruous, is the game of dice that figures in the funeral rites of the Canelos Indians. Only the men participate in this game. Divided into two rival groups and lined up on either side of the deceased, they take turns casting their dice *over* the corpse. The sacred spirit, in the person of the dead man, determines the outcome of each throw. The winner is awarded one of the dead man's domestic animals, which is slaughtered on the spot, and the women prepare a meal from it for the assembled mourners.

Jensen, in citing these facts, remarks that the games are not simply additions to established religious practices.[1] If one were to say that the Canelos Indians "play at dice during the funeral rites of their parents," one would be conveying the wrong idea of the ceremonies. For this game takes place only in conjunction with these funeral rites. It is modern man who thinks of games of this sort as exclusively secular, and we must not project that idea onto the Canelos Indians. This is not to say that our own games have nothing to do with rites; in fact, they

---

[1] Jensen, *Mythes et cultes chez les peuples primitifs*, pp. 77–83.

originate in rites. But, as usual, we have got things reversed. For us, games of chance are a secular activity upon which a religious meaning has been superimposed. The true state of affairs is precisely the opposite: games originate in rites that have been divested, to a greater or lesser degree, of their sacred character. As I have already remarked, Huizinga's famous theory of play should be inverted. It is not play that envelops the sacred, but the sacred that envelops the notion of play.

Death, like any passage, entails violence. The passage into the beyond by a member of the community may provoke (among other difficulties) quarrels among the survivors, for there is always the problem of how to redistribute the dead man's belongings. In order to meet the threat of maleficent contagion the community must have recourse to the universal model, to generative violence; it must attend to the advice of the sacred itself. In this particular case, the community has perceived and retained the role of chance in the liberating decision. If violence is given free play, chance alone is responsible for the ultimate resolution of the conflict; and the rite tries to force the hand of chance before violence has had the opportunity to act. The rite aims straight at the final result, achieving, as it were, a minimum expenditure of violence.

The Canelos dice game offers a clue to the reason why the theme of chance recurs so frequently in folklore, myth, and fable. Oedipus, it will be remembered, refers to himself as the son of *Tychè*—that is, Fortune or Chance. There were towns in the ancient world in which the selection of magistrates was made by drawing lots, for the power bestowed by ritually regulated chance always contains a sacred element, the sacred "fusion of opposites." Indeed, the more we reflect on this theme of Chance, the more universal it appears. In popular legend and fairy tale Chance is often invoked to "find" kings or, conversely (and the converse is always the other face of the same coin), to designate someone to undertake a difficult or perilous mission, a mission that might involve self-sacrifice for the general good—someone, in short, to assume the role of surrogate victim:

> On tira-t-à la courte paille
> Pour savoir qui serait mangé.[2]

Yet is there any way of proving that the motif of Chance has its origin in the arbitrary nature of the violent resolution? There are numerous instances in which the drawing of lots so clearly supports the meaning proposed here that it is virtually impossible to doubt the connection. One such example is the Old Testament Book of Jonah. God tells Jonah to go forth and warn the people of Nineveh that their

[2] From *Il était un petit navire*, folkloric French song (ed).

city will be destroyed if they do not repent of their ways. Hoping to evade this thankless task, the reluctant prophet embarks on a ship sailing for Tarshish:

> But the Lord sent out a great wind into the sea, and there was a mighty tempest in the sea, so that the ship was like to be broken.
>
> Then the mariners were afraid, and cried every man unto his god, and cast forth the wares that were in the ship into the sea, to lighten it of them. But Jonah was gone down into the sides of the ship; and he lay, and was fast asleep.
>
> So the shipmaster came to him, and said unto him, What meanest thou, O sleeper? Arise, call upon thy God, if so be that God will think upon us, that we perish not.
>
> And they said every one to his fellow, Come, and let us cast lots, that we may know for whose cause this evil is upon us. So they cast lots, and the lot fell upon Jonah.
>
> (Jonah 1:4–7)

The ship represents the community, the tempest the sacrificial crisis. The jettisoned cargo is the cultural system that has abandoned its distinctions. The fact that everybody calls out to his own particular god indicates a breakdown in the religious order. The floundering ship can be compared to the city of Nineveh, threatened with destruction unless its people repent. The forms may vary, but the crisis is always the same.

The passengers cast lots to determine who is responsible for the crisis. Chance can always be trusted to reveal the truth, for it reflects the will of the divinity. The lot designates Jonah, who proceeds to confess his culpability:

> Then the men were exceedingly afraid, and said unto him, Why hast thou done this? For the men knew that he fled from the presence of the Lord, because he had told them.
>
> Then they said unto him, What shall we do unto thee, that the sea may be calm unto us? for the sea wrought, and was tempestuous.
>
> And he said unto them, Take me up, and cast me forth into the sea; so shall the sea be calm unto you: for I know that for my sake this great tempest is upon you.
>
> (Jonah 1:10–12)

The sailors attempt to gain the shore by their own efforts; they would like to save Jonah's life. But they finally recognize the futility of their efforts, and address themselves to the Lord—even though he is Jonah's Lord and not their own:

> Wherefore they cried unto the Lord, and said, We beseech thee, O Lord, we beseech thee, let us not perish for this man's life, and lay

not upon us innocent blood: for thou, O Lord, hast done as it pleased thee.

So they took up Jonah, and cast him forth into the sea; and the sea ceased from her raging.

Then the men feared the Lord exceedingly, and offered a sacrifice unto the Lord, and made vows.

(Jonah 1:14–16)

What we see here is a reflection of the sacrificial crisis and its resolution. The victim is chosen by lot; his expulsion saves the community, as represented by the ship's crew; and a new god is acknowledged through the crew's sacrifice to the Lord whom they did not know before. Taken in isolation this story tells us little, but when seen against the backdrop of our whole discussion, each detail acquires significance.

Modern man flatly rejects the notion that Chance is the reflection of divine will. Primitive man views things differently. For him, Chance embodies all the obvious characteristics of the sacred. Now it deals violently with man, now it showers him with gifts. Indeed, what is more capricious in its favors than Chance, more susceptible to those rapid reversals of temper that are invariably associated with the gods?

The sacred nature of Chance is reflected in the practice of the lottery. In some sacrificial rites the choice of victim by means of a lottery serves to underline the relationship between Chance and generative violence. In an essay entitled "Sur le symbolisme politique: le Foyer commun," Louis Gernet cites a particularly revealing ritual, which took place in Cos during a festival dedicated to Zeus:

> The choice of victim was determined by a sort of lottery in which all the cattle, which were originally presented separately by each division of each tribe, were mixed together in a common herd. The animal ultimately selected was executed on the following day, having first been "introduced to Hestia," and undergone various rites. Immediately prior to the ritual presentation, Hestia herself receives homage in the form of an animal sacrifice.[3]

At the close of the previous chapter I noted that Hestia, the common hearth, in all probability marked the place where the original act of communal violence was perpetrated. It seems more than likely, therefore, that the selection of the victim by lottery was meant to simulate that original violence. The selection is not made by men, but left to divine Chance, acting through violence. The mixing together of the cattle that had originally been identified by tribe or by division of

---

[3] Gernet, *Anthropologie de la Grèce antique*, p. 393.

tribe is particularly revealing. This deliberate confusion of distinctions, this merger into a communal togetherness, constitutes an obligatory preamble to the lottery; clearly it was introduced to reproduce the exact order of the original events. The arbitrary and violent resolution that serves as a model for the lottery takes place at the very height of the sacrificial crisis, when the distinctions delegated to the members of society by the cultural order succumb to the reciprocal violence and are merged into a communal mass.

A TRADITIONAL DISCUSSION of Dionysus involves a demonstration of how he differs from Apollo or from the other gods. But is it not more urgent to show how Dionysus and Apollo share the same characteristics, why the one and the other should be called divine? Surely all the gods, despite their differences, have something in common, something from which all their distinctive qualities spring. Without such a common basis, the differences become meaningless.

Scholars of religion devote themselves to the study of gods and divinity. They should be able to provide clear and concise definitions of these concepts, but they do not. They are obliged, of course, to decide what falls within their field of study and what falls outside it; yet they leave the crucial and most decisively scientific task of *defining* their subject to uninformed public opinion. Even assuming that it is possible—or justifiable—to stretch the concept of divinity to include each and everybody's idea of the divine, the so-called science of religion can neither do without this approach nor provide a convincing defense of it.

There is no true science of religion, any more than there is a science of culture. Scholars are still disputing about which cult Greek tragedy should be ascribed to. Were the ancients correct in assigning tragedy to Dionysus, or does it rightfully belong to another god? Undoubtedly this is a genuine problem; but it is also, I think, a secondary one. Far more important, but far less discussed, is the relationship between tragedy and the divine, between the theater in general and religion.

Whether my theory proves to be true or false, it can, I believe, lay claim to being "scientific," if only because it allows for a rigorous definition of such terms as *divinity, ritual, rite,* and *religion.* Any phenomenon associated with the acts of remembering, commemorating, and perpetuating a unanimity that springs from the murder of a surrogate victim can be termed "religious."

The surrogate victim theory avoids at once the impressionism of the positivist approach and the arbitrary and "reductivist" schemata of psychoanalysis. Although this theory brings together many crucial aspects of man's experience, it offers no simple substitute for the "wondrous profusion" of the world's religious systems. Indeed, one ought perhaps to ask whether this "profusion" is really as wondrous as all that; in any case, the mechanism proposed here carries us beyond the mere cataloging of characteristics. The endless diversity of myths and rituals derives from the fact that they all seek to recollect and reproduce something they never succeed in comprehending. There is only one generative event, only one way to grasp its truth: by means of my hypothesis. On the other hand, there are innumerable ways of missing it; hence the multiplicity of religious systems. My thesis results from an eminently positive line of inquiry. I have a certain confidence in language—contrary to some modern thinkers who, at the very moment when truth becomes accessible in language, declare that language is incapable of expressing truth. This absolute distrust of language, in a period of mythic dilapidation like our own, may well serve the same purpose as the excessive confidence that prevailed before the dilapidation, when no decisive truth was in sight.

Our theory should be approached, then, as one approaches any scientific hypothesis. The reader must ask himself whether it actually takes into account all the items it claims to cover; whether it enables him to assign to primitive institutions an origin, function, and structure that cohere to one another as well as to their overall context; whether it allows him to organize and assess the vast accumulation of ethnological data, and to do so in a truly economical manner, without recourse to "exceptions" and "aberrations." Above all, he must ask himself whether this theory applies not in single, isolated instances but in every conceivable situation. Can he see the surrogate victim as that stone initially rejected by the builders, only to become the cornerstone of a whole mythic and ritualistic edifice? Or as the key that opens any religious text, revealing its innermost workings and rendering it forever accessible to the human intellect?

∽◷ THAT INCOHERENCE TRADITIONALLY attributed to religious ideas seems to be particularly associated with the theme of the scapegoat. Frazer treats this subject at length; his writing is remarkable for its abundance of description and paucity of explanation. Frazer refuses to concern himself with the formidable forces at work behind religious significations, and his openly professed contempt for religious themes protects him from all unwelcome discoveries:

> The notion that we can transfer our guilt and sufferings to some other being who will bear them for us is familiar to the savage mind. It arises from a very obvious confusion between the physical and the mental, be-

tween the material and the immaterial. Because it is possible to shift a load of wood, stones, or what not, from our own back to the back of another, the savage fancies that it is equally possible to shift the burden of his pains and sorrows to another, who will suffer them in his stead. Upon this idea he acts, and the result is an endless number of very unamiable devices for palming off upon some one else the trouble which a man shrinks from bearing himself. In short, the principle of vicarious suffering is commonly understood and practised by races who stand on a low level of social and intellectual culture.[4]

However, the disrepute in which he is held today is far from justifiable, for few scholars have labored so diligently in the field or set forth their findings with such admirable clarity. And many later writers have in effect done little more than repeat in somewhat different form Frazer's own profession of ignorance.

Anyone who tries to subvert the sacrificial principle by turning it to derision invariably becomes its unwitting accomplice. Frazer is no exception. His work contributes to the concealment of the violent impulse that lurks within the rite of sacrifice. Such phrases as "physical loads" and "bodily and mental ailments" recall nothing so much as the platitudes of second-rate theologians; and Frazer treats the act of sacrificial substitution as if it were pure fantasy, a nonphenomenon. Yet authors closer to our time have done the same and with considerably less excuse, for the Freudian notion of transference, inadequate as it is in some respects, should at least have alerted us that something vital is missing from the picture.

The modern mind still cannot bring itself to acknowledge the basic principle behind that mechanism which, in a single decisive movement, curtails reciprocal violence and imposes structure on the community. Because of this willful blindness, modern thinkers continue to see religion as an isolated, wholly fictitious phenomenon cherished only by a few backward peoples or milieus. And these same thinkers can now project upon religion alone the responsibility for a violent projection of violence that truly pertains to all societies including our own. This attitude is seen at its most flagrant in the writing of that gentleman-ethnologist Sir James Frazer. Frazer, along with his rationalist colleagues and disciples, was perpetually engaged in a ritualistic expulsion and consummation of religion itself, which he used as a sort of scapegoat for all human thought. Frazer, like many another modern thinker, washed his hands of all the sordid acts perpetrated by religion and pronounced himself free of all taint of superstition. He was evidently unaware that this act of hand-washing has long been recognized as a purely intellectual, nonpolluting equivalent of some of the most an-

[4] J. G. Frazer, *The Golden Bough*, 1 vol., abridged (New York, 1963), p. 624.

cient customs of mankind. His writing amounts to a fanatical and superstitious dismissal of all the fanaticism and superstition he had spent the better part of a lifetime studying.

The *sacrificial* character of this misunderstanding should remind us that today, more than ever before, we will encounter resistance when we try to rid ourselves of ignorance—even though the time has come for this ignorance to yield to knowledge. This resistance is similar to what Freud calls resistance, but far more formidable. We are not dealing with the sort of repressed desires that everyone is really eager to put on public display, but with the most tenacious myths of modernism; with everything, in short, that claims to be free of all mythical influence.

What I have said of Freud holds true for all modes of modern thought; most particularly for ethnology, to which Freud was irresistibly drawn. That ethnology is alive today, when the traditional modes of interpretation are sick unto death, is evidence of a new sacrificial crisis. This crisis is similar but not identical to previous ones. We have managed to extricate ourselves from the sacred somewhat more successfully than other societies have done, to the point of losing all memory of the generative violence; but we are now about to rediscover it. The essential violence returns to us in a spectacular manner—not only in the form of a violent history but also in the form of subversive knowledge. This crisis invites us, for the very first time, to violate the taboo that neither Heraclitus nor Euripides could ever quite manage to violate, and to expose to the light of reason the role played by violence in human society.

Bibliography

Arrowsmith, William. "The Criticism of Greek Tragedy." *Tulane Drama Review* 3, no. 3 (1959).

Bataille, Georges. *L'Erotisme*. Paris: Minuit, 1965.

Bateson, Gregory; Jackson, Don D.; Haley, Jay; and Weakland, John. "Toward a Theory of Schizophrenia." In *Steps to an Ecology of the Mind*. New York: Ballantine Books, 1972.

Battistini, Yves. *Trois Présocratiques*. Paris: Gallimard, 1970.

Beidelman, T. O. "Swazi Royal Ritual." *Africa* 36 (1966): 373–405.

Benveniste, Emile. *Le Vocabulaire des institutions indo-européennes*. 2 vols. Paris: Minuit, 1969.

Boas, Franz. "Tsimshian Mythology." *Report of the Bureau of American Ethnology* 31, 185, no. 25.

Caillois, Roger. *Man and the Sacred.* Translated by Meyer Barash. Glencoe, Ill.: Free Press, 1960.

Canetti, Elias. *Crowds and Power*. Translated by Carol Stewart. New York: Viking Press, 1966.

Chagnon, Napoleon. *Yanomamö, the Fierce People*. New York: Holt, Rinehart and Winston, 1968.

Cook, P. A. W. "The Inqwala Ceremony of the Swazi." *Bantu Studies* 4 (1930): 205–10.

Delcourt, Marie. *Légendes et cultes des héros en Grèce*. Paris, 1942.

———. *Oedipe et la légende du conquérant*. Paris, 1944.

Derrida, Jacques. "La Pharmacie de Platon." In *La Dissémination*, pp. 71–179. Paris: Seuil, 1968.

Diels, Hermann, and Kranz, Walter. *Die Fragmente der Vorsokratiker*. Berlin, 1934–35.

Dostoievski, Fiodor. *The Double*. In *Three Short Novels of Dostoevsky*. Translated by Constance Garnett, revised and edited by Avhram Yarmolinsky. New York: Anchor Books, 1960.

Douglas, Mary. *Purity and Danger*. London: Penguin Books, 1966.

Dumézil, Georges. "Lecture de Tite-Live." In *Horace et les Curiaces*, Paris, 1942.

———. "LesTransformations du troisième triple." In *Cahiers pour l'Analyse* 7 (1967).

———. *Mythe et Epopée*. Paris: Gallimard, 1968.

Durkheim, Emile. *Les Formes élémentaires de la vie religieuse*. Paris: Presses Universitaires de France, 1968.

Eliade, Mircea. *Aspects du mythe*. Paris: Gallimard, 1963.

———. *Rites and Symbols of Initiation*. New York: Harper & Row, 1965.

———. *The Sacred and the Profane*. New York: Harper & Row, 1961.

Elkin, A. P. *The Australian Aborigines*. New York: Doubleday & Co., 1964.

Euripides. *Euripide.* Edited and translated by Marie Delcourt-Curvers. Paris: Gallimard, 1962.

Evans-Pritchard, E. E. *The Nuer.* Oxford: Oxford University Press, 1940.

———. *Social Anthropology and Other Essays.* New York: Free Press, 1962.

Farber, Bernard, ed. *Kinship and Family Organization.* New York: John Wiley & Sons, 1966.

Frazer, J. G. *The Golden Bough.* 1 vol., abridged. New York: Macmillan Co., 1963.

———. *Totemism and Exogamy.* 4 vols. London: Macmillan & Co., 1910.

Freud, Sigmund. *The Standard Edition of the Complete Psychological Works.* Edited and translated by James Strachey. 24 vols. London: Hogarth Press, 1953–66.

Gernet, Louis. *Anthropologie de la Grèce antique.* Paris: Maspero, 1968.

Gluckman, Max. *Order and Rebellion in Tribal Africa.* Glencoe Ill.: Free Press, 1960.

———. *Politics, Law, and Ritual in Tribal Society.* New York: Mentor Books, 1968.

———. *Rituals of Rebellion in South-East Africa.* Manchester, 1954.

Harari, Josue, ed. *Textual Strategies: Criticism in the Wake of Structuralism.* Ithaca, N.Y.: Cornell University Press, 1977.

Heidegger, Martin. *Early Greek Thinking.* Translated by David Farrell Krell and Frank A. Capuzzi. New York: Harper & Row, 1975.

Henry, Jules. *Jungle People.* 1941. Reprint. New York: Vintage Books, 1964.

Heusch, Luc de. *Essai sur le symbolisme de l'inceste royal en Afrique.* Brussels, 1958.

———. "Aspects de la sacralité du pouvoir en Afrique." In *Le Pouvoir et le sacré.* Brussels: Institut de sociologie, 1962.

Hölderlin, Friedrich. *Poems and Fragments.* Translated by Michael Hamburger. Ann Arbor: University of Michigan Press, 1967.

———. *Lettres.* Translated by D. Naville. In *Oeuvres.* Edited by Ph. Jaccottet. Paris: Gallimard, 1962.

Hubert, Henri, and Mauss, Marcel. *Sacrifice: Its Nature and Function.* Translated by W. D. Halls. Chicago: University of Chicago Press, 1964.

Huizinga, Johan. *Homo Ludens.* Boston: Beacon Press, 1955.

Huxley, Francis. *Affable Savages.* New York: Capricorn Books, 1966.

Jeanmaire, Henri. *Dionysos: Histoire du culte de Bacchus.* Paris: Payot, 1970.

———. "Le Traitement de la mania dans les 'mystères' de Dionysos et des Corybantes." *Journal de psychologie,* 1949, pp. 64–82.

Jensen, Adolphe E. *Mythes et cultes chez les peuples primitifs.* Translated by M. Metzger and J. Goffinet. Paris: Payot, 1954.

———. *Myth and Cult among Primitive Peoples.* Translated by Marianna Tax Cholsin and Wolfgang Weissleder. Chicago: University of Chicago Press, 1963.

Kantorowicz, Ernst H. *The King's Two Bodies.* Princeton: Princeton University Press, 1957.

Kluckhohn, Clyde. "Recurrent Themes in Myth and Mythmaking." In *Myth and Mythmaking.* Edited by Henry A. Murray. Boston: Beacon Press, 1968.

Krige, H. J., and Krige, J. D. "The Lovedu of Transvaal." In *African Worlds.* London, 1954.

Kuper, H. "A Ritual of Kingship among the Swazi." *Africa* 14 (1944):230–56.

———. *The Swazi: A South African Kingdom.* New York: Holt, Rinehart and Winston, 1964.

Lacan, Jacques. *Ecrits.* Paris: Seuil, 1966.

Laplanche, Jean. *Hölderlin et la question du père.* Paris: Presses Universitaires de France, 1961.

Laplanche, Jean, and Pontalis, J. B. *Vocabulaire de la psychanalyse.* Paris: Presses Universitaires de France, 1967.

Leach, Edmund, ed. *The Structural Study of Myth and Totemism.* London: Tavistock, 1967.

Lévi, Sylvain. *La Doctrine du sacrifice dans les Brahmanas.* Paris: Presses Universitaires de France, 1966.

Lévi-Strauss, Claude. *The Elementary Structures of Kinship.* Translated by James Harle Bell, John Richard von Sturmer, and Rodney Needham. Boston: Beacon Press, 1969.

———. *Structural Anthropology.* Translated by Claire Jacobson and Brooke Grundfest. New York: Basic Books, 1963.

———. *Totemism.* Translated by Rodney Needham. Boston: Beacon Press, 1963.

———. *Tristes Tropiques.* Translated by John Weightman and Doreen Weightman. New York, 1975.

———. *The Savage Mind.* Chicago: University of Chicago Press, 1966.

———. *The Raw and the Cooked.* Translated by John Weightman and Doreen Weightman. New York, 1969.

———. "La Geste d'Asdiwal." *Annuaire de l'école pratique des hautes études* 6 (1958–59).

Lévy-Bruhl, Lucien. *Primitive Mentality.* Translated by Lilian A. Clare. New York, 1923.

Lorenz, Konrad. *On Aggression.* Translated by Marjorie Kerr Wilson. New York: Harcourt Brace Jovanovich, 1966.

Lowie, Robert. *Primitive Society.* New York: Liveright, 1970.

Maistre, Joseph de. *Works.* Translated by Jack Lively. New York, 1965.

Makarius, Laura. "Les Tabous du forgeron." *Diogène* 62 (April–June 1968).

———. "Le Mythe du trickster." *Revue d'histoire des religions* 175, no. 2 (1969).

———. "Du Roi magique au roi divin." *Annales* 25, no. 3 (1970):668–98.

Malinowski, Bronislaw. *Argonauts of the West Pacific.* New York: E. P. Dutton & Co., 1961.

———. *Crime and Custom in Savage Society*. Totowa, N.J.: Littlefield, Adams & Co., 1967.

———. *The Father in Primitive Society*. 1927. Reprint. New York: W. W. Norton & Co., 1966.

———. *Magic, Science, and Religion*. New York: Doubleday & Co., 1954.

———. *Sex and Repression in Savage Society*. New York: Meridian Books, 1955.

Métraux, Alfred. *Religions et magies indiennes d'Amérique du Sud*. Paris: Gallimard, 1967.

———. *La Religion des Tupinamba et ses rapports avec celles des autres tribus Tupi-Guarini*. Paris, 1928.

Nilsson, Martin P. *A History of Greek Religion*. New York: Norton, 1964.

Norbeck, E. "African Rituals of Conflict." *American Anthropologist* 65 (1963):1254–79.

Otto, Rudolf. *The Idea of the Holy*. Translated by John W. Harvey. New York, 1958.

Otto, Walter. *Dionysus: Myth and Cult*. Translated by Robert B. Palmer. Bloomington: Indiana University Press, 1965.

Radcliffe-Brown, A. R. *The Andaman Islanders*. New York: Free Press, 1964.

———. *Structure and Function in Primitive Society*. New York: Free Press, 1965.

———. "The Study of Kinship Systems." *Journal of the Royal Anthropological Institute* 71 (1941).

Radcliffe-Brown, A. R., and Forde, Daryll, eds. *African Systems of Kinship and Marriage*. Oxford: Oxford University Press, 1950.

Rohde, Erwin. *Psyche, Seelencult, und Unterblichkeits-glaube der Griechen*. 1893.

Shärer, H. "Die Bedeutung des Menschenopfers im Dajakischen Totenkult." *Mitteilungen der Deutschen Gesellschaft für Völkerkunde* 10 (Hamburg, 1940).

Sousberge, L. "Etuis péniens et gaines de chasteté chez les ba-Pende." *Africa* 24 (1954).

———. "Structures de parenté et alliance d'après les formules Pende." *Mémoires de l'Académie royale des sciences coloniales belges* 4, no. 1 (1951).

Smith, W. Robertson. *Lectures on the Religion of the Semites*. 2d. ed. London, 1894.

———. *Kinship and Marriage in Early Arabia*. London, 1903.

Storr, Anthony. *Human Aggression*. New York: Bantam Books, 1968.

Thompson, Stith, ed. *Tales of the North American Indians*. Bloomington: Indiana University Press, 1968.

Turner, Victor. *The Forest of Symbols: Aspects of Ndembu Ritual*. 1967. Reprint. Ithaca, N.Y.: Cornell University Press, 1970.

———. *The Drums of Affliction*. Oxford: Clarendon Press, 1968.

———. *The Ritual Process*. Chicago: Aldine, 1969.

Vaillant, George C. *The Aztecs of Mexico.* New York: Pelican Books, 1950.

Van Gennep, Arnold. *Les Rites de passage.* Paris: Nourry, 1909.

Vernant, Jean-Pierre. *Mythe et pensée chez les Grecs.* Paris: Maspero, 1966.

————. "Ambiguïté et renversement: sur la structure enigmatique d'*Oedipe Roi.*" In *Echanges et communications.* Edited by Jean Pouillon and Pierre Maranda. The Hague: Mouton, 1970.

Wilson, Monica. *Rituals of Kinship among the Nyakyusa.* Oxford: Oxford University Press, 1957.

Index

Abraham, 4–5
Achilles, 9
Adrastus, 62
Adultery, 52, 126
Aeschylus, 46
Agauë, 126, 128, 137
Ajax, 9
Alternation: of *kudos*, 153; of Love and Hate, 163; and madness, 156; of *thymos*, 154; in tragedy, 149–51, 153 155. *See also* Duality; Reciprocity, violent
Ambivalence, 1, 181–85
Amphitryon, 40
Anathema, 27, 84
Anaximander, 307–8
Ancestors, 254, 256
Andaman Islanders, 16
Andromache, 80, 153
Anger, 68; collective, 80, 106–7, 123–24, 139; divine, 87, 130–31, 155, 259–60; and serenity, 149–50
Animals: as differentiated from man, 2–3, 10–11, 128, 283; instinctive limits of, toward violence, 145, 221; as sacrificial victims, 9, 97, 110; substituted for man, 5–6, 106, 110
Antifestival, 121–22
Anthropology, science of. *See* Ethnology
Apollo, 315
Arbitrary, 236–37, 311–12
Aristotle, 207, 295; *Poetics*, 73, 290–92
Arouet, François Marie, 203
Arrowsmith, William, 293
Athens, 9, 94, 296
Aztec, 301–2
Avant-garde theater, 107

Bacchanal. *See* Festival
Bacchantes, 126–28, 131, 137
Bachelard, Gaston, 37
Bataille, Georges, 222
Bateson, Gregory, 147
Beidelman, T. O., 111
Benveniste, Emile, 152, 262–64, 297
Beyle, Marie Henri, 91, 246
Blood: beneficent, 36–38; in childbirth, 35; maleficent, 38, 104–5; menstrual,

33–36, 289; ritual, 104–6; and violence, 34–36
Boaz, Franz, 248
Bones, white, 244, 247, 256
Book of Rites, 8
Bororo culture, 140, 243
Bouphonia, 98, 307
Brothers, 4, 59–61, 63; as enemies, 61–65, 71, 73, 109, 150, 158, 160, 203, 212–13, 279; -in-law, 62, 279

Caillois, Roger, 119–20
Cain and Abel, 4, 61
Calderon, 192 n
Cambridge Ritualists, 95–96, 292
Canelos culture, 311–12
Cannibalism, 274–80, 283, 294 n. *See also* Ritual
Cape tribe, 121–22
Castration, 184, 248–49
Catharsis, 30, 81, 99, 102, 120, 161–62, 267, 271, 273; and tragedy, 290–92, 294. *See also* Katharsis
Ceram Islanders, 100
Cervantes, Miguel de, 248
Chagnon, Napoleon, 140
Chance, 149, 311–15
Chomsky, Noam, 230–31
Chukchi culture, 16–17, 25–28
Cithaeron, Mount, 126, 128, 139
Classification, 195, 293
Clytemnestra, 11
Colonus, 85
Consciousness. *See* Unconscious
Contagion: of individual "in passage," 281–82; of Oedipus's monstrosity, 75; of sacred king, 268; of twins, 57–58. *See also* Diseases, contagious; Impurity; Violence, contagious
Contamination. *See* Contagion
Contests, 93, 109, 151, 311. *See also* Ritual
Corneille: *Le Cid*, 44; *Horace*, 42
Creon, 46, 48, 62, 68, 73, 76, 78, 127, 150, 159, 252, 279
Creusa, 37–38
Cyclops, 6, 100
Cyclothymia, 154–55, 158

325